Before speech

The beginning of interpersonal
communication

Before speech
The beginning of interpersonal communication

EDITED BY
MARGARET BULLOWA

CAMBRIDGE UNIVERSITY PRESS

CAMBRIDGE
LONDON · NEW YORK · MELBOURNE

Published by the Syndics of the Cambridge University Press
The Pitt Building, Trumpington Street, Cambridge CB2 1RP
Bentley House, 200 Euston Road, London NW1 2DB
32 East 57th Street, New York, NY 10022, USA
296 Beaconsfield Parade, Middle Park, Melbourne 3206, Australia

© Cambridge University Press 1979

First published 1979

Printed in the United States of America
Typeset by Ward Partnership, Widdington, Essex
Printed and bound by Vail-Ballou Press, Inc., Binghamton, New York

Library of Congress Cataloguing in Publication Data

Main entry under title:
Before speech.

Bibliography: p.
Includes index.
1. Interpersonal communication. 2. Nonverbal
communication. 3. Parent and child. 4. Infant
psychology. I. Bullowa, Margaret.
BF723.C57B43   155.4'22   78-51671
ISBN 0 521 22031 9 hard covers
ISBN 0 521 29522 X paperback

To all the parents and their infants who, by allowing us to invade their privacy and study their intimacy, have helped us toward an understanding of the beginning of human communication.

Publisher's note

Margaret Bullowa was taken ill while she was editing this book, but she did not allow this to deter her from carrying on the work with meticulous care. She died before proofs were available.

Contents

I

Introduction
Prelinguistic communication: a field for scientific research[1]

MARGARET BULLOWA
Massachusetts Institute of Technology

1 Introduction

This is primarily a book about a field of research: about how scientists
go about finding out how infants and adults communicate with one
another. This topic is now exciting the interest of investigators. Until
recently most scientifically minded people in our culture considered
infants incapable of communication since they don't talk. Of course
most mothers know otherwise but scientists and other 'experts' haven't
always taken them seriously.

I have been looking into the development of communication from a
'scientific' point of view for nearly two decades. While helping with
the preliminaries for the Third International Child Language Symposium in London in 1975 and preparing to chair the section called
'Prespeech' it occurred to me that a book about prelinguistic communication would be timely and useful. As others enter this area of investigation, or have an interest in it, they should be able to find in one
place an account of how some of us have gone about investigating it.
But this isn't a 'how to' book. There is no simple formula for finding
answers to the questions which arise as soon as one starts to think
seriously about communication between infants and adults. (Studies
are already being started on communication between infant and infant.)
At this point the best I could do was to assemble examples of ways in
which some successful investigators have gone about reducing our
ignorance. Therefore I invited a number of colleagues who study the
communication of prelinguistic infants to join me in this enterprise.
Nearly everyone I consulted or invited to participate responded with
enthusiasm. A few had to beg off because of prior commitments, but
none said this couldn't or shouldn't be done yet.

As editor I've urged my colleagues to be terse without sacrificing

1

ideas. I've asked as many of them as possible to say something about what led them to this field of inquiry, about how they go about it and what they have learned. Each chapter is therefore an exemplar of how a researcher, or in a few instances a team of researchers, has gone about looking into some aspect of prelinguistic communication. We haven't concealed the difficulties in this kind of research. There isn't any one right method any more than there is any one right theoretical viewpoint, although there are methods and viewpoints which might be less appropriate or fruitful than others. We are all in agreement that infants communicate, so among us I haven't found anyone asking whether infants participate in communication, although that question is still being asked or a negative answer to it assumed. On the other hand we don't all agree on the definition of communication, although meaning and intention are nearly universally included, nor on exactly what counts as communication. I feel that the field at this stage of its development is better served by not imposing a uniform definition but by letting diverse points of view find expression.

A book such as this with related contributions by a number of authors is often the result of a conference and papers are published after being revised in the light of the discussion between participants and by commentators. We have not held a conference nor had the benefit of group discussion. Some of us are personally known to one another and sometimes refer to each other's work. But I am probably the only one of us who is personally acquainted with everyone else. I have tried to get representation of different kinds of work from members of different academic disciplines and schools of thought and from as many different places as possible, though obviously I couldn't ask everyone I know or know of who works on anything to do with the topic to contribute. I didn't intend to confine the representation to Britain and the United States, although these are the relevant research communities I know best. I have found a few people in other countries working in the field. Yet this is for the most part an Anglo-American book. I did inquire of knowledgeable persons in many parts of the world about who was doing research in this or related areas. While I found out about a number of interesting developments by this method, I turned up hardly any completed research which would be appropriate in this collection. But, too late to make use of it, I visited some continental research centers where through personal contact I did find work which would have been appropriate for inclusion.

1.1 Precursors and influences on our research

I have been curious as to why research on this topic is more advanced at this time in these English-speaking countries than elsewhere. I'm not at all sure that I know the reason, although I have been offered a number of explanations. My hunch — and it is only a hunch — is that the emergence of prelinguistic communication as a field of inquiry represents the intersection of several research trends of the recent past in the United States and Britain. *Infancy* research has been moving from infant as isolated organism through infant as interactant, mainly in mother—infant dyads, toward infant as communicative partner. *Language acquisition* research has been reaching back from the study of children producing recognizable sentences at least two words long through holophrase and one-word 'sentence' production toward any detectable sound—meaning correspondence. At the same time there has been an extension of research attention by child language investigators from 'sound-track' alone to the observed interactional context and the term 'communicative competence' has become prominent. There have also been contributions from *cognitive psychology* as it has looked to younger and younger children for origins of intelligence, and found them. I would guess that trends in these three areas in the United States and Britain have been largely responsible for convergence on infant communication.

It might at first seem that this is simply an extension of the mother—infant interaction field. Therefore it is necessary to explain why it is not, even though there is an area of overlap. Few, if any, would claim that all interaction is communication, although communication is recognized as taking place in interactional contexts. Richards (1974a: 123) states that he regards 'communication as something beyond interaction'. The mother—infant interaction literature, most of which has appeared in the past five years or so, has a different thrust from the concerns we are dealing with. It has usually focussed on socialization or on personality formation rather than on communication. When we consider communication, we are basically concerned with shared meanings (enculturation). Interaction can occur without having the same meaning for each interactant. Since communication occurs only in the course of interaction with other people, we are in a sense all doing interaction studies. And investigators of mother—infant interaction have pioneered methods (described in detail below) which lend themselves to studies of how meanings are shared before language is available for the purpose. Admittedly this does leave us with a grey area between the two concepts, for how can we tell, we who are so dependent on words, that an infant, who cannot say what he means, shares meaning with another person?

The same issue might arise in relation to the other fields (language acquisition and cognitive psychology). Why isn't this language acquisition pushed still further back? In a sense it is, but the issues which require consideration when we look into the infant's 'total communication' seem to me broader than those which have been taken as their province by students of language acquisition, traditionally linguists and cognitive psychologists. Their question has been: how does a child acquire his mother-tongue? — with adult language as the target. So the development of phonology, syntax and semantics has been studied from the point of view of what the child as an individual knows and how he applies it. Recent interest in how a child uses language extends the field in the direction of communication, but it is still focussed on what the child as an individual knows and does, rather than on the exchange of meanings between child and partner implied by communication. It is possible to use language all by oneself, though not to learn it. It is not possible to communicate, in the basic meaning of the word, alone.

The three fields just discussed are not the only ones which have made significant contributions to these investigations. The impact of the field of ethology, as people trained in animal behavior research brought their concepts and skills to bear on problems of human development (Blurton Jones 1972), shows clearly in the background in biology and medicine of a number of contributors to this volume and to the field. Furthermore, concepts and terminology derived from ethology are quite pervasive throughout this volume. Almost everyone in this book tends to interdisciplinary thought and practice and, if only by some slight allusion, brings biological or ethological ideas into his discourse.

There is an inescapable resemblance between the problem of investigating communication between infra-human animals, especially other primates, and that of investigating communication between human adults and their prelinguistic infants, since language in the linguist's sense is not available as a guide to meaning in either case. At the level of signalling behaviors the relationship is especially strong. But there is probably also resemblance at a deeper level. Social animals share with us states of 'being in communication'.

Another influence which has become so pervasive in modern thinking that it is often not mentioned explicitly is cybernetics (systems theory, e.g. Bertalanffy 1933, Chappell & Sander this volume). Most of us recognize the mutual regulation which takes place between mothers and infants in communication and we use language which stems from systems thinking while seemingly oblivious of its source. Even when the influence of one or the other of the communicants is seen as predominant, it is never suggested that one partner is unresponsive to the other's behavior. Thus we acknowledge feedback loops whenever we consider communication or interaction.

The concern with turn-taking is dealt with specifically in chapters by Bateson, Fraiberg, Kaye, Newson, Snow et al., Trevarthen and Tronick et al. The writings of a group of social psychologists known as 'ethnomethodologists' (e.g. Garfinkel 1967, Sudnow 1972) may have contributed to this concern, although their literature deals mainly with adults and is not generally referred to by investigators of infant communication.

1.2 About this book: in general

When I undertook this project I expected to find a great deal of diversity of viewpoint among these widely scattered investigators with such differing backgrounds. It came as a surprise to me to discover the extent to which we are in basic agreement on a number of fundamental issues. That meaning and intent are fundamental to the definition of communication is nearly universally acknowledged, even though we might not all define communication in identical terms. Everyone of us who has anything to say about the relation between prelinguistic communication and language sees continuity when meanings and intentions, at first expressed through extralinguistic means, are transferred to language. Relations between context and content, while variously conceived in detail, are universally recognized as important in understanding the developing system of interpersonal communication, which is itself seen as constructed through the joint effort of mother and infant. Timing and sequencing are acknowledged significant aspects to investigate.

These ideas must be 'in the air'. It is true that there are traceable intellectual relations between some of the contributors, especially among those who at one time worked at the Harvard Center for Cognitive Studies.[2] But there are also contributors who have come by different routes with minimal if any contact with that seminal source. My own contact with it, even though it was only two miles from where I was working most of the time, was quite peripheral. At the time I was unaware of possible influence from the occasional colloquia I attended 'up the river', in what seemed to me the alien area of cognitive psychology, on ideas I was developing in virtual isolation. Others were even more isolated both by geography and by intellectual provenance and affiliation. Our relative unanimity suggests that we are in step with the *Zeitgeist* of this field.

This book will of necessity raise more questions than it can answer. It can, however, be useful at this stage of our inquiry for us to face up to the kind of problems, both theoretical and practical, inherent in the research consideration of infants as partners in communication.

The topic of infant communication is an emotionally, and I suspect even politically, loaded one. This implies that it will fall to the low end on a scale of objectivity. Since Heisenberg, we as scientists no longer claim total objectivity even in the 'hard' sciences. We have invented all sorts of ways to try to circumvent our tendency to project our personal ways of perceiving onto human objects (so-called 'subjects') of scientific investigation, as though what two or more people agree they perceive is in some sense more valid than what each alone perceives, and we throw out as 'data' observations which are considered too deviant from those we can agree on in common. It is as though we believe that two heads are always better than one, forgetting that the two heads have usually developed a common perspective and that, even if they don't communicate directly about their perceptions until after they have recorded them, their work in a common frame of reference inevitably leads to mutual calibration. I'm not saying that this is 'a bad thing' but rather that we should recognize it as inherent in the perception of people, whether the people are infants, school children, psychiatric patients or any other class of humans under scrutiny.

How such knowledge may be applied is, as with all knowledge, a problem in wisdom and responsibility. I want and hope that whatever we learn will benefit people, but I am disposed to be very cautious about giving advice. I feel that we are looking into a Pandora's box, the contents of which are exceedingly complex and all interrelated. I want to know. I feel very far from being ready to do. And yet some of what we are learning about the 'normal' process may suggest ways to help those individuals who are communicatively most handicapped, children who have or acquire sensory, motor or central nervous system defects. This concern is prominent in the chapters by Brazelton, Condon, Fraiberg, Newson, Plooij, Ricks and Stensland Junker. To me this seems a different sort of application from tampering with social institutions, such as educational systems, on the basis of fragmentary knowledge.

1.3 About this book: some technicalities

These chapters and the work they are based on are interrelated in so many ways that it is impossible to classify them in any straightforward sequential arrangement; therefore the chapters are presented alphabetically by first author.

The extent to which some of these accounts of research are personalized is my responsibility. I have encouraged my co-authors to use the first person where appropriate, since research is always thought out and executed by a particular living person and is the product of his personal life-history and experience interacting with the situations in which he lives and has lived. I have tried to find out what led the authors to do the kind of work they report here and describe this in section 6; some of the authors have included personal accounts in their chapters. For at least five of them (Bateson, Halliday, Ricks, Stensland Junker and Trevarthen) the direction of their research was shaped by experience with children of their own.

In order to aid readability I have asked everyone to conform to a few simple conventions in the use of personal pronouns. Babies, unless a girl-baby is specifically referred to, are by convention 'he' to acknowledge personhood but avoid the cumbersome he/she. This does not seem to me to be a 'sexist' way of dealing with the issue but simply an acknowledgement that English uses a masculine form for the general case. Caregivers are conventionally 'she', without implying that men can't function well as caregivers, so as to leave sentences with both infant and adult unambiguous when pronominalized. Authors in generic usage are 'he' for the same reason as the infants. Conventions of spelling, however, have been made uniform only within chapters, not throughout the book.

The notes for each chapter are numbered sequentially and are placed at the chapter ends. The references for the entire book are combined in one alphabetical list, which also serves as a citation index, at the end of the book.

This introductory essay encompasses both my personal view of the field of research we are presenting and what I hope will prove a useful guide to the chapters which follow. Rather than introduce them one by one, I will refer to them repeatedly in context as I review some of the themes and methods of investigation I have found in them. When authors are named without a date in this introductory essay, the reference is to a chapter in this book.

I suggested to the other authors that it might save them space for presentation of their own work if they left the review of the literature to me, since I felt sure there would be a good deal of overlap between chapters. In fact most chapter authors did take up the work of others, as it customary. Therefore, instead of grouping the literature review in one section in this introduction, I will take up writings which I have found relevant as I discuss the themes I have identified in the chapters along with clues to where more references are to be found. My purpose throughout the introduction is to supply additional leads rather than to be exhaustive.

2 Prelinguistic communication

The explicit concept of communication between infants and adults is of fairly recent appearance in the pertinent Anglo-American literature: child development, pediatrics, advice on child-rearing and language acquisition, to name the most obvious. Although there have been studies of the signalling behavior of infants during the past century (dating auspiciously from Darwin's *Expression of the emotions* (1872)), I feel that communication, with emphasis on interpersonal process, is a more modern concept.

In book indexes, tables of contents of journals and lists of abstracts covering these fields one searches in vain for the term 'communication'. Even a 1300-page compendium of research, *The competent infant* (Stone et al.) published in 1973 does not have the term 'communication' in its index nor even 'interaction', and yet it is not hard to find relevant material there in a large section called 'The social infant'.

One can make a case for the thesis that the concept of communication *with* infants has newly emerged in Anglo-American child development studies. There is evidence, too extensive to present here, that disregard for infant communication by professionals has not been uniform throughout the world (e.g. Luria 1957; Lezine 1972; Lisina 1974).

But if one searches in the literature with one's mind tuned to nuances, there is some evidence that at least some people recognized all along that it is possible to communicate with infants. In early psychoanalytic writings about infants, the term 'empathy' seems to have overtones of communication. Burlingham (1972), in a paper published originally in 1935, writes: ' . . . empathy between infant and mother, mysterious and almost uncanny as it used to appear formerly, is here shown lodged to a large degree in the acuteness of the child's perception' (69). Freud & Burlingham in *Infants without families* (1944: 14) attributed the slower development of the five- to twelve-month-old infants in their wartime nursery to 'reduction in emotional interplay and the intellectual stimulation which results from it' when many infants had to share the available adults in contrast to the one-to-one relationships of home-reared babies.

A child starts to learn mother-culture even before he starts to learn his mother-tongue. Infancy is the great opportunity to learn about people without distractions. At first an infant's world is almost exclusively a world of people and what they do with and to and for him. The people he is learning from and about are the members of his own household. These are the people who give an infant his start toward enculturation.

The anthropologist Edward T. Hall (1976) equates communication and culture:

What is characteristically man — in fact what gives man his identity no matter where he is born — is his culture, the total communication framework: words, actions, postures, gestures, tones of voice, facial expression, the way he handles time, space and materials, and the way he works, plays, makes love, and defends himself. All these things and more are complete communication systems with meanings that can be read correctly only if one is familiar with the behavior in its historical, social and cultural context. (37)

This is a very broad definition of communication indeed, but one which makes sense to me. For each culture, in its specific way of dealing with all dimensions of the lives of its adherents, supplies the contexts needed to comprehend the meaning of all interpersonal communication.

I believe that one of the things which has delayed the study of the earliest human communication is our habit of thinking of communication as consisting mainly of language. Students of language acqui-

sition are just now coming to recognize that to understand child
language requires a great deal of attention to pragmatics — to the
contexts in which it is used. This includes not only the situation but
also all extra-verbal communication. What is content at one time
becomes context later. I suspect that this has a developmental
sequence.

This may be illustrated with data from a study on the development
of pointing (Murphy forthcoming). Infants and toddlers at nine, fourteen, twenty and twenty-four months were video-taped while on their
mother's laps sharing picture books. Looking, pointing and vocalizing
of both mothers and infants were among the behaviors located and
timed precisely. At nine and fourteen months infant pointing and
vocalizing were not well integrated with each other. Frequency of
vocalizing at the same time as pointing reached a peak at twenty
months and then consisted mostly of naming, whereas the twenty-
four-month-olds and their mothers were looking 'more earnestly' at
individual pictures and defining more detail: not just 'kitty' but tail
and whiskers. What interests me in this developmental sequence is the
way in which manual pointing developed within the context of shared
visual attention and then was overtaken by vocalization which became
naming of the objects looked at, and, when language came in, whole
objects became contexts for their parts in turn. What had been content had moved from central focus to periphery, from figure to ground.

One can find such developmental sequences almost anywhere one
looks among longitudinal studies which involve shared meaning. The
illustration just cited is based on indication. I am offering another
based on demand, the other major category of early performative
utterances (Gruber 1973). Starting with younger infants I noted such
a sequence in reviewing two series of monthly sequential films of two
babies and their mothers from around three to fifteen months in
'naturalistic' observations searching for 'demand' behavior (Bullowa
1977). At first visual fixation on an object communicated the baby's
attention to it, then visual attention became the context for manual
reaching and still later the babies could point to out-of-reach objects
to 'request' them (the issue here is not whether the pointing gesture
is a modified reach–grasp gesture but that it serves to specify an
object in the environment in a communicative situation, a different
issue); and finally vocalization, which at first tended to accompany
the hand gestures, would displace them in the form of language as a
way of communicating the topic of discourse. I conceptualize such a

developmental sequence as a progression in which what at one time stands for the entire message gradually falls into place as context for more detailed, complex and abstract (symbolic) ways of presenting a message. The earlier form doesn't get lost. It becomes first obligatory, and later optional, context, for example, designating the required object by means of gaze is at first sufficient by itself, then gaze accompanies a hand movement with or without vocal utterance. Later gaze and gesture may be omitted entirely if a verbal request is made when the partners are spatially separated. A message can become totally independent of its situational ties, as, for instance, in its written form.

It is my conjecture that in order to use language or to use any linguistic device, for example a word or a syntactic marker, productively, an individual must have passed through a period of having its meaning in focus.[3] This meaning need not have been in linguistic form and may even have come into focus before speech. This would be true for all aspects of language, not just for nominals. As adults we experience this whenever we encounter a new word or usage or in learning a foreign language. Experience with words and ideas makes it possible for them to recede into the background where they may come to serve as context for other words and ideas. In the course of development what was message becomes context and context comes to encompass more and more as each individual experiences his enculturation. Meaning and language, then, are highly person- and culture-bound. If one believes this, then one cannot start too early in life to look for roots of meaning.

With this point of view about the development of communication it follows that I welcome the fact that students of language acquisition now reach back earlier and earlier in individual experience for the beginning of language. I started to look into language acquisition while working as a psychiatrist expecting to find insights into the miscarriage of communication characteristic of psychiatric patients, imagining that their problem was one of language. Fortunately I disregarded the received wisdom of the day which told me that there was nothing to study before the child had begun to talk. I wanted to observe the onset of language at its earliest. I sought guidance from Heinz Werner, one of the pioneers in child development studies. He advised me that the way to find early precursors of a phenomenon was to locate it in clearly recognizable form and to trace it backward through longitudinal data to find its origin. I started recording as early as I could, in the delivery room when possible, in order to have records which would include the earliest seeds of language. I had no idea when to expect to find them. Only gradually did it dawn on me that my records on tape and film from the long prelinguistic period all contained relevant information which was fundamental to understanding what is termed language acquisition. I now think 'language emergence' might be a more accurate way to characterize it, at least in its early phase. I also came to realize that the problems of my patients were not so much linguistic as communication problems.

The shared understandings which are built up between an infant and his familiars constitute the indispensable basic context for all his later interpersonal transactions, including the ones utilizing verbal language. We need to learn all we can about this substrate while it is still visible on the surface if we are ever to understand not only language but all aspects of social and psychological development. Chapters by Bateson, Brazelton, Chappell & Sander, Condon, Fraiberg, Kaye, Pawlby (Newson), Snow et al. and Tronick et al. have bearing on this very early communication.

We have been slow in coming to realize that extra-linguistic cues must aid the child in his learning what the speech he hears is about. Even now that the importance of context is more generally recognized, the underlying attitude is often that nothing less than speech really counts as communication. We know that this is far from the case. Most human beings in most places at most times have used language (in the linguist's sense) as a face-to-face medium of communication embedded in its full complement of vocal, bodily, social and situational contexts. These are all there right from the start, albeit often in rudimentary form (Trevarthen), and they become more, not less, elaborated as the infant turns into a speaker and language user.

The transition to speech (examined in detail by Halliday and Ricks) is indeed an important turning point in individual development. Traditionally, we find it difficult to accord a person without speech full human status. We as adults are so language-oriented that we fail to notice a large part of the communicative means we habitually employ. For us it is merely background. The very term *non*-verbal communication, introduced recently to cover a wide range of extra-linguistic human communicative modalities, emphasizes by its negative form the supremacy of verbal communication in our habits of thought. Despite recent popularization of the concept of 'body language', the whole field of human extra-linguistic communication is still greatly underdeveloped as a scientific discipline. It is true that some fragmented parts of it have been studied recently, much as language has been studied, as self-contained systems. There have been studies and books on gesture, facial expression, proxemics etc., each dealt with in isolation. The time is becoming ripe for a more comprehensive view. So long as we don't know what is common with older children and adults, we are likely to think anything we observe in infancy unique to that time of life.

Some of the interest in these communicative systems stems from the field of ethology and its successes in decoding various aspects of animal communication. This may have led to the recognition that man as a primate may well share in at least some of the means of communication we find well developed in the primates and especially in the great apes. Unfortunately, from the point of view of understanding basic human communication, a lot of effort goes into 'proving' that chimpanzees could speak if they but had the right sort of vocal articulatory equipment. I feel that it is more pertinent to learn as much as possible of how they actually do communicate with one another and especially how communicative ability develops in individual members of a primate species (Plooij). Language has been thought to be that which makes us uniquely human. Whenever evidence is presented which suggests that great apes may share with us some features of linguistic communication, there is a rush to the defense of man's uniqueness, as Fouts (1975) has pointed out, and the definition of language is respecified in such a way as to exclude the intruders.

At the present stage of our knowledge of extra-verbal communication there is no basis for ascribing all the levels of complexity which are found in language to other communicative modalities. While I know of no attempt so far to assemble an integrated account of the development of non-verbal communication from birth to maturity, I would not expect that an account of the complete mature system and the processes by which it is achieved will reveal complexity, including the many levels of embedding, to rival that which linguistics has brought to light in language. However, Kendon (1972) has shown something akin to the hierarchical structure of discourse in the organization of the body movements accompanying narrative speech. I expect that we will find mainly, as Ekman (Ekman et al. 1972) has for emotive facial expression, a limited set of basic message types which can be combined and blended in graded series to express degrees of meaning. Except for sign languages of the deaf, which are structured similarly to spoken language and presumably draw on the same cognitive capacities, extra-vocal communication accompanying speech between adults tends to carry the background messages, the context which highlights the verbal. For the most part this remains confined to the here-and-now 'performative' level (as animal communication does) and most of it refers to the participants and how they feel toward one another. It can extend to include reference to someone or something beyond the communicating dyad, as when pointing specifies an external topic of communication. Such a system can be very rich in texture and subtle in its overtones but it cannot achieve the intellectual accomplishments of language unless it is converted into an art form through the use of some medium. Much detail can be conveyed when a self-conscious code is expressed through movement, as in the hand movements of oriental dance. This I believe is more like sign language, an intellectual accomplishment. But it is my impression, as proposed earlier, that the untaught extra-verbal communication, which is part of everyone's enculturation and may be built on biologically given forms, not only starts to develop ahead of language but provides a foundation for the emergence of language.

Studying the course of total communicative development from its beginning can furnish clues to understanding the mature system. Studies of developing and matured communicative systems complement one another. But we must not expect to identify only mature aspects of communication from the beginning. That can lead up blind alleys in the way that investigating infant vocal sound as if it were composed of adult speech elements impeded developmental phonology. Here, however, as we deal with early phases of the developing system we cannot avoid some reference to the mature condition, usually exemplified by the mother or other caregiver. We are beginning to realize that the speech and behavior addressed to infants differs from adult-to-adult communicative behavior in systematic ways (Collis, Snow et al., Trevarthen, Tronick et al.). Bateson deals with the problem of communication between people using disparate codes, a prime problem for investigators of infant communication. The problem is thrown into relief where an infant is significantly defective.

Why should it be so difficult for us to conceptualize a communication system, albeit in a developing phase, which is intrinsically functional in its own right without benefit of language? Is it because the senior partner is not only capable of speech but uses it even when she expects no response in kind in her transactions with her infant (Snow

et al.)? Whatever the reason, this looking ahead may be blinding us to
what is going on at the time, especially during the first four to six
months when much richer communication is taking place than has
yet been studied. Yet it is hard to imagine what a model for mother–
infant communication would look like if it were not based on a
linguistic model. It is difficult for us as adult language users to appreciate the prelinguistic infant's experience. Why should language be the
prototype for all human communication, a great deal of which is
extra-lingual, even among adults? Even the engineers, who have given
us mathematical models of communication and realized them in computer technology, have perpetuated the linguistic model as though it
were the only one possible.

I am not advocating that we entirely rule out linguistic modeling
and analogy in our study of early communication, only that we recognize it when we are using it. Knowing that an infant is destined to
become a speaker, it is hard not to anticipate. There are obvious links
between speech (a motor act) and the remainder of communication
as demonstrated by Kendon (1972) and by Condon. This even includes
aspects of language at the syntactic level.

2.1 The communicative state

For an infant to enter into the sharing of meaning he has to be *in* communication, which may be another way of saying sharing rhythm. A
great deal of work on interaction with infants during their first half
year considers shared attention. This is probably the key to rhythm-
sharing underlying also fully elaborated interadult communication,
even though it is often overlooked in our preoccupation with details
of the codes for transmission of messages, as Condon's work suggests.
The problem is how two or more organisms can share innate biological
rhythms in such a way as to achieve communication which can permit
transmission of information they do not already share. (The concept
of 'continuates' described by Tronick et al. appears to belong to a way
in which the communicative state can be kept on an even keel.)

The study of communication between persons has been very much
influenced by contributions from electrical engineering and information theory. We tend to emphasize a sender–message–receiver
model or one of its variants. This model has been very successful in
solving communications engineering problems. It has its place in consideration of biological communication too (Denes & Pinson 1963)
since we are all equipped with sending and receiving organs. I make

use of this model in the next section as a convenient way of presenting studies of infant capability. However, we must pay attention not only to the coded message and the details of transmission and reception but also to the overall properties of the system which make interpersonal communication possible. This has more to do with being 'in communication' than with the what and how of communication, and pertains to fundamental properties of animal and human communicative systems, properties less obvious than the nature of the codes and how they are used. The problems are biological ones. Often those who investigate them have been trained as ethologists, physicians or anthropologists. However, it is possible to reverse the process and draw a physical analogy. I once (1967) compared establishing communication to tuning to a carrier wave (as one does when tuning to a radio station) in trying to express what I meant by getting into communication.

This is the aspect of communication referred to by the anthropologist, musician and photographer Byers (1976: 160) when he writes:

if we find that the variations or modulations of underlying rhythms at multiple levels are systematically related to biological processes, we can envision a human or animal world that is communicationally related through the sharing of time forms in multiple levels of behavioral organization.

And further:

the information carried by interpersonal rhythms does not move directionally from one person to another. Thus information cannot easily be conceptualized as 'messages' since the information is always simultaneously shared and always about the state of the relationship.

Although Byers and Sander (1975) are probably unaware of one another's work, I suspect that they are both fundamentally concerned with the same issue.

Byers' research method consists in detecting the beat in each communicant's speech or activity as one would in assigning the 'signature' to a stretch of music. It is then as easy to see when two or more co-present individuals share rhythm as it is when looking at the scoring for more than one musician (see also Hall 1976). Byers suggests one way in which the communicational phenomena expressed in both the speech and movement which he has studied can be related to the more commonly observed ones:

While the 10 cycles/second rhythm found underlying speech and movement behavior is clearly a biological rhythm, these temporal units are the building blocks for such culturally determined behavior as pauses between speakers or listener interjections in a speaker's pauses.

Byers' analytic procedure has not yet to my knowledge been applied to communication between infants and caregivers, but it would certainly be feasible. The study by Condon & Sander (1974a, b, see also Condon this volume) on neonatal synchrony of movement to adult speech is not unrelated but has focussed on the overt aspect of synchrony between communicants rather than on the underlying rhythms both partners share. Trevarthen's criticism of Condon seems to me to stem from a way of looking at the phenomenon closer to Byers' than to Condon's. In any case, Trevarthen too is reaching for a similar concept when he discusses the probable neural mechanisms underlying intersubjectivity.

Although rhythms involved in interpersonal communication are biologically based, they may be modified by the impact of culture mediated by already acculturated individuals. Byers himself (1972), and E.T. Hall (1976), also an anthropologist and pioneer in the study of communication, have explored rhythm-sharing, mainly between adult members of various cultures and between members of disparate cultures. Hall cites evidence that rhythmic incompatibility exists between members of different cultures and underlies much mistrust and misunderstanding. I wonder how it comes about that a newborn baby, capable of synchronizing his body movement with adult speech from any culture (Condon & Sander 1974a, b) becomes enculturated in the course of his growing up to the point where he feels strange and uncomfortable in any cultural setting but his own? When does this come about? And is it linked to his entry into his language community? Or perhaps to the maturational events at puberty beyond which second language learning is said to become more difficult (Lenneberg 1967: 176)?

This aspect may also have bearing on questions of bilingualism, an area in which educators are now seeking to find out what is optimal for a child's development. Shouldn't we be looking into the effects of early, even prelinguistic, exposure to more than one rhythmic pattern early in life, since we know that speech rhythm is linked to other body rhythms? Perhaps how incommensurate the several rhythms are might underlie whatever problems arise for children confronted with more than one language. On the other hand, early mastery of the ability to synchronize with adults using very different rhythmic patterns might facilitate bilingual learning.

2.2 Some issues which concern researchers

There is some confusion in the literature about what counts as communication. For some what qualifies must be not only directed to someone but intended as a message. This involves questions about how and when conscious intentionality may be considered to have begun. This concern draws a distinction between biological and psychological phenomena and appears to rest on a philosophical attitude which accepts mind—body dualism. For others the infant may be considered capable of communication from birth, for to them communication is part of his biological makeup. The problem does not seem to exist for students of animal behavior.

Another issue, discussed in terms of a musical analogy by Tronick et al., concerns which partner controls the joint performance which results in communication. Trevarthen, working with quite similar methods, reaches a seemingly opposite conclusion. At first it seemed obvious to everyone that adults, being more experienced, must be the leaders and teachers of babies who could only follow and never innovate without some model or assistance. Perhaps this is our heritage from the *tabula rasa* concept of infant mind. Then, with the emergence of the concept expressed in *The effect of the infant on its caregivers* (Lewis & Rosenblum 1974) came a tendency to see the infant as very powerful in shaping his relationship with his 'significant others'. Brazelton utilizes this view of the infant to help assuage parental guilt which escalated in response to the overemphasis by psychiatrists and other child-rearing 'experts' on the serious consequences of early psychological trauma. As is usual with extreme dichotomies, both of these opposing views are probably simultaneously valid. Both partners in a communicating dyad contribute to the relative success or failure of their intercourse, to the history of their relationship and to the outcome in communicative competence when the infant enters the wider social world beyond his own family circle.

Even before speech there is an issue as to whether successive infant achievements in communication are arrived at by analytic or by synthetic processes.

A prominent issue in discussion is the relation between early co-action and alternation patterns during mother—infant interaction, and there has been some discussion (Aaronson & Rieber 1975) as to whether they are precursors of adult forms. Both occur from very early in mother—infant dyads. The alternating pattern, when expressed vocally, has been labeled 'proto-conversation' (M.C. Bateson 1971) or vocal dialogue. Fraiberg and Kaye also deal with it. Behavior is always continuous, as is communication for all its participants so long as they are 'in communication', i.e. sharing mutual attention (see fig. 1). Behavior in individual modalities may have an on—off character, e.g. mutual gaze or vocalization, or be episodic, e.g. gestures. The message may be carried in multiple channels or switch channels without interrupting communication. Once the hierarchical organization of behavior, interaction and communication is recognized, the problem of coaction versus reciprocity takes its place as a relatively superficial issue, as Bateson explains.

One aspect of these studies on which all the authors agree, sometimes only implicitly, is that the object of their studies is rule-governed behavior. No matter to what extent small numbers of cases lead to descriptions of what is recognized as idiosyncratic styles, the suspicion is nowhere expressed that any of the communicative systems described is chaotic or that they cannot be described in terms of observed regularities. We have been through a period when it was usual for infant behavior to be described as random, which may in part account for its neglect by scientists for so long.

2.3 Pathology

So far we have been considering, at least by implication, questions relating to communication with intact infants. One of the reasons for studying the 'normal' is to throw light on how to bring help to individuals who, for whatever reason, do not function normally. In addition study of defective individuals can help us understand normal processes. We have among our chapters some which deal with pathology affecting interpersonal communication. Ricks and I both undertook our research on the normal developmental process out of concern for groups of patients: his were autistic children; mine, both autistic children and schizophrenic adults. Richer (forthcoming) has investigated the communicative defect of autistic children by means of experiment and clinical observation. Several authors have studied infants with defects which interfere with communication. Fraiberg's longitudinal study of blind babies has been particularly enlightening in regard to the significance of vision in normal communicative development as well as teaching us a great deal about communicative modalities less often studied. Newson describes research by several co-workers on infants with severe pathology: Jones with Down's syndrome children

Fig. 1 The beginning of a proto-conversation: consecutive frames taken
automatically in black and white at ½-second intervals (12 seconds elapsed
time) using a Kodak Ciné Special camera with 16mm XX film under
room lighting (observation no. M032). The mother has positioned her
infant on the edge of the kitchen table after bathing and dressing him
and has squatted to bring her head nearly level with his. The sequence
illustrates some of the phases of face-to-face communicative interaction
described by Tronick et al. (this volume: section 3). Because the frames
are spaced out (in a way which differs from ordinary cinema or video
technique) it is easy to identify successive states of mother—infant communication as it develops. Face-to-face contact is not continuous eye-
to-eye contact but there is no lapse in mutual awareness and the maintenance of the communicative state.

and Mogford with a diagnostically mixed group of retardates. Condon has applied his special analytic technique with an unexpected result to infants and children with a variety of conditions which impede learning, including autism. Plooij argues from chimpanzee observations to a possible analogy in human psychopathology. Two authors (Brazelton and Stensland Junker) describe the development of assessment procedures for identifying conditions which interfere with communication in the newborn period and at eight months respectively. The purpose behind developing such procedures is the belief that early detection and remediation effort improves an infant's chances for having the defect corrected or, if that is not possible, for being offered ways to compensate for it.

3 The infant we study

The very term *infancy* focusses attention on the issue of communication. Literally it is the period before speech (etymologically *infans* = Latin 'speechless'). The word has come to have a very wide and diverse meaning in regard to the period of life it designates. Since the onset of speech is not a true event (Bullowa 1970) like the onset of unassisted walking, but rather a process, the exact boundaries must remain a bit fuzzy. Here we will hold to the fundamental meaning and deal with infants mainly before their first birthdays.

The chapters cluster around three age periods (identified in section 5). A few deal with the first few days after birth, the neonatal period. A number are concerned with infants in the first three to four months, before they sit without support. (This is probably what is meant when the imprecise term 'young infant' appears in scientific literature.) In our culture they tend to spend a great deal of their time alone, lying or propped except when actively engaged with an adult in caregiving or social activities which offer opportunities for communication. In many cultures infants at this age spend a great deal of time in bodily contact with an adult or older child, sometimes receiving full attention, sometimes nearly ignored as the caregiver goes about her everyday business. Contact is maximized for the Fore infants described by Sorenson. In some cultures infants are swaddled or on cradleboards, but often placed so that they can see the activity around them. A third age group from six to seven months on are beginning to move around if allowed the opportunity but are not yet walking. (This is

the age at which, it is generally agreed, infant vocalization changes.)
Once they walk alone we would call them 'toddlers'.

In what follows I will sketch some aspects of infancy which have
emerged from recent research, mainly by psychologists. Since I am
not a psychologist by training but rather a consumer of their findings,
my perception of how their field developed may contain some distortions. In the subsections immediately following I refer to some
findings from psychological research and a few pediatric studies which
I have found relevant to a concern with infants as communicators.
Where chapter authors have reviewed such literature, I refer to their
presentations rather than duplicate them. The way in which we as
investigators of communicative development make use of these findings is presented in section 4.

3.1 Signal production

Motility. In order for anyone (or even any organism) to participate
in communication with another it is necessary for him to have some
way to signal and some way to receive and interpret signals. (This
refers to the message aspect, not to the aspect of being in a state of
communication.) Signal or message production requires ability to
produce change. A continuous and undifferentiated state produces
no signal. That requires contrast. Usually this change is produced by
motion. It could be by change in something which appears static,
e.g. blushing, but this too is due to motion at a more microscopic
level. What moves may be sound waves set in motion by the 'vocal
apparatus' or it may be some more visible part of the body.

The possibilities for human-to-human communication are limited
only by human motor and perceptual capacities. Ultrasound is not a
basis for human communication because we are not biologically
equipped to send or receive it, as bats are. Voice, gaze, facial
expression and gesture are the motor functions most frequently
investigated, to the relative neglect of those used mainly when bodies
are near or in contact, the ones of prime importance with small
infants.

Even newborns are able to see and to aim their gaze. The biological
importance of vision and eye movement is attested by their extensive
representation in the human central nervous system and their early
maturation. Together with orienting movement, gaze is the first means
by which we can detect to what infants are paying attention. It is

usually easy to detect what someone else, including a baby, is looking at and to recognize unfocussed gaze. While inanimate displays, especially changing and moving ones, are known to hold the babies' visual attention, for the purpose of communication studies the significant findings are in regard to babies' looking behavior toward people. Robson (1967) did pioneer work on mutual gaze involving infants and their mothers. He pointed out its significance in relation to the formation of emotional bonding (attachment) and to the pathology associated with blocking or withholding this form of communication. Since mutual gaze is the context for a great deal of communication in other modalities at the beginning as well as throughout life, it should be considered a very fundamental form of human communicative behavior. While it may have underlying biological significance as with other mammals, only humans use it for intimacy as well as to enforce submission (Robson 1967).

Until recently descriptions of infant and child facial expressions have been largely impressionistic. Although smiling has been extensively researched, what was needed was a way of describing all infant facial movement in a more 'objective' way based on underlying anatomical structure. Harriet Oster (Oster & Ekman forthcoming), working in Ekman's laboratory, the laboratory which has taken the mystery out of adult facial expression, has done the same for infants. At last we have a way of looking at the faces of infants which takes into account the underlying bone structure (quite different in its proportions from that of adult faces) as well as differences in the overlying 'soft parts', especially the fat pads in the cheeks (sucking pads) which account for the characteristic infantile appearance that adults have been shown to find irresistible (Eibl-Eibesfeldt 1971). Although we have no difficulty in extreme cases in knowing from either his voice or his facial expression whether an infant is contented or distressed, up to now a good deal of the intermediate behavior in both media has been ambiguous. Oster has given us an analysis based on the action of individual facial muscles acting alone and in combination using the FAC (facial action code) units Ekman & Friesen (1976) have established for adults. Plooij has compared human and chimpanzee facial expression, especially smiling, and cites additional literature.

While the patterns of gross motor development, especially in regard to locomotion (Gesell 1934, McGraw 1943), have been well known for some time, attention to details of motor patterns of expressive gestures, such as pointing (Murphy & Messer 1977), is a more recent interest stemming from concern with cognitive issues and communication.

Vocalization. Although vocalization is produced by a form of motility, because of the extensive research attention it has received and the special techniques associated with its study, it warrants separate treatment. Just as attention to language and speech have overshadowed attention to non-verbal forms of communication, so until recently attention to infant vocal behavior seems to have provoked as much scientific attention as all other potentially communicative infant behavior combined. Sophisticated technical methods for the study of speech devised by acoustic engineers have been exploited for recording and analyzing infant sounds. Very detailed studies were done on infant crying in a co-operative study involving scientists from a number of disciplines in Sweden and Finland in the 1960s. The summaries of their findings, published in English, are in Lind (1965) and Wasz-Höckert et al. (1968). This much-researched area deserves fuller treatment: more of its literature (prior to 1973) is reviewed in Bullowa et al. 1975.

We are now entering on an even more advanced engineering attack on the problem, based on the hope of using cry analysis diagnostically. Ostwald (1972) has contributed in this field and reviewed its literature. Michelsson (1971) in Finland showed the feasibility of detecting brain damage in babies who had suffered anoxia at birth through electronic acoustic analysis of their cry patterns.

Study of prelinguistic vocalization (sometimes termed 'prespeech', I believe unfortunately, since the word suggests continuities which have not been established and is, moreover, used in a different and specific sense by Trevarthen) was a major topic at two recent meetings in addition to the section of the International Child Language Association Symposium in London mentioned above, p. 1 (Waterson & Snow 1978). The second Colloque International d'Audiophonologie devoted to 'Prélangage' was held at Besançon, France, in November 1973 and was published in its entirety in three volumes (Lafon 1974). In April 1974 the sixth annual Child Language Research Forum at Stanford University in California held a panel discussion with five participants on 'From babbling to speech' (Clark 1974) and had an invited address by Sinclair-de Zwaart (1974) of the University of Geneva on 'Prespeech'. While a great deal of effort has gone into minute analysis of vocal sound without context, there also are some attempts to relate vocalization to other aspects of psychological devel-

opment (e.g. Sinclair-de Zwaart 1974) and to communicative development (e.g. Peters 1976). Such studies bring us closer to the findings
of Ricks and Halliday.

There has been a tradition of considering infant vocal noises,
especially non-crying ones, as precursors of speech and attempts to
categorize them in terms of phonetic elements recognized in adult
speech. This was undoubtedly implemented by the weight of the
reputation of the internationally celebrated linguist, Roman Jakobson,
whose *Kindersprache* (1941) propounded the theory that infants universally may babble all the human speech sounds of the world before
they narrow down to the phonemic elements of the mother-tongue.
Since he worked from paper and pencil records mainly by linguists
recording their own infants in phonetic notation, it was inevitable
that he should have arrived at this conclusion. This theory is widely
quoted and has led to a popular misuse of the term 'phoneme' which
is inapplicable to prelinguistic vocalization, since it implies a certain
minimal element in a language, and cannot be identified in the sounds
made by a child who does not yet speak a language. Jones is a linguist
who made a pioneer attempt to consider early infant socialization in
its own right (Bullowa, Jones & Bever 1964). At least one group of
linguists is now undertaking such an analysis: Koopmans-van Beinum
(forthcoming) and her co-worker, van der Steldt.

For Grace de Laguna, who published a now classic study of
language and its acquisition half a century ago (1927), the cry of
infant or animal is 'at once a specific response to a situation and an
act directed toward another member of the group' (262), whereas the
'sentence-word' 'is a response to the situation *perceived* or otherwise
cognized, and not as *felt*' (262). While we still tend to look on infant
prelinguistic vocal sounds as largely 'emotive expressions', many of
the authors of this book find evidence in infants' developing vocal
behavior of a much more advanced state of intelligence than the
psychologists of almost any school would have accorded them in the
1920s.

Walburga von Raffler-Engel (now professor at Vanderbilt University
in Nashville, Tennessee) was an early proponent of the communicative
value of prelinguistic vocalization. Her major work on this appeared
in Italian (*Il prelinguaggio infantile* 1964) and so has been largely
overlooked by the English-using child language community. She studied
the vocal development of her infant son during his first year of life in
1960—1. A relevant passage from her English summary of her book

presents her theory of the 'carrier sound':

It was apparent that within the first months of life the little boy was beginning to understand rudimentary statements from their sentence melody. At four months he started to use a 'basic sound' m̥ while pointing at objects. The intonation of this sound *passe-partout* was varied according to whether the baby wanted the object or simply wondered what it was. Only at five months did he perceive phonemic distinctions. At seven months he uttered his first word *ča*, for the Italian colloquial good-by, 'ciao'. Then, at nine months, the child began to acquire many new words, none of which happened to contain the semi-vocalic m̥. Still, the 'basic sound' m̥ continued to serve him whenever he did not know the proper word or was unable to pronounce it. Consequently, the m̥ is not to be considered a phoneme, but rather a base for tone variation.

She also observed this phenomenon in six additional infants. Von Raffler Engel has insisted all along on the need to study language acquisition in the context of interaction and cultural influences and to include the gestural behavior which develops along with the vocal behavior as data. For her, infant vocalization has a communicative function from the start.

Other channels. The means of signal production by infants already mentioned are those most extensively researched. This by no means exhausts the possibilities. At close range infants can produce signals perceived through olfaction, temperature sensation, pressure and other modalities. These are so far best known to science as medical signs, but are probably taken into account by caregivers, even if not with focussed attention (see section 4).

3.2 Signal reception: perception

Communication requires not only production of signals but also their reception and processing. Reception depends on sensory organs (collectively 'the sensorium') and their connections with the central nervous system. Registration of the input from the sensorium is called 'perception'.

When I was a medical student I was taught that infants were born blind and deaf. If true, this would have foreclosed a lot of communication with the newly born (and we would have no chapter by Brazelton or Chappell & Sander). Even somewhat older infants were not credited with much ability to perceive the world around them. Not only pediatricians but also psychologists consigned them to a world of blurred confusion. This had to change before anyone would have considered doing the studies reported here. In fact it has by now been demonstrated that vision and audition are functioning at birth, even though there is still some rapid development to be accomplished in the early postnatal period of fullterm infants. Newborns can fixate visually and follow a moving test object with gaze as demonstrated by Brazelton et al. (1966). Previously they had been tested with objects so bright that they protected themselves by refusing to look. Similarly inappropriate overloud stimuli had led to underestimating their auditory acuity. Careful studies such as those of Eisenberg (1975) have mapped infant audition. All other sensory modalities of the newborn have been subjected to study and none have been found wanting. We now know what to expect of intact neonates. This information forms part of what underlies the neonatal assessment procedure developed by Brazelton and the early intervention program of Stensland Junker. Perceptual studies of developing infants, especially on presentation of sound, are at the basis of Stensland Junker's assessment procedure at eight months. Perceptual functioning is a necessary, but not a sufficient, condition for interpersonal communication.

In the course of studying other modalities investigators have seemed indifferent to the presence or absence of body contact, not to mention its quality and quantity. Some infants are observed in cribs and infant seats, others in their mothers' arms or on their laps. Researchers have usually disregarded this as a factor which might modify results in other areas.

3.3 Cognition

Not so long ago infants were hardly credited with having any minds at all, at least in most American academic psychology. By now cognitive psychology has reached back practically to the moment of birth, if not earlier. In order to consider exchange of meanings between persons there must be persons, and it is very hard for us to conceive of persons apart from minds. Psychologists, at least in the United States and Canada, have tended to explore thinking and feeling as if these were independent functions. It seemed to me when I was engaged in the practice of psychiatry that there were two different kinds of psychologists: those concerned with intelligence who used test procedures which could be scaled to obtain IQs and those concerned with personality who used projective tests to find out about emotions. This is, of course, a caricature and no doubt stems from the fragmentation of academic psychology in the United States and from the affiliations of psychologists with other professional groups, including psychiatrists. Be that as it may, there is a real difference between images of infancy stemming from people concerned with precursors of thinking and those stemming from people concerned with precursors of feeling. This has contributed to an impression of fragmentation in infancy research. It often seems, as one reads the 'literature', that the infant who learns has no feelings, or at most experiences pleasure and pain, while the infant who is developing his personality or becoming a social being is not concerned with learning anything except who will gratify him and who frustrate him. It is difficult to put these findings and pronouncements together to produce the image of a unified person — infant, child or adult.

Until recently an infant starting on the path toward intelligence seemed in scientific writings to be concerned mainly with the physical properties of the world in terms of what distinctions he was able to make, usually demonstrated by experiments on 'conditioning'. In these studies the infant was very like any other laboratory animal and regrettably capricious. I have to admit that it was always hard for me to understand how such 'science' would help me to understand how infants communicate, even when the statistics were impeccable and the findings stood up to replication.

The work of Bower began to show me why I needed to pay attention to the psychologists who looked into infant perception, motor development and cognition. Two articles in *Scientific American* (1966, 1971) summarize parts of his elegant studies on the perceptual world of infants. His book, *Development in infancy* (1974), gives an even more complete picture of what has been discovered by his tightly structured experiments dealing with what the infant experiences of the physical world through his sense organs, how he demonstrates this to his investigators through his behavior and what is called his cognitive development — his developing understanding. Here Bower is very clear on what has been learned and what suspected and what still remains equivocal, either because it has not been looked into or because the studies done so far have not considered all possible factors. He gives us some very useful pointers which are as applicable in our field of interest as in his: 'The point is that different functional behaviors use the same behavioral components. It is risky to infer one particular functional behavior from occurrence of a behavioral component that is used in a variety of situations' (91). This came up in a discussion of arm extension in the development of reaching and grasping. He says: 'Pointing and reaching both involve arm extension; one must there-

fore be certain that the *intent* of an extension is reaching and not
pointing or some other activity' (91). An infant who can have intentions is getting close to one who can communicate, an infant I can
think of as a person. (Tronick et al. include further discussion and
reference on infant information processing.)

It becomes very difficult (and perhaps irrelevant) to draw a line
between biological and psychological levels of functioning (see beginning of section 2.2). We tend to assume that things which happen very
early in life must be 'just' biological reflexes, but when does cognition
'really' start? Which way do we account for the visually guided reaching which Bower (1972) demonstrated for one- to two-week-old
infants? Ordinarily this function disappears quickly to surface again
at four months, but he showed that with practice it could continue
during the period when it is usually in abeyance. This turned out to
be of no advantage to the practiced babies just as practice had been
of no advantage in locomotor achievement to the practiced one of
McGraw's famous twins (1935). But the potential is there.

Language acquisition has been the province mainly of linguists and
cognitive psychologists. With the recognition of the need to seek
language beginnings earlier, these studies have dealt with data beginning
at younger ages. A characteristic example is a study based on records
taken at home of 'naturalistic interaction' combined with simple test
procedures of three Italian children by Bates et al. (1975). They
studied language acquisition longitudinally by recording three girl-
infants beginning at two, six and twelve months and following each
until she had overtaken the point at which the next older had started.
They were seeking precursors of 'performative' imperative and declara-
tive sentences in the infants' actions and gestures. The recent volume
edited by Lock (1978) contains a number of studies of language
acquisition bridging the period between prelanguage and language.

3.4 Interaction

Cognition studies, however, traditionally consider the infant essentially
as an isolated individual. The step to interest in interaction seems to
me the great divide. The infant is no longer alone in his crib or infant
seat or even on his mother's knee undergoing tests of his functions. At
last he has a companion who is recognized as part of what is being
investigated. It is not obvious to me why this shift took place, but I
can perceive the seeds of it in some of the less 'interactive' work. Rob-

son's infants (1967) controlled their gaze to look at the faces of adult caregivers. Somehow the 'other' had been lurking there all along.

Jerome Bruner has been a bridge-builder between the cognitive psychology of infancy and mother—infant interaction studies, having attracted to his laboratory, first at Harvard and then at Oxford, investigators who have pioneered the interaction field. His own orientation seems to me focussed on the cognitive basis for communication rather than on the communicative process itself (1977). Brazelton, Kaye, Trevarthen and Tronick all worked at the Harvard Center for Cognitive Studies while Bruner was director there (see the center's Annual Reports). Bower, Papoušek, Richards and probably a number of others to whom reference is made in this volume are veterans of that laboratory.

Hanuš Papoušek has established at the Max-Planck-Institut für Psychiatrie in Munich, beginning in 1972, a laboratory for the study of the preverbal period of mother—infant communicative interaction equipped with audio-visual recording and analyzing apparatus representing the most advanced 'state of the art' of the early seventies. Here with co-workers he is beginning to combine the results and techniques he formerly used in Prague and Cambridge, Massachusetts for the study of early cognitive development with studies of social communication in the early months of extra-uterine life. An important feature of his approach is the bridging of interdisciplinary and subdisciplinary gaps, first between association learning and operational learning and then between the infant's individual cognitive processes and the unfolding of communicative interaction between mother and infant (Papoušek & Papoušek 1975, 1977). Parental behavior is included in his studies.

3.5 The infant as a person

This topic has bearing on both scientific and lay attitudes toward infants. Lately the infant has been discovered to be human and so more able to communicate with other humans than was formerly thought. Why should it need mentioning, much less discovering, that human young are human too? Simply because the 'experts' seem to have forgotten it for a time while they were busy being scientific. Pediatricians and others who gave advice to parents went through a phase of talking of an infant with so fragile a nervous system that it was dangerous for him to be picked up and 'stimulated'. Less than half a century ago affection was supposed to be detrimental to babies.

In 1944 an American pediatrician mother (Whipple) could confess in print that she cuddled her baby and that it hadn't led to disaster. She admitted to having been influenced by a book called *Babies are human beings* by a pediatrician couple (Aldrich & Aldrich 1938). This book was influential in the United States in the 1940s in breaking the temporary hold of restrictive 'science' on child-rearing advice. An analysis of successive editions of *Infant care*, a bulletin of the US Children's Bureau distributed in millions of copies, traces the reversal of child-rearing attitudes (Wolfenstein 1955). Newson & Newson (1974) discuss this change in child-rearing attitudes, including more of the British experience.

Among the present-day students of communication with infants the trend toward acknowledging the humanity, or personhood, of infants is carried still further. Some are calling attention to the consequences of treating babies like persons even before they act like persons (Shotter 1974, Shotter & Gregory 1976). Snow et al. call attention to this aspect of what they term the 'ideology of child-rearing'. At least in cultures in which mothers think of their babies as people, babies are talked to and behaved to in a special quasi-conversational mode right from the start. This phenomenon ('baby talk') and infant response to it is now a focus of research attention (see section 4). It is included in the field of 'talking to children', the subject of a research conference in 1975 and of a volume (Snow & Ferguson 1977).

3.6 Relevant literature

There remain a number of large areas in the rapidly accumulating infancy literature which I have not touched on. There is the important and relevant field of developmental neurology, the older work still probably best represented by Peiper's *Cerebral function in infancy and childhood* (1963). A few more recent writings are mentioned in the chapters by Condon and Trevarthen. I have mentioned the psychoanalytic literature and that on attachment, separation and fear of strangers which stems from it only occasionally in passing. A good way to find the trends in these areas is to search the annual series *Psychoanalytic Study of the Child*, already past its first three decades. Bowlby's report (1951) to the World Health Organization (WHO) on the deleterious effects of 'maternal deprivation' took its original inspiration from psychoanalytic concepts and engendered studies which led into the whole field of interaction between infant and caregiver. An updated version of that report (1965) is available in paperback and his writings on 'attachment' (1969, 1973) are also widely distributed. There is also a part of the literature on socialization which borders on and partially overlaps that on interaction, including such works as Schaffer's *The growth of sociability* (1971a). Richards (1974b) has edited a collection of papers on early socialization and Stern (1977) has written a popular book on socialization during the first half year.

Since there is not scope here for an exhaustive review of the relevant investigations and literature which led to our present focal area, I am including a brief directory to English-language writings. The task of locating the bulk of this literature has recently been made easier by the appearance of several compendia focussing on infancy. *The competent infant* (Stone et al. 1973) is a mammoth collection of readings with commentary. Items cited in this book which have been reprinted in it are indicated in the bibliography. *Exceptional infant* vol. I, *The normal infant* (Hellmuth 1967) is the first of a series of volumes of review papers dealing with all aspects of infancy. These two large publications cut across disciplinary and sub-disciplinary lines and are virtually encyclopedias for those concerned with non-medical aspects of infancy. The two volumes of Cohen & Salapatek's *Infant perception from sensation to cognition* (1975) present up-to-date infancy research in its more restricted area. A volume of papers on infancy from a cross-cultural viewpoint has recently appeared (Liederman et al. 1977). An earlier symposium on 'Cross-cultural studies in mother—infant interaction: description and consequences' chaired by M. Lewis was held at the Minneapolis meeting of the American Society for Research in Child Development in 1971 and published in *Human Development*, 15 (1972). A *Handbook of infancy* (Osofsky) is forthcoming. Semi-popular accounts of results of recent infancy research are to be found in some of the chapters of *Child alive* (Lewin 1975) and in some of the small books of the *Developing child* series edited by Bruner, Cole & Lloyd (1977–). Another useful publication is a collection of reprints from *Scientific American* (Greenough 1973).

The development of non-medical infancy research during the past quarter century can be traced in publications stemming from small conferences (Mead & Byers 1968) held during this period. Their titles and sponsorship are revealing of trends. In 1952 an international seminar organized by the World Federation for Mental Health was held at Chichester, England. This was a three-week training course attended by fifty-one professionals from thirty countries, some of whom were designated 'faculty'. Child development patterns in different cultures as well as health services and education of the public were taken up. Two volumes entitled *Mental health and infant development* (Soddy 1955) contain the papers, discussions and case reports.

A WHO study group on the 'psychobiological development of the child' met annually in Geneva from 1953 through 1956 supported by the Josiah Macy Jr Foundation. Four volumes (Tanner & Inhelder 1956a, b, 1958, 1960) were later consolidated into one paperback volume (1971).

The Ciba Foundation, London, has been hosting conferences of experts on infancy since 1959. A series of four organized for a Tavistock Study Group by John Bowlby and J.A. Ambrose met every second year. The prepared papers and discussion appeared under the title *Determinants of infant behaviour* (Foss 1961, 1963, 1965, 1969) testifying to the extent to which infants were then viewed as isolated emitters of behaviors. In the foreword to the first volume Bowlby wrote: 'considering it was intended to be a Study Group on mother—infant interaction, material on the behaviours of human mothers and their interaction with their infants was noticeably absent' (xiv).

In 1967 the Developmental Sciences Trust was founded in Britain with the purpose 'to promote the growth of knowledge about the development of human behaviour and the factors that influence it' (Huxley & Ingram 1971: xi). Five international study groups with the general theme 'Origins of human behaviour' were organized by the Centre for Advanced Study in the Developmental Sciences (CASDS). These too represented collaboration with, and met at, the Ciba Foundation. The first meeting, held in 1967, was reported in Ambrose 1969. Papers and discussions of subsequent meetings were edited by Robinson (1969), Connolly (1970), Schaffer (1971b) and Huxley & Ingram (1971). Subsequent conferences of the trust were also held at Ciba; the first of these, for which Connolly & Bruner (1974) were responsible, received additional support from the Carnegie Foundation. While much of the development discussed at most of these meetings extended well beyond infancy, the series introduces a great deal of the most up-to-date research on many aspects of infant behavior. Since 1974 The Ciba Foundation has itself sponsored meetings, in 1974 on 'Parent—infant interaction' (Ciba 1975), and in 1976 on 'Breast-feeding and the mother' (Ciba 1976).

In 1975 the British Social Science Research Council financed a

meeting organized by Rudolph Schaffer of the University of Strathclyde, Glasgow (Schaffer 1977a), bringing government support to this
enterprise after decades of sponsorship by private foundations. The
pattern of government bodies taking over responsibility from foundations for successful demonstration projects is a familiar one in the
public health and welfare fields.

Meanwhile in the United States conferences dealing with research
and teaching of infant development have been held annually since
1957 by the Merrill-Palmer Institute of Human Development and
Family Life at Detroit, Michigan and the papers have been published
in the *Merrill-Palmer Quarterly*, which also publishes submitted papers
on infancy research. Five volumes of the series *Review of Child Development Research* have been published irregularly since 1964 (see
bibliography) and include review articles covering aspects of infancy,
notably Caldwell's in vol. I (1964). Vol. V (1975) includes a history
of the child development movement. Starting more recently another
conference series sponsored by the Educational Testing Service of
Princeton, New Jersey, has been documented in volumes on origins
of behavior under the general editorship of Lewis & Rosenblum.
Advances in Child Development and Behavior is an annual which has
appeared since 1963.

This account covers only some of the meetings and resulting publications devoted specifically to non-medical aspects of infancy,
aspects which are receiving increasing attention in other meetings and
publications as well. While infancy is not accorded a separate heading,
it is fairly easy to find the relevant titles from the subject index in
Child Development Abstracts and Bibliography published three times
a year by the (American) Society for Research in Child Development.
Around 150 journals from most of the industrialized countries, including a number from Eastern Europe, are abstracted regularly and current books are briefly reviewed. Yet the coverage is predominantly of
American research. The journal *Developmental Medicine and Child
Neurology* is less biassed toward American contributors. Spastics
International, which sponsors this journal, is also responsible for the
monograph series Clinics in Developmental Medicine, several volumes
of which deal with aspects of infancy relevant to communication.
There are numerous national and international journals which occasionally carry papers on infancy research. Only a few can be mentioned
here. The journal *Early Child Development and Care* began publication
in 1971. It is interdisciplinary and international and includes trans-

lations into English of descriptive and evaluative articles including
'special monograph' numbers on early child care in various countries
compiled by professionals in each country. The individual monographs are also available as separate volumes in hard cover; they preserve a uniform format in an attempt to promote comparability. The
Journal of Child Language (Cambridge University Press) publishes
papers on prelinguistic vocalization.

Early Human Development and Care, 'an international journal concerned with the continuity of fetal and prenatal life' (Amsterdam:
Elsevier) began publication in June 1977. Its articles so far are mainly
physiological and medical. The *International Journal of Behavioral
Development* has been announced as the official journal of the International Society for the Study of Behavioral Development (ISSBD)
to start publication in January 1978 (North Holland Publishing
Company).

The most comprehensive source of documentation on all aspects
of infancy and childhood throughout the world is to be found at the
library of the Centre Internationale de l'Enfance housed in their conference center in the Château de Longchamp in the Bois de Boulogne,
75016 Paris.

Thus it is not difficult to obtain reasonably up-to-date information
about many aspects of infancy. On the other hand, I have found that
in order to follow research in what seem to me to be the fields relevant to communication in infancy I have had to range very widely
into areas which do not bear an infancy label. Some of this literature
is reviewed in Bullowa 1975.

4 What we investigate

A pervasive problem in researching communication is that we are
always trying to find out what those we are observing experience from
outside their communicative system. We are eavesdropping on something going on between others and, when those others are an intimate
pair, like the mothers and babies who are our most frequent subjects,
there is a limit to what we can find out from our peripheral position.
We are able to deal most comfortably, and so far most extensively,
with the things both we and our subjects can perceive by means of
'distance receptors' — eyes and ears.

4.1 The modalities studied

One way of categorizing communication is according to the organs or modalities employed in sending and receiving signals (see section 3).

Aurally perceived modality. What both caregivers and investigators perceive by ear is also picked up and preserved when electronic recording devises are used: tape-recorders and film or video sound-tracks. These forms of recording acoustic data make it possible to listen repeatedly to fleeting events and to share at least part of the direct experience at another time and in another place. Instrumental analysis of vocal sound has been discussed in section 3 and sound-recording is discussed in section 5.

The ability to work without sound-recording devises requires training and experience. Often, except for phoneticians (as discussed in section 5), the record of infant vocalization is reduced to simple presence or absence or at most a few easily distinguished categories. In the past much early non-cry sound was left out of the record because it has such low intensity that one had to be very near the source to hear it.

In attempting to transcribe the content of recorded adult speech, there is likely to be a good deal of ambiguity, since we adults don't always enunciate clearly, especially in the intimate situations of caring for infants. The person who was actually there when the recording was made is probably the best interpreter of what was said, for he is more attuned to the caregiver than someone listening 'cold'. However, unless the exact words used are of critical importance to a study, how it was said is probably of much greater communicative significance than what was said — and this is rarely ambiguous.

The vocal– (or oral–) aural modality is represented here by attention to both infant and caregiver vocalization. Halliday and Ricks have analyzed infant vocal development in entirely different ways: Halliday 'naturalistically', Ricks experimentally. Ricks also experimentally probed parental recognition of the meaning and source (own or other infant) of certain infant sounds and infants' ability to imitate their own sounds (from tape) and those of others. Bateson submitted an infant's contribution to 'proto-conversation' to acoustic analysis and measured the duration of the sounds and their timing in relation to maternal speech sounds (M.C. Bateson 1971, 1975b). Chappell & Sander coded maternal vocalization to newborn infants during caregiving. Brazelton and Stensland Junker both make use of adult vocalization to infants in their procedures. The Snow et al. chapter deals with mothers' speech directed toward infants in two cultures. Even in Plooij's study of mother–infant chimpanzee pairs,

vocalization was one of the behaviors coded. There is some mention
of vocal behavior in every chapter except Sorenson's (owing to his
use of silent film).

Visually perceived modalities. To an interactant it does not seem
possible to assess the direction of another's gaze without gazing oneself but, from the observer's point of view, individuals may not only
look into one another's eyes (mutual gaze) but may simultaneously
look at the same other thing or person. Collis is investigating how this
comes about when, for instance, the mother's gaze locates the object
the infant on her lap is looking at when she cannot see his face. I
wonder whether this would be possible if the baby were not in intimate contact with the mother. Collis (1977a) is investigating deictic
gaze as a form of communication in this and other ways. Stensland
Junker in her screening test uses the visual attraction of a red stick as
an intermediate step between the infant's attention to the tester's
face and search for the hidden source of a sound. Brazelton too uses
gaze engagement in his assessment procedure. There is some mention
of gaze in nearly every chapter; Collis supplies additional references
on several aspects of gaze as well as of some other modalities used in
interaction with infants.

'Face to face' implies mutual gaze. Because mutual gaze is (except
for the blind) the context in which early vocal exchanges usually take
place, it is implied in every study which deals with this. Collis analyzes
data relating mutual gaze to both vocalization and gesture. Fraiberg
in describing the blind infant tells us a great deal about the significance of mutual gaze in normal communication. She has described
how upsetting the lack of visual focus in blind babies is for their
mothers. Plooij reports absence of eye contact early in the chimpanzee mother—baby relationship.

Facial expression, also involving the visual modality except for the
blind, is coded by Collis, Tronick et al. and, for chimpanzees, by
Plooij. Trevarthen and Tronick et al. experimentally ask mothers to
hold a blank expression and note infant response to this unnatural
situation. Trevarthen discusses the significance of infant facial
expressions including those he believes prefigure speech. Substitution
of fingering for vision by blind infants is described by Fraiberg.

Movement of the rest of the body, which people perceive visually
when they are not in intimate contact, is part of communication, not
only as isolated gestures, such as pointing (the one most often studied
in infancy because of its apparent relationship to naming in early

language use), but also in many other ways. Classifications of non-
verbal means of communication are to be found in Ekman & Friesen
(1969) and Poyatos (1975) among others. Condon's entire investigation deals with the relation between body movement and speech.
Collis has analyzed the response of 'older' infants to the mother's
pointing gesture, as well as the infant's own movements. Halliday
takes note of his subject's gestures as well as his vocal sounds as he
traces his exploration of meanings. It is of course of special significance to Fraiberg where absence of sight leads to increased body
movement, especially at intimate range. A list would not properly
represent the pervasive attention to gesture and body movement.
Even when it is not specifically coded, we take note of it. As we
become better at watching babies, less of what they do appears random and so we can interpret more.

Posture (orientation of the body in space) is a very important factor in interpersonal communication which is dealt with explicitly in
the chapter by Chappell & Sander. They also deal with the distance
between bodies, coding posture and proximity between mother and
newborn every 5 seconds during caregiving procedures. Most laboratory studies were done with seated or propped infants. Bower (1972)
had demonstrated that a supine infant is at a great disadvantage. Posture may be considered also in relation to body parts so that postural
shifts of head or hand, for instance, may act as signals, as Papoušek &
Papoušek (1977) found for infant hands between waking and sleep.
Tactile communication. Communication through the skin is the first
modality activated in prenatal life and is heavily involved in the birth
process, as Desmond Morris points out graphically in the first chapter
of *Intimate behaviour* (1971), and remains prominent throughout
infancy. We have tended to overlook dermal communication, possibly
because it is difficult to devise discrete research methods with which
to study it and also because northern cultures have until very recently
placed a taboo on public skin contact between adults. The appearance
of scientific (Montagu 1971, Morris 1971) and popular books and the
rise of cults and 'therapies' which focus on contact between bodies
shows that we are now in the pendular swing away from this neglect
and taboo. This climate should be more favorable to the investigation
of tactile experience and communication of infant—adult pairs. Most
of this work remains to be done, even though a pioneer paper by
Frank was published in 1957.

In the revolution against the scientific sterility of our hospital obstetrics, doctors and nurses have come to question aspects of 'modern' procedures which separate infants from their mothers the moment the cord is cut and allow them access to one another only for brief scheduled periods of nursing or bottle feeding. This has led to such studies, changes in procedure and recommendations as those of Klaus et al. (1975). Newborn infants were placed naked beside their mothers in a warm environment and the mothers' behavior as they began to become acquainted with their infants was noted. These investigators describe a uniform sequence of maternal approach beginning with fingertip touch and progressing by stages to holding and enfolding. A number of workers in various countries are in the process of replicating these observations. The French obstetrician Leboyer (1974), in his campaign to alter obstetric practice, lays great stress on tactile communication, as he does in his more recent *Shantala* (1976) in which he describes and advocates a ritualized form of massage of babies performed by mothers in India.

Although touch has been little researched in the laboratory, since we have not developed techniques for measuring it, it is the subject of Sorenson's entire chapter based on field observation. It is also prominent in Fraiberg's chapter on blind babies and receives mention in others.

A paper to be published (Bullowa & Putney in preparation) suggests ways in which we might at least surmise a more inclusive picture of the communication taking place between an infant and his mother from the audio-visual record. We looked for places where messages based on pressure, movement, taste, temperature etc. were probably passing between mother and infant during feeding. In the material we studied from this point of view there appeared to be an alternation between 'steady states' with either no perceptible change or only rhythmic oscillations and, usually briefer, change periods during which messages in many modalities appeared to be exchanged in clusters. This could have been characteristic of the feeding activity but it is one possible pattern in the structure of communication viewed more comprehensively than usual. However, extraction of even a small amount of such data is very costly in time and is likely to become even more so with more refined methods. This is likely to discourage many from attempting it. Nevertheless, I hope it presages the direction which our studies of prelinguistic communication will take as we seek a more comprehensive view of how infants find out

about the human environment into which they were born and which
they have to understand if they are to survive.

This by no means exhausts the possibilities for communication,
which are as varied as the human sensorium permits. The sense considered the most primitive in evolution, that of olfaction (usually
classified with the distance receptors), is available to both partners.
MacFarlane (1975) is one of the few students of mother—infant interaction who considers it. Brazelton considers temperature change in
his assessment procedure. Taste too has been studied in terms of what
the individual perceives, but not to my knowledge as a communication
channel in infancy. There are possibilities for communication involving
the richly supplied tiny sensory organs embedded in the skin which
can detect deep and superficial pressure, tickle sensation, pain and
temperature and which may be stimulated when bodies touch or
approach, but these have been largely disregarded as communicative
modalities for infants and caregivers. Ashley Montagu has begun to
open up this area in a book called *Touching* (1971). But so far this
has been an area more for poetry than for science.

4.2 Phenomena

Communicative experience is often described in terms of the phenomena observed. Some of them cannot be easily classified by sensorimotor modality. When this classification deals with items of behavior,
it fragments the flow but picks out events which engage attention,
which may then be described as patterned behaviors. We also sometimes treat as phenomena background states which are necessary for
communication but have low message content.

In the latter category, attention is probably the most important
for communication since it signals a receptive state. Mutual attention
or orientation is the context for communication based on conscious
intention. Attention may be expressed by combinations of gaze, by
facial expression of interest, and posturally and kinesically by orienting postures and movements. Fraiberg vividly describes how blind
babies share attention through their hands while their faces remain
inexpressive. Selective attention, the ability to attend to one thing in
the presence of other things, is the concept on which Stensland Junker
based her test. The concept and the phrase come up independently in
the chapters of Bateson and Brazelton.

Body contact or intimacy is another contextualizing phenomenon.

The proximity dimension (Hall 1969) and relative position (Scheflen 1964, 1975) specify what sort of communication may take place. Chappell & Sander code interpersonal distance. Collis, studying older infants, also attends to proximity. It is mentioned or implied in a number of the other studies. It makes a difference, rarely taken into account, whether an infant is on an infant seat facing his mother who may or may not touch, reposition or support him, as in the chapters by Newson, Tronick et al. and Trevarthen, or is seated on her lap as in that of Collis. If the infant is on the lap during laboratory studies he tends to be facing in the same direction as his mother, but if he is in the infant seat, they are face to face and usually recorded with 'split-screen' technique (see Tronick et al. section 2.2). Thus at least body contact and gaze differ. Collis points out that mothers try to monitor baby faces. It is possible for the baby to be on the mother's lap or in her arms in a position which permits mutual gaze, as I too have often found in 'naturalistic' film. Stensland Junker assesses eight-month-olds seated on the mother's lap while she sits facing the baby with her head at his level. Brazelton picks up the baby himself.

Certain isolated behavior patterns have attracted research attention to their communicative significance. One such is greeting (Kendon & Ferber 1973). Mothers and infants do a great deal of greeting. The relation between these early greeting behaviors and the more elaborate adult acts of greeting is not known. Tronick et al. have coded mother and infant greeting and Halliday refers to it.

A phenomenon which receives increasing attention and gives rise to questions as to its origin and significance is the special slowed down behavior adults and even quite young children show in their intercourse with infants. It is the topic of the chapter by Snow et al. and is discussed by Bateson (who described it as part of proto-conversation in 1971), Collis, Newson, Trevarthen and Tronick et al., Collis cites additional literature. A research field is developing around it.

Applicable here only to the newborn is attention to 'state' (meaning conditions of the central nervous system producing various levels on a sleep-to-fully-awake scale (Prechtl & Beintema 1964)). The research dealing with newborns considers state in relation to communication (Brazelton, Chappell & Sander).

Episodic behavior occurring in the course of communication with infants is often noted. Sometimes this is labeled 'burst–pause' pattern as in describing infant sucking and maternal jiggling (Brazelton, Kaye). It is mentioned in relation to maternal speech by Tronick et al.

4.3 Integration

Human communication may be analyzed in terms of means (communication channels) and of isolated phenomena, but it is fundamentally an integrated system. Whole persons communicate with other whole persons. The way in which this is orchestrated is what we must aim at understanding, even though we must analyze a great deal of intricate detail along the way. At this level timing and rhythm-sharing become salient. This has been introduced already in section 2. In some ways it is implicit in all the studies. It is brought into especially clear focus in the chapters by Chappell & Sander and Condon and in each there is speculation about the way in which integration takes place in the central nervous system.

4.4 Other possible categorizations

There are other ways in which I might have divided up the topic of what we investigate. For instance we could consider occasions (or contexts) for communication as they specify what sort of communication takes place within them. Snow et al. consider this. Communication when no other activity is taking place, what Bateson calls 'proto-conversation', Snow et al. 'talking for fun' and Tronick et al. 'play dialogue', is frequently brought under inspection because researchers feel that the communicative behavior is less likely to be confounded with behavior stemming from 'instrumental' activities such as feeding, bathing and dressing. However, caregiving activities can also be occasions for communication, even though it is possible to carry out some procedures on a drowsy or sleeping infant with little if any communication.

Subject matter (topic) of communication is another aspect which could provide categories for investigation. At first this tends to be related to the relationship itself (and is known as phatic communication), then to the ongoing caregiving activity, but soon expands as infant and caregiver come to share more interests in common. As students of language acquisition become more concerned with pragmatics and semantics, this aspect is seen as more significant in prelinguistic communication also, and that is the area in which Ricks deals with it. Trevarthen reports the absence of reference to the ongoing caregiving in the content of a mother's speech to a two-month-old, indicating the phatic nature of very early communication.

5 How we investigate

Here we get to the nitty gritty of our research. I will outline some of
the methods we have employed, but first I want to try to communicate the *sine qua non* of this work: the prepared mind and the practiced eye and ear. There is no instant way to become an effective
researcher in this area (and it isn't for everyone). It takes years of
living with live subjects, and the films and tapes which allow those of
us who use them to relive the original experience, to understand what
is going on and to come up with insights as to how to get a grip on it
for analysis. Condon and Sorenson make this explicit in their chapters. All of us know it from experience. Such work may seem unpro-
ductive for a long time and this turns people away from it. Since it
doesn't yield quick results, it often fares poorly with granting agencies.
But once one becomes attuned to observing the way mothers and
babies communicate, there is no limit to what one can explore. At
first one seeks special subjects and special observation conditions.
Then comes a time when, while this is desirable, it is no longer absolutely necessary except for experimental procedures. The prevalence
of mothers and infants is very high and babies are taken into public
places from a very early age (although this differs from culture to
culture, see Snow et al.). It is quite easy to gain access to mothers
and their newborn babies in hospitals and in their homes by approaching mothers near term in an appropriate way. This makes it possible
to follow the developing relationship from the beginning, or to come
in on it at any point. Anderson (1972b) observed toddlers and their
mothers in a public park. I have come to insights during, or afterward
in thinking about, informal observations which could be checked by
searching my stored tapes and films later and which might have
become the basis for experimental procedures. Having recorded my
observations on tape and film in the early 1960s and having no opportunity to record so extensively again, I feel the need to return from
time to time to the living situation. It is always rewarding and sometimes sends me back to new searches through old data.

It would be nice if we could honestly say that the method of the
investigator is always logically designed to match the question he is
investigating. It would be more realistic to acknowledge that many
non-rational factors often play a part. Sometimes it is largely a matter
of opportunity. A particular research design has been successful in
solving other problems or a kind of equipment is available or a popu-

lation from which to draw subjects is at hand. This can lead to very fruitful research if the thinking behind the design is on target. Sometimes one just stumbles onto it. The important thing is to recognize when something useful is emerging and then to exploit one's opportunity.

5.1 Notes on methods and techniques

As to methods of investigating mother—infant communication, it depends on who does the investigating. Chappell & Sander and Collis discuss methodological alternatives. Each discipline has its characteristic tools which tend to become traditional and so help to standardize the sort of study which is done by those raised in that discipline. One might say that the tools most characteristic of this field are sound film or video and the capability of studying these records in slow motion, techniques taken over from interaction studies, but these are by no means the only techniques we employ (see fig. 1).

Several broad classifications of our chapters can be made in regard to method and technique. The details are described in each chapter. On the dimension descriptive versus experimental, some are clearly one or the other and some manage a combination. Mainly descriptive studies are found in chapters by Bateson, Chappell & Sander, Collis, Condon, Fraiberg, Halliday, Newson, Plooij, Sorenson and Snow et al., although some of them set up situations and then observe what happens. Kaye, Ricks, Trevarthen and Tronick et al. make use of experiment in addition to observing naturally occurring events. Brazelton and Stensland Junker might be considered experimental since they have both devised and standardized tests. Fraiberg, among others, uses tests in addition to describing natural situations.

Some observe many babies of about the same age or at several ages (cross-sectional study) while a number follow the same babies over significant periods of time (longitudinal study). The latter include Fraiberg, Halliday, Kaye, Newson, Plooij and Snow et al.; Chappell & Sander achieve a longitudinal study in the first week. Brazelton also reports successive phases of recovery of the baby during the neonatal period.

Classified by where they observed their subjects, we find Fraiberg, Jones reported by Newson, Kaye, Ricks and Snow et al. going into people's homes and Halliday staying in his own. Bateson visited homes by means of pre-existing film and tape. Many prefer to control the setting by inviting mothers to bring their babies into their laboratories

for short observation sessions (Collis, Newson, Trevarthen, Tronick et
al.). But these laboratories do not look like our usual stereotype of a
scientific laboratory. They are specially constructed home-like rooms
carefully arranged with unobtrusive cameras and microphones for
recording. Often one wall is a one-way mirror so that the observers
are not noticeably present. Everything is planned: where each person
will be, what objects will be available etc. Often mirrors are arranged
so that a pair who face one another can be recorded side by side on a
'split screen' (see also Tronick et al. section 2.2). A timing devise is
often placed in the background so as to be included in the picture.
The neonatal studies took place in hospitals (Brazelton, Chappell &
Sander and Kaye's first observation) because that is where their newborn subjects could be found, but nothing about their procedures
depended on the hospital setting. Kaye used hospital, home and
laboratory successively with the same babies. Stensland Junker tested
babies in the well-baby clinic. Brazelton has reported using his neonatal assessment scale under 'primitive' conditions in underdeveloped
countries (see his chapter). Still more primitive conditions were
encountered by Plooij and Sorenson who found their subjects in
jungle and rainforest.

The age range of subjects fell into three groups described in section
3: neonates (Brazelton, Chappell & Sander and Kaye at the start),
under six months (Bateson, Kaye, Snow et al., Trevarthen, Tronick
et al.) and six months and over (Collis, Newson (mainly), Ricks).
Some of the authors don't fit this classification because they follow
infants from one age range to the next (Fraiberg, Halliday, Pawlby
reported by Newson). Stensland Junker tested behavior at many ages
before standardizing her procedure for eight months. None of us
seems to have been particularly concerned about the sex of the babies,
although sex is usually stated, despite reports that mothers behave
differently toward their babies of different sexes.

How many subjects are required to obtain meaningful answers?
Bateson, after preliminary scanning of a great deal of data, based her
demonstration of the mutual influence of the vocal behaviors of the
mother and infant on data which represented only 10 minutes of 'real
time' recording. Thus what seems like a minute amount of data, carefully studied and placed in a relevant theoretical frame, could lead to
principles of wide applicability. Halliday, in his meticulous and per-
ceptive longitudinal study of one child, produced a model of what

needs to be done with many children, one at a time. He correctly recognized the idiosyncratic aspect of a single case study. As such studies accumulate, we can begin to recognize common patterns and develop typologies. Longitudinal studies are costly in time and materials, not only for recording the data, but even more in their study if it is to be done at a fruitful level of detail. Kaye's longitudinal study of fifty mother—infant pairs has the most subjects among those reported here. With a different kind of problem, Stensland Junker used hundreds of babies, each tested once, to develop her assessment procedure. In our work the significant amount of data depends on the way they are recorded and analyzed, not on the number of subjects, as Chappell & Sander point out.

One of the inevitable restrictions of this collection of studies is the limited variety of cultural backgrounds. Snow et al. do give us a comparison between British and Dutch pairs which show minor differences, and of course Stensland Junker's infants were Scandinavian. She points out a significant difference in an immigrant population. But the only drastically different cultural setting reported here is Sorenson's from the Fore of New Guinea. Bateson cites a cultural difference in an attitude toward children in Iran, and Kaye one in an American Indian culture.

It is notable that all of these studies deal with whole individuals in relationship with other persons, either the investigator (Brazelton, Halliday, Kaye in part, Stensland Junker) or another caregiver, most frequently the infant's mother. There is no testing of isolated functions even though what is taken note of may focus on some special aspect of the ongoing communication, e.g. Halliday and Ricks on vocal behavior, Collis on gaze behavior. While Brazelton and Stensland Junker appear to be testing functions in isolation, their concern with context and sequence differentiates their work from that of perceptual psychologists.

The degree of dependence on predetermined categories varies. Some authors employ behavior catalogues (ethograms in ethological usage), Chappell & Sander and Plooij as almost the sole means of preserving data. Snow et al. and Tronick et al. apply their catalogues to replayable data.

Techniques employed for data collection range from paper and pencil recording (Chappell & Sander, Halliday, Stensland Junker) to film and video tape often studied in great detail (Collis, Condon,

Kaye, Newson, Sorenson, Trevarthen, Tronick et al.). A few employ the latter as auxiliary methods, e.g. Fraiberg. I will discuss the relative merits and problems of these techniques below.

A linguist, especially a 'field worker', characteristically uses pencil and paper. He has been trained to record simultaneously in 'real time' (that is, as it occurs) a number of aspects of speech so that he can tell from his record not only what was said but how it was said, i.e. both linguistic and paralinguistic features. He can take down the vocal product he hears even if it is in an unfamiliar language (such as baby). This is how Halliday was able to make a record of all the vocal noises he heard his son make and sort it out afterward without benefit of tape-recorder. Only a highly trained and experienced phonetician can do this. The counterpart of this skill is that of the field anthrolopogist and field ethologist who until recently always made notes during observation. This requires a stable system of categorization based on preliminary exploration of the repertoire of the people or animals observed. A checklist may be used (Chappell & Sander, Snow et al.). Without some sort of code many things happen too fast to be recorded, but having a code tends to channel one's observing.

Modern technology has given the field observer new freedom. Sorenson describes how he uses his ciné camera to record anthropological data, including unforeseen categories. Sound can also be recorded on tape under field conditions, providing an opportunity to bring sounds heard in the field back to the laboratory for analysis. This has been done for both animals and humans. Audio-tape can be used not only to record the subjects under observation but also to preserve the observer's notes, leaving his eyes and even his hands free. Plooij followed his chimpanzees through jungle with a tape-recorder strapped to his chest. Under less stringent conditions I dictated descriptions of ongoing behavior and interaction into a microphone as I observed babies, who were being filmed simultaneously, in their own homes. I used a second microphone to record their vocal noises, the mother and other environmental sounds on a parallel track of the same tape. Bateson studied data I had obtained in this way. Ricks used two tape-recorders in his experiments, letting babies and parents listen to sounds and recording their responses on the other machine.

Video recording has solved some technical problems while creating others. Since small video-recorders which give good resolution without floodlighting became available, they have been widely used in interaction and communication studies. They guarantee synchronization of picture and sound track, a technical problem which I could not resolve readily under field conditions with the ciné camera and tape-recorder of the early 1960s in an economically feasible way. With a 'Portapack' one can even go outdoors away from connections with electrical outlets. But video-tape is not as easy to manipulate as film when it comes to recovering the data. The image from tapes taken on one machine may distort when played back on another. It is not possible to alter the playback speed of video as flexibly as that of film. Film may be viewed at the desired speed by means of a film 'editor' or a more elaborate 'analyst' film projector. Relatively expensive equipment can overcome the problem of slowing and 'freezing' images on video. Some of our laboratories have used it to good advantage, e.g. those of Collis, Newson, Trevarthen and Tronick et al. Tronick et al. discuss data recovery by means of the 'dynamic second'. Condon takes some of his data on video-tape and converts it to 'kinescope' to analyze as film. He manipulates the relation between film and sound track and also projects sound film backwards to investigate certain problems. Speeding up film can be useful for surveying long sessions and locating passages of special interest.

One consequence of these technical developments has been the emphasis on what can be seen and heard (i.e. vocal and kinesic behaviors) by observers usually at a fixed distance from the subjects, at the expense of attention to other channels of communication. We use our distance receptors to look at what our subjects themselves deal with largely through their own distance receptors. I have tried, by analyzing some of my film from an unusual point of view, to call attention to some of the rest of the communicative possibilities in the experience of mother and baby in addition to what they can see and hear of one another (see section 4). There is a whole area of communication using more intimate sensory modalities which went unexplored as we focussed on voice, gaze direction and gross movement. I was pleased to find Collis (1977a) adding body movement to his concern with seeing and hearing to build up appreciation of a richer communication network between a mother and the infant on her lap.

How the data, once collected, are analyzed is, obviously, as varied as the data and the questions put to them. Most of the methods are not specific to this field of inquiry, but one aspect is characteristic: most of the research deals with communicating pairs as participants in a system. So, while we need to analyze the behavior each individual contributes, we aim at reassembling individual behaviors into a representation of the flow of the system over time. We are interested in sequence and timing. Incidentally, the unnecessary controversy about reciprocal (alternating) and simultaneous (coaction) patterns arose from this concern (see section 2.2). Chappell & Sander, Collis, Condon and Kaye among others have discussed various aspects of data analysis in some detail. I have discussed the presentation of audio-visual data and supplied a sample data analysis elsewhere (Bullowa 1975).

The availability of computers in the research centers where many of these studies are done, usually connected with institutions of higher learning or medical schools, tends to channel data handling and analysis into forms compatible with computer languages and programs. Some ingenious investigators manage to automate the collection of data as well as their analysis, e.g. the early studies by Sander and co-workers using electronic transducers to keep track of when the caregiver was with the infant etc. Such devises make it possible to obtain round-the-clock records of relatively simple but very significant aspects of communication. It is also possible to put data coded by a researcher in the field or from film into computer storage for subsequent manipulation and comparison. Since computers are very literal in assigning meaning, it is likely that there will always be room for human investigators in handling data as well as in devising ways of studying interpersonal communication. There is still a great deal to be learned from sensitive observation.

5.2 About categories

It is not possible to investigate (or even to use language) without some sort of categorization. How we slice up a universe of discourse sets conditions, often unintended, on what we can find. Gesell (1940), a pioneer developmental psychologist and pediatrician, created a systematic procedure for developmental assessment, still in use, based on careful observation. Four major fields of behavioral development were defined and age norms were established for items in each of them. 'Language' and 'personal–social' were two of these fields. Language starts with vocal sound in earliest infancy and proceeds to speech. Personal–social embraces the child's reactions to other persons and to the impact of culture. By separating essential components of communication, this system made it impossible to achieve an integrated concept of communication in the sense used here. Yet Gesell's systematic longitudinal studies stressing maturational factors provided a major contribution to our understanding of child development.

Whenever we define the categories we use in investigation, we inevitably gain access to some relationships while risking foreclosure of access to others, a problem which is of course not peculiar to the particular field of scientific investigation with which this book is concerned.

6 Authors

What draws a scientific investigator trained to work in an orderly way to seek order in what would seem so unpromising and apparently disorganized a field as the study of infants in communication? Obviously there are as many paths as there are investigators. Because each of us is the product of his own personal history with its specifics of time, place and accident, it seemed to me that knowing a bit more about the authors than the customary names of the disciplines and the institutions with which they are affiliated could add a dimension of meaning to their contribution. I have therefore asked each of them for a curriculum vitae and publications list and whatever he is willing to share of the paths and motivation which led to the work described here. I draw no conclusions since I feel none are warranted. This is not a 'random sample' of any sort of population. The order, as with the chapters, is alphabetical except that joint authors are grouped together.

Mary Catherine Bateson (b. New York, 1939; BA in Semitic languages, 1960 and PhD in linguistics and Middle Eastern studies, 1963, Harvard University) was born into a family in which both parents were anthropologists and researchers on child development and character formation. She was professor of anthropology and of linguistics in the United States, the Philippines and Iran before becoming dean of social sciences at the new Reza Shah Kabir University, Mazandaran, and she has been continually active in planning and organizing conferences and educational projects. Her approach is an original personal one: for example, her account of the Burg Wartenstein Symposium on conscious purpose and human adaptation is no sterile abstract but a book which reads like a novel (M.C. Bateson 1972), describing each of the participants and how their discourse developed. She wrote her chapter for this volume in Tehran without access to the books and records of research that lie behind it, and this enabled her to place it in a wider frame of reference than is available to those of us who are still closely involved in the day-to-day details of our research.

T. Berry Brazelton (b. Waco, Texas, 1918; AB Princeton University, 1940; MD Columbia University, 1943) has since 1945 been in Boston and Cambridge, Massachusetts, where he has established himself as the pediatrician other doctors send their children to; at Harvard Medical School he is associate professor of pediatrics, and he has established a postgraduate training center in developmental pediatrics. He is well known to the general public as well through his books, articles and frequent television appearances. He chose to study child psychiatry at the Putnam Children's Center because he felt dissatisfied with pediatrics without psychodynamics. There he was able to observe well babies as well as sick ones, and was impressed with how the baby shapes his mother; he used this awareness in helping to free parents from the guilt they were encouraged to feel by the current climate of opinion. The child psychiatrists John Benjamin and Sally Provence of Yale were his most influential mentors. His 'neonatal assessment scale', the basis of his chapter, is the result of a long collaborative effort which culminated in its publication in a standardized form. He and co-workers have applied it in a number of countries world-wide and the findings make cross-cultural and cross-racial comparison between newborns possible. He is a prolific contributor to both clinical and research literature of infancy and early childhood and is active in many organizations concerned with both strictly professional matters and human welfare.

Margaret Bullowa (b. New York, 1909; AB in mathematics and science, Barnard College, 1930; MS in public health, Columbia University, 1935; MD New York University College of Medicine, 1942; d. Boston, Mass., 1978). After several years spent exploring workers' education, a commercial biological laboratory, public health statistics and medical economics I studied medicine and began to specialize in psychiatry. Being impressed with the pervasiveness of misunderstandings between persons labeled patients and their families, the outside world and those who were trying to help them I proposed research focussed on language at clinics where I worked, but this was not considered 'psychiatric research' in the 1950s. However, I attended courses in linguistics at Harvard and in 1960 obtained a grant from the National Institute of Mental Health to study normal language acquisition. This enabled me to work out the methods and to collect the extensive longitudinal audio-visual records of a few children on which most of my studies have been based. When I proposed studying behavior and interaction between mothers and children my grant was not renewed; I and my data were rescued by the Speech Communication Group at Massachusetts Institute of Technology. Since retiring from psychiatric practice I have been engaged full time in research on the ontogeny of human communication.

Patricia F. Chappell (b. Kentucky, 1930; BA in English, 1966, MA in English and psychology, 1967 and PhD in developmental psychology, 1972, George Peabody College, Nashville, Tenn.) came via an interest in language acquisition to realize the mother's role in the development of communication and to realize further that the study of the development of communication should begin at the beginning – with the neonate in early interaction with the mother. At this point she participated in a project to develop a newborn state scale in order to study the behavioral organization of the newborn infant and to assess those characteristics of the infant which affect maternal behavior. Then she was ready to study organization and control in mother–infant interaction, first in the rhesus mother–infant pair and then in human mother–infant pairs. In each species she was interested in the mutual control of behavior during the interaction. In 1972 she came to Boston University Medical Center, where she studied the organization of interaction in both humans and squirrel monkeys. She is now assistant professor in the Department of Child Psychiatry and Child Development there.

Louis W. Sander (b. San Francisco, 1918; AB University of California, Berkeley, 1939; MD University of California Medical School, San Francisco, 1942; Boston Psychoanalytic Institute 1961) has studied early mother–infant interaction and communication since 1954, when, having completed his training in child psychiatry at the Judge Baker Guidance Center and the Putnam Children's Center, he was invited by Eleanor Pavenstedt to join her group at the Boston University Child Guidance Clinic as a research psychiatrist. He was connected with the Department of Psychiatry of the Boston University Medical School from 1947 to 1977, latterly as professor of psychiatry, and

then became visiting professor at the University of Colorado, where
he was appointed professor of child psychiatry in 1978. In his research
he has focussed more and more sharply on the initial infant–caregiver
system and its sensitivity to change, finding evidence of the embedded-
ness of the human infant in a microscopic interactive regulative system
as well as a macroscopic one. His current research projects are aimed
at the further documentation and confirmation of regulatory models
which have emerged from earlier studies.

Glyn Collis (b. Isle of Wight, 1947, brought up in London; BSc 1969
and research for PhD on behavior of ducks 1969–72, University of
Leicester) began work on mother–infant interaction as a research
fellow at the University of Strathclyde in the laboratory of Rudolph
Schaffer, who, with Uli Weidmann, has had the strongest influence
on his research attitudes. He has become interested in patterns of
integration of behavior between two or more individuals on a moment-
to-moment time scale, and is committed to the idea that to establish
the existence of a pattern it is necessary to specify rather carefully
how the observed events deviate from a random 'non-pattern'. The
combination of his liking for babies and liking for theory produces
elegant research, characterized by a striking independence of thought
in the face of external trends.

William S. Condon (b. Sligo, Pa., 1925; BA Gannon College, Erie, Pa.,
1949; MA 1956 and PhD 1962 in philosophy, University of Pittsburgh) became associated with the Western Psychiatric Institute in
Pittsburgh while still a graduate student and taught courses in philosophy. He credits a two-week course in linguistic and kinesic analysis
with Ray L. Birdwhistell and Albert E. Scheflen with directing his
interest to human communication, and he spent a year in postdoctoral
study of linguistics with Norman McQuown at the University of
Chicago. His intensive study of sound film, begun in Pittsburgh in
1962 and continued from 1971 at Boston University Medical School,
has led to basic discoveries about the microstructure of human and
also mammalian behavior and interaction. His techniques and the discovery of self- and behavioral synchrony are introduced in his chapter.
He describes his sound/film micro-technique as constituting a behavioral microscope with many medical applications. It is being used at
Boston University Medical School, where he is now associate professor
of psychiatry and director of human communication research, to

study normal communication and behavior, family interaction, group processes, cross-cultural communication and psychotherapy and a number of psychiatric conditions. He also uses his findings and techniques in training medical students and psychiatric residents in interviewing and psychotherapy.

Selma Fraiberg (b. Detroit, 1918; BA 1940 and MSW 1945, Wayne State University) is a child psychoanalyst and social worker. After teaching at Wayne University, Tulane University and Baltimore Psychoanalytic Institute she moved to the University of Michigan, where she became professor of child psychoanalysis in 1968; concurrently she acquired wide experience of casework with children. She initiated systematic developmental studies of blind infants with David Freedman in 1960 in New Orleans, out of concern for the grave developmental problems she saw in a clinical caseload of older blind children, and this became the basis of her research at the University of Michigan (1965–75). Beside her work with blind babies she is widely known as the author of a book directed to parents, *The magic years.*

Michael Halliday (b. Leeds, 1925; BA in Chinese language and literature, University of London; graduate studies, University of Peking; PhD on fourteenth-century colloquial Mandarin, University of Cambridge, 1955) held appointments at the universities of Cambridge and Edinburgh and as director of the Communication Research Centre at University College, London, before becoming professor of linguistics at the University of London (1965–70), the University of Illinois and (from 1976) the University of Sydney, where he founded the Department of Linguistics. His wide-ranging publications cover modern Chinese, machine translation, literary texts, teaching of English, and the sociology of language, as well as strictly linguistic topics. Recently he has published a number of studies based on detailed observation of the language development of his son, of which his chapter is one. His current work is concerned with various related aspects of the study of language in a social–functional perspective, including the semantics of modern English, language development in early infancy, language in education, style and 'texture' in speech and writing, language variation, and the relation of language to social context and social structure.

Kenneth Kaye (b. Brooklyn, N.Y., 1946; AB in English and American literature, 1966 and PhD in developmental psychology and education, 1970, Harvard University) worked as a graduate student with Roger Brown on language acquisition and with Jerome Bruner. In Bruner's laboratory he was impressed by the work of Brazelton, who considered the infant part of an interactive system, not just a cognitive mechanism. Martin Richards, on a visit to the Center for Cognitive Studies, called his attention to a mother's behavior as she restrained herself from helping the baby on her lap in an object permanence experiment; Richards' advice was crucial in shaping the direction of his research, and in 1969 he spent a year at Richards' laboratory in Cambridge, England. He is now assistant professor in the Department of Education at the University of Chicago.

John Newson (b. London, 1925; BSc in mathematics and physics, University of London, 1948; PhD in psychology, University of Nottingham, 1957) is joint director with his wife, Elizabeth Newson, or the Child Development Research Unit at the University of Nottingham where he holds a personal chair in child development. He and his wife are well known for their series of studies on child-rearing practices in an urban community, but have more recently become preoccupied with the transcription of video-recordings showing mother—infant interaction because they are interested in the basic problem of interpersonal communication including its origins in human infancy. He credits John Shotter, also from the Department of Psychology at Nottingham, with providing a philosophical underpinning to much of their empirical work. This has been expressed in the definition of infants as persons and interest in the consequences of this in the way in which mothers, by anticipating infant intentions, help them to succeed and advance. In addition to research and teaching, the Newsons are active in clinical work with handicapped and disturbed children and in organizations and direct approaches to the public on child-rearing and educational issues.

The four studies described in Newson's chapter were done under his direction by students or former students in the unit. Susan Pawlby and Olwen Jones have moved to clinical and research posts in London hospitals. Susan Gregory and Kay Mogford have stayed in the unit to undertake a longitudinal study of interaction between deaf infants and their mothers.

Frans Plooij (b. 1946, Schiedam, The Netherlands) studied biology with the intention of eventually applying work on the biochemistry and ultrastructure of cell-membranes to cancer research. He completed his initial research, but, disliking the practical side of the work, decided to change direction, and interest in behavior led him to study the biology of behavior. After analyzing the message content of amphibian vocalizations in the field under the supervision of Dr Oomen and Dr van Gelder, University of Nijmegen, he was attracted to the evolution of behavior and comparative studies of higher primates and entered the University of Amsterdam to study ethology under Dr Kortlandt. There he did (unpublished) research on the formation of the number concept in captive chimpanzees. Meeting researchers returned from Africa and reading primate fieldwork led him to study long-distance communication and interaction between groups of chimpanzees in the wild at the Gombe National Park. Finding that such a study was already under way, he turned his attention to infant development and mother—infant interaction, a topic in line with Jane van Lawick-Goodall's long-term research and made urgent by the imminent clos-ure of this field station because of political unrest. Since then he has been closely committed to the study of early development, and is now studying preverbal interaction of human babies and their mothers at the University of Nijmegen; his chapter, which contains more about his motivation, is part of his dissertation research.

Derek Malcolm Ricks (b. London, 1928; BA 1952, MD 1972, Univer-sity of London). Interest in how things develop took him from study-ing the growth of towns to studying the growth of people and, com-bined with interest in the human brain, led to his thesis study (1965) at the University of London Institute of Psychiatry and Maudesley Hospital which forms the basis for his chapter. His interest has been greatly enhanced by discovering how little we know about children's early acquisition of basic skills. This became apparent to him when, as a working clinician, he concentrated on attempting to promote these skills in children who were without them, and discovered that no one seemed to know how normal children acquire them. Dr Ricks is in charge of the Children's Department of Harperbury, a large hospital for the mentally handicapped, and teaches pediatrics and psychiatry at University College Hospital, London.

Catherine Elizabeth Snow (b. Toledo, Ohio, 1945; BA in psychology, Oberlin College, Ohio; MA 1967 and PhD 1971 in psychology, McGill

University, Montreal) has been concerned with language acquisition since her student days and is especially known for her work on mothers' speech to children. She and Charles A. Ferguson organized a conference on this topic and co-edited the resulting volume, *Talking to children*; she was also co-editor of the proceedings of the Third International Child Language Symposium. Her research has covered second language learning and aphasia as well as the effects of malnutrition on maternal behavior in rats. In 1975 she was a visiting scientist in the Unit for Research in Medical Applications of Psychology with Martin Richards at the University of Cambridge where she made the observations for the English part of the cross-cultural study reported in her chapter. From 1971 she taught in the Institute of General Linguistics at the University of Amsterdam, and in 1978 she took up a post at Harvard Graduate School of Education.

Akke de Blauw and Ghislaine von Roosmalen (both b. The Netherlands, 1949; BA in Dutch language and literature, MA in linguistics) became interested in early language acquisition through their participation in a research project on the language of five- to seven-year-olds and carried out a program of observation of three- to six-month-olds designed by Catherine Snow. Van Roosmalen then returned to Dutch studies while de Blauw became Snow's assistant and did follow-up work on the same babies, adding to the sample to investigate sex and class differences, before embarking (1978) on a three-year longitudinal project on the relationship between early interaction and the development of communication.

E. Richard Sorenson (b. New York, 1929; BA in philosophy and history, University of Rochester, 1956; PhD in anthropology, Stanford University, 1971) has spent twelve years studying child behavior and human development in cultural isolates on expeditions of the National Institutes of Health, Stanford University and the Smithsonian Institution. It was on such an expedition that he first noted the extraordinary situation reported in his chapter, felt it deserved attention and set about documenting it. Since 1974 he has been director of the National Anthropological Film Center which he founded at the Smithsonian Institution in Washington, D.C. He also directs the study of child behavior and human development in cultural isolates and the world ethnographic film sample there. He has developed and written about the theory and method of research film with a view to maxi-

mizing the scholarly potential of film records of human behavior in
changing and vanishing ways of life and culture; he has worked on
such studies in Papua New Guinea, Micronesia, Brazil, Mexico,
Afghanistan, the Cook Islands, Nepal and the New Hebrides.

Karin Stensland Junker (b. Lidingö, Sweden, 1916; economics and
English, 1934–6, MA in psychology, pedagogics, German and phonetics, 1958 and PhD in phonetics and linguistics 1968, University
of Stockholm; Med. Sci. D. Karolinska Institutet, Stockholm, 1972),
after a career in public service dealing with issues ranging over abor-
tion, alcohol, foreign affairs, secret service and building research, and
while also being an actress and novelist, has developed an overriding
interest in communicatively handicapped children. This stems from
the experience of having mothered two such children of which she
has written in *The child in the glass ball* (1964). In the early 1950s
she and her late husband founded the first auditory training program
in the community for very young children. Subsequently she returned
to the university and her studies and research led to the development
of the BOEL assessment procedure and program described in her chapter; she was appointed professor on the Medical Faculty of the Karolinska Institute in Stockholm in 1972. With a colleague she founded
the first therapeutic toy library for children with communicative
handicaps. She is active in organizations with this and other welfare
concerns on a world-wide basis.

Colwyn Trevarthen (b. Auckland, 1931; MSc in biology, University
of Auckland, 1954; MSc in physiology, University of Otago, 1956;
PhD in psychobiology, California Institute of Technology, 1962)
studied visual–motor functions in split-brain monkeys in California
and Marseilles. Watching his first child develop he became convinced
that developmental studies might be, if not a more powerful alternative method to brain surgery for understanding the organization of
intelligence, at least a highly important complementary one. Invited
to the Harvard Center for Cognitive Studies by Jerome Bruner, he
was amazed at the social skills of young infants. Since 1971 he has
been in the Department of Psychology of the University of Edinburgh,
where he has turned almost entirely to research on infants, becoming
more and more interested in their interpersonal functions for which,
he finds, we appear to have no brain anatomy at all. Nevertheless, he
sees promise of a close connexion between these two fields of work.

Edward Tronick (BS in industrial and labor relations, 1964 and MS in comparative psychology, 1965, Cornell University; PhD in developmental psychology, University of Wisconsin, 1968) went to the Harvard Center for Cognitive Studies in 1968 where he started to study visual perception in infants with Jerome Bruner. His contact there with T. Berry Brazelton and the behaviors he could demonstrate in infants, together with his own work as educational director of an infant daycare center, led to dissatisfaction with his model of infant behavior based on perceptual processing since it left out function, emotion and the social context. Since then he has been trying to come to a more biologically based viewpoint while attempting to see how the adult–infant communication system is structured. He directed Brazelton's research group at the Children's Medical Center, Boston (1971–7), where he pursued the line of study represented in his chapter including participation in studies in various parts of the world. In 1977 he became associate professor in the Department of Psychology of the University of Massachusetts in Amherst.

Heidelise Als (b. Krumbach Schwaben, West Germany, 1940 (now an American citizen); BS, Friedrich-Maximilian Universität, Wurzburg, and Pädagogische Hochschule Eichstatt, 1963; MS in education, 1968 and PhD in human learning and development, 1975, University of Pennsylvania) worked initially as an elementary school teacher. In the United States she became research assistant to Sandra Scarr-Salapatek at the University of Minnesota and then at the Graduate School of Education of the University of Pennsylvania. After a year in the Behaviour Development Research Unit at St Mary's Hospital, London with J.A. Ambrose she joined T. Berry Brazelton and Edward Tronick in the Child Development Unit at the Children's Medical Center, Boston, where she participated in the studies reported here. Her dissertation was an ethological study of the interaction of the human newborn and his mother.

Lauren Bernstein Adamson (b. Saranac Lake, N.Y., 1948; BA Swarthmore, 1970; MA 1972 and PhD 1977 in psychology, University of California, Berkeley), starting from a base in cognitive and developmental psychology and psycholinguistics, has during the last five years become particularly interested in the patterns of developmental change during early infancy. She has been focussing on the transformations occurring in skill development, with particular reference to early defensive behavior to visual and tactile barriers, and on the changes in organization in communicative systems. During the three years 1972—5 these studies were pursued through association with the Child Development Unit at the Children's Medical Center, Boston. She is now assistant professor in the Department of Psychology at Wellesley College, Massachusetts.

Notes

1. I gratefully acknowledge the support of Professor Kenneth N. Stevens, director, laboratory of the Speech Communication Group of the Research Laboratory of Electronics, Massachusetts Institute of Technology, under National Institutes of Health grant no. NB 04332. I would also like to thank Jeanne Chall, Colin Fraser, Elena Lieven, Lise Menn, Martin Richards, Maureen Shields and Grace Shugar, who generously gave advice and criticism but are in no way responsible for any errors that remain; Hedy Kodish, for help in typing the manuscript, and Andrea Stevens, for help in compiling the bibliography; and the staff of the Cambridge University Press, especially the subeditor concerned with this book.
2. I have been asked by the editor to add a brief note on what proved to be something of a watershed in the evolution of research on preverbal communication. My judgement about its importance must, of course, be qualified by the fact that I was a participant observer and am a working scientist — not a historian of the subject.

   The Center for Cognitive Studies at Harvard University has been directly or indirectly a major influence on many of the people working on preverbal communication. In 1966 there was a shift in interest at the Center from work with older children (reported in *Studies in cognitive growth*, Bruner et al. 1966) towards infancy. And in the following year Professor Bruner received a substantial grant to support work on voluntary action, perception and attention and the transition from babbling to language in babies. In this year and the following many of the broad concepts and ideas that have shaped the field of mother—infant interaction were elaborated. I was at the Center for the summers of both these years. My memory of the first is of talk, argument, discussion and excitement. People from several different backgrounds had found an area of common concern (and one they all held to be potentially of great importance) and they wanted to understand it. Discussion seemed to fill each day and often continued late into the evening.

   The mood of the second summer was different. The excitement of the previous summer was still present but ideas had found a temporary stable form and the cry was for data. People would emerge blinking from long sessions of analyzing films with a 'Perceptoscope'. The discussions still persisted, although now much of our conversation involved the technicalities of film making and the everyday problems of working with babies and their parents in a laboratory.

   All who participated showed a strong sense of involvement, not least the undergraduates who, in theory at least, were the general factotums around the laboratory. Often they proved to be major contributors to the debates and were responsible for teaching some of us a good deal of psychology. More formal accounts, including lists of those who participated, are contained in the Annual Reports of the Center for 1966 and 1967.

Various research traditions had come together. Bruner's interest in infancy grew out of his earlier work in a Piagetian tradition on perception, attention and motor skills in children. Like so many of us, having tried to understand functions at one age point, he was led to search for earlier origins of what he saw. Piaget's work was an ever-present background and there was more or less constant dialogue with colleagues in Geneva. Another major influence was the work on child grammars of Roger Brown and his co-workers. Attitudes to this altered a good deal as the infancy research got underway. The search for grammars of action in preverbal children gave way to a much greater interest in the semantics and pragmatics of language, a shift that marked the movement to concern with communication. Many things helped to bring about this change. Among the linguists themselves was the growing reaction to Chomskian nativism which was in part brought about by the growing knowledge of child speech and the difficulties in constructing grammars for the early phase of acquisition. Those who began to analyze what went on between adults and preverbal children were struck by the richness of what they saw and became committed to the idea that the key to understanding acquisition of speech lay in the period before children began producing words.

The work during that period relied heavily on observation rather than experiment. This perhaps was the contribution of those who had worked with animals and had begun to study humans in the tradition of attachment theory. By this time the limitations of attachment theory were very plain and the search was underway for better theoretical frameworks. Also it was these workers who had experience of research with small babies and they were able to contribute some practical know-how about how to get the best out of babies in the constraining environment of the laboratory. Curiously in those days few of us left the laboratory very often to see our subjects in their own homes.

Biological thinking was an important part of most discussions — not only evolutionary concerns and knowledge of primate behaviour but also neuro-anatomy and physiology. I don't think anybody actually engaged in animal work at the Center in these years but some of us certainly visited local zoos and were in close contact with animal workers in the surrounding universities.

Perhaps most important were the varied experience and background (and nationality) of those involved, the fact that most of us were learning for the first time whole areas of work that suddenly seemed relevant to our concerns and the fact that by and large we shared common concerns. Few of us formulated the problems we were investigating out of our own research traditions. I think we all felt rejuvenated by the experience.   MARTIN RICHARDS

3. After this was written I became aware of the concept of language as a problem area for children, expressed by Karmiloff-Smith (forthcoming). The concept seems to be related also to one implicit in Blank & Allen (1976) in connexion with the three-year-old's investigation of what 'why' means.

2

'The epigenesis of conversational interaction': a personal account of research development

M.C. BATESON

Reza Shah Kabir University, Mazandaran, Iran

1 Background

The journals present us with dozens of highly specific research projects, described with only the most modest statement of the broader intellectual path that led to them, and most restrained projections of the implications spreading from that narrow research activity. Since in this paper I will be discussing a piece of research that has already been fully described according to the conventions of scientific reporting,[1] I propose to approach it here in a different way: to describe the miscellany of curiosities and interests that led to that research and to reflect on its broader implications. An awareness of these double shadows cast by any piece of reported research can enrich the process of research and clarify the way in which differences of theoretical orientation and personal experience inform it, especially in a field like the study of infant communication and language acquisition that tends to be populated by researchers of distinct and diverse orthodoxies.

In 1969–72 I did a relatively limited study of mother–child communication, concerned with the epigenesis of conversational interaction. When it first appeared, this study took a very different approach from most other studies then being done by psychologists and linguists, an approach that was related to work being done by some anthropologists and psychiatrists but not extensively applied to questions related to language learning. In a sense it was an accident that I applied that approach to mother–child communication, an accident that occurred through meeting Margaret Bullowa and being about to produce a child myself so that I was looking for a way of applying whatever heightened sensitivity this might bring to my work. The research I did on mother–child communication was from one

63

point of view 'time out' for me — a brief foray into a new field. From another point of view, it was in direct continuity with most of the work I had done before, research dealing with the structure of events and with communicational contexts.

During the preceding decade I had been pursuing a set of interests that were closely related at an abstract level and yet very different in terms of specific subject matter. In effect, I had concerned myself with the structure of mutually sustained performances ranging from neocharismatic prayer meetings to psychiatric interviews through the work of Scheflen (1972) and Birdwhistell (1970) to the Arabic odes that I studied for my dissertation. I had also been involved in various ways with language learning and teaching and had come increasingly to think of the learner's problem as learning how to participate in and sustain joint performances, in spite of differences in competence from native speakers, and had come to focus on participation as providing contexts for the development of this competence. A psychiatric interview uses joint participation to bring about change, and so in a different way does a prayer meeting which is concerned with episodes of religious healing and conversion.

Thus, by the time I began to read the literature on child language learning, as a post-doctral fellow at Brandeis in 1968–9, I had a set of rather special biases. One was towards the study of performances as events, events with several participants, communication in several modalities and a contextual structure, rather than the study of a single competence like language in the abstract spheres of Mind. Another was towards an emphasis on the phatic function of communication of any kind, for language cannot be used for any other purpose unless some agreement is established that one is 'in touch'. I was also concerned that much of anthropological and linguistic theory seemed to suggest such highly interlocked and interdependent structures that change was unimaginable. Even the successive grammars that some linguists had written about their own children presented the same problem: how did one get from grammar to grammar?

My interests in the problems of change were sharpened by my own experiences, as I became convinced of the biological bases of learning to be a mother, after the birth of my own child. I became convinced that the ethologists, whose work had first interested me when I was trying to understand the nature of ritual, had a great deal to offer to our investigation of human learning.

2 The research

Shortly after I gave birth, I began working with the films and tapes
Margaret Bullowa had collected of babies, from birth on, taken in
their homes. Within a few weeks, I had selected for study a type of
episode that occurred in the films. I selected five filmed and taped
interactions between a mother and her infant (between the ages of
forty-nine and 105 days) for intensive analysis, including analysis of
the temporal and sequential relationship between maternal and
infant vocalization. Each was very brief, so the total time of analyzed
interactions was less than 10 minutes. They occurred spontaneously
in longer filmed sessions. In selecting brief sections for intensive
study, I was partly building on the model of previous research in
kinesics (Pittenger et al. 1960; Birdwhistell 1970; McQuown et al.
1971).

A study of these sequences established that the mother and infant
were collaborating in a pattern of more or less alternating, non-
overlapping vocalization, the mother speaking brief sentences and
the infant responding with coos and murmurs, together producing a
brief joint performance similar to conversation, which I called 'proto
conversation'. The study of timing and sequencing showed that certainly the mother and probably the infant, in addition to conforming
in general to a regular pattern, were acting to sustain it or to restore
it when it faltered, waiting for the expected vocalization from the
other and then after a pause resuming vocalization, as if to elicit a
response that had not been forthcoming. These interactions were
characterized by a sort of delighted, ritualized courtesy and more or
less sustained attention and mutual gaze. Many of the vocalizations
were of types not described in the acoustic literature on infancy, since
they were very brief and faint, and yet were crucial parts of the
jointly sustained performances.

The details of that research, including the instrumentation and the
statistical and acoustic analysis, have already been published (M.C.
Bateson 1971, 1975b). That description primarily emphasized parallels between these prelinguistic interactions and adult conversation.
Here we will presume on that description and go further afield, examining such sequences of interaction as contexts for learning and for
whatever they may suggest about the contextualization of learning
in infancy. We will be looking at ways in which both parent and child

are prepared for engagements of this sort, and ways in which the patterning of these interactions itself facilitates further learning, by providing contexts of variation and heightened attention, structured by the behavior of both participants. The development of the capacity for participation in complex sequenced behavior must lay the groundwork for participation in games and for the development of playful patterns of imitations, and so the study of such performances can shed light on a variety of types of learning, including language acquisition. Thus, having found in the proto-conversations contexts suitable for a certain type of accelerated learning, I shall consider a range of evidence on whether they really have that function and what its biological basis might be, which should suggest further research.

3 Contexts for learning

The ethologists have been able to demonstrate a considerable range of innate species specific mechanisms for learning. One example, which highlights some of the theoretical issues involved, is that very rapid type of learning called 'imprinting' which takes place in genotypically highly specified contexts, best described for various birds (Lorenz 1970—1). In fact, imprinting can be regarded as working by the genetic specification of a context for learning.

Imprinting is similar to the instructions sometimes given for finding one's way: 'When you get to a big square with a sort of little park in the middle, ask again', or, alternatively, 'I don't know which turn you should take, but it will be the one with buses running along it'. Thus, a duckling coming out of the egg, already able to walk, needs to learn to recognize its mother, an individual whose idiosyncratic and accidental features could not economically have been specified for recognition at the genetic level. So it emerges from the egg with a structured pattern of attention, knowing *when and how to learn* what its mother looks like.

The specification of a crucial period for imprinting is extremely efficient, for even where survival does not require speed, the setting up of specified periods for learning to take place seems to accompany learning of extraordinary rapidity and intensity — one brief exposure producing accurate and almost inextinguishable learning, with structured attention excluding irrelevant material.

The possibility of innate patterns that prepare human beings to learn, rapidly and efficiently, what needs to be learned at a specific stage of development, raises interesting and important questions for the study of language learning. Since Chomsky refuted the possibility of learning language according to the behaviorist model in his famous review of Skinner (Chomsky 1959) and since Chomsky's argument (1967) that linguistic performances in the child's environment are so muddled and incomplete that they would not allow language learning by imitation, we are aware that only an organism with rather specific characteristics would be able to develop complex linguistic competence. One approach is to regard some important part of linguistic competence as innate. A great deal of the response to this proposal depends on how fundamental a particular theorist considers the differences between languages to be. Human behavioral and adaptive diversity provide the prime argument against innate knowledge, unless we can express that knowledge as an innate, perhaps highly specific, ability to learn. In fact, imprinting and other such innate learning and teaching mechanisms are what we should expect to find in human learning, because imprinting is precisely a way of taking advantage of the economies of genotypic programming in species whose patterns of adaptation require flexibility and variation. The instructions for finding one's way from the great square are likely to take that form just because the square is the sort of place from which many possible different paths diverge. In situations of this sort, rigid pre-formulated instructions may not be useful, but alerting the traveler to how and when to discover the appropriate path is. The capacity to learn always depends on a biological given, so the ant hatches knowing what to do, and the duckling hatches knowing how to find out what to do, and the human being is born knowing . . . how to find out how to find out what to do? . . . over a very long period of time (G. Bateson 1972).

The duration of human childhood allows for massive, gradual and variegated learning, whereas the duckling must learn to follow its mother immediately because a fox may appear at any moment. However, it is reasonable to expect variations in the learning texture, where special contexts may be genotypically defined as appropriate for intensified learning — where, so to speak, the stage for rapid learning is set. Cultural definitions of contexts or models for learning could be expected to build on those that are genotypically defined. Thus, e.g., the acceptance of parents as appropriate models for imitation is certainly based on biological patterns, and then the culture elaborates on that by inventing school teachers and psychoanalysts. We do indeed know that human learning, cognitive and affective, takes place according to certain schedules, and that certain types of learning, if not achieved at the appropriate period, never will be achieved. We need, however, to discover a great deal more about how contexts for learning are structured during development. We know that development is gradual and discontinuous, but little has been done to define the variations in texture and the way in which, in any stage of development, certain moments may be moments of especially intense or focussed learning. An understanding of the early contextualization of human learning is essential in order to under-stand the cultural elaboration of this contextualization, and the kinds of interactions that develop and sustain it.

To sum up, I am suggesting that many of the dilemmas that face the description of human language acquisition may be resolved if we ask whether the infant has a rather highly specific *readiness* to learn language — or, to put this in other words, to take the appropriate steps, in the appropriate sequence, that will lead to a knowledge of language. Since the task is a massive one, we should expect to find contexts of very high mobilization (such as in imprinting) simply for the sake of economy, as well as structured patterns of attention and inattention, and sequences where what is learned at one stage keys in to what is learned at the next stage.

When we consider the form that might be taken by such sequences, certain intellectual strategies suggest themselves, some of which are already very much a part of the discussion of how infants learn language. Thus, there has been considerable discussion of when a child is able to perceive differences between various types of stimuli. It is clear that such abilities may be a precondition for some learning — but *lack* of such abilities may also facilitate learning at a previous stage, giving priority or selective attention to something that needs to be learned first, blocking out confusing distraction. In the case of proto-conversations, where sentences spoken by the mother are struc-turally equivalent (in terms of the rules of alternation) to monosyl-labic murmurs by the infant, learning to participate in the give and take may depend on perceiving the mother's vocalizations as unitary. Similarly, using one part of experience to parse another part may depend on innate patterns, in terms of selecting what experience, in what modality, gives a handle on something else. After all, even the capacity to be reinforced depends on knowing how to relate two events (Lorenz 1970—1: xv). Again, we need to consider the possibility that out of the continuum of experience certain intervals are marked for especially intense learning. In whatever internal analysis is taking place, the experiences of those intervals would have very high preference, just as certain models take precedence for imitation.

Thus, we are looking for cases where patterned materials provided by the environment meet a patterned receptivity. This receptivity can be innate and species specific, but it need not be an elementary linguistic competence — rather it needs to be a way of arriving at linguistic competence. However, considering the economies of genetic programming, where we continually learn that more and more is provided by the environment, we must expect the patterned receptivity of each stage to have been built up incorporating components learned in the previous stage. This drives us inexorably back to the very earliest experiences.

4 Readiness for proto-conversation

In what follows, I will consider, from the point of view of a structured readiness to learn and the provision of patterned stimuli by the environment, some of the background of those brief moments when mothers (and perhaps other caretakers) and infants 'converse' with one another. It is not reasonable to suppose that the infant is 'programmed' to learn in an especially intense way from such interactions unless their occurrence is also provided for, perhaps in some 'programming' of the mother, presumably with cultural variations. This may also serve to underline the propriety and relevance of ethological analogies.

First to review a few familiar and general ideas. Human infants, unlike ducklings, cannot walk away, are in fact extraordinarily helpless. Therefore, the immediate biological task is not to teach the infant to recognize the mother but to teach the mother to recognize, acknowledge and care for the infant — to mobilize a set of maternal behaviors or, alternatively, to set the stage so that she will learn these very fast. She must meet both the infant's physical needs and his emotional and communicational needs, thus structuring the environment so that the infant can learn. Thus, in addition to asking how the mother is triggered to nurture the infant and protect him (documented by a whole library of material on how nursing is established), we must ask how she is triggered to provide those stimuli that will allow the infant to learn according to his internal schedule. One of

the simplest examples of this would be the establishment of mutual
gazing, if it can be shown that once a pattern of mutual gazing is
established, the mother tends to behave in a given way within mutual
gaze episodes. This would seem to be the case with proto-conversations:
mutual gazing sets the stage for maternal vocalization which sets up
the possibility of an unfolding process of learning, probably
strengthened by selective attention. I would assume that my rapid
focus of interest on the proto-conversations was also a case of such
triggering carried over from my own post-partum state and transferred
to research.

Most of the genotypically given guidelines for mother and child in
this early adaptation are apparently extremely evanescent — rapidly
replaced or modified by new learning — for instance, the sucking
reflex which is shaped so rapidly by experience to adapt to breast or
bottle. The period immediately after delivery when such patterns
might be visible has, until very recently, been so drastically tampered
with for most Western births that we have been almost completely
ignorant of the normal pattern of development of mother–child communication. Since the mother is the one who should be initially
highly programmed for learning appropriate maternal behaviors, post-
partum depressions may be due to this disruption. This is also perhaps
the real function of the extreme suggestibility or influencibility of
women in the early post-partum period — an adaptively useful biological readiness to learn how to be a mother, to grasp on every clue
offered by the environment or by the infant. It seems possible that
many cognitively very important experiences of order in the caretaking environment occur because of the mother's willingness to learn
from the infant and respond to his patterns — again, a matter of selectively intensified attention. Thus, the mother's observation of regular
rhythms in the child's hunger, which become reflected in her readiness
to nurse, may instruct the infant on the nature of order sooner than
the arbitrary order built into a nursing schedule.

Even the process of learning to recognize one's own infant, the
basis for the pleasures of mutual gazing and recognition, probably has
a biological basis. In 1966 I had a premature delivery of a boy who
died after 5 hours, whom I saw for only a few seconds. Many women
who have had such experiences describe how the image of the infant
was etched on their memory, recurring with perfect ineradicable
detail in dreams and in waking hours for months and even years afterwards. Surely here we have an example of imprinting, and instead of

dismissing it by saying that the emotional stress of the moment and the significance of the event were bound to leave a sharp and vivid memory, we should search reports of other such vividly etched memories for comparative study, to evaluate them as learning and consider their possible adaptive significance. This vividly etched image of the newborn is surely, under normal circumstances, immediately overlaid with multiple images, but must provide a basic foundation for the developing relationship.

Another element in the readiness of mother and child for proto-conversation concerns rhythm. Movement, sound and rhythm make up much of the common experience infant and parent bring to their meeting – patterns of synchrony and potential patterns of counterpoint and syncopation. Just as we don't recognize the dog's behavior as instinctive when we see him digging in the forest, the ways in which mothers tap and jiggle their infants to soothe them (and hold them with their heads against their hearts) seem self-evidently reasonable and effective and are only recently being intensively studied. However, when the dog begins to paw at the living-room rug, we begin to wonder about the basis for the behavior. I was fascinated after the more felicitous birth of my daughter in 1969 to find that for about 36 hours after birth, if I was not holding my daughter but could see or hear her, I was likely to start tapping and jiggling anything I held, a book, or my own knee.

This is only an example of a range of patterns that can be understood as ways in which the mother is activated to care for the infant, ways in which nursing is initiated and regulated, and so on – all areas where very rudimentary and quickly extinguished or developed patterns provide a starting place for rapid mutual learning, where maternal commitment and infant need must be orchestrated very rapidly in trustworthy common events in time. My purpose here is to discuss the way in which they also provide the framing and internal structure for contexts of further learning. Thus we can integrate them into the more general topic of what order of pattern must already be present in order for learning to take place and, when the two interactants are so very different, what order of commonality must exist in that pattern?

5 The establishment of conversational patterns

The proto-conversations I studied reached, by forty-nine days after birth, a length and complexity that made it possible to use statistical methods to study sequencing and temporal spacing of vocalizations. However, on the tapes much briefer examples could be found, when the infant was slightly less than one month old, and it was when she was approximately one month old that I became aware of such sequences in my interactions with my own daughter. I say 'aware' because I know that before that period I certainly talked to her and gazed into her eyes and found the process meaningful, but only when she was about one month old did I begin to have the sense of complex sequenced joint participation in interaction in two or more modalities. Bullowa describes such sequences beginning within a few hours after birth: 'It seems to be a spontaneous behavior of mothers in our culture[2] to initiate such behavior and for the infants when awake and in the appropriate position vis-à-vis the adult to gaze at the mother's face and vocalize softly. Such exchanges are usually brief.' (Bullowa forthcoming b).

Infant gazing behavior — and infant fascination with even simplified models of the human face — has been extensively studied. Jaffe et al. (1973) argue that infant gazing should be seen as a precursor to later gazing patterns rather than to verbal conversational patterns. This is obvious but somewhat misses the point. Conversation, whether for adults or for parent—child pairs, is a highly complex activity, involving communication in many (or all) modalities, according to varying rhythms. Speech is characterized by very short signals, with the communicationally useful characteristics of discreteness and rapid fading (Hockett 1960). Kinesic behavior (communicative body motion) contains a great many sustained signals which provide transfixes to the stacatto of speech: a gaze, a cocked eyebrow, a tension in one shoulder modifying and unifying a long stream of speech (Birdwhistell 1970). These signals would not be communicative if they were not varied and terminable. The essence of conversation is in fact the possibility, provided in ordinary conversation by kinesic behavior and paralanguage, of organization into units larger than the syntactic sentence, so that both participants are included in an ongoing pattern. Infant gazing is indeed a precursor of adult gazing, infant gesticulation a precursor of adult gesticulation, and infant vocalization a precursor of adult vocalization. But would learning in each of these types of signalling occur if they were not juxtaposed and their communicative functions were not complementary? Maternal imprinting to an individual infant's face and the infant's genetically given liking for faces bring them into mutual gazing; mutual gazing provides the *framing* for a context of learning and perhaps also triggers or is connected to an intensification of attention and readiness to learn.

Neonates are 'old hands' at sound and rhythm, which form part of their environment before birth, although in a very global kines-thetic way. Mothers are skilled at the sounds and rhythms of speech, and some at least are equipped with translations of the cadences of their lullabies and endearments into the same whole-body experiences of sound and rhythm that preceded birth, tapping and jiggling. Can we think of the tapping and jiggling, intelligible and satisfying to the infant in terms of earlier experience, as a sort of carrier wave that gives him more access to the new types of sounds and rhythms of song or speech? Both mothers and infants seem to move rapidly into patterns of mutual gaze of varying intensity and duration. Following the carrier-wave metaphor, these periods of mutual gaze may provide contexts in which vocalization becomes increasingly meaningful. Such contexts would serve as frames of attention within which pattern can be discerned in otherwise fragmented and inchoate material, and the translation from perceptions of the frame to perceptions of internal structure may be facilitated by experiences of interlocking rhythm (cf. Condon this volume). When I was looking for additional examples of 'proto-conversation' to study in my research, I located them by scanning through stretches of film at accelerated speed, look-ing for mutual gaze, and then checking with the sound to see if I found alternating vocalization. That may be, in a sense, what both infant and mother do — take the mutual gaze as the signal that identi-fies the nature of the framed material, and identifies the period as a valuable period of intensified attention.

My interest in this has in part been focussed by a striking phenom-enon in patterns of child care I have observed in Iran, with older but still pre-verbal children. Iranians act as if they believed that children, when *not* in interaction with adults, are in a sort of neutral gear, a sort of suspension, doing nothing. Although, as a cultural perception of childhood, this seems to miss a great deal that goes on in the child's mind *out* of interaction with adults, it lays a very great stress on the significance of episodes of intense interaction. This may be a cultural prolongation of the perception of an infant condition in which atten-tion is swamped by physical events most of the time but there are brief periods of high attention (Wolff 1966: 84). One of the things that creates or contextualizes those periods is interaction with an adult, as in proto-conversations. For a Westerner, used to thinking about the child's mental activity outside of interaction, it is a useful reminder of the greater potential significance of the interactional sequences.

Another way in which we can find interesting evidence of the high learning significance of the proto-conversations of infancy is by looking at the most closely equivalent events of later childhood. Proto-conversations tend to take place after feeding, caretaking, bathing, dressing — at a moment when the bustle is over and physical needs are met and sleep is not yet urgent. These are the moments that in many households in our culture are kept almost ritualized for the most intimate converse of parent and child. Perhaps prayers are said, perhaps the day is reviewed and the morrow planned and concerns of the day put into perspective, perhaps sudden questions of God or love, death or sex are trusted to speech as at no other hour of the day: conversation, which occurs framed and with a sustained commitment of attention, represented in earliest childhood by mutual gaze.

6 Conversation and ritual

From the very beginning of my research on child communication, I was aware of a convergence of key ideas in this research with a different strand of interest in ritual, approached through a study of neo-Pentecostal or 'charismatic' prayer groups (M.C. Bateson 1975c). Initially I was primarily interested in glossolalia, or 'speaking in tongues', as a form of 'regression in the service of the ego' such as crops up in relation to many different kinds of religious and mystical experience, harking back to meaningful experiences of vocalization combined with communion in pre-verbal infancy — much the kind of experience provided by a proto-conversation. (All studies which I have seen depict glossolalia as non-meaningful phonation, sometimes highly repetitive and simple in structure, sometimes more varied, corresponding generally to the phonology of the tongues-speaker's native language and the rhythms of speech, without the grammatical structure).[3]

From this point of view, the connection of non-semantic vocalization and a sense of religious communion, the study of glossolalia provides supporting evidence for the apparent pleasure of proto-conversation in infancy. But there is still another connection, and this is through the notion of ritual contexts as contexts for learning. The study of charismatic prayer meetings presents a number of analogies with proto-conversations. These, too, are performances framed in time, with several participants interacting in various modalities and using various different codes. In the prayer groups, vocalizations vary from glossolalia to memorized prayers through spontaneous prayers of various degrees of stereotypy. Whereas proto-conversations present the theoretical problem of how two persons with disparate codes can orchestrate their behavior in a common performance, the prayer groups provide examples of a group of persons each of whom is capable of performing in several different codes, orchestrating those codes within a joint performance — that is, code switching is not tied to individual participants. Each case raises the question of *codes governing performance*, and the further question of whether performance codes might not provide frameworks for changes in competence. I have described changes of this sort occurring in the prayer group context as aspects of the process of *ritualization* — that is, the meaning and structure of certain types of vocal and other behavior are progressively altered by their performance in ritual contexts (M.C. Bateson 1968, 1975c; Hymes 1964). In ritual, sequences of behavior become fused so that they are no longer generated anew each time, nor do they any longer mean what an analysis of their components and structure would suggest. Our question here is whether the contexts provided by proto-conversations are not contexts for the opposite process, a process of fission — that is, contexts in which the infant can participate in terms of large, fused chunks of behavior (treating the complex utterances of the mother as single counters in an exchange), while at the same time allowing for a progressive analysis and potential recombination of smaller elements.

7 Conclusions

The original research on which this paper is based focussed intensively on five interactions between a single mother—infant pair, totalling no more than 10 minutes. The striking thing about these brief interactions was that mother and child, in spite of the vast differences between them, were able to participate jointly in performances that seemed to give great pleasure to both. Infant and mother may enter into such interactions because previous experience combined with phylogenetic characteristics prepares them to do so. The particular kind of preparation, as well as a comparison with other kinds of contexts in which rapid and intense learning takes place, suggests that interactions of this sort have a very high potential not only for pleasure but also for learning. This is highly suggestive. The inadequacy of linguistic performances in a child's environment for the learning of language has been a major issue in attempts to evaluate the level of innate knowledge needed for language learning. However, the evidence from animal ethology strongly suggests the need for study of specific ways in which the young organism is equipped to *select* from among environmental stimuli and to match them selectively with phylogenetically given patterns. A concept of structured receptivity or readiness to learn, as we are able to define it, casts a totally different light on the value and usefulness of environmental input. Specifically, in this case, we are suggesting that mother and child, long before speech, have the potential for developing joint vocal performances (although these will clearly take different forms in different cultures), which function as contexts for learning.

Further we are suggesting that in addition to the advantages for learning given by intense attention and pleasure, the infant's participation sets the stage for learning: once he knows the 'rules of the game' and can anticipate patterns, he can also deliberately and playfully vary them and he has a 'handle' on what he is trying to understand. Here at the prelinguistic level we can see the child playing a 'grammatical' game. This should cast new light on our data on games playing, imitation and mother–child interaction at later stages of development. Indeed, it provides an analogy for understanding a wide variety of interactions in which change or learning takes place, from psychotherapy to religious ritual to the ordinary pleasures of conversation, and the general phenomenon of active participatory learning.

For purposes of this volume, it seems important to emphasize the way the special interests and personal experience of the researcher influenced the research. Vast as is the range of human adult behavior, it all grows from potentials for development that infants, in general, have in common, and we can expect contributions to our understanding from scholars with all sorts of specialized interests in the human sciences. At the same time, the researcher's skills in observing behavior are also closely akin to the capacities he or she has needed to mature as an individual human being, and this too can contribute to our expanding knowledge.

Notes

1. This research was conducted at the Research Laboratory of Electronics at the Massachusetts Institute of Technology and supported by the National Institutes of Health (Grant 2 RO1 NB-04322). Preliminary versions of parts of the research were reported in M.C. Bateson 1971 and presented at the 1971 meetings of the Society for Research in Child Development. A sequence from the visual material analyzed is shown in the Introduction, fig. 1. Collis (this volume, section 2.1) summarizes the research; a complete summary of its empirical aspects may be found in M.C. Bateson 1975b.
2. Bullowa rightly emphasizes the culture (mainly American and British) in which the observation has been made; although we don't know that such interactions do not occur in other cultures, we do know that in one case at least, that of Japan, they are statistically less frequent at later stages of childhood — mothers and infants simply vocalize less (Caudill 1973).
3. Further references on the structure of glossolalia may be found in M.C. Bateson 1975c and in other papers in the same volume.

3
Evidence of communication during neonatal behavioral assessment[1]

T. BERRY BRAZELTON
Children's Hospital Medical Center, Boston

The old model of thinking of the newborn infant as helpless and ready to be shaped by his environment prevented us from seeing his power as a communicant in the early mother–father–infant interaction. To see the neonate as chaotic or insensitive provided us with the capacity to see ourselves as acting 'on' rather than 'with' him. Perhaps this model served a purpose in an area when it was necessary to experiment upon him in order to gain some medical control of his environment and of his physical well-being. But by now we have gained a certain amount of control over infection and respiratory and cardiac disease, and even over survival for very high risk neonates.

The rule of the day in the past had been to assess neonates as if they were functioning at a reflex or midbrain level, and the resultant predictions were never very rewarding. As the potential for early intervention increases, it becomes more and more important that we be able to evaluate infants at risk as early as possible with an eye to more sophisticated preventive and therapeutic approaches. Early intervention may prevent a compounding of problems which occurs all too easily when the caregivers cannot adjust appropriately to the infant at risk. Quiet, undemanding infants do not elicit necessary mothering from already overstressed parents and are candidates for kwashiorkor and marasmus by virtue of their neonatal behavior in poverty-ridden cultures such as are found in Guatemala and Mexico (Cravioto et al. 1966; Lechtig et al. 1975). Hyperkinetic, hypersensitive neonates may press a mother and father into a kind of desperation which produces child-rearing responses from them that reinforce the problems of the child so that he grows up in an overreactive, hostile environment (Heider 1966). Parents of children admitted to the wards of the Children's Hospital in Boston for clinical syndromes such as failure to thrive, child abuse, proneness to repeated accidents and ingestions, and infantile autism are often successful parents of other children. Parents associate their failure with this one child to an inability to communicate with him from the neonatal period onward, and they claim that he differs from their other children in his earliest reactions to them.

If we are to improve the outcome for children who have difficulty in communication, we must identify them. Assessment of the risk for non-communication in early infancy is necessary in order to mobilize preventive efforts and programs for intervention before the neonate's problems are compounded by an environment that cannot understand him. This calls for more sophisticated methods for assessing neonates and for predicting their contribution to possible failure in caregiver—infant interaction. We also need to be able to assess noxious environments. As a practical matter, we need to select target populations for our efforts at early intervention. With better techniques for assessing strengths and weaknesses in infants, we might come to understand better the mechanisms for failure in development which result in some of the above-mentioned syndromes.

Twenty-five years ago I first became aware of the amazing individual differences in neonates which were bound to shape their caregiver's responses to them. In addition, I realized that the newborn baby's behavior reflected his physiological integrity. For example, one could tell whether he was ill or stressed by whether he could alert to an auditory or visual stimulus. In a baby with even a mildly damaged nervous system, or a depressed sensorium due to maternal drugs, one saw a real interference in behavioral responsiveness. This seemed to point to the interaction between physiological and psychological responses, and, in my mind, behavioral responses afforded a new window into physiological and neurological integrity. Over the following twenty-five years I have been attempting to sort out these behavioral responses.

In order to record and evaluate some of the integrative processes shown in certain kinds of neonatal behavior, we have developed a behavioral evaluation scale (Brazelton 1973) which tests and records the infant's use of state behavior (state of consciousness) as well as his other responses to various kinds of stimulation — both social and non-social.

Since his reactions to all stimuli are dependent on his current 'state', any interpretation of his reactions must be made with this in mind. His active use of state to maintain control over his reactions to stimulation from within and from his environment reflects his potential for organization. His capacity to control state in order to communicate with his environment is a further measure of a well-integrated baby. His ability to quiet himself in order to pay attention to his caregiver gives evidence of his potential for development within his environment.

The Neonatal Behavioral Assessment tests for neurological adequacy with twenty reflex measures and with twenty-six behavioral responses to environmental stimuli, including the kind of interpersonal stimuli which a mother uses in handling her infant as she attempts to help him adapt to his new world. In the examination there is a graded series of procedures designed to soothe and alert the infant: talking, hand on belly, restraint, holding and rocking. His responsiveness to animate stimuli, e.g. the examiner's voice and face, and to inanimate stimuli, e.g. rattle, bell, red ball, white light and temperature change, are assessed. Vigor and attention are also estimated and motor activity and tone and autonomic responsiveness are assessed as he changes state.

By giving this examination on successive days, we have been able to define (1) an initial period of alertness of several minutes or hours immediately after delivery, presumably the result of the stimulation of labor and of the new environment after delivery; (2) a period of depression and disorganization which follows and lasts for 24—48 hours in infants with uncomplicated deliveries and no medication effects (but for longer periods up to three to four days if they have been compromised with medication given their mothers during labor); (3) the gradual recovery to 'optimal' function after several days. Each of these periods signals the caregivers 'I'm ready to interact' or 'Leave me alone'. Thus, stages of recovery supply a base for communication with caregivers and behavioral recovery can be seen by a nurturing environment as the result of its successful nurturance. As such, recovery becomes the first communication signal calling for further nurturing.

The main value of neonatal behavioral assessment is that it attempts to elicit and record the neonate's behaviors as he communicates with a caregiver. Since the goal of the examination is to establish the 'strengths' of the neonate and his capacity to respond in a way that elicits attachment and nurturance from his caregivers, the twenty-six behavioral items become a measure of his capacity to interact with social and to respond to non-social stimuli.

In performing the examination, we attempt to reproduce a mother's best efforts to communicate with her new baby as we elicit state changes and behavioral responses. The first part of the evaluation tests his ability to protect himself from disturbing non-social stimuli, such as bright light, a bell and a pinprick to the foot. In order to attend to important social stimuli, the newborn must be able to shut out disturbing stimuli. The fact that he can shut off his responses to intrusive, negative stimuli is a proof of this strength.

1 Communication during neonatal assessment

Let me describe how a neonate communicates with me as I examine him. One of the most remarkable performances that one can observe in a neonate is seen as he changes from a quiet state to a state in which he could become distressed if he were not able to control himself. As he begins to rouse, he makes real efforts to turn his head to one side, then performs a cycle of hand-to-mouth movements (Babkin 1958). When he is able to bring his fist up to his mouth and to hold it there, and even to suck on it, he quiets down, his agitated motor activity subsides, and, as he relaxes, he begins to alert, looking for auditory and visual stimuli around him. This active attempt to control disturbing motor activity, and to maintain an alert state using his ability to get his hand to his mouth, seems to be a process designed to allow him to attend to his environment. The observer who watches a neonate achieve this becomes struck with how he is 'programmed' for interaction with his environment.

When he is alerted, he responds with periods of active fixation on an attractive visual stimulus such as a bright, shiny red ball. He will quiet, and maintain a quiet inactive state in order to follow the ball through complete 180° arcs of movement, turning his head as well as his eyes to follow it. If, then, he is presented with a human face, he will act 'hungry' as he follows the human face laterally and vertically. When the infant begins to register his preference for human stimuli, it is impossible for an adult interactant not to become 'hooked' to him. His ability to communicate this preference by facial and eye 'softening' and his increasing attention is reflected in prolonged suppression of motor activity in the rest of his body, as well as in increased state control. The examiner or adult interactant becomes aware of his own involvement with the infant, as he too maintains an intense period of eye-to-eye and face-to-face communication.

In the same way, an infant can register auditory preferences. He can react to the sound of a bell or a loud rattle by turning away from it, with startling, jerky movements which propel him either into a crying state or into an inactive state resembling sleep. In such a state, he shuts out stimuli, his extremities and body tightly held, his eyes tightly closed, his face masked, and his respirations deep, jagged and regular (Brazelton 1961). Thus sleep can be a protective state. And in the same way he can use crying as another way of regulating his environment, as he attempts to control the input of stimulation from those around him. If in either of these shutting-out states, crying or sleep, he is offered a sound of a soft rattle or a soothing human voice, he is likely to quiet from agitation or rouse from light sleep and to become alert, gradually turning toward the attractive sound. If the stimulus is non-human, he will search for it while maintaining an alert facial expression and all of his extremities quietly inactive. When the stimulus is the human voice, the neonate not only searches for the observer's face but, when he finds it, his face and eyes become wide, soft and eager, and he may even crane his neck, lifting his chin gently toward the source of the voice. As he does so, his body tension gradually increases, but he is quietly inactive. A nurturing adult feels impelled to respond to these signals by picking the baby up to cuddle him.

As the well-organized alert neonate is held in a cuddled position, he molds into the adult's body, turning gently toward the chest. He may even grab hold of the adult's clothing with his free hand and his legs may mold around the side of the adult's body. This molding response cannot help but become a reinforcing signal to the adult for more active cuddling, for looking down at him to engage him in face-to-face contact for rocking or singing to him.

When he is held upright at the adult's shoulder, he first lifts his head to look around. As he does so, he actively holds on more tightly with all four extremities. After a period of alert scanning of the environment, triggered by the vestibular stimulation of the upright position (Korner & Thoman 1972), he is most likely to tire and put his head against the adult's shoulder, nestling his head in the crook of the adult's neck. Mothers tell me that as the soft fuzz of the infant's head makes contact with the skin of the crook of the neck, it causes a tightening sensation in the breasts followed by a 'let-down' reflex of milk. No adult is likely to resist the feeling of a soft head resting on the shoulder.

Another powerful set of communicative signals occurs as the infant builds up to crying. If an adult keeps on talking at one side of the infant's head, he will probably stop crying, quiet down, and gradually turn toward the voice. The adult can use the infant's capacity to alert to voices by changing her own vocal behavior. If her voice softens, the infant will maintain his focussed searching and scanning. He will remain quietly alert, and may smile or his face may soften into the precursor of a smile face. As they continue to communicate, the adult can bring him up to a more active state by gradually increasing the pitch and timbre of her voice, or she may cause him to 'overload' and return to a crying state by changing her tempo to a staccato rhythm, or she may help the infant maintain the quiet alert state by speaking softly in a slow rhythmic fashion which allows the newborn to become active and then to withdraw and recover in rhythmic fashion, allowing for a kind of quiet reciprocity which is rhythmic and provides feedback of attention and recovery for the neonate as well as for the adult. This model of reciprocal communication is seen later in infancy in intense play situations such as 'games' (Brazelton et al. 1974; Stern et al. 1977; Kaye this volume).

We (Kaye & Brazelton 1971) have described the communication value of the pauses in the burst—pause pattern of sucking seen in a normal feeding. Although the pauses have signal value to the mother, eliciting activity from her in turn, such as jiggling or rocking the baby, or looking down at him to talk or to prod him to return to sucking, the infant seems to be programmed to utilize the pauses as opportunities for communication. We found that when the duration of the pauses in which the mother did react were compared with the duration of the pauses when she did not react, her reaction appeared to prolong the pauses. The baby seemed to wait for more response in each pause in which she responded.

2 Discussion

From such experiences while testing neonates we have come to feel that the newborn infant comes equipped with a series of complex behaviors for communication and for eliciting the appropriate nurturing responses from the adults around him. Further, we feel that these behavioral items give important evidence of cortical control and responsiveness, even in the neonatal period. The neonate's capacity for managing and overcoming the physiological demands of this adjustment period in order to attend to, differentiate, and habituate to the complex stimuli of an examiner's maneuvers may be an important predictor of his future central nervous system organization (Tronick & Brazelton 1975). His regulation of his states of consciousness becomes the behavioral basis on which a caregiving adult knows how to adjust her timing. The adult learns when it is appropriate to play with the neonate and when to leave him alone. And then, within this basic communication system, she learns which signals are appropriate to his ambient state; which auditory, visual, tactile or kinesthetic responses will elicit an alerting response from the baby which says, 'Now we are in communication'. The developing clarity of the baby's states and of his responses to his caregiver becomes a firm reinforcer of further communication and for the development of affective bonds between them.

Bowlby (1969) has stressed the importance of observing the earliest interactions between mother and infant as predictive of the kind of attachment a mother may form for the infant. He suggests that there is a kind of 'imprinting' of responses from her which may be triggered by the neonate's behavior. Moss (1965) and Goldberg (1976) point to the trigger-like effect of the newborn's small size, helpless appearance and distress cries in setting off mothering activities. Klaus & Kennell (1970) have described the kinds of initial contacts which mothers make with their newborn infants and the distortions in this behavior if a mother is depressed by abnormalities in the baby: prematurity, deformity, illness in the neonatal period etc. We may predict a mother's capacity to relate to her new baby by observing her eye-to-eye contact, touching, handling and nursing behavior. Change in these behaviors over time should be considered indicators of the degree of recovery or non-recovery of capacity to attach to the baby by a mother who has been depressed and unable to function optimally after having produced an infant considered to be at risk (Klaus et al. 1972).

Infant behaviors seem to reflect intrauterine experience. We studied a group of 157 babies in Guatemala whose mothers were on inadequate protein-calorie diets during pregnancy (Brazelton et al. 1977). Since we found we could predict marasmus or kwashiorkor from appearance and behavior at birth with a high degree of accuracy, it seemed important to document the behaviors which were affected by undernutrition in the uterus. Neonatal behaviors such as lack of vigor, immature, jerky motor behavior and decreased responsiveness to visual, auditory and kinesthetic cues and to handling by the examiner were found to be correlated with inadequate maternal diets and lowered socio-economic status of the parents. In addition, these behaviors were correlated with maternal height and head circumference, reflecting the mother's experience in her own mother's uterus and her own stunted growth. The behaviors were also correlated with the infant's size at birth, his gestational age, and the number of hypoxic episodes around delivery. Hence the neonates' behavior reflected their own depletion and correlated with their tendency to be vulnerable babies. The fact that their behavior correlated with the inadequacy of their own mothers made it appear that this was already a three-generation effect. Furthermore, these depleted babies remained limp and unresponsive throughout the first month of our observations. For all of that month, they moved into alert states of arousal slowly and showed little vigor in these states. They were unrewarding babies to hold or to play with. They rarely cried out for feedings and their already depleted mothers were found to be feeding them and handling them only three to four times a day throughout the neonatal period!

Although they thrived marginally throughout infancy, they were easily tipped over into a marasmic condition by any infection in the first year and into kwashiorkar when they were weaned from breast-feeding in the second year. We could predict which neonates were at rick by their inadequate behavioral responses when they were handled. One could then be sure that the feedback from the babies was sufficiently rewarding to get these undernourished mothers to respond with adequate nurturing. Neonatal behaviors, then, both reflected intrauterine inadequacy and predicted the baby's future outcome.

Interactive behaviors are found to be predictive of the baby's future central nervous system function (Tronick & Brazelton 1975). To assess the effectiveness of the behaviors in our examination as predictors of neurological function we compared its predictive value with that of a standard neurological examination for fifty-three neonates seen in 1962. These infants had been rated 'abnormal' or 'suspect' at three days by staff pediatricians at a maternity hospital during a longitudinal study designed to detect cerebral palsy, mental retardation and other neurological and sensory disorders of infancy and childhood (National Institutes of Health Project no. BP2372). The labeled infants were examined repeatedly in a neurological follow-up clinic for seven years.

The predictive value of the two types of examination was assessed by comparing outcomes at seven years. They were found comparable in their capacity for detecting abnormal infants. The neurological examination correctly diagnosed thirteen of the fifteen neonates who later turned out to be abnormal and the behavioral assessment examination diagnosed twelve of these fifteen abnormal infants. However, there was a striking difference between the two examinations in mislabeling normal infants, i.e. 'false alarm' rates. The neurological examination classified forty-three 'abnormal' or 'suspect' in the neonatal period, of whom thirty later turned out to be 'normal'. Thus the neurological examination achieved its 'hit' rate of 87% for detecting abnormal infants by misclassifying a large number of normal infants. All of these labeled neonates were followed in the neurological clinic for seven years. In contrast, the behavioral examination labeled twenty-one neonates as 'abnormal' or 'suspect'. Only nine of the latter turned out to be normal. Behavioral assessment achieved its hit rate of 80% in detecting abnormality in neonates without assigning as many normal infants to abnormal or suspect categories during the neonatal period.

The abnormalities recorded by the neurological examination reflected reflex function rather than central nervous system (CNS) integration or adaptability. The behavioral examination found the same neurological signs but weighed them against the infant's ability to perform integrated social behaviors that pointed to higher-level CNS functioning. Thus, despite apparently questionable functioning, infants categorized as suspect neurologically were able to be classified successfully as normal by a behavioral examination. Despite worrying CNS signs, these infants showed an ability to (1) alert and attend to auditory, visual or other social cues, (2) organize and control states of consciousness, with self-quieting, (3) produce smooth, fluid movements when in alert states, (4) shut out disturbing stimuli and (5) improve significantly over the first few days.

These differences may have to do not only with the level of CNS functioning but with differences in the manner in which the examinations are carried out. The behavioral examination is designed to encourage an infant's optimal performance over the 20- to 30-minute period of assessment. Behaviors are elicited in appropriate states, and several attempts are made to produce optimal responses. The examiner comforts the infant and supports his attempts to maintain motor control and thereby enhances his states of alertness, unlike the more standardized approach used in neurological evaluations. As a result an apparently disorganized infant may be helped to demonstrate controlled periods of alertness which indicate his capability for future recovery and optimal performance. This kind of interactive assessment is especially important with temporarily disorganized infants, such as those whose mothers have had large doses of drugs during delivery.

Interactive behaviors, then, can be elicited in the neonatal period which reflect intrauterine experience, predict future neurological functioning and reflect the kind of behavioral feedback a newborn will offer to his caregivers. These behaviors are powerful predictors of future development.

Note

1. This work was supported by grants from the William T. Grant Foundation, Inc., New York, and the Robert Wood Johnson Foundation.

4

Mutual regulation of the neonatal – maternal interactive process: context for the origins of communication[1]

PATRICIA F. CHAPPELL
Boston University Medical Center
LOUIS W. SANDER
University of Colorado Medical Center

1 Introduction

In considering the ontogenesis of human communication, especially over that span of time before speech appears, much attention is currently being directed toward the characteristics of the interactions and exchanges which take place between the infant and those about him. Well before speech can be said to have begun, a working arrangement of interactions between the infant and his caregivers, familiar to each, will have become established and will be accomplishing a great number of functions, essential not only for the maintenance of the continued existence of the infant, but also for the development of an increasingly complex repertoire of infant behaviors coordinated with or adapted to specific features of both the personal and non-personal world in which the infant is living and growing. The question being asked is whether there is some systematic relationship between these early coordinations and the development of communication between the infant and others. In what way do interactional coordinations which are achieved in the caregiving situation relate to the ontogeny and differentiation of the more specific process designated as communication?

Although at the present time we must leave the answers to these questions for the future, we can at least examine the empirical details of preverbal exchange between the infant and those around him, define their characteristics, and formulate, if possible, lawful regularities in their organization. The hunch is that, somewhere in the principles of organization of exchange in biological systems, bridging principles will be found which will relate the organization of inter-

acting elements at the more advanced levels of complexity to those
at the simpler levels.

Over the past two decades the Child Development Unit of the
Department of Child Psychiatry of Boston University Medical Center
has been engaged in the investigation of interaction between infant
and mother from birth onwards, at various levels of detail and over
different longitudinal spans of time. From this work a perspective has
been gained, or a point of view, which had undergirded subsequent
research and has led to new questions, some of which bear on the one
we are interested in here, namely how early interaction may be related
to later communication. We will describe this perspective and a
research project stemming from it which can then be discussed in
relation to the beginnings of human communication.

There have been three major projects and a number of more specifically focused investigations with which the Boston University group
has been engaged. These began in 1954 with a ten-year naturalistic
longitudinal study of thirty mother—infant pairs followed from the
prenatal period through the first year at school (Pavenstedt 1961,
1964; Sander 1969). The next effort beginning in 1965 focused on
detailed aspects of mother—infant interaction within the first two
months of life and has been reported in part in Sander (1975), Burns
et al. (1972) and Sander et al. (1969, 1970, 1972). The third, which
began as a collaborative project of the authors in 1972, and from
which we are reporting the study here, has centered about mechanisms of change in the organization of events within the first week of
life.

The questions of the first project were clinical ones raised by child
psychiatrists concerning the effects of maternal character organization
(assessed prenatally) on the organization of maternal behavior observed
subsequently in the rearing interaction with the child, and in turn the
relation of these observed events to the course of the child's development. The questions of the second project derived from the way we
had begun in the first project to deal with the task of assembling the
data of multiple variables related to different functions of the interacting members of a dyad, and of identifying the changes they showed
over time. This was, indeed, the problem of organization, and as such
required the adoption of an organismic or holistic perspective. To
provide a way of thinking about exchange and development, we
needed to think of infant and caregiving environment as a biological
system, one in which both its maintenance and its changes depend on

regulatory mechanisms which govern the interactions between participating elements or components. Our attack on the problem of
organization became a search for mechanisms of regulation.

Beginning early in the 1964 longitudinal study, we had been
impressed with the uniqueness of each mother's characteristics and
each infant's characteristics at the very outset of their life together.
Obviously, the ensuing interaction itself could only be unique, as
could be the ways it changed over the course of development. But
uniqueness always combined elements of both stability and of variability. The research task we set ourselves gradually moved away
from the analysis of cause and became a study of the process of
change — one depending first on the identification of variables common to all infant–mother pairs, which could be measured continuously or repeatedly day after day.

The third project, then, of which this report forms a part, was
designed as an investigation of change within the first week of life
based on two methods of quantitative measurement: one concerned
with observed behaviors in the interaction and the other with the
continuous monitoring of infant states along the sleep–awake continuum. The questions we wanted to ask of these variables and
methods were suggested by the point of view which had been emerging from reflections about the biological system. How does the
organization of the system, its integration, depend on processes of
adaptation between its participating elements, and how do these in
turn depend on the mechanisms of regulation of their essential functions? There are powerful conceptual advantages for discovering such
relationships among a complex array of variables if the *system* becomes the unit of analysis rather than the *individual*. In the examination of process and the search for mechanism, economy is introduced
by the possibility of a basic relation between regulation, adaptation
and organization within the biological system, each living system at
some level of conceptual analysis possessing features common to all
living systems.

One such basic feature of life process is the characteristic of synthesis or integration of more elementary components and their functions. If one is looking for mechanisms by which such integration is
achieved, one finds a great array of them built into the system at
many levels — a feature which has often been overlooked in our eager-
ness to analyze causal relationships and to isolate 'determining' factors. When we begin from the basic elements of the biological system,

e.g. from the living cell, we begin with elements which already show spontaneous endogenous activity and are each actively self-regulating. To some extent basic organic units from the cell upward can be thought of as machines which are already running. Events may influence or perturb their ongoing activity but do not start it. Rather, each such element, as a component of a system, *interfaces* with other elements by complex yet highly specific and closely governed or regulated sets of exchanges between them. Exchange, and coordination of exchange between components, characterizes biological systems in general. This suggests the possibility that if exchanges can be examined closely, common governing mechanisms by which interfacing is accomplished may become evident. The structures of exchange interfacing neonate and mother at the outset of postnatal life may illuminate the structures of exchange at the level of communication and even possibly of the organization of language.

We have focused on two large categories of principles governing exchange in our search for mechanism. One is related to biorhythmicity and the other to cybernetics and its related area of information processing theory. In regard to the former, the significance for us of biorhythmicity lies in its role in the determination of biological organization as a matter of time and timing. The problem of organization in the living system can be viewed first of all as a problem of temporal organization of its semi-independent endogeneously biorhythmic elements. Regulatory mechanisms related to biorhythmicity, such as entrainment, phase-shifting and phase-synchrony, govern the interaction between elements and harmonize disparate elements, thus providing integration to the system. In this light, mechanisms related to biorhythmicity contribute to regulation, adaptation, synchronization, organization and integration. In regard to the infant—mother system, biorhythmicity also has fundamental relevance to the distribution of states of the infant on the sleep—awake continuum. This distribution generates the 24-hour pattern of sleep—awake states which must harmonize, in turn, with key cyclic or recurrent features of the infant's environment.

Our emphasis on the second category of governing principles, namely the cybernetic, includes not only the notion of feedback control but that of guidance or goal-oriented action. Although basic to any consideration of biological regulation, these concepts have particular relevance if individual elements of the living system are viewed as possessing a primary endogenous activity, a feature which imposes the consequent necessity of active self-regulation. Adapted action is guided action, being governed by cybernetic principles. Initiation of action, goal direction and criteria of goal realization are essential elements interfacing the exchange between infant and mother. They can be studied also at the level of interactions which can be observed in the more immediate sequence of behaviors mother and infant engage in when together. For a particularly clear description of the way these principles can be applied to an analysis of the adaptive behavior of living systems the reader should turn to Ashby (1952). His model of the 'ultrastable' system allows one to visualize the way the state of the infant contributes to the regulation of the sensory-motor sub-systems in their exchanges with the caregiver during the process of adaptation.

2 The study

In turning now to a description of the third project, centered about the investigation of change in the infant—caregiver system over the first week of life, we are describing essentially a pioneering attempt to explore mechanisms involved in the initial organization of a system at the immediate postnatal period. The event of birth represents a disruption in the fabric of temporal organization for the fetus, on the basis both of a termination of the previous exogenous (maternal) sources of rhythmicity in the fetus prenatally and of the institution of a new set of powerful endogenous determinants of rhythmicity postnatally, e.g. hunger—feeding—satiation, respiration, elimination. The task of caregiving over the first two or three weeks of postnatal life is to establish the new bases for temporal organization for both the infant and the infant—caregiver system. This process is difficult to discover on the basis of small time samples of interaction, the traditional method of study. Temporal organization is a 24-hour matter in which variations around the clock are of especial significance. It is just in dwelling together, continuously around the clock, 24 hours per day, that the real stress is placed on mother and on newborn, requiring the mutual modifications upon which their initial adaptation or coordination is based. Central to this is the coordination of 24-hour patterns of sleeping both for mother and infant — i.e. a proper organization of night and day distributions. This is based on placement of a longest sleep and a longest awake period per 24 hours, as well as of the remaining shorter naps in relation to day and night partitions. These shifts in placement of sleep and awake periods are all taking place within the first two or three weeks of life. Increasing stability in durations and placement of periods establishes a familiar time framework by which the 24 hours become organized for both mother and infant. The framework of temporal organization is largely beyond the mother's awareness but it provides a shared congruence in time as the context for the more specific sequence of behaviors of each in relation to the other. These data have been reported (Sander et al. 1975).

There is also a temporal organization of the events taking place in these more specific sequential behavioral interactions, which we can observe minute by minute between mother and infant during the course of the infant's awake periods. A familiar sequence soon becomes based on the time course of infant state change over the full extent of the awake period. Regularly recurring infant and caregiver behaviors become related to that time course. Here again, as with the 24-hour span, we have chosen the complete duration of awake periods as our unit of analysis rather than sampling interactional events during part of an awake period. The time course of changes in infant state introduces the factor of directionality to the interactional sequence, i.e. which event is likely to lead to which next event. Events will move in a given direction depending on durations of infant states tending toward arousal or sleep and how stable or changeable they are at different points in the overall time course of the awake period. As the direction of the mutually shared sequence becomes familiar, it provides the basis for interpretation of meaning or intentionality in specific actions of the partner.

There are many positions which can be taken regarding a connection between the mutual regulation of early behavior and its relation to the onset of communication. There seems to be a certain agreement that, among others, two elements are essential to exchange which qualifies as communication; these elements may be traced to their origins in early interaction. They are (1) a basic congruence of mind between the individuals communicating, i.e. a shared commonality of context or background within which each is functioning, and which contributes the context for the meaning of the more specific events constituting the foreground of the communication; and (2) an accurate reading of the intentionality governing the employment of communicational events. In undertaking this project we follow the hunch that the ontogeny of both these essential elements of communication can be examined in infant and caregiver when the empirical data are arranged in terms of change over days in the organization of events in the system.

3 Methods

Data being reported are from observations of four mothers and their female infants who were roomed in in the hospital lying-in unit during the infants' first week of life, ending with their discharge on the morning of the infants' eighth day. Reported here are observations of each infant's first full awake period after 8 a.m. on days 2, 5, 6 and 8 and of each infant's second full awake period on days 2, 5, 6 and 7. Thus, eight full awake periods comprise the observations for each mother—baby pair. The first awakening on day 7 is not discussed because a substitute caregiver cared for the infants at that time; no observation was made of the second awakening on day 8 because of the discharge of the pairs following the first feeding and subsequent return to sleep of the infant. No observations were planned or executed on days 3 and 4 in order to protect the developing relationship between the mother—infant pair during this early vulnerable period in the first week of life.

Beginning with the awakening of the baby, and continuing until the baby returned to sleep and reached a state of quiet sleep, the mother's and infant's behaviors were recorded on a checklist every 15 seconds.[2] The observation was organized in this manner in order to study the structure of the interactive process between mother and infant, and to study the course of state change between sleep and waking in the baby over the full awake period vis à vis caregiver behavior. State was the primary focal behavior under study in regard to the infant because of the importance of state regulation in the regulation of interaction between mother and infant; the degree of success and the manner in which the issue of state regulation is resolved between infant and caregiver determines in part the manner and success of the negotiation of later issues (Sander 1969). State patterning of the infant was viewed as context for the occurrence of other behaviors. Also recorded were measures of distance between the pair members and posture of the infant. (See appendix for definitions and listing of the behaviors reported.) Other behaviors were recorded but not reported here: feeding behaviors and other social behaviors, such as caress, touching etc. The observer stood in the room with the interacting pair but at a distance always of at least 4 ft. All mothers were Caucasian, primiparous women who had normal pregnancies and deliveries; all infants were judged normal at birth and were bottle-fed.

4 Findings

The values reported represent events which occurred from the time the mother first touched the infant at its awakening, throughout the interaction until the infant was returned to its bassinet. The findings presented are from analyses of the distribution of separate behavioral events over days, of the distribution over days of the cooccurrence of behavioral events within 15-second epochs, and from analyses of contingent relationships between events. The frequency of occurrence or cooccurrence of behavioral events is reported in relation to the number of 15-second epochs per day within the total observation time across pairs. Although these findings are based on observations of only four mother—infant pairs, the population, e.g., of posture change/state change associations analyzed totaled 426 (changes 158, non-changes 268).

The proportion of total observation time that infants maintained a state of alertness increased over days, beginning with 44% time in alertness on day 2 and increasing to 79% by day 8. Tests of differences in proportions show statistically significant changes to have occurred between days 2 and 6 and between days 7 and 8 ($p<0.05$). (See fig. 1.)

There were also increases over days in the proportion of the observation time that mothers held infants in the closest proximity, beginning with 42% on day 2 and increasing steadily until day 8 when during 70% of the total observation time the infant was held against the mother's ventrum — coded as Proximity 1. Significant changes occurred between days 2 and 5 and between days 7 and 8 ($p<0.05$). (See fig. 2.)

Concomitant with the independent increases in the proportion of alertness and Proximity 1, there was an increase in the proportion of the cooccurrence of these two variables within 15-second epochs across days. Beginning with a proportion of 24% on day 2, cooccurrence of alertness and Proximity 1 increased across days to 57% on day 8 in proportion to the total observation time. Significant points of change in proportion occurred between days 2 and 6 and days 6 and 8 ($p<0.05$). (See fig. 3.)

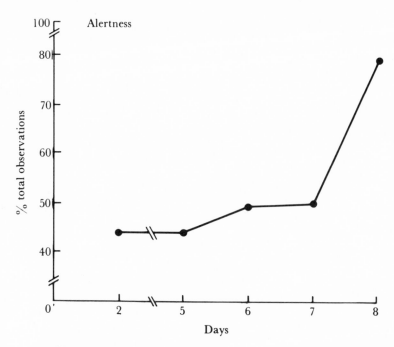

Fig. 1 *Alertness*. The proportion of total observation time that infants were alert on each of the observation days.

Similarly, the cooccurrence of maternal verbalization and alertness increased significantly across days. The values of cooccurrence were low, beginning with 1% on day 2 but increasing across days to 16% on day 8. Points of significant change were between days 2 and 5 and days 5 and 8 ($p < 0.05$). (See fig. 4.)

To understand the development of the wakefulness in the infants, and in order to identify the sources of environmental influences on infant wakefulness, the contingent relationship between infant state change and maternal behavior was examined. State changes were identified by examining successive 15-second epochs and examining those areas where two different states were immediately contiguous. The analysis was limited to one maternal behavior, posture change of the infant; the posture of the infant was judged at one of three levels every 15 seconds, upright, sitting or lying. When in two successive 15-second epochs two different postures occurred, a posture change was considered to have occurred, and entered into the analysis irrespective of the direction of the change. Thus, the relationship between state change and posture change could be determined. The

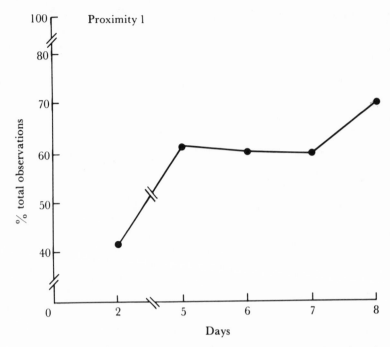

Fig. 2 *Proximity 1*. The proportion of total observation time that mothers held infants in the closest proximity on each of the observation days.

first level of analysis was executed to determine the value of state change in the infant as a cue to the mother to change the infant's posture. The results showed that state change in the infant did *not* cue the mother to change infant posture within the next two 15-second epochs. An analysis to examine the posture change in the infant as the antecedent of state change showed the contrary to be true, although this relationship could be seen only if state of the infant when the change in posture occurred was considered. If the infant was in a state of alertness and posture change occurred, no state change was probable; but if the infant was in any state other than alertness when posture change occurred, a state change followed the posture change significantly often ($X^2 = 73.85$; df, 1; p<0.001).

The next level of analysis was done to determine the appropriateness of the effect of posture change on the infant's state. This determination of appropriate effect was made possibly only by positing what an optimal effect should be, or what the optimal state of the infant would be according to specific periods as defined by the

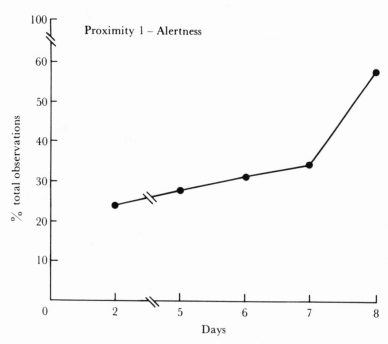

Fig. 3 *Proximity 1 — alertness*. The proportion of total observation time that alertness and proximity 1 cooccurred on each of the observation days.

sequence of events in the interaction. That is, the appropriateness of the effect of maternal manipulation on infant state would be judged according to whether the events occurred at the beginning, middle or end of the interaction between the pair members. The questions concerning appropriateness of effect of mothers' manipulation of posture on state change could best be answered by generating a hypothetical model of the sequence of events over the total interaction period. At least for this analysis, implicit in the hypothetical model is a continuum of states ranked according to level of arousal (as ordered in the appendix) from sleep to waking. In addition, for this particular analysis of the data generated in this study, the model has as its beginning the point at which the observation began. The beginning of the observation was determined by the mother who summoned the observer when she decided the infant was awake. Because of this restriction, the period of infant awakening is not represented in this model; thus, the observation began when the mother first touched the baby, and the hypothetical model is structured to reflect this

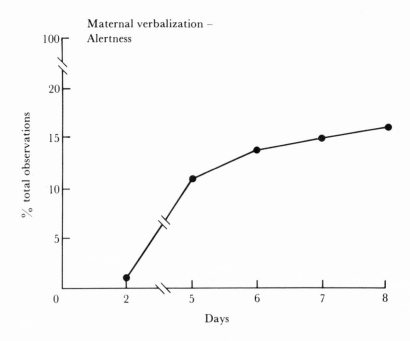

Fig. 4 *Maternal verbalization – alertness*. The proportion of total observation time that maternal verbalizations to the infant and infant alertness
cooccurred on each of the observation days.

restriction. Basically, the model states that in optimal state functioning over the interaction period, the infant will awaken and alert,
remain alert to feed and return to sleep. The interaction period was
thus divided into three periods, before feeding, during the feed and
after the feed (see fig. 5). The hypothesized optimal effect could then
be classified in relationship to the period in which a change of state
occurred: if the mother changed the infant's posture during the first
phase of the interaction, an optimal effect of this manipulation would
be to bring the infant from either a higher or lower state toward alertness; if the infant were fussing or crying, or drowsing when manipulation occurred, the optimal state change would be to alertness, or to
an adjacent state if two or more defined states intervened (see appendix). During the feed, the same definition holds as for the first period.
During the third period, a manipulation of posture by the mother
would be followed by an optimal state change if it were in the direction of sleep, so that if the infant were fussing, alert etc. at the point
of manipulation, state change would be judged optimal if the resultant

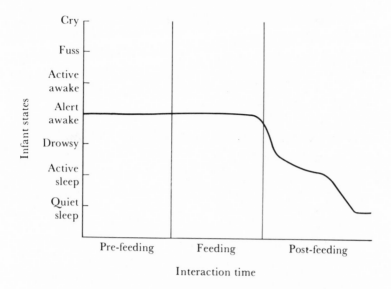

Fig. 5 Hypothetical model of the optimal course of infant state functioning over the interaction period, i.e. from the time the mother first made
contact with the infant until she returned the infant to the bassinet.

state following the manipulation were drowsiness or sleep. Non-
changes of state were also evaluated according to the same model;
if state did not change (i.e. if state was maintained) following a
manipulation of posture by the mother it was deemed an optimal
state condition if, during the first two phases, alertness was maintained, or, during the third phase, no elevation of state occurred,
that is, if the infant's drowsy or sleep state was maintained. With
these definitions as criteria, each posture change/infant state relationship was examined in order to plot the change in optimality of maternal
control of infant state over the course of the first week of life.

In order to separate out the endogenous control of state by the
infant from exogenous control by the mother, the population of posture change/infant state relationships was separated into two groups:
those in which no change occurred, which were deemed points at
which endogenous control was little affected by the maternal manipulation, and those in which infant state functioning was affected by
maternal manipulation, which were considered points at which endogenous factors controlling state regulation in the infant were manipu-
lable by exogenous factors. The analyses provided the following
results: an increase was found across days in the proportion of

maternal manipulations effecting a *state change* in the infant which was concordant with the definition of optimal as defined by our model, beginning with 40.5% on day 2 and increasing across days until day 8 when 71% of the posture change/state change relationships were deemed optimal. Significant points of change occurred between days 2 and 6 and between days 2 and 8 ($p<0.05$ for each). (See fig. 6.) Across days, the proportion of maternal manipulations (i.e. posture changes of the baby) resulting in an optimal state condition due to *non-changes* of state decreased from 78% on day 2 to 53% on day 5, increased to 73% on day 6, with a further increase on day 7 (78%) and day 8 (90%). Significant changes in proportions occurred between days 2 and 5, days 5 and 6 and days 6 and 8 (all changes at $p<0.05$). (See fig. 7.) In sum, these analyses show that optimality of the effect on infant state condition by maternal manipulation of the infant, at least as indexed by posture change of the baby, increased steadily across the week. Similarly, the infant's capacity to maintain state

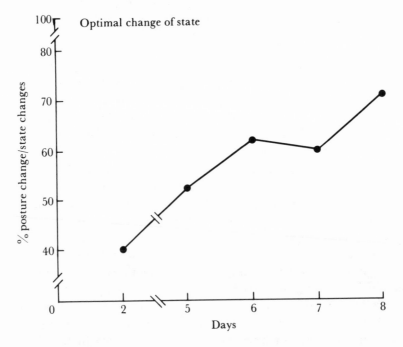

Fig. 6 *Optimal state changes.* The proportion of state changes following posture changes of the infant by the mother which result in an optimal state as defined by the hypothetical model; the proportion is relative to the total number of posture changes/state changes per day.

increased between day 2 and day 8, but with a period during the middle of the week which suggests some factor preventing optimal state regulation by endogenous means.

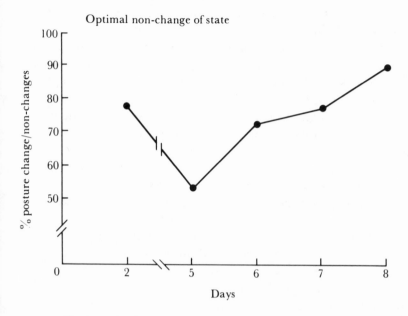

Fig. 7 *Optimal non-change of state*. The proportion of non-changes of state following posture changes of the infant by the mother which result in an optimal state as defined by the hypothetical model; the proportion is relative to the total number of posture changes/non-changes of state per day.

5 Discussion

The observations of these mother–infant pairs provide evidence of significant changes occurring in the organization of the interactions over the first eight days of the infants' lives. In this setting, infants showed significant increases in alertness over days, and, concomitant with the increased alertness, close maternal holding and verbalization cooccurred with alertness increasingly across the week to provide more frequent opportunity for close face-to-face interaction and to facilitate perceptual and affective development in the infant. These findings show that an increasing coordination of activities emerged over the eight days between infant alertness and maternal behaviors.

The work just described represents a pioneering effort in a number of ways. The study of change from day to day over the first week of life of infant and maternal variables representing different modalities of function and interaction, and the independence or cooccurrence of these changes begins the analysis of neonate and mother as a system in process. The attempt to relate fluctuations in variables of infant state with the linear sequence of interactional events begins to examine mechanisms of integration in the system. The increase in cooccurrence of change which has been demonstrated begins to document the manner by which the commonly shared events necessary for a basic congruence of context may be acquired initially by infant and mother. Finally, the use of the hypothetical expectancy model for analysis of the interactive regulative system can now be investigated. It is a structure of directionality shared by both infant and mother, which, over subsequent weeks, differentiates into an increasingly complex sequence (see Sander 1977), one which in providing basic elements of context provides an anchoring framework for the interpretation of intention in the behaviors initiated by either partner.

A word of caution must be added to those who would translate this research model of assessment of appropriateness of maternal behavior into a clinical model in the name of intervention. Underlying this model is the assumption that the organization and integration of the mother—infant interactive system exists at a preconscious level, and that attempts to bring this integrative mechanism into consciousness (e.g. to bring it to the mother's attention through training) would necessarily change the integration of the mother's behavior as well as the integration of the total system, thus placing undue stress on a very vulnerable organism, the neonate—mother system. The judgment of appropriateness of maternal manipulation on infant state was made in order to assess the effect of the mother on the infant's changing patterns of state over the first week of life, and was made independent of the obvious appropriateness or inappropriateness of maternal behavior at the time of observation; in this sense, the judgment of appropriateness as reported here can be considered a data analytic procedure, and as such, it differs in purpose and procedure from assessments of maternal behavior such as those reported by Ainsworth (1972) and labeled 'maternal sensitivity'.

A number of investigations have provided data which inform the issue of the adaptation of the human infant to its environment in regard to sleep—wake cycles (e.g. Sander et al. 1970) but few findings are available which relate to the changes in infant state patterning during the wakeful period which result from environmental manipulation. The results of the analysis evaluating optimality of the effect of maternal manipulation across days enlightens the process of adaptation of the infant to the environment during wakefulness. The finding not only shows that the caregiver does influence and facilitate state regulation during this period, but further identifies points at which state can be manipulated by environmental events. During the ordinary course of the full awake period, minor state fluctuations occur; during alert periods, short periods of drowsiness occur; during the shift to sleep, brief periods of alertness are interspersed with drowsiness. It is at these points of shift within the larger phases of the interaction as defined by our model that manipulation facilitates a state change concordant with the model. During alert periods when the infant shifts to a more active state or into drowsiness, a posture change brings the infant back to alertness to conform to the phase-defined appropriate state. During the shift to sleep, when the infant becomes alert or active, a change in posture can facilitate the shift to sleep in concordance with our definitions.

The effect of such manipulations on the durations of the awake period can easily be seen. This plays a direct role in the synchronization of the pattern of infant sleep and awake cycling with major environmental periodicities, i.e. a day—night differentiation with day having morning, afternoon and evening subsegments (Sander et al. 1970). In addition, the dynamics of the adaptation process and its role in the socialization of the infant and in the acquisition of communication are illustrated. With the coordination of the phases of the interaction (as defined by the mother's behavior) with infant state deemed appropriate to each interaction phase, each pair member gives tacit agreement to the type of events permissible at a particular point in time. The basic synchrony of events in the neonatal period gives birth to the acquisition of meaning, not only for the infant but also for the mother, for it is only through mutual agreement that meaning exists. More explicitly, the context for interaction is agreed upon.

The demonstration given here of the matching of infant state to the hypothetical model suggests that mothers have at least a gross plan for the interaction that parallels the hypothetical model of infant state change across the interaction that has been proposed, that is, they expect the infant to awaken, stay awake to feed and then to return to sleep. It suggests further that the temporal placement of

maternal behaviors, which define the different phases of the interaction, is made relative to infant state. The infant's wakefulness determines the activities of the mother, the activities of the mother determine in some degree the course of infant state over the interaction
period, and the modifiability of infant state by maternal manipulation
determines the mother's further activities. Her judgments for actions
and plans are based on her immediate 'reading' of the infant, on her
present knowledge of the temporal course of the interaction and
experience with the infant in prior interactions. Moreover, the
sequence of maternal behavior is well fixed: preparing for the feeding
(diapering, picking up the infant) precedes the feeding, feeding in
short periods is followed by change in posture for burping which
always follows the feeding bouts, posture change in a different direction which follows burping, and finally a settling back for social interaction followed by the infant's shift to sleep and then to bed. The
sequence of these events is all but unaltered and the changes in the
mini-cycle of feeding/posture change/burping is altered only by infant
state condition and the amount of food taken by the infant. The
implication for the infant is that with each successive awakening his
interaction with his environment becomes increasingly stable, thus
predictable, and particularly so in the effect of the environment on
him, as we have seen. Moreover, experience with a predictably ordered
sequence of events is basic preparation for later management of information processing in any communication code, and with the management of all serially ordered activities. If the predictable order be shared
between interacting partners, a common *context* is provided for the
more variable *content* of the events which take place between them,
setting up the conditions under which such events also gain in meaning common to both.

In regard to the application of the term 'communication' to the
interactions occurring between the newborn and his mother, the data
presented here refer to interactions which could be considered communication only at the biosocial level and the interactive processes
which demonstrate mutual regulation have been demonstrated here
only at this level, at least as reflected in the variables reported here.
The findings demonstrate the kind of synchrony which can develop
in the mother—infant pair at the biosocial level of interaction during
the first week of the infant's life, a level upon which a hierarchy of
levels of interaction builds, among them a level of interaction appropriately termed communication. To cite an example from McKay

(1972) (but see also Ryan 1974 and Glasersfeld 1974), we should distinguish between the cry of an infant who cries in such a way as to get attention and the cry of an infant who cries *in order* to get attention, i.e. who has achieved *intention*; our goal is to study the responses of the mother which are instrumental in the change over time toward purposiveness of the cries. This admonition holds for other behaviors as well. The assumption is that neonatal signals reflect a condition of the infant, a symptom of underlying status, and are not at the outset purposively directed toward the caretaker; it is the response of the mother appropriate and contingent to the infant's 'symptoms of underlying status' that gives meaning to her response for the infant and elevates the infant's expression of under-lying status to the level of a goal-directed signal that allows the infant to reveal internal state *in order* to bring about the desired environmental outcome. We propose that intentionality in the behavior of the infant develops in this manner.

In addition, each manipulation of the infant by the mother pro-vides her with feedback information of the effect the manipulation has on her infant; this information gives her an estimate of the appropriateness of her behavior — whether she has asked the ques-tion of appropriateness or not. The gain to the pair is in the co-ordination of activities or harmony out of which the mutuality of *intention* develops, a level of interaction which can theoretically be considered communication.

Notes

1. The authors wish to acknowledge the support provided by the Grant Foun-dation for this project and the Chelsea Naval Hospital Departments of Obstetrics and Pediatrics for their kind cooperation in the execution of this study. The authors wish also to acknowledge the assistance of Ms Patricia Snyder in the collection of the data. Dr Chappell is supported by a Medical Foundation Fellowship from the Medical Foundation Inc., of Boston, Massachusetts and Dr Sander is supported by a USPHS Research Scientist Award no. K5-MH-20505-09.
2. The time for recording information is taken from the beginning of each 15-second epoch and does not involve more than 5 seconds and usually less. In any event, the reliability is not depressed as a result of this method. These reliabilities are reported in appendix 1. Epochs are marked by a transistorized tone-generator which delivers the tones to the observer every 15 seconds through an ear jack.

Appendix:
Behavioral variables[1]

Infant state

(A judgment was made to determine which of the following states was characteristic of the infant during the majority of each 15-second epoch. Earlier versions of this scale appeared in Chappell 1970, Chappell et al. 1973 and Boismier et al. 1970. Observer agreement: 92%.)

1. Quiet or non-REM (rapid eye movement) sleep: regular respiration; eyes closed; no facial movement; no vocalization; no motor activity except an occasional reflex movement, e.g. startle or sobbing inspiration.
2. Active or REM sleep: irregular respiration; eyes closed with ocular motility; facial movement; vocalization can occur; peripheral movements.
   Active sleep without REM: all of the above with the exception of ocular motility.
3. Transitional sleep: irregular respiration; eyes closed, with or without ocular motility; facial movements; vocalization can occur; trunk and gross limb movements.
4. Drowsiness: regular or irregular respiration; eyes close and open slowly; ocular motility can frequently be seen; facial movements absent; no vocalization; no movements.
5. Alertness: regular or semi-regular respiration; eyes open and bright; no facial movement; no vocalization; no or peripheral movements.
6. Active wakefulness: irregular respiration; eyes open; facial movements can occur; vocalizations can occur; mild or gross motor activity.
   Fussy wakefulness: all of the above except the eyes can be closed and the vocalizations are 'fussy' in nature.
7. Crying: irregular respiration; facial movements; eyes closed; crying vocalizations; gross motor activity can occur.

Proximity

(Judgments were based on occurrence for the major portion of the 15-second epoch. Observer agreement: 89%.)
1. The infant is held against the mother's ventrum.
2. The infant is held at forearm's length from the mother.
3. The infant is held at extended arm's length from the mother.

Infant posture

(Judgments were based on occurrence for the major portion of the 15-second epoch. Observer agreement: 98%.)

1. The infant is held in an upright posture, as in standing, perpendicular to the mother's lap.
2. The infant is held in a seated position, defined as an angle of 45—90° relative to the mother's lap.
3. The infant is held in a lying position, defined as an angle of less than 45° relative to the mother's lap.

Maternal verbalization

(Observer agreement: 89%.)
1. Mother verbalizes *to* the infant any time within the 15-second epoch.

Note

1. Details of observational methodology may be requested from the first author.

5

Describing the structure of social interaction in infancy[1]

GLYN M. COLLIS
University of Strathclyde

1 Introduction

In this chapter I shall be concerned with the discovery, description and investigation of the structure of social interaction in infancy and the patterns that comprise this structure whereby the actions of each individual are composed into a sequence and related to the actions of other participants. I am interested, in other words, in what may loosely be called behavioural synchrony. My main emphasis will be on patterns revealed by micro-analysis, that is, I shall focus on time scales of the order of seconds or fractions thereof. Although in most of the examples to be discussed two individuals are involved, an infant and his mother, it is to be hoped that the kind of analysis advocated will be extended to include interaction with peers, sibs, father etc., and to groups larger than a dyad.

I want to avoid the issue of whether these patterns of interaction *are* communication. My primary aim is more descriptive than taxonomic. To borrow a phrase from Tinbergen (1963) I am inclined to ignore the term and get on with studying the phenomena. However, it is fair to say that I believe that the micro-structure of interaction is absolutely basic to the theme of this book: such patterns are at least an essential component of any normal social exchange that is at all likely to be considered worthy of the label 'communication'.

In laying the foundation of a descriptive analysis of mother—infant interaction there are two ways in which we can follow up initial impressions of what is going on in the dyad. Suspicions that certain actions serve as cues or signals that affect the other individual's behaviour can be checked systematically or, having noticed patterns where the two individuals' activities are co-ordinated, we can proceed to examine how these co-ordinations are brought about (Menzel 1973). Either approach, applied to observational data, requires

111

descriptive and analytical techniques that do justice to the timing and sequencing of the two individuals' behaviour. As a rule in social inter-action, a number of cues pass from one participant to the other and, most often, these cues are integrated into a coherent organisation. Hence it is necessary to examine organisation within, as well as between, individuals' behaviour: intrapersonal as well as interpersonal integration.

By far the greater part of the literature on mother—infant inter-action is outside our focus on micro-structure. A large proportion of this research still is concerned almost exclusively with measurements of crude amounts (frequencies, durations or unspecified) of various activities performed by one of the participants (usually the infant) in the presence of the other (the mother). At the end of the observational session these amounts comprise the score(s) of the individual or, more properly, of the relationship. This approach often follows the concep-tualisation of the activities in question as *indices* of some kind of trait, disposition or capacity that the subjects possess to a greater or lesser degree. A consequence of this is that, with a few noble exceptions, activities that have not been considered as indices of some kind of psychological construct are largely neglected and not considered as worthy of investigation in their own right. To get to grips with the complexity of mother—infant interaction there is a need for a series of descriptive analyses, quantitative where appropriate, of as large and as representative a sample as possible of the multiplicity of ways in which the activities of mother and infant are integrated together in time. Paralleling the compilation of an ethogram in classical ethology, where the aim is to produce an inventory of behaviour patterns shown by individuals of a species, the suggested programme may be thought of as an approach toward building a *dyadogram* of the mother—infant relationship. An account of the mutual organisation of mothers' and infants' behaviour during interaction will complement, and should validate, the present rather one-sided body of knowledge on infants' responses to 'social' stimuli and their production of a limited range of social signals such as crying and smiling.

1.1 Models and methods of analysis

How are we to set about studying the sequential organisation of mothers' and infants' behaviour? We are interested in evidence that the occurence of action x by individual A is associated with the occurence of action y by individual B. Further, we may wish to use this evidence to support the stronger causal hypothesis that *x* affects the likelihood of *y*. Such inferences logically precede more global categories where *B*'s response is related in some specified way to *A*'s (for instance, imitatively) or where *B* responds in *any* way to any action by *A*. Particularly with linguistic data, a degree of congruency in the content of *x* and *y* may be sufficient to satisfy us that it is unlikely that they would be juxtaposed by chance. In other cases we will want to test this numerically.

In a very simple model (fig. 1a) mother and infant are considered to perform actions alternately, the one affecting the other as a stimulus—response chain. The quantitative data base would comprise frequencies of two-step infant—mother and mother—infant sequences. Crude transition frequencies such as these are usually uninterpretable until they are compared with those 'expected' from the relative frequencies of the various actions considered singly (Slater 1973). Intra-individual sequences can be measured in a similar way and incorporated into the model (fig. 1b). Organisation over more than one step in the sequence can also be assessed (S.A. Altmann 1965).

Conceiving the interaction as a series of discrete events occurring

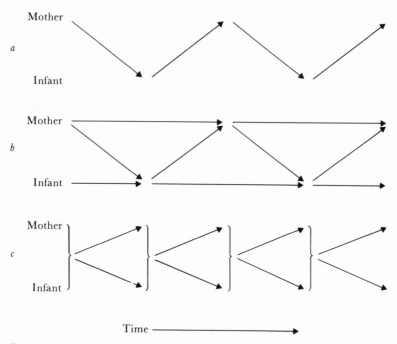

Fig. 1 Conceptual models of interaction sequences.

one at a time has obvious limitations: patterns such as mutual gaze and vocal turn-taking, where the degree of alternation or simultaneity is the subject of enquiry, can not be examined from this perspective. To accommodate the possibility of simultaneous action by the two participants one can consider each individual's action or inaction as following from the preceding *joint* action state (fig. 1c). To match this model with an empirical procedure we might sample, at discrete points in time, the current dyadic state as defined by the combined activity states of the two individuals. Such an approach has been used to good effect by D.N. Stern and his colleagues. Studies of interpersonal gaze (Jaffe et al. 1973; Stern 1974b) showed how analysis of transitions between successive dyadic states illuminates the pattern of mutual influences between the two individuals' behaviour. In addition, the proportion of sampling instants occupied by joint states such as mutual gaze (Stern unpublished) or simultaneous vocalising (Stern et al. 1975) can be compared with the proportion expected on the basis of the gaze or vocalising of each individual considered separately. This is analogous to calculating 'expected' amounts of joint activity from duration data; with both methods estimates of expected amounts may be improved by taking other factors into account (Argyle & Ingham 1972).

Inevitably, the utility of the dyadic state approach depends on the nature of the data. Lewis (1972) and his colleagues used data based on the occurence or non-occurence of selected events in 10-second time intervals, a procedure referred to by J. Altmann (1974) as one-zero sampling. When several events occurred within any one such interval the order of events was noted. However, the dyadic state analysis could only cope with patterns of occurence of combinations of events between successive intervals and the important within-interval patterning was lost (Lewis & Freedle 1973; Lewis & Lee-Painter 1974).

With suitable data this approach can be very powerful, particularly when it can be shown that a small number of parameters are sufficient to model the sequential structure of some facet of interaction as in the study by Jaffe et al. (1973; see also Jaffe 1968; Jaffe & Feldstein 1970). Often, however, this is not the case, particularly when the pattern changes over time, that is, when the process is non-stationary. In such cases we may have to be content with rejecting null hypotheses of non-deviation from some random model. A generally useful technique that retains provision for simultaneity of action is to ask: at the moment of *onset* of activity *y* by individual *B*, is the *ongoing* behavioural state of *A* more likely to be *x* than it would at other times? For example, when a mother looks at a particular toy, is the infant especially likely already to be looking at that toy (Collis & Schaffer 1975)? Again, we might suspect that a mother's vocalisations prompt the infant to look at her, an idea that would be supported by the finding that, say, 25% of his looks started while she was vocalising whereas, in all, she vocalised for only 10% of the total time available. However, this might merely reflect a tendency for looking and vocalising to be associated with each other in a bout of relatively intense interaction. One might then compare rates of looking during the child's own vocalising with rates while his mother was vocalising and find, particularly with an older infant, that his looks were more likely during his own utterances (Schaffer et al. 1977).

Particularly when activities do not overlap, much can be learned from the distributions of intervals between events. The methods outlined by Delius (1969) for within-individual sequences can be extended to between-individual effects (Kloot & Morse 1975) and have been used in this context by Kaye (1977). A major problem with many sophisticated methods of analysis is the relatively large amount of data required. In all cases careless pooling of data can be disastrously misleading.

2 Some patterns of interaction

2.1 Vocal interaction

By association with speech, the vocal—auditory channel is normally considered to be of greatest importance in human social interaction. Most recent research directly concerned with the dyadic structure of vocal interaction between mothers and infants has been in terms of on—off patterns of vocalisation. The interest here stems from the fact that in adult conversation, participants normally take turns to speak; is this true of interactions involving young children?

Schaffer et al. (1977) looked for evidence of turn-taking in vocal interaction between mothers and their one- or two-year-old children by carefully listening through recordings so as to detect episodes of vocal overlap between the two participants' utterances. Although speaker-switch pauses were mostly very brief, there were rather few instances of actual overlap between a mother's and child's vocalisations.

The data were not subjected to formal statistical analysis to see whether the amount of overlap was less than chance expectation but the impression that turn-taking was indeed occurring was supported by the finding that the few instances of simultaneous vocalising that did occur were mostly confined to special contexts where a break-down in turn-taking seemed intuitively reasonable. Thus a mother might interrupt the child when some undesirable turn of events seemed imminent, when the mother was trying to slot her utter-ances into nearly non-existent pauses in the child's distressful vocal-isations, or the mother and child might laugh together or unite in a chorus of 'ooooh's or 'aaaah's.

In a study of vocal interaction between mothers and their three- and four-month-old twins, Stern et al. (1975) presented data suggest-ing that *co-actional* vocalisation predominated over a turn-taking pattern. Probabilistic evidence was presented that showed that mothers and infants tended to vocalise together *more*, not less, than they might have been expected to do by chance. Examination of dyadic state sequences to determine the immediate cause of co-actional vocalisation showed that mothers were more likely to initiate and less likely to terminate vocalisations when the infant was himself vocalising than when he was silent. Similarly, infants were more likely to initiate a vocalisation while the mother was vocalising than while she was silent. Precisely the same set of effects was reported by Strain & Vietze (1975).

One should, perhaps, be cautious in comparing the studies of Stern et al. and Schaffer et al. in view of the methodological differences, particularly the type of interaction examined and the means employed to detect simultaneous vocalising. Schaffer et al. made an effort to discriminate instances of actual vocal overlap from very rapid non-overlapping speaker-switches which were often faster than might be expected from thinking in terms of reaction times, and hence could appear as simultaneous vocalisation when the data were extracted by observers operating pushbuttons. This point is particularly important for the Strain & Vietze data where the analysis was based on one-zero sampling (J. Altmann 1974) of 1-second time intervals rather than the instantaneous sampling used by Stern et al. The majority of speaker-switch pauses in the Schaffer et al. study were less than 1 second in duration and thus, in the frame of a 1-second interval, could appear as instances of vocal co-action.

Stern et al. made a point of stating that they did not believe that vocal co-action was simply a primitive pattern of vocal exchange to be wholly replaced by turn-taking at a later developmental stage. It was demonstrated that co-actional vocalising tended to occur when, according to the mothers' judgement obtained after the observation session, the infants were in a high state of arousal. The contexts of simultaneous vocalising described by Schaffer et al., especially those of laughter and distress, could perhaps be described in terms of high arousal but it may well be more productive to think in functional terms, especially in relation to the information content of the vocalisations. This is particularly attractive if turn-taking is seen as an adaptation to some kind of constraint on processing auditory input during the production of vocal output. Vocal exchanges between mothers and very young children are rather simple and little useful information would be lost if, during periods of simultaneous input and output, the incoming signal was not monitored continuously. As the child develops and messages become more complex, the turn-taking pattern will become more important; however, simple signals such as laughing, crying, 'ooooh's and 'aaaah's could still occur in a co-action pattern.

There are other issues in the sequence and timing of mother–infant vocal interchange as well as turn-taking. M.C. Bateson (1975b), having established that there was minimal vocal overlap in her recordings, examined the sequencing of mother and infant vocalisations. There was a greater tendency for infant vocalisations to be followed by mother vocalisations and mother vocalisations by infant vocalisations than would be expected if the sequential arrangement of mother and infant vocalisations were random – an alternating pattern in a sense different from non-simultaneity.

Bateson also found that onset-to-onset times of adjacent maternal vocalisations were longer than those when a maternal vocalisation followed an infant vocalisation or vice versa. This suggests that the mothers tended to wait for a reply from the baby before themselves vocalising again. In a similar vein, Schaffer et al. (1977) showed that mother–child speaker-switch pauses tended to be longer than child–mother ones. This was interpreted in terms of the bout structure of the vocal interaction, the child being more likely to initiate a new bout, after a lengthy pause, than the mother whose main role it seemed was to reply. (Sequences with such long pauses were probably not analysed by Bateson.) Thus it is clear that the mother and child do not play equal roles in vocal exchanges, yet what part of the conversation-like structure of these early interactions is contributed by the infant still remains to be discovered.

2.2 Interpersonal gaze

Most of the work on the dynamics of gaze in the mother–infant dyad is the product of Stern and his co-workers (Stern 1971, 1974b; Jaffe et al. 1973). In the study by Jaffe et al., sequence analysis showed that mother and infant appear to make statistically independent decisions on whether or not to gaze on the basis of the immediately preceding gaze state. Were their decisions not independent, it would imply that, in making his decision, one of the participants was taking into account the *anticipated* outcome of the other's decision process. Stern (1974b) showed that infants were more likely to start or continue looking at the mother if she was looking at her infant. As would be expected, the proportion of time occupied by mutual gaze generally exceeds the product of the proportions of time occupied by each individual's gaze (Stern unpublished); that is, there is more mutual gaze than would be expected from a random juxtaposition of the two individuals' gaze sequences, at least according to this simple model.

2.3 Deictic gaze

Deictic gaze refers to gaze directed not at the other member of the dyad but at some other object in the environment. Deictic gaze has the potential of directing the recipient's own attention to the same object, although there is no implication in the term that such an effect is necessarily intended. When both individuals look at the same thing at the same time they are in the state of co-orientation, which is analogous to mutual gaze in the interpersonal sphere.

Collis & Schaffer (1975) described and quantified observations demonstrating that during interaction mothers monitor their infants' gaze at objects and establish co-orientation, as easily replicated finding (Collis 1977b). No conclusions could be drawn from these studies about the cues that the mother was using to establish co-orientation, although it was clear that mothers were not always in a position to see the child's face and would have to rely on gross changes in the orientation of the head and/or body. In any case in these studies, as in the real world, the structure of the environment was such that infants were not equally likely to be looking at a large number of different points in any one general direction, making the mother's task very much easier.

On the other side of the coin there seem to be no observational data on mother—infant interaction showing that infants follow the direction of their mothers' visual regard. A number of experimental studies have, however, tackled the issue from the point of view of discovering when infants are *able* to do this. Scaife & Bruner (1975) presented evidence suggesting that, during the second half of the first year, infants would turn their heads in the same direction as an experimenter who, having established eye contact in an *en face* position, turned to look 90° to his left or right. These data are some-what difficult to interpret as there were no control trials which would allow an assessment of the likelihood that the infant would look in the same direction as the experimenter merely by chance (Collis 1977b) — a particularly important point when the criterion for a successful response was fairly lenient. However, Lempers (1976) reported that although only five out of twelve nine-month-olds responded correctly according to a strict criterion in a similar situ-ation, none looked in the *wrong* direction.

Lempers et al. (1977) found that about half of the one-and-a-half-year-olds did not succeed in a task where the experimenter's eyes, *but not the face*, were directed at the target toy. In this study the experi-menter's eyes were closed to conceal from the subject the actual movement of the eyes toward the target toy but, according to Lempers (1976), allowing the subject to see the movement of the experimenter's eyes made the task possible for one-year-olds even in the absence of facial orientation cues. Thus it is apparent that cues from head orientation, eye orientation and eye movement all have a role to play.

There is evidence that members of other species, particularly pri-mates, use information from other individuals to locate or identify objects in the environment (Menzel 1971; Menzel & Halperin 1975). Gaze direction appears to be one of the cues operating: according to Marler (1967) baboons follow the gaze of troop 'sentinels' to locate a potential source of danger and, in the realm of mother—infant inter-action, Harlow (1963) mentioned that young monkeys follow their mothers' visual regard to objects outside the cage. In view of the likely importance of this kind of mechanism it is strange that it has received so little attention compared with the massive amount of work done on interpersonal gaze (Argyle & Cook 1976).

In groups larger than a dyad, gaze may be interpersonal from one individual's perspective, and deictic from another's. Among primates,

displays are commonly accompanied by gaze that indicates which
individual out of several potential recipients is being addressed (S.A.
Altmann 1967). Similarly with *Homo sapiens* gaze accompanying
gestures or vocalisations gives onlookers an indication of whom the
signal is being directed toward or, especially with young children,
that it is other-directed than egocentric (Bates et al. 1975).

2.4 Gaze and gesture

In a detailed observational analysis of the use of the pointing gesture
in the mother—infant dyad, Murphy & Messer (1977) described how
the mother's own gaze was remarkably well synchronised with her
pointing. In most cases the onset of a point was accompanied, to an
accuracy of a fraction of a second, by the mother starting a look at
the target toy. In a remarkably consistent way, this was followed by
looking back at the baby, a tendency that peaked 1.1 seconds after
the start of the point. This was, presumably, to monitor the baby's
response to the gesture. When fourteen-month-old infants pointed
toward objects they too looked at the target toy but in only five out
of seventy-five instances was there a look at mother.

Turning from intrapersonal to interpersonal integration, it was
found that in addition to infants' looking where their mothers pointed,
mothers sometimes pointed where their infants were already looking!
Without the benefit of stop-frame viewing and repeated play-back of
a video recording, this effect could easily have been missed, the events
probably being recorded as 'infant follows mother's point'. In investigating the infants' visual responses to their mothers' gestures, Murphy
& Messer compared the likelihood that, immediately after the onset
of the point, the infant would look at the target toy with the likelihood of the infant's looking at that toy on the basis of the distribution
of his looks among the various toys throughout the observation session.
In this way it was possible to take account of the possibility that an
infant might appear to follow a point whereas, in fact, his look at the
toy coincided with a point by chance. The results showed that some
spatial arrangements of toy, infant and pointing limb could be coped
with easier than others. Points *across* the baby's face could be followed
by fourteen-month-olds but not by nine-month-olds whereas points
away from the baby's face were followed equally well by both age
groups. Other workers have approached infants' abilities to follow
points from an interest in their cognitive capacities (Lempers et al.
1977; Lempers 1976). Lempers' (1976) results confirm that the nine-

month-old's capacity to follow a point depends on distances and
spatial arrangements.

2.5 Gaze and vocalising

A number of studies have examined the integration of gaze and vocalising. Schaffer et al. (1977) showed that two-year-olds tended to
initiate looks at their mothers while they themselves were vocalising.
In mothers too, looking at the infant tends to co-occur with vocalising (Stern unpublished). Although the one-year-olds in the Schaffer
et al. study did not tend to look at their mothers while vocalising,
giving the impression that their vocalisations were not other-directed,
neither did they tend to look while the mother was vocalising. In contrast, Stern, with his three- and four-month-olds, found that infant
gazing-at-mother was likely to co-occur with maternal vocalisations.
Apparently the infant's gaze was more likely to be initiated and maintained when the mother was herself vocalising and/or gazing back.
Moreover the influence was reciprocal; a mother was more likely to
initiate and maintain vocalising when the infant was looking at her.

Going beyond simple on—off patterns of vocalising, there is also
some information available on fine temporal relationships between
gaze and the *content* of maternal speech to infants. Collis (1977b)
demonstrated that mothers tended to name toys that both their
infants and they themselves were looking at. In accordance with this,
a mother's own looks at the toys were more likely to be accompanied
by her naming a toy if, by looking, she had followed the infant's line
of regard. In other words, naming toys was associated with visual co-
orientation between mother and baby — just the kind of pattern to
be expected from Bruner's exposition (1975a) of the use of joint
reference in establishing the topic in a 'proto-conversation'. Other
kinds of maternal utterance, for instance questions about the toys,
were as likely to result from mothers' own initiative as from the
infants'.

It is of considerable interest to extend this kind of analysis of
maternal speech to contexts other than gaze. Murphy & Messer (1977)
showed how the types of utterance that mothers use in conjunction
with pointing differed from the overall distribution of utterance types
in their observation sessions. In addition, Messer (forthcoming) has
examined how the content of maternal speech is integrated with the
temporal structure of play with toys by mother—infant pairs. Similarly, Howe (1975) showed that the semantic content of maternal

utterances to young children depended on the proximity of the object being referred to.

These admittedly few data on the relationship between the content of maternal speech and other activities being pursued by the dyad offer considerable promise of a major advance over traditional treatments of maternal speech data in terms of rather global indices of verbal style. It is, after all, widely believed that context is of great importance in helping the child to understand speech. Hence, it is clearly desirable that the relationship of speech to micro-context be measured directly.

2.6 Kinesics and posture

Even those body movements that are less well defined than orthodox gestures may be presumed to play a role in infant—adult interaction. Perhaps the most well-known work here is the extension, into infancy, of studies on the synchronisation of speech and body movements in adults. Using sound-film micro-analysis Condon & Sander (1974a) provided evidence of *interactive synchrony* between adult speech and the fine structure of motility in neonates. Other work in this area includes that of Stern et al. (1977) who examined the hierarchical organisation of the kinesic behaviour of adults playing with three- and four-month-old infants.

The movement patterns described by Stern et al. appear to be mostly 'playful' and for the entertainment of the two participants in the interaction. We must not forget, however, that many aspects of bodily movement with more 'sensible' functions are also important in the ongoing interaction: consider, for instance, Birdwhistell's analysis (1970) of the highly task-directed body movements of a mother in a nappy-changing episode. I have recently been following up an impression that in certain situations much of a mother's body movement when interacting with her baby can be understood in highly functional terms as postural adjustment to permit a reasonably good view of the infant's face.

That mothers are extremely watchful of infants is attested by the very reliable finding that mothers watch infants more than infants watch mothers (e.g. Schaffer et al. 1977; Stern 1974b). Moreover, studies of visual co-orientation and the synchronisation of maternal speech with infant's gaze (Collis 1977b) show that mothers do indeed use the information that they gain from so carefully watching their babies. Particularly in conditions of close proximity it is the face, as the most expressive region of the body, that is monitored most closely. When the couple are positioned opposite each other facial monitoring is simple, particularly as mothers neither require nor demand continual full frontal *en face* position with their infants. Even so, as Stern (1971) has described, patterns of body movement involving infants and mothers turning toward and away from one another are subtle and fascinating, with mothers apparently adapting to the likely response of the infant to their attempts to establish *en face* position. Consider, though, the older infant seated on his mother's lap. In this and many other settings mother and baby are both facing in the same general direction rather than toward one another. To get even a side view of the baby's face the mother has to lean round to one side of the baby and, should the infant turn away from her perhaps in response to some object of interest, she will only be able to see the back of his head unless she shifts her body so that she can lean round the other side of the infant (fig. 2).

In order to check the reliability and generality of this kind of phenomenon I have analysed a number of 5-minute video recordings, made for a different purpose, of infants seated on their mothers' laps at a table on which there was a set of coloured, plastic, nesting cubes. The mothers were recruited from a list of names supplied by Glasgow Child Welfare Clinics with predominantly upper-working to middle class catchment areas. They were told that we were interested in examining how infants played with the toys with mother.

Data were extracted from the video recordings by stages. The basic method was to view the video recording being replayed at normal speed while operating pushbuttons controlling equipment programmed to register the desired variables. Two observers were used throughout, each recording different parameters on any one run through the recording. They then exchanged roles for a second run so that there were, for each subject pair and from each stage of the analysis, data obtained by two observer assignments from which to calculate reliability estimates in terms of product moment correlations.

The first stage of the analysis was devoted to recording the cumulative durations of head positions of mothers and infants and the durations of these positions in combination. The infants' head positions were facing left (IL) or facing right (IR). (Throughout, left (L) and right (R) refer to the observers' point of view.) Care was taken to concentrate on the position of the child's head relative to rotation about the vertical axis irrespective of gaze direction; the relative visi-

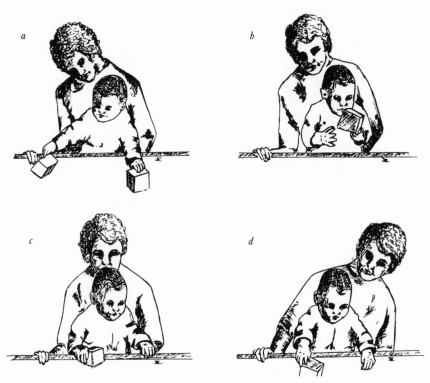

Fig. 2 A mother changes her posture to match the facial orientation of her eleven-month-old infant: drawings from video frames 1 second part. (*a*) Infant facing left, mother's head on left of infant's head, mother viewing infant's face in profile. (*b*) Infant turns to face right, the back of his head is toward mother. (*c*) and (*d*) Mother shifts her position to right of infant and once more has a profile view of the infant's face.

bility of the two ears was a most useful cue in this respect. The head positions of the mother were recorded as either to the left (ML) or to the right (MR) of the baby's head, irrespective of her facial orientation or gaze direction. Mothers spent rather little time in the intermediate 'middle' position whereas the infants faced 'midline', that is, not discernibly left or right, a little more.

The 'expected' amounts of time spent by a mother on the same side of her infant as he was facing were calculated as follows: *expected IL and ML = IL × ML / T: expected IR and MR = IR × MR / T*, when *T* is the total duration of the session. As table 1 shows, observed durations exceed those expected in every one of ten pairs of a mother with her eleven-month-old infant (six males, four females). An eleventh

Table 1 Cumulative durations in seconds of positions of mother and infant, singly and in combination (means of two observer assignments)

Subject pair	ML	MR	IL	IR	ML and IL		MR and IR	
					expected	observed	expected	observed
i	50.9	244.3	86.4	153.0	14.7	38.8	124.6	151.6
ii	129.7	145.4	92.0	134.1	39.8	64.9	65.0	97.7
iii	92.7	182.5	107.2	115.8	33.1	57.9	70.4	103.9
iv	16.2	260.1	112.8	127.5	6.1	16.1	110.5	130.7
v	10.3	280.9	120.2	114.4	4.1	10.6	107.1	119.3
vi	64.4	237.9	122.3	80.0	26.2	30.8	63.4	73.8
vii	104.2	175.5	82.7	157.3	28.7	54.3	92.0	128.7
viii	66.0	199.9	190.4	41.2	41.9	58.9	27.4	30.9
ix	214.5	44.7	110.1	71.2	78.7	92.8	10.6	25.2
x	19.0	271.6	190.8	48.4	12.1	17.0	43.8	47.9
reliability	0.991	0.968	0.944	0.961	—	0.952	—	0.977

pair was also examined but the mother remained always on one side of the infant, making this analysis pointless — more on this below.

Though informative, these calculations of expected durations are crude and give no indication of which partner brings about the apparent effect. Hence, on a second run through the recordings, the equipment was programmed to answer the question: when a mother shifts her position (the moment of onset of ML or MR) where is her infant facing, and when the infant shifts where is the mother positioned? If a mother shifted to her least preferred side (LPS) irrespective of the child's facial orientation, we would expect minimal difference between the proportion of those shifts which occurred while the infant was facing the mother's LPS and the proportion of the total session that the infant was so orientated. In fact, in every subject pair the former proportion exceeded the latter (see table 2), indicating that each mother's shifts to her LPS tended to coincide with the infant's already facing that side, just as would be expected if she were shifting in order to view the infant's face. Table 2 also shows a similar analysis of the mother's position when each infant turned to his LPS. There was clearly no tendency for the infants to turn across midline to the side where their mothers were.

The obvious next question was whether older children would turn toward the side where mother was, perhaps to look at mother more often. With this in mind, we examined recordings of thirteen children aged twenty-four months (seven males and six females) with their mothers. We counted the number of times each pair established an *en face* position with mother and child directly facing one another as if to establish mutual gaze but not necessarily immediately preceded by a change in the infant's orientation from IR to IL or vice versa. There were slightly more instances of *en face* in the older group (mean 3.6, range 0–8) than in the younger group (mean 1.5, range 0–5) although this was not statistically significant. Low frequencies of *en face* are to be expected in an object-centred setting.

However, when the type of analysis shown in tables 1 and 2 was attempted with the older group, we found, much to our surprise, that there was little point in proceeding as nine of the thirteen mothers never shifted from one side to the other, a markedly different proportion from the one out of eleven mothers of younger infants ($p < 0.005$, Fisher test). Inspection of the video recordings suggested that this difference was correlated with the mothers of two-year-olds paying less attention to the childrens' faces and more to their hands and what they were playing with. When we measured the cumulative

Table 2 *Mothers' shifts relative to infants' position and infants' shifts relative to mothers' position*

Subject pair	Mother's shifts to her least preferred side (MLPS)[a]			Infant's shifts to his least preferred side (ILPS)[b]		
	No.	% when infant facing MLPS	% time infant facing MLPS[c]	No.	% when mother on ILPS	% time mother on ILPS[d]
i	3	100	36	16	19	17
ii	10	80	41	24	46	47
iii	6	100	48	14	43	34
iv	5	100	47	23	0	6
v	2	100	51	19	100	96
vi	2	100	60	18	78	79
vii	6	66	34	15	53	37
viii	10	100	82	17	76	75
ix	6	83	39	19	16	17
x	4	100	80	12	92	93

a Omits shifts occurring while infant facing 'midline'.
b Omits time while infant facing 'midline'.
c Omits shifts while mother in 'middle' position.
d Omits time while mother in 'middle' position.

durations of the mothers' visual regard of the children's hands (a few
of the video recordings did not permit this) the following results were
obtained (reliability = 0.98):

	11-month group	24-month group
n	10	8
mean duration (secs)	206	267

The difference between the two groups was in the expected direction
and statistically significant ($p<0.001$, Mann—Whitney), and it seems
likely that the replacement of face regard with hand regard contributed to the decline in the mothers' readiness to adjust their bodily
position. Other factors are probably operating too. An obvious candi-
date is the growing importance of vocal communication which, in this
type of situation, may lessen the need for facial—visual signalling.

3 Discussion

In surveying the known patterns of interpersonal integration we should
have been able to focus on many other aspects of behaviour in the
mother—infant dyad. Two glaring omissions are facial expression and
interpersonal proximity. Despite a fair amount of descriptive material
on static facial expressions (e.g. Blurton Jones 1971), next to nothing
is known of its dynamics in interaction, possibly because expressions
become rather intangible when subjected to micro-analysis. This is not
the case for proximity. Although we know that various environmental
features affect the young child's proximity to his mother (Rheingold
& Eckerman 1970), we know little of the factors associated with the
ebb and flow of proximity in a stable environment (Anderson 1972a, b).

It is clearly desirable that an attempt should be made to relate the
diverse patterns of interpersonal integration in a broader conceptual
scheme that transcends the variety of activities and sensory modalities
employed. One possibility is to focus on aspects of interactions that
characterise mother—infant relations. Stern has pointed to the exaggerated nature and slow tempo of adult activities directed toward
infants (1974b) and to their repetitive nature (Stern et al. 1977).
Similarly, adults' speech to young children is simplified in various
ways (reviews: Landes 1975; Vorster 1975), as may be the relationship between verbal and non-verbal channels (Collis 1977b). Whereas
these principles focus on the behaviour of one individual in the dyad,

Fogel (1977) has highlighted a *timing* relationship that characterises many mother—infant interactions. Infants' activities tend to occur with rather short phase lengths and hence are often *framed* by the relatively steady behavioural state of the mother. Thus, when an infant breaks mutual gaze by looking away from his mother it is highly likely that, when he looks back at her, she will still be looking at him. Similarly, when an infant temporarily departs from the mother, the chances are that when he returns she will still be in much the same position.

There are also a number of ways in which different kinds of mother—infant interaction can be characterised. Focussing on behavioural content, we might ask whether mother and infant are performing the same actions (*reciprocating*) or activities that *complement* one another (Hinde 1976). There is an analogous question to be asked about timing: do mother and infant act at the same time (co-action, simultaneity) or exhibit turn-taking (alternation)? We have already referred to this distinction with reference to vocal behaviour but it has been suggested that the basic concept can be extended to other modalities. Stern et al. (1975) argue that vocal co-action is analogous to simultaneity in other channels. Similarly, Schaffer et al. (1977) and Kaye (1977) suggest that turn-taking is not confined to vocal exchanges but that it also characterises patterns of integration at other levels of analysis and in other modalities. Having found various patterns that involve individual A's being relatively inactive while individual B takes the more active role in the interaction, with a subsequent and repeated exchange of roles, we have to examine the nature of the similarities between the various patterns. Is there anything beyond analogy? The chances are that there could never be an answer to such a general question and that answers to more specific questions on this theme are unlikely to converge in a simple manner. Nonetheless, there is little doubt that the specific sets of data so generated will provide valuable insights into the structure of mother—infant interaction: such is the role of broad principles of synthesis.

Doubtless, our present understanding of social interaction in infancy is primitive, but progress can be made only on a firm descriptive foundation precise enough to be communicated, verified and examined for its implications. The endeavour is important, not merely in view of what babies will become but for our understanding of babyhood in its own right.

Note

1. I am grateful to Charles Crook, Christine Howe, David Messer, Cathy Murphy and Rudolph Schaffer for discussions around the theme of this chapter, to David Messer for allowing me access to his video recordings, to Margaret Hunter for aid with data analysis and to Dawn Collis for fig. 2. The work was supported by a (UK) Social Science Research Council grant to H.R. Schaffer.

6

Neonatal entrainment and enculturation[1]

WILLIAM S. CONDON
Boston University School of Medicine

I did not start out with an intention to study infant behavior. Back
in the early 1960s when I first began to study human communication
using sound films, little was known about the nature of speaker or
listener behavior at the micro (frame-by-frame) level. No one had
systematically examined the organization of behavior that minutely.
This required the development of a new way of conceptualizing the
organization of the 'units' and the levels of organization of behavior.
My major area of study thus became the micro-organization of individual and interactional behavior. This led to the view of human behavior and interaction which will be presented below. The emphasis here
will be on how this might contribute to an understanding of the
enculturation of infants.

In time I discovered that one of the very basic characteristics of
normal individual and interactional behavior was temporal synchrony.
Such integration (or organization) is manifested in the synchronized
timing or changing together of the aspects of behavior with each
other, including both speech and body motion. The most startling
discovery was that this synchronization is not limited to individual
behavior but also occurs between people when they interact, including infants. Listeners move in precise synchrony with the articulatory
pattern of a speaker's speech. It is like a remarkable sort of dance. I
became interested in how early in life this phenomenon I had discovered was established. Speech is not present at birth but body movement is.

In order to present my recent work on both normal and dysfunctional infants and children, I must first give some account of my
earlier work with adults. This will be reviewed in sections 1.1 and 1.2.
Section 1.3 will discuss infant synchronization. In section 2 I will discuss the extension of these methods and concepts to the study of
infants and older children with certain forms of dysfunction.

131

1 Previous micro-analytic studies

My many years of intensive micro-analysis of sound films led to the emergence of several basic hypotheses about human behavior and communication at the micro level. The perspective used was similar to that of the ethologist. Sound films of natural human interaction were viewed over and over, frame by frame, until forms of order began to be seen. I began by analyzing behavior at a relatively macro level, examining the relation of gestures to words and word sequences of natural speech. There were always movements detectable at finer levels which remained unaccounted for. In essence, a whole domain of body motion had never really been carefully examined. Therefore, I analyzed movement at the frame-by-frame level, using 24, 48 and 96 frame per second (fps) sound film. I spent several years in the systematic study of body motion and speech at this level, carefully seeking to determine the nature of the units. Out of this a new concept of the nature of behavior emerged.

1.1 Self-synchrony

When a speaker is conversing several body parts are often moving *at the same time*. This occurs while the speaker articulates the syllables, words and phrases of his utterance. He may use both hands to emphasize his statement or he may reach for an object. This prompts many questions. What is the relationship at this level between the parts of the body as they move together? If the eyes, fingers, legs and arms are all moving, what is the relationship of change between them? And further, how are the relationships between these different moving body parts related to features of the speech which the speaker may be uttering at the same time? When several body parts are moving at the same time, which one of them can be said to deserve unit status in preference to the others? Frame-by-frame analysis led to the observation of 'forms-of-order' in the way these simultaneously moving body parts of the speaker change in relation to each other *and* to his speech.

Fig. 1 is based on a sound film of two men who are seated and talking. They have known each other for several years. They were told that the film (taken at 48 fps) was being made to study human communication. The speaker is saying, 'I was gonna ask you, why do you . . . um . . . have difficulty keeping your late appointments?' The word 'keeping' /kkkiiipppiiŋŋ/ and the co-occurring body motion

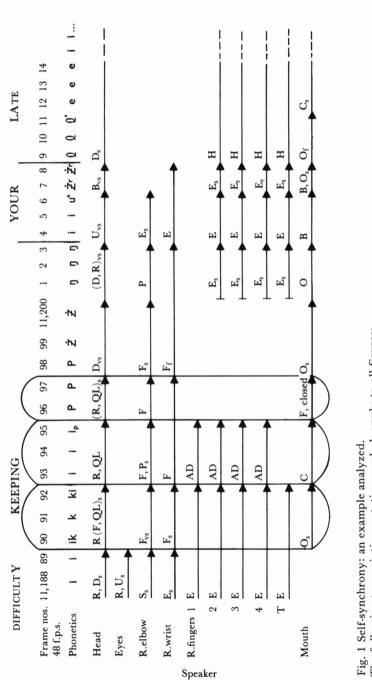

Fig. 1 Self-synchrony: an example analyzed.
The following transcription notation symbols apply to all figures:

AB = abduct   E = extend   O = open   RI = rotate in
AD = adduct   F = flex   P = pronate   RO = rotate out
B = back   H = hold or non-movement   Q = incline   S = supinate
C = close (mouth)L = left   R = right   U = up
D = down

illustrate the characteristic self-synchrony that has been observed in *normal* speaker behavior. Each frame of the film has been numbered for identification. The flow notation which describes this sequence uses horizontal lines for frames during which movement in a given direction is sustained and arrow points at the frame in which movement terminates or changes direction. The vowel sound /iii/ lasting three frames (93, 94, 95) or $\frac{1}{16}$ of a second will be used to illustrate the precision of self-synchrony. During the emission of /iii/ the speaker's head moves right and inclines left (R, QL), while the right elbow flexes and pronates slightly (F, Ps), the right wrist flexes (F), the fingers of the right hand adduct (AD) and the mouth closes (C). All of these movements sustain a relationship together across the three frames of /iii/ forming a 'movement bundle' which has a form of unity that contrasts with similar movement bundles across /kkk/ and /pp/. The fingers, for example, which had been extending, adduct together precisely during the emission of /iii/ and cease movement exactly as this segment ends. The body parts are often moving in different directions and with different velocities but they maintain a relationship with one another, creating these movement bundles which constitute a unitary form which may be considered a unit of behavior. A unit is not defined by its content but by its order. This involves a new usage of the term 'unit'.

This order appears to be an organized process emanating from the central nervous system. The adduction of the fingers, for example, does not cause the head to turn right simultaneously. The synchronization of these movements with one another and with speech must be orchestrated in the central nervous system. Schmitt et al. (1976) in their paper on the revolution in neurological conceptualization suggest that the electrotonic coupling between neurons may provide a basis for the synchronized firing of cell assemblies. Higher order neurological operations may be a manifestation of the integration of such synchronized assemblies functioning as sub-systems in relation to one another and to simultaneously larger assemblies. Such an organization model was forced on me by the nature of the structure that behavior presented when examined naturalistically. I am trying to state this in a way which avoids a discrete or part—whole view of behavior.

The principle of 'relational sustaining' as illustrated in fig. 1 is characteristic of both individual and interactional behavior. It appears to be a feature of the basic structural logic of the organized processing of nervous systems in general, at least at the mammalian level. The flow of behavior of a lioness chasing prey illustrates this principle. How and where one body part is moving at a given moment and where it will be moments later is not separate from where the other body parts are and where they will be moments later. Yet this can all change and be redirected in a split second as the lioness swerves suddenly in pursuit of her prey.

Behavior is also integrated hierarchically in that *while* lower order organizations are sustaining their relationships there are concomitant temporally longer sustainings which continue to maintain an ordered relationship with the temporally shorter sustained ones. Thus behavior is both sequentially and hierarchically continuous at the same time. It is all organized together and each aspect is discriminated as a pattern of relationship in contrast to the rest. No one of these forms or patterns has a privileged position or exists in isolation. A form is described to be what it is by the order it manifests in contrast with the other simultaneously ongoing forms of which it is an aspect. The other patterns provide a contrastive backdrop. The concept of discrete units interferes with finding out how behavior flows. This description of forms of behavior as relationships of patterns of change in relation to one another is derived through a process of intensive re-viewing of sound film. In the course of this the patterns emerge and are recognized.

To return to the analysis of the behavior related to the word 'keeping', fig. 1 also illustrates the rhythmic, *hierarchic integration* of this relation of patterns of change of body motion with those of speech. There are five short sub-forms of body motion which co-occur with five short articulatory features. These are /kkk/, /iii/, /pp/, /p̊ɨɨ/ and /ŋŋŋ/. Higher order body motion forms also occur is omorphically with the syllabic aspects /kkkiiipp/ and /p̊ɨɨŋŋŋ/; there is an incline left (QL) of the head accompanying /kkkiiipp/; and a downward movement of the head (D) plus rapid wrist flexion (Ff) accompanying /p̊ɨɨŋŋŋ/. The word as a whole is also precisely accompanied by flexion of the right wrist. That wrist had been extending but flexes exactly at the onset of 'keeping' and continues flexing until the end of the word, when it again extends. Behavior is thus integrated during its immediate occurrence and also hierarchically as it emerges across longer spans of time. These integrated levels of organization are 'hidden' in the behavior. A spoken sentence has both discrete and continuous features simultaneously, and without contradiction. This was clearly the case with respect to the speaker's body motion and speech described in fig. 1, suggesting that the neurological processes mediating that behavior were similarly organized. This would imply that the speech was also emerging in terms of that same neurological organization. Words (which appear discrete) are unified in the continuity of the sentence by the hierarchically integrated nature of neurological processing. The discrete and continuous are equally essential for meaningful discourse. My view is that the hierarchic syntactic unity of language is also a function of the hierarchic unity of the neurological process. This unity has been shown to break down in pathology with concomitant loss of language skill and intelligibility.

Since this organization is apparently a universal process in adult speaker behavior the question arises as to how it is expressed in infancy. The infant does not seem to exhibit a rhythm hierarchy in the longer adult form, i.e. covering phone, syllable, phrase and sentence as illustrated in fig. 1. In the course of enculturation individual behavior is molded through interactional participation toward forms characteristic of the particular culture, including language. During the process of growing up and learning to speak infant behavior changes from a relatively simple organization to the longer, rhythmic, hierarchic adult form illustrated in fig. 1. The process described in the following section appears to account for this. It has been found that before speech the infant's body motion reflects certain aspects of the speech around him. Such movement synchronization appears to be a process well suited to facilitate enculturation, particularly language acquisition.

1.2 Interactional synchrony (responsive entrainment)

Intensive frame-by-frame micro-analysis of the *listener's* behavior led to the unexpected observation that a listener moves synchronously with the phones, syllables or words of the speaker's speech (Condon 1963, 1964). Since listener behavior had never been intensively analyzed at this micro level either, this phenomenon had remained unknown. I called this phenomenon 'interactional synchrony'. When I first presented this concept in 1963 it was not readily accepted, but it is now acknowledged, particularly among those who analyze sound films of behavior. Interactional synchrony refers to the phenomenon as it can be observed in human interaction. The term 'responsive entrainment' refers to inferred processes inside the individual which bring about such synchronization. The listener was found to move in organizations of change which parallel the articulatory patterning and intensity of the speaker's speech. A listener moves in synchrony with the speaker's speech almost as well as the speaker himself does. There is physical continuity in the flow of sound between interactants as the sound waves perturb the air between them. Assemblies of cells in the listener's auditory system reflect and carry on the physical structure of the sound which is being received. Within a latency of 50 milliseconds or less the organization of change of the body motion of a listener holistically reflects the organizations of change in the structure of the speech he is listening to.

Fig. 2 illustrates the precision which is characteristic of interactional synchrony. The word 'pressure' from another film of adult interaction exhibits a contrasting sequence of voiced and unvoiced segments. An oscilloscopic display of the speech is presented to illustrate how the sound pattern can be displayed visually. The voiced /ʌ/ sound terminating 'the' (just preceding but not shown in fig. 2) is followed by /p/ which is unvoiced and lasts two frames ($\frac{2}{24}$ of a second). This is then followed by voiced /re/ also lasting two frames which is then followed by the unvoiced /š/ lasting three frames. Finally, the voiced /r/ occurs,

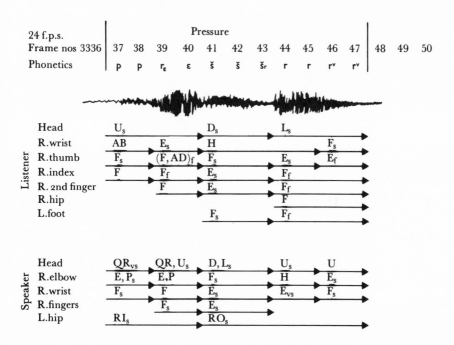

Fig. 2 Interactional synchrony: speaker phonetics, listener and speaker movement.

lasting four frames. The total word lasts eleven frames or just slightly under half a second. The body motion of the listener exhibits organized movement bundles which parallel or entrain with the lengths of the units of the speaker's speech. This is seen particularly well in the listener's movement bundle that co-occurs with /ššš/ in 'pressure'. Fingers 1 and 2 of the right hand had been flexing. They change direction and extend slightly across the three-frame duration of /ššš/ and then flex again at the end of this segment.[2]

A relatively continuous yet constantly varying stream of speech is simultaneously, continuously and organizationally tracked as expressed in the varying body motion configurations of a listener. The example in fig. 2 shows how the organization-of-change of the body motion of the listener changes in a parallel tracking fashion with the forms of change of the word 'pressure'. The precision and speed with which the listener's body moves in synchronized organization with the speaker's speech led to the postulation of a primary, short-latency entrainment phase in the human responding process (Condon 1977). This appears to be an organized process like self-synchrony. The synchronization of the listener's movements in relation to each other in patterns that are isomorphic with the incoming pattern of the speaker's speech are probably centrally orchestrated in the listener as well. If a person can be seen to be moving while he is listening, his body motion organization is found to be entrained with the sound patterns of the speech of the person he is listening to. It may be essential, in order for speech and sound reception to take place, that the listener entrain with the structure of incoming signals through organized, neurological tracking processes.

The infant, even though moving in synchrony with the flow of speech, must eventually become aware of the discrete features within that flow. The postulated primary entrainment phase may also therefore simultaneously involve an incipient discrimination process. Since the listener is reflecting the structure of the incoming sound, his brain must also be tracking its structure. Since such incoming structures contain the linguistic *segmental units*, tracking provides a basis for discriminating them. The speaker provides the listener with the speech elements already organized into larger integrated forms. The listener does not have to assemble them for himself. The listener processes speech across several levels simultaneously. Thus it is possible for the listener to process incoming speech at both discrete and continuous levels simultaneously without contradiction. These processes may be as much outside of awareness as digestion.

The hypotheses of self and interactional entrainment have been examined by other investigators using similar techniques and they have corroborated my observations (Kendon 1972; Mair personal communication; Hall 1976). Mair used a Laryngograph and also studied the changes of body motion of the interactants. He reports, 'Gross interactional synchrony is evident as well as self-synchrony'. Linguists have also had to deal with the problem of the very great speed with which speech is processed by the normal listener. An entrainment model similar to mine has been proposed by Martin (1972): 'It is on this basis that one might say not that the listener "follows" the speaker but rather that the listener, given initial cues, actively enters into the speaker's tempo.' Later on in the same article he says, 'Further research may determine the extent to which efficient perceptual processing involves actively locking into the temporal flow of the speech signal.'

1.3 Infant entrainment

Since I had already observed this responsive entrainment in a three-month-old infant I wished to find out how early in human life it might begin. To most people an infant looks quite unco-ordinated in his movements. That is only a superficial appearance. Micro-analysis indicates that a newborn infant is quite well co-ordinated and self-synchronous although he does not exhibit the stylized movements of adults. Sixteen one- to four-day-old awake, normal neonates were filmed in their cribs while being addressed by male and female adults. In one instance a Thai nurse used her native language. To rule out visual synchronization each infant was also presented with audio-taped adult speech in his own language and Chinese (language tapes). All of the infants exhibited marked entrainment with both tape recorded and live human voices (Condon & Sander 1974a, b). This has subsequently been observed as early as 20 minutes after birth. It is likely that it exists in utero but this has not yet been investigated.

A very young infant entrains with the structure of adult speech almost as well as an adult listener. The organization of the infant's body motion is sustained in parallel with the duration of a speech sound and changes to a new organization when that sound changes. This is particularly marked where silence follows vocalization, which gives a clear sound change point. The infant moves very rapidly at this point as if released from a guiding force. When a film is played in reverse the ends of sounds then appear as onsets. Of course the infant's movements are reversed also so that any movement changes which occurred at the ends of sounds in real life (or when the film was played forward) now appear as movements occurring at an onset of sound. The infant, as predicted, then moves in precise synchrony with these sound change points. This demonstrates the reality of entrainment since it is precisely predictable from either direction. The neonate's precise sustaining of movement in relation to speech sounds strongly suggests that this postulated entrainment phase is also simultaneously a discrimination process.

Fig. 3 illustrates neonatal entrainment with live adult speech. The adult says 'Come over and see who's over here' to the infant. All of the infants exhibited similarly precise entrainment.

The short-latency entrainment phase (synchronization) could be considered pre-cognitive evidence of response. Such an entrainment/ discrimination phase potentially fulfills many of the properties postulated by Stevens & House (1972) as part of a model of auditory perception and articulation. They suggest that all signals may undergo transformations in the peripheral auditory structures. Such processing may provide information concerning the signal which is relevant to the discrimination of linguistic categories. They also feel that there are close ties between the processes of speech production and speech perception and that there may be components or operations that are common to both processes. The hypotheses of speaker self-synchrony and of listener entrainment would support such a conception since both involve a unity of speech and body motion. Behavioral timing and the self-synchrony of the speaker's behavior may be related to hearing his own voice. Frame-by-frame analysis of sound films of subjects under delayed auditory feedback indicates that a speaker is thrown out of phase by delay in the feedback of his own voice.

What the child hears, what he is turn says and how he hears what he says provides a means for comparing his intent with his product. This would include the minimal units as well as the longer pitch/stress rhythm forms. Stevens & House suspect that the relation between the articulatory and auditory processes is established early. The view presented here is that the linkage between articulation and audition has a neurological basis related to a postulated entrainment/discrimination phase which appears to be present at birth.

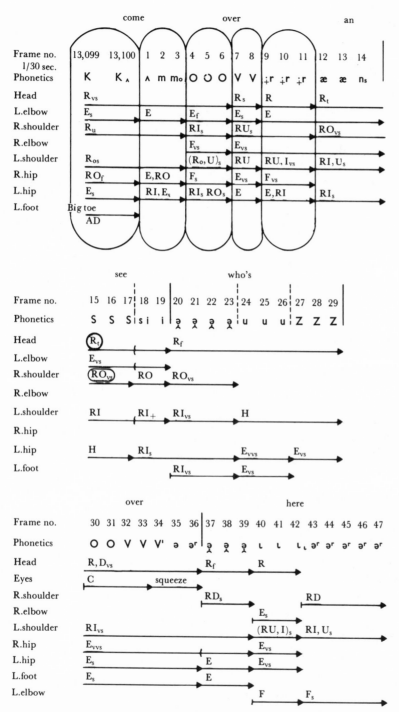

Fig. 3 Neonatal entrainment to adult speech: infant movement and adult phonetics.

2 Multiple entrainment to sound

The frame-by-frame, micro-analytic approach described above was utilized in the study of sound films of children with learning difficulties. This led to the observation that after sound stimuli their body motion was disturbed in a way not found in normal children. Specifically, they appear to entrain repeatedly to the same sound. This is what I call multiple entrainment. In contrast, normal children entrain only once. The dysfunctional children seem plagued and at times overwhelmed by 'reverberations' which may last as long as a full second. Multiple entrainment has been observed in the following diagnostic categories: autism, mental retardation, aphasia, cerebral palsy, hyperactivity and reading disability (dyslexia). An example from the behavior of an autistic-like child following sound stimulation illustrates the phenomenon. On film a four-year-old girl is playing with blocks at a table with her mother. She sits back in her chair, remaining relatively still. Her mother drops a block on the table, making a loud sound. Although the child responds only minimally to this sound at the time, at approximately 1 second (precisely 23 frames) after the sound has occurred she jerks her head sharply as if slapped. No other sounds or events occurred which might account for this sudden strange movement. It is certainly conceivable that she just happened to move at this time. But I found such movements precisely 23 frames after most sounds in the film. A movement was judged to be occurring at a particular frame if an organized movement boundary occurred there. I could count out to the 23rd frame after the onset point of almost any sound and find that the child jerked or moved at precisely that frame. In other words, the child seemed to be moving synchronously with these sounds just like the normal listener except that the movement was far too late and intense. This child also exhibited several additional delayed entrainments following sounds, hence the hypothesis of *multiple* entrainment. I found that later body motion of all these children follows a movement pattern that is timed precisely and in parallel with the pattern of earlier, actual sound, but delayed by constant time intervals. The body appears to move synchronously with the sound, but as if it were occurring later when there is actually silence.

Very convincing audio-visual demonstration of multiple entrainment is obtained by printing a film with the sound delayed by the number of frames found between sound and body movement. In the present case it was 23 frames. When this altered film was viewed the child was seen to move in precise synchrony with the sound and no longer appeared bizarre. It is not possible from the present evidence to assert that these children are actually hearing sound several times. All that can be said is that they move as if this were happening. Much of the bizarre movement behavior of these children could be accounted for by the hypothesis of multiple entrainment. Recent thinking favors the view that childhood autism is basically a perceptual and comprehension defect, primarily related to abnormal processing in the auditory modality (Rimland 1964; Rutter 1968; Simon 1975). These findings could provide an explanation.

Thus two interrelated hypotheses dealing with sound processing are involved in this aspect of my research. The first and most general hypothesis is that there is a post sound-stimulus perturbation in the body motion of dysfunctional children in contrast to normal children. This appears in the form of slightly delayed, startle-like movements or jerks in the body following environmental sounds. A second and more specific hypothesis is that this pathological perturbation takes the form of multiple response to each sound. In other words, these jerks (which may occur in any part of the body) occur at specific intervals following a sound and not just at random points. The results of the research strongly indicate that the body motion pattern following sounds in autistic-like children does indeed differ from that in normal children. It also supports the contention that there are peaks of body motion at various fixed intervals following a sound, indicating a multiple response. These findings will be described below.

2.1 Sound analysis

Sound and picture are recorded independently when a sound film is made. The sound is recorded continuously and in parallel with the discrete pictures. The sound can therefore occur at any point in relation to these pictures. It is important to be able to determine as precisely as possible where these sound events occur in relation to the pictures. This is obviously critical since the body motion changes of the subjects in relation to sounds constitutes the central focus of the research. We developed techniques for reliably determining the point of onset of a sound to $\frac{1}{4}$ of a frame accuracy. In order to determine the point at which a sound event occurs it must be correlated with a visual event, in this case the numbered frame. It is much easier to attain high reliability in analyzing sound than it is in analyzing body motion.

2.2 Body motion analysis

Obtaining high reliability in the micro-analysis of body motion has been the most difficult part of this research. The ease with which sound could be accurately segmented in contrast to the difficulty in micro-analyzing body motion suggests that sound changes may be more precisely detectable by humans than visual changes. This may, however, be only an artifact of the technique. An initial reliability study between two independent judges in segmenting body motion frame by frame resulted in agreement at the 91% level. Subsequent reliability studies between two judges were not clear cut: one was 76% and the other 94%. Since I was often working alone I also conducted a variety of self-blind reliability studies which were above the 90% level of agreement. Further studies will need to be conducted.

2.3 The research on autistic children

Children were sound-filmed at 30 fps through a small glass partition. They were accompanied by their parents and a researcher who presented tape-recorded sound stimuli. A synchronized frame counter in the camera field insured frame numbering of the film. This was essential to enable correlation of a sound onset point with a specific film frame which stored the body movement.

For analysis twenty separate sounds were selected for each subject and the response to each sound was analyzed for accompanying body motion at the point the sound onset actually occurred (called I or immediate sound) and for the next 10 frames or $\frac{1}{3}$ of a second following the point of onset of the sound. A response was considered to have occurred if a body motion boundary change point occurred at any of these frames. A body motion boundary change was defined as a detectable change of direction in a body part or parts, e.g. extension of the arm changing to flexion. There were usually several such changes at the same moment but even a single change was accepted as evidence. The concept of body motion bundles as organized forms of change at the micro level was described in detail in section 1.1. They are the natural units in terms of which behavior occurs and by which it must be described, at least at the micro level. This was illustrated by the motion analyzed in relation to the word 'pressure' in fig. 2. This is the special criterion of 'response' used in this research. It provides a basis for comparing normal and autistic-like behavior and opens up a way to study the universe of these children. There are multiple delayed responses in the behavior of the autistic-like children manifested by a large number of such change points occurring at later frames in relation to sounds. The timing of these change points is specific for each child. Normal children, in contrast, do not show later peaks.

For purposes of illustrating the research, let us assume that a tap sound occurred at frame $99\frac{1}{2}$. This would be the real sound. Any body motion change boundary that might be related to that sound could not be detected in frame 99 since the shutter is already closing by $99\frac{1}{2}$. A change in movement could only be detected in frame 100. The body motion would be analyzed carefully at frame 100 to see if a body motion boundary change point occurred there. For example, the right arm might be seen extending through frame 99 and then be seen beginning to flex at frame 100. This would then be entered as a body motion response at frame 100. The body motion would be analyzed for subsequent frames up to and including frame 110. Any body motion boundary change points that occurred at any of these later frames would be transcribed. For each child response to all twenty sounds was studied in this fashion for the 10 frames following I.

In terms of the basic hypotheses which are being examined, this frame-by-frame analysis of the body motion following sounds should show the following results.

(1) The graphs of the normal children should show the greatest number of responses at I or actual sound. This follows from the hypothesis of interactional entrainment.

(2) The graphs of the autistic-like children, conversely, should show body motion response patterns at multiple intervals following sounds which characteristically exceed those of their normal controls. This would indicate that a post sound-stimulus perturbation exists.

Six autistic-like and six normal children (matched for age and sex) were studied in the manner described above. The body motion responses of the normal children were greatest in relation to I sound. This is as predicted. The results showed marked additional post sound-stimulus body motion peaks in the autistic-like children and the absence of such peaks in the normal children. What is even more surprising is that most of the dysfunctional children have post sound-stimulus peaks which are higher than their peaks at I sound. Fig. 4 illustrates this using one matched pair (studied for 15 frames following

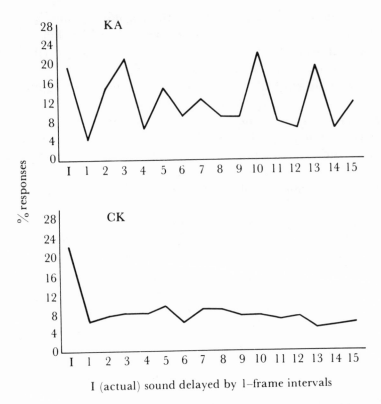

I (actual) sound delayed by 1–frame intervals

Fig. 4 The mean of the analyses of autistic-like child KA contrasted with the mean of the analyses of normal control CK.

I sound) as an example. It shows the heightened peak of body movement of the normal at I sound and the marked later peaks in the autistic-like, indicating perturbation.

2.4 Multiple entrainment to sound in infant behavior and other forms of dysfunction

Multiple entrainment was clearly demonstrated in an infant at two months of age. This infant had been anoxic for 7 minutes at birth and sustained brain damage in the right hemisphere. She was sound-filmed at two months and every month thereafter for thirty months. There was consistent marked response at a 14-frame delay. The analysis was conducted in the same fashion as those presented earlier.

Thus far, sixty-one cases of childhood dysfunction have been analyzed and all exhibited multiple response to sound. They all also

exhibited varying degrees of self-asychrony. Existence of the multiple entrainment phenomenon across a wide diagnostic spectrum
suggests a dysfunctional continuum from severe (autism) to mild
(reading disability). However, there is a marked difference in the
nature of the multiple entrainment between autism and reading disability. The autistic children seem much more controlled by the
sound and jerk much more intensely following sounds. My recent
observations indicate that the orienting response in the more severe
autistic children appears to be entrained or locked to sound stimuli.
These children display searching behavior, looking this way and that
several times in response to the same sound, and do not appear able
to inhibit this. This occurs constantly in response to almost all the
sounds around them. In this respect they are enslaved to sound
stimuli. They do not seem to be able really to focus on anything
because they focus on everything.

3 Summary

An attempt has been made in this chapter to present some of the
emerging information about the perceptual and responsive entrainment of human beings with the universe of which they are a part.
This linkage has been revealed by micro-analysis of naturalistic sound
films of human interaction. Listeners were discovered to move in
holistic, body-motion organizations of change tracking the ongoing
articulatory patterns of the speaker's speech within 50 milliseconds.
This suggests a very rapid process of entraining on the part of the
human organism. This may occur in relation to visual and possibly
tactile modalities as well. An infant as early as 20 minutes after birth
is capable of precise entrainment with the flow of human speech and
sound. Such interactional entrainment appears to play a wide role in
the human enculturation process. It is like a beautiful, rhythmic
dance. It is probable that at some level the mother is aware of this
responsive entrainment of her infant with herself. Synchronization
may facilitate establishing essential human relationships such as that
between mother and infant even while, or because of, being an aspect
of the perceptual and response processes of both.

The normal infant entrains with the speech sounds of the adults
around him, participating vitally in the language rhythms and shared
interactional experiences which this entails. His total being is in participation with the order surrounding him and this participation is

mediated by his normal brain which reflects and processes stimuli adequately. In the light of the potential importance of this infant— caretaker synchrony one can speculate about the possible effects of impairment in such synchronized entrainment. One such effect seems to be some degree of learning disability. As the previous research illustrates, a wide range of children with learning disabilities were discovered to have some degree of difficulty in moving synchronously with sound, including human speech. The greater this disturbance seemed to be, the greater the autistic-like isolation from people and the world also seemed to be.

Notes

1. W.S. Condon is partially supported by the Medical Foundation (through the Dr Charles H. Weed Memorial Award) which is the Research and Community Health Agency of United Way of Massachusetts Bay.
2. For greater accuracy in segmenting speech a sound film was made of an oscilloscopic display of this speech with the sound of the speech being simultaneously re-recorded onto the sound track of the new film being made. Speech was then easily segmentable down to the level of $\frac{1}{60}$ of a second. Because of the nature of recording, sound can be segmented much more precisely than body motion. At this laboratory we have developed techniques to analyze sound with high reliability down to $\frac{1}{4}$ frame using 30 fps film.

7

Blind infants and their mothers: an examination of the sign system[1]

SELMA FRAIBERG
University of Michigan Medical School

In this chapter I bring together observations from our longitudinal studies of infants blind from birth, which describe the elements of communication between baby and mother that must be derived from a nonvisual vocabulary of signs and signals.

Before describing our sample, our methods and our observations of mothers and their blind infants, I propose to introduce the problems under consideration by first choosing a neutral frame of reference: observations of myself, self-observations of our research staff, and observations of visitors to our project in response to blind babies.

Understandably, there will be questions as we introduce our findings. A mother who has just delivered a blind baby, or who has just learned that her baby is blind, must cope with immeasurable grief and despondency. When we describe the extraordinary problems of a blind baby and his mother in finding a sign vocabulary, how can we know what belongs to the obliteration of a visual sign system and what belongs to psychological pain as a deterrent to the mother's reading of signs? The self-observations of the researcher and observations of visitors to our project may offer some measure of the meaning of blindness to an adult where blindness it not a personal tragedy.

1 Self-observations

I began the developmental study of blind infants twelve years ago. I gradually became aware of many differences in my behavior toward blind infants when I watched myself with sighted infants. Many of these feelings are still with me, and catch me by surprise. Yet I think I am reasonably without prejudice toward the blind and, as far as I can judge, my feelings have not been an impediment in my work.

The first self-discoveries came to me in New Orleans when David

Freedman and I began our study of a five-month-old blind baby, Toni. We had been visiting Toni for six months when we were asked by a social agency to evaluate another blind baby, Lennie, then nine months old. We arranged for a home visit.

Somebody had made a mistake. Lennie was not blind. We found a neglected baby lying in a filthy crib. If we exerted ourselves in testing, we elicited brief regard of our faces and tracking. It was the absence of sustained fixation that had led someone to believe that Lennie was blind when he was three months of age. Since that time he had been reared as a blind child and as the unwanted fourteenth child in an impoverished family.

After concluding our testing and a long discussion with the mother, I began to write up notes for a social agency referral. As I put the observations in sequence, I made notations on the conditions that elicited visual regard. I was describing Lennie's responses to my voice when something struck me as strange. It was my monolog. But I always talk to babies, I told myself. No. I don't always talk to babies. I don't talk to Toni in the same way.

I searched my memory. It was true. I did very little talking when I was with Toni. This troubled me. Toni was a responsive and endearing child. Lennie depressed me. I enjoyed holding Toni. I had to overcome some feelings of revulsion when I held Lennie. But I talked to Lennie. What was the reward? When I searched my memory again, I came up with two pictures. When I talked to Lennie long enough, I elicited brief moments of visual fixation of my face and a meeting of eyes. When I sustained his fixation long enough, I elicited a ghost of a smile.

Later, I could make use of this self-observation when I was with Toni. I talked to her more frequently, but always I had the sense of something missing, something that should be coming back to me from Toni. There was of course no fixation of my face. And something else was missing. Although Toni smiled frequently in response to her mother's voice, she rarely smiled in response to the voices of us as observers. Later, in the course of years, I was to learn much more about the stimuli that evoke smiling in the blind infant. The voice, even the voice of the mother, does not automatically evoke smiling in blind infants. I missed that in Toni. I still miss it in blind infants, and my team members share this feeling with me.

Twelve years later there are still surprises for me. A few months ago five-year-old Karen, who is blind, was visiting our office. I saw Karen playing in one of the offices and stopped to talk with her. Her back was turned to me. When she heard me speak to her she stopped her play for a moment and listened. She did not turn around immediately. Then as I continued to talk, Karen slowly turned around and met me full face. I had a moment's shock. The words came into my mind, 'She's blind!' But I had known for nearly five years that Karen was blind.

Sometimes when we have professional visitors at the project to look at films or videotapes, I steal glances at their faces when the child is seen on the screen. With sighted children it is always interesting to see the resonance of mood on the viewer's face. We smile when the baby on the film smiles; we are sober when the baby is distressed. We laugh sympathetically when the baby looks indignant at the examiner's sneakiness. We frown in concentration as the baby frowns when the toy disappears. When he drops a toy, we look below the movie screen to help him find it.

But the blind baby on the screen does not elicit these spontaneous moods in the visitor. Typically, the visitor's face remains solemn. This is partly a reaction to blindness itself. But it is also something else. There is a large vocabulary of expressive behavior that one does not see in a blind baby at all. The absence of differentiated signs on the baby's face is mirrored in the face of the observer.

One afternoon recently our staff devoted a session to the discussion of self-observations in relation to blind infants. Our consensus, as a team of researchers and clinicians who have worked with blind children for several years, was that we have never overcome this sense of something vital missing in the social exchange. And yet our rewards from blind children have been very great. All the staff members have strong attachments to children we have known since the first year of life. With rare exceptions the babies have grown into preschool children who are healthy, active, freely mobile, talkative and mischievous, surely a group of highly personable and attractive youngsters. Among ourselves we talk about them the way proud parents do. We are never aware that something is missing in our response until a sighted child comes to visit.

When a sighted child comes to visit, there is spontaneous rapport and we trot out our repertoire of antics with babies. We are back in the tribal system where the baby plays his social game and we play ours. If one has worked very largely with blind babies for many years, as we have, the encounter with a sighted baby is absurdly like the experience of meeting a compatriot abroad after a long stay in a country where the language and customs are alien. The compatriot, who can be a perfect stranger asking for directions, is greeted like a friend, his regional accent and idiom are endearing, and with nothing more in common than a continent two strangers can embark upon a social exchange in which nearly all the tribal signs are understood and correctly interpreted.

What we miss in the blind baby, apart from the eyes that do not see, is the vocabulary of signs and signals that provides the most elementary and vital sense of discourse long before words have meaning.

In this chapter, I describe through our observations some of the unique problems of a blind infant and his mother in finding a vocabulary of signs.

2 The sample

The data summarized in this report are derived from a longitudinal study of ten babies, five boys and five girls. So far as possible we have brought babies into the study soon after birth, but the actual age at the point of first observation has ranged from twenty-three days to seven months for eight children, and two children were first seen at nine and eleven months. Within the range of medical certainty, we have selected babies who have been totally blind from birth or who have light perception only and no other defects.

Our sample, then, is highly selective, and our findings cannot be generalized for the total blind infant population. (A typical blind population includes children with a range of useful vision, who are still legally classified as 'blind', and children who have other sensory and motor handicaps and neurological damage.) Our babies, then, are advantaged in a blind child population by the intactness of other systems and are disadvantaged as a group by having no pattern vision. (These restrictive criteria have given us a very small population, even though we called upon the referral network of a major medical center.)

It is important to note that we have provided a concurrent educational and guidance service for all babies in the research program. We know that the early development of blind babies is perilous. In the general blind child population there is a very high incidence of deviant and nondifferentiated personalities and arrested ego development (even when we exclude cases of brain damage and multiple handicaps

which are also common to this population). As our own research pro-
gressed, we were able to link certain developmental road blocks with
a clinical picture seen in the older blind child (Fraiberg 1968; Fraiberg & Freedman 1964). As these findings became available to us,
they were readily translatable into a program of prevention and education. We felt that no benefits to the research could justify withholding this knowledge and began to provide a home-based educational program which has been highly effective in promoting the
development of our blind babies (Fraiberg 1971a; Fraiberg et al.
1969).

We can say then that the observations in this report are derived
from a group of healthy, otherwise intact infants; their families represent a good range of socioeconomic conditions; their mothers are
at least adequate and, in four cases, are rated as superior. The development of these babies has probably been favored by our intervention. See table 1 for sample characteristics.

3 Observational procedures

3.1 Observers

Each baby is assigned to a team of two observers. The primary
responsibility for observation is given to the senior staff member who
is present at each visit.

3.2 Methods

The baby is visited in his home at twice-monthly intervals for a 1½-
hour session. (We travel within a radius of 100 miles to cover our
home visits.) We try to time our visits to coincide with a morning or
afternoon waking period, and to fit our observations into the normal
routine of that period. Nearly all the data required for our study can
be obtained through observing a feeding, a bath, a playtime with
mother, a diapering or clothes changing, and a period of self-occupation
with or without toys. A small amount of time in each session may be
employed for testing procedures by the examiner in the areas of prehension and object concept.

The observers record a continuous narrative with descriptive detail.
Once monthly we record a 15-minute, 16 mm film or video sample
covering mother—child interaction, prehension and gross motor development, which is employed for close analysis by the staff.

Table 1 *Sample characteristics*

Criteria	
Total blindness from birth or only minimal light perception	
No other known handicaps of neurological damage	
Less than 1 year old	
Within fifty miles of our office	
Description	
Sex	5 boys, 5 girls
Age at referral	1 to 11 months
Age last seen	2 to 6 years
Ordinal position in family	
Only	(5)
First of two	(1); of three (1)
Second of two	(1)
Fifth of five	(1)
Sixth of six	(1)
Diagnosis	
Hypoplasia of optic nerve	(3)
Retrolental fibroplasia (three months premature birth)	(3)
Infantile glaucoma	(2)
Ophthalmia neonatorum	(1)
Resorption of vitreous humor	(1)
Social class by father's occupation[a]	
Managerial	(1)
College student	(2)
Skilled	(2)
Semiskilled	(3)
Unskilled	(2)

[a]Based on Edwards Occupational Index.

Since the areas we are studying have not been previously researched, our data collection procedures had to insure coverage of hundreds of items for comparative study, yet needed to be open, flexible and rich in detail for qualitative study.

Our study of human attachment was of course one of the central areas of this study. Since nothing was known regarding the characteristics of human attachments in the blind infant, we had to design a study that permitted the blind baby to teach us what kinds of sense information he uses when he makes selective responses to his mother, his father and other familiar persons, how he differentiates mother and stranger, how he reacts to separation from his mother, and how he demonstrates affection, joy, need, grief, anger, and the range of human emotion that normally tell us about the quality of human bonds during the first eighteen months.

Our observations, then, covered differential responses (smiling, vocalizing, motor responses) to the human voice, to touch, to holding and to lap games, with familiar and unfamiliar persons, with mother present and, when appropriate for testing, with mother absent. The data covering the first eighteen months of life were classified, yielding twenty-five categories which were employed for analysis of differential responses.

4 The absence of an eye language

I have described some of the reactions of professional observers in social exchanges with blind babies. The blind eyes that do not engage our eyes, that do not regard our faces, have an effect upon the observer which is never completely overcome. When the eyes do not meet ours in acknowledgment of our presence, it feels curiously like a rebuff. Certainly, mothers attribute 'knowing' and 'recognition' to a baby's sustained regard of the face long before he can actually discriminate and recognize faces, and this is only because the engagement of the eyes is part of the universal code of the human fraternity, which is read as a greeting and an acknowledgment of 'the other' long before it can have meaning to the infant.

It is a potent sign. Robson (1967) describes the role of eye-to-eye contact in eliciting maternal responses to the infant. In his report mothers speak of the first feelings of love in response to the infant's fixation of the face, of the sense of the baby 'becoming a person'. Roskies (1972), in her work with the mothers of thalidomide babies, describes two mothers who were considering institutionalization of their deformed babies soon after birth. The baby's eyes 'looking back', the eyes 'talking' to the mother, were moments recalled by both mothers as compelling. The decision to keep the baby was remembered by both mothers within the context of this engagement of the eyes.

'How will he know me?' This question, sometimes explicit, sometimes implicit, may come to us from the mother soon after she has learned of her child's blindness. And while we know that under all favorable circumstances the blind baby will come to know his mother and that the course of human attachments will closely parallel that of a sighted child, the imagination of the mother may be strained to encompass a 'knowing' without vision. Discrimination, recognition, preference and valuation are signs that the mother normally reads through visual responses of the infant. And while a mother can acknowledge that there can be recognition, 'knowing' through tactile, kinesthetic and auditory experience, the registration of this 'knowing' is normally interpreted through differentiated facial signs. Eye contact connotes greeting and acknowledgement. Eye contact elicits the smile. Visual discrimination leads to preferential smiling. In the case of the blind infant, a large vocabulary of signs is either obliterated or distorted for the mother, as I describe in the sections that follow.

Vision affords the sighted child an elementary form of initiative in human partnership long before there can be intention. From the responses of the mother of a baby under two months of age, we can say that the baby woos his mother with his eyes. He elicits social exchange through the automatic smile in response to the human face gestalt. At five months of age, the sighted child extends or uplifts his arms in the gesture 'Hold me', 'Pick me up', which most mothers find irresistible, even an imperative.

But the blind baby has a meager repertoire of behaviors that can initiate social exchange and, beyond the vocal utterances of need and distress, he has virtually no sign vocabulary that elicits an automatic response from his mother. Instead, the absence of eye contact gives the negative sign of 'no interest'. The absence of a smile in response to the presentation of the human face has the negative value of 'not friendly'. The smile to mother's voice, which is in the repertoire of the blind baby, is not an automatic smile and is not employed to initiate a social exchange. The gesture 'Hold me', 'Pick me up', does not appear, even among our most adequate blind babies, until the end of the first year, at which time the voice of the mother can elicit a directional reach and the reach becomes a meaninfgul gesture to the mother.

Our records document the extraordinary problems for a mother in reading the nonvisual sign language of the blind baby. Only two mothers among our group of ten found their way unaided by us. Both were extraordinary mothers, and both had had extensive experience with babies. Other mothers in our group, including those who had older children, showed us at the time of our first meeting that they found their blind babies perplexing and 'unresponsive', that it was hard to know what the baby 'wanted'. No criticism is implied here. A sighted baby does not need an extraordinary mother in order to make the vital human connections and to find the developmental routes in infancy. We provided much help to all the parents of our blind infants. As we ourselves became experienced in understanding the nonvisual vocabulary of the blind baby and the developmental road blocks, we were able to become the translators for the blind baby and his perplexed parents. When the mother learned the language, the rewards for the baby and his parents were very great.

5 The smile language

Our observations on smiling in blind infants were reported in an earlier article (Fraiberg 1971b). The material that follows is a summary.

As early as the fourth week, we have observations in which a blind baby responds to his mother's and his father's voice with a smile. Our findings show close correspondence with those of Wolff (1963), who demonstrated that the sighted baby shows a selective smile to the sound of his mother's voice as early as four weeks of age.

At this age, as Emde & Koenig (1969) point out, the familiar voice, as well as several other stimuli, can irregularly elicit a smile in the sighted child. And while it is impressive to see how the blind baby can respond selectively to the voices of his mother and father, we should note that this is not an automatic or a regular response. As the number of babies in our sample increased, differences between the characteristics of smiling in blind and sighted infants appeared in a clear pattern.

At two to two and a half months, when for the sighted child the visual stimulus of the human face evokes an automatic smile with a high degree of regularity, there is no equivalence in the blind baby's experience. Thus the blind baby's smile becomes more frequent, and although the pattern of selective smiling becomes increasingly demonstrated in favor of the mother, even the mother's voice does not regularly elicit a smile. There is no stimulus in the third month or later that has true equivalence for the human face gestalt in the experience of the sighted child.

For the mother of the blind baby, the selective response smile to her voice signified 'knowing' and 'preference', and the first fears of 'How will he know me?' were diminished by appearance of the universal sign. When observers tried experimentally to elicit a smile through their voices, they were only rarely rewarded, and we used our failures to help the mother to see the smile for her as being 'special' and the beginning of 'knowing' the mother.

But the smile was not automatic. In our records and on film we see the mother coaxing a smile. Sometimes several repetitions of her voice were needed before the smile appeared. Clearly, something was needed that was not automatically given.

Then, in our records of this period, we begin to see that the most reliable stimulus for evoking a smile or laughter in the blind baby is gross tactile or kinesthetic stimulation. As observers we were initially puzzled and concerned by the amount of bouncing, jiggling, tickling and nuzzling that all of our parents, without exception, engaged in with the babies. In several cases we judged the amount of such stimulation as excessive by any standards. We had rarely seen among parents of sighted babies, in such a range of homes, so much dependence upon gross body stimulation. Then we began to understand; these games provided an almost certain stimulus for a smile, while the parents' voices alone provided at best an irregular stimulus. The parents' own need for the response smile, which is normally guaranteed with the sighted child at this age, led them to these alternative routes in which a smile could be evoked with a high degree of reliability.

When we exclude vision as a factor in the socialization of the smile, other differences in smiling emerge. Once a familiar voice is heard, the blind child may respond by smiling, but he does not initiate contact through a smile. The smile to initiate, the automatic greeting, is largely mediated through visual signs and is normally reinforced through visual rewards (the return or exchange smile of the partner).

This leads us to the observation that our blind babies do not smile as frequently as sighted babies do (the consensus of our staff and a very large number of independent observers who have reviewed films with us over the years). And even when we have all the criteria for a mutually satisfying mother–child relationship, the smile of the blind infant strikes us as a muted smile. The joyful, even ecstatic smile that we see in a healthy sighted baby is a comparatively rare occurrence among blind babies. This suggests that the smile on the face of 'the other' is a potent reinforcer — even in infancy — of one's own smile.

The effects upon the human partner of a baby who does not greet with a smile, who smiles infrequently and without predictability to the social stimuli presented to him, are best seen in the judgments

made upon the blind baby's personality and his state by both clinicians and laymen who have not had experience with blind babies.

'She looks depressed', says a visitor watching one of our blind
babies on film. 'No affect! The face is so bland. No expression.' The
visitor wonders if the mother is giving the baby enough stimulation.

The baby in question is a perfectly adequate blind girl (seventeen
months) who has given a demonstration on film of her attachment
to and preference for her mother, of locomotor achievements close
to sighted norms, and a rapt exploration of a new toy with her
sensitive fingertips. The amount of 'stimulation' provided by the
mother must be judged as adequate to produce this kind of investment in persons and things in a blind baby of this age.

Yet we understand what the visitor is experiencing. The visitor
misses the signs of affectivity, of investment, of social response which
register on the face of a sighted baby and are automatically translated
by us. Only when we see a blind baby do we fully appreciate that
most of these signs are differentiated through vision.

6 The absence of differentiated facial signs

In the range of pleasure—displeasure, we can read the signs at both
ends of the arc for a blind baby. A blind baby who smiles 'looks
happy'. A blind baby who is crying for a delayed dinner 'looks unhappy'. But between the contrasting states, which everyone can read,
there is a tremendous range of modulated affect and attitudes which
is normally discerned by human partners through expressive facial
signs. By any reasoning the modulations must exist for blind babies
as states of feeling, but we cannot easily read these states by scruti-
nizing the face.

If we make a brief inventory of expressive facial signs in the sighted
child, at six months of age, we can immediately see how the child's
own eyes lead the way and give us the signs we read as 'affect', 'investment' and 'attention'.

(1) 'He looks attentive' (attention inferred from sustained visual
regard).

(2) 'A look of longing' (can be read through the baby's prolonged
visual fixation, visually oriented postures).

(3) 'He looks quizzical' (visual inspection of an unfamiliar phenomenon).

(4) 'He looks doubtful' (visual inspection with mixed positive and negative emotion).

(5) 'A coy look' (a visual peek-a-boo game: now you're here; now you're not).

(6) 'She is bored' (restless or unfocused searching or scanning with the eyes).

The list can be compounded for the sighted child before he has reached six months of age. In the third and fourth quarters, imitative signs begin to enter the repertoire for the sighted child (Piaget 1946), giving personal style to the face and extending the differentiated vocabulary of facial expression. All this is closed out in blindness.

The blind baby, by contrast, has an impoverished repertoire of facial signs. The blind baby does not 'look attentively', 'look quizzically', 'look doubtfully', 'look coyly'. He has no object of visual fixation that can elicit these differentiated signs. This leads the uninitiated mother or observer to feel as our visitors do, 'He looks depressed', 'Nothing interests him'.

The absence of signs is misleading. We have no reason to believe that the affective state of longing, for example, does not exist for the healthy blind baby, but the motor expression of longing which is read by us through sustained visual fixation (and visually oriented postures) is not available to him. Since we normally read affective states through expressive facial signs, the absence of the differentiated sign on the blind baby's face is misread as 'no affect'.

(There are of course blind babies who are, properly speaking, depressed, withdrawn and apathetic. But to make the clinically valid diagnosis, we need much more than a reading of the face.)

For the healthy, adequately stimulated blind baby, there are registrations of affective states with motor expression. But we have to turn our eyes away from the face to discover them. To do this is so alien to normal human discourse, that we might not have discovered the other signs if we had not been looking for something else.

7 The hand language

Our developmental observations included the study of prehension in blind infants. Very early in our work we saw that adaptive hand behavior followed another route in blind babies. There was no adaptive substitution of the ear for the eye in reaching and attaining an object at five months of age. Our question was 'How does the blind baby achieve the coordination of ear and hand which leads him to localize a sound object in space, to reach directionally for the object and attain it?' We were to find that 'reach on sound' was not achieved by any baby in our group until the last quarter of the first year (Fraiberg 1968; Fraiberg et al. 1966).

We became 'hand watchers' as a staff. To examine the sequential patterns in adaptive hand behavior, we analyzed many thousands of feet of film on a variable-speed projector, viewing at one-third speed. Our prehension film samples were always photographed under circumstances in which the full range of the baby's experience with human partners as well as inanimate objects could be included.

As we watched the baby's hands, we found what we were looking for, and we also found a large number of things that we were not looking for.

We began to see the expressive motor signs in the hands themselves. We began to read 'I want' and intentionality through fleeting, barely visible motor signs in the hands. Our staff film reviews took on a curious aspect. When we examined mother–child reciprocity, we looked at the mother's face and the baby's hands. (The baby's face told us very little.) When we studied investment in a toy or toy preference, we looked at the baby's hands. When we examined emotional reactions to momentary separation from the mother, or toy loss, we looked at the hands. It was — and still is — a bizarre experience for us to read hands instead of faces in order to read meaning into emotional experience. (As a clinician with sighted children, I normally read faces for signs of emotionality. I picked up cues from the hands either peripherally or as an alternative when the face masked emotionality.)

As we ourselves became sensitive to the motor expressions in the hands themselves, we began to read them as signs and responded to them as signs. What we saw we could easily help the mother to see too, and some of our mothers became as adept as the observers in reading and translating the baby's hand language.

Since it took us a considerable time as professional observers to 'read hands', we should now fairly consider the dilemma of the mother of a blind baby without professional guidance. In the absence of a repertoire of expressive facial signs, the mother of the blind baby had no differentiated sign vocabulary in which modulated affective states or wants were registered, and from which an appropriate response from the mother was elicited. And since many of the baby's signs could not be 'read' by his mother, his own experience in eliciting specific responses to need was largely restricted to elemental need states. 'Hunger', 'contentment', 'fussiness', 'rage' and 'sleepiness' could be read by the mother, but the full range of affective expression which becomes socialized in the first year could not be exploited until the signs could be read by the mother.

Let me give a few examples of the problem.

Toni is ten months old. Her mother (a very experienced mother with five older children) tells us 'She's not really interested in her toys.'

We assemble a group of Toni's crib toys, stuffed animals and dolls, and invite the mother to present them to Toni, one by one. As each of the toys is placed in her hands, Toni's face is immobile. She gives the impression of 'staring off into remote space'. Naturally, the totally blind child does not orient his face toward the toy in his hands. Since visual inspection is the sign that we read as 'interest', and averted eyes and staring are read as the sign of 'disinterest', Toni 'looks bored'.

Now we watch Toni's hands. While her face 'looks bored', her fingers scan each of the toys. One stuffed doll is dropped after brief manual scanning. A second doll is scanned, brought to the mouth, tongued, mouthed, removed, scanned again. Now we remove doll no. 2 and place doll no. 1 in Toni's hand. A quick scanning of fingers and she drops it again. She makes fretful sounds, eyes staring off into space. We return doll no. 2 to her hands. She quiets instantly, clutches it, brings it to her mouth and explores its contours.

In short, there is no message from the face which Toni's mother can read as 'interest' or 'preference'. But the behavior of the hands showed clear discrimination and sustained exploration of one toy and not another.

Examples such as this multiply throughout our records. The immobile face, the vacant eyes, 'no interest', but the fingers explore the tiny crevices of the rattle, the clapper of the bell, the bumps on the soap dish, the bristles of the pastry brush.

The problem is compounded when the mother needs to read 'wanting' or intention in her blind baby. No mother of a sighted baby at six months is at a loss in reading 'I want' from a very large number of visually directed behaviors. At this age the sighted child is very good at getting what he wants within range. He also reaches for things out of range, with eyes fixed determinedly on their target, hands and

torso extended, and urgent vocalizations just in case somebody cannot read sign language. He has in fact a differentiated vocabulary of
motor signs in orientation of the head, and extended arms and hands,
which we read instantly as 'I want', 'Gimme', 'Pick me up', 'No, not
that', 'Oh, please'. All these signs are mediated by vision (e.g. eye and
hand) and depend upon visual fixation of the target and a motor
expression of want or supplication for a quick reading of intention by
the adult partner. If, for example, we had the implausible situation in
which a six-month-old sighted baby produced the motor sign of
'Gimme' and the eyes did not fixate a target, we would not be able
to read intention.

This means of course that, even when the blind baby reveals his
wants or his intentions through the motor expression of his hands,
not only does the sign require fine reading by us or by the parents,
but there are many wants that cannot be expressed through the
hands without orientation and gesture to identify the target. It is
only at the close of the first year, when the sound object is localized
and the blind baby begins to make a directional reach for the object,
that we begin to see the sign of 'I want' through the extended hand,
and the sign of 'Pick me up' through extended arms.

A toy drops from his hand and the blind baby at six months may
make no sound of complaint, no gesture of retrieval. The face registers
nothing that we can read as disappointment. In the blind baby's world
of evanescent objects, the manifestation of a toy, its comings and
goings, are subject to a capricious fate. Things materialize out of a
void, manifest themselves when grasped, heard, mouthed or smelled,
and then are lost, swallowed in a void. The sighted child of this age
can follow the trajectory of a falling toy, and the registrations of 'I
want' on the face and in the hands are sustained through visual contact with the toy that has left his hand.

The blind baby 'looks bored', 'not interested', as we read his face
when the toy drops from his hand. But if we watch his hands, another
story emerges.

The toy drops to the floor. Robbie 'looks bored'. But now Robbie's
open hand can be seen sweeping across the table surface, and then
sweeps back. The 'hand watchers' read this instantly as a search. The
play table surface is the place where toys are usually found; a toy
'belongs to' this space, as it were; it materializes from this space. The
exploratory sweep of the hand is the sign of 'I want' for the blind
baby.

When Robbie is eight months old, if we bring his muscial dog within easy reach of his hands and play its familiar music, he will not reach for the toy. Does he want it? His face does not register yearning or wanting. But now as the music plays we see his hands in an anticipatory posture of holding, grasping and ungrasping.

When Robbie is nine months old, we ring our test bell within easy reach of his hands. The bell is a favorite toy for Robbie. He does not reach for the bell. Does he want it? We watch his hands, and then we see the hands execute a pantomime of bell ringing as he hears the bell 'out there'.

This leads us to consider the more central problems for the blind baby and his mother in establishing the vital human connections. The alien sign language of the blind baby is not only an impediment to the reading of want and intention in the baby. The baby's sign vocabulary of selective interest, preference and valuation of his human partners, which constitute the earliest language of love, is distorted for the mother of the blind baby. The blind baby's face does not reveal signs of discrimination, preference and recognition.

Yet once again, if we shift our attention from the face of the blind baby to his hands, we can read an eloquent sign language of seeking, wooing, preference and recognition, which becomes increasingly differentiated during the first six months.

We have observations and film records of three of our ten babies during the first quarter. In the early weeks the behavior of the hands does not yet differentiate, for my eyes, a blind baby and a sighted baby. In a film of a blind baby being fed in his mother's arms we see his hands making chance contact with the mother's face or hands, grasping or lightly fingering. In the second month we see the beginnings of active seeking of contact with the mother, the hand, for example, returning to a point of prior contact after interruption. This behavior corresponds to Piaget's protocols for Laurent at the same age (Piaget 1936). The number of examples of manual tactile seeking begins to proliferate for two of the children between two and five months of age. The hands, not engaged, seek engagement with the mother's hand or her body. The hands linger, lightly finger or grasp, withdraw, and return. Sometimes we catch on film a kind of ballet in which the baby's hands seek and find the mother's hand, and the mother's hand sustains or responds to the signal.

I am sure we can see an identical hand language in watching sighted babies and their mothers. But the sighted child, even at two months, sustains an eloquent dialogue of eyes, smiles and motor responses to invite and sustain contact with his mother. To a very large extent the blind baby is dependent upon his hands to woo, to maintain contact and to affirm the presence of the mother. During the period two to six months, we can follow the blind baby's adaptive exploitation of the hand in establishing human connections.

Between five and eight months of age (as reported for eight children in the sample), we have examples for all the children in which the blind baby's hands explore the mother's or father's face, the fingers tracing features with familiarity and giving the sense to the viewer of anticipation of what he will find. The film record gives strong evidence that these exploring hands are discriminating, and that the information from the fingers brings recognition as well as nonrecognition.

In one example on film, I hold Toni at age seven months two days, to test her reactions to me as a stranger. She begins to strain away from me and to whimper. Then her hands seek my face, finger my nose and mouth in a quick scanning of this unfamiliar map; she cries louder, and clutches my arm in frozen terror. When I return her to her mother's arms, she settles, still crying, then scans and rescans her mother's face with her fingers, and finally is comforted.

This tactile language can speak eloquently to the mother who 'knows' it. The two mothers who found their way unaided by us in intuiting their blind babies' needs were mothers whose own tactile sensibilities were large, and who not only provided abundant tactile experience for their babies but responded with spontaneity to the baby's tactile sign language. Other mothers needed our help both in understanding the blind baby's need for tactile intimacy and manual tactile experience, and in interpreting the tactile sign language of the blind child.

What we ourselves learned from hand language we brought to the mothers of our blind babies. It was most welcome help. When the baby's expressive signs could be read, the dialogue between mother and baby was facilitated with predictable rewards. The mother who felt out of contact, uncertain, not competent, found her way as a mother who could minister to her child's needs. Even grief could be managed when the baby brought his own rewards in response, in diversity of social exchange, and in becoming an active partner in the love relationship — a partnership that is really possible only when the language of need and intention can be understood.

8 The vocal dialogue

The vocal dialogue that is available to the blind baby and his parents is, finally, the one channel that remains open and available as a relatively undistorted language system between mother and child. Even in this area we see some qualitative differences (and, we think, some differences in quantity too), but our data do not suggest that blindness is an impediment to the acquisition of language in the first and second years. Here, again, we are speaking of our highly selective and advantaged group of blind infants. Scales available for the larger blind population show marked delays by sighted child standards.

Within our own sample the expressive vocalizations, the emergence of vowel—consonant syllables and imitative sounds, 'mama', 'baba', 'dada' and so on, appear within the Bayley ranges for sighted children. Two of our children used the words 'mama', 'dada' and 'bopple' (bottle) as correct referents between the ages of eight months and twelve months (Bayley median fourteen months). In the second year, which is not under consideration in this article, naming, expression of wants and simple sentences appeared within the range for sighted children. A linguistic study of one of our children conducted by Eric Lenneberg showed that her language competence at two years of age compared favorably with that of sighted children (reported in Fraiberg & Adelson 1973).

Yet, throughout the first year, it seemed to us that the spontaneous vocalizations of our blind babies were sparse. In the absence of quantitative measures for sighted children of comparable age, we can only offer our impression and that of several independent observers that our babies seemed 'very quiet' in comparison with sighted babies, that vocalization for self-entertainment was infrequent and scant (even among the high vocalizers of our group), that vocalizations to greet were rarely recorded, and that the initiation of a 'dialogue' with mother or other partners was rarely observed. However, response vocalizations in 'dialogue' with the mother are recorded for all the children in our group.

These differences, which we can support only impressionistically, may reflect the poverty of eliciting stimuli in a blind child's world. Where visual stimuli afforded by people, food, toys, a colorful object and a moving object can produce a volley of utterances from the sighted child, even under four months of age — and these stimuli are omnipresent from the moment the child opens his eyes — there is no equivalence among the exogenous stimuli in the blind child's world. Sound, voices and tactile–kinesthetic stimulation are not 'at the disposal of' the blind child in the way that visual stimuli are available from the moment the eyes open. The sound–touch stimuli of the blind child are actually at the disposal of someone outside the infant self, the human partners whose voice and touch are not constant components of the waking hours. (Only a nonstop talking and touching mother could provide equivalence in quantity of stimuli.)

There may be other factors not explored in our study that have bearing on the seeming poverty of spontaneous vocalization in our blind babies. We do not know, for example, if blindness is an impediment for the mother in her vocalizing to the infant. Does the absence of eye contact and of the automatic smile reduce the spontaneity of utterances on the part of the mother (as I reported in my self-observations at the beginning of this chapter)? Is this a reciprocal effect of blindness on discourse between the two partners in which a reduced level of utterances from the mother has correspondence in a reduction of vocalizations in the baby?

Our blind infant observations during the four- to eight-month period show that the mother's or father's voice is the prime elicitor of vocalizations. We have a large number of examples of 'dialogues' between parent and baby which do not distinguish our blind babies from sighted babies under circumstances in which the adult himself initiates the dialogue.

Vocalizations to initiate contact appear later (in the second year) for our blind children. It is not easy to understand why. In families in which the rewards for vocalizations are very large, with much parental 'talking to' the baby and echoing of his sounds, we are still struck by the absence of initiative in the baby. We can only guess that vision is a potent elicitor of vocalizations and that what appear as 'greeting vocalizations' in sighted babies are stimulated by and reinforced by visual signs (e.g. the human face gestalt). But why, in the circular causality available to the blind infant at six to eight months, doesn't he vocalize with the magical expectation that his sound-making will produce sounds from his partners?

I realize that in the area of vocalizations and language in the first year I am raising more questions than I can answer.

When we consider how many social signs are obliterated by blindness, and how resourceful and inventive the mother of the blind baby must be to read her baby's alien sign language, no comment is needed from me on the significance of the early vocalizations and the blind baby's discovery of the spoken language in the partnership of mother and baby. With the first words there is, for the first time, a common language.

9 The achievement of human bonds

From this discussion we can see that the mother of a blind baby faces extraordinary problems in learning the alien language of her child. Grief and self-recriminations which come with the first shock of blindness are compounded by the sense of estrangement from a baby who cannot communicate in the universal code. The perils to the baby are very large. In the general blind population, there is a significant number of blind children, otherwise intact, who show grave impairment in their human—object relationships. In our consultation service (a separate program not reported in this chapter), we see blind children in the second, third and fourth years who appear to have no investment in persons or things. These are children of families for whom no guidance was available in the crucial sensorimotor period.

Our research sample can tell us more fairly about the capacities for human attachments in blind infants when the nonvisual vocabulary of the infant 'speaks to' the mother and the mother responds and is rewarded by her baby.

For those mothers (the majority) who could not find their way unaided into the alien experience of the blind baby, we shared our own understanding. The benefits to the baby and the mother were demonstrable in all developmental areas. In the area of human attachments, I briefly summarize our findings.

In the course of the first year, the characteristics of human attachments in the blind infants of our research group closely paralleled those of sighted children. Discrimination, preference for and valuation of the mother were seen in differential smiling, differential vocalization, manual tactile seeking, embracing, spontaneous gestures of affection and comfort seeking. In the period seven to fifteen months, negative reactions to a stranger (avoidance, manifest distress) are recorded for nine of the ten babies. During the same period the unfamiliar person was refused as a substitute in feeding, in comforting, as a game partner and in vocal exchanges. As with the sighted child, the stranger was an intruder into the magic circle.

In the second year anxiety at separation from the mother and comfort at reunion spoke for the blind baby's valuation of the mother as the indispensable human partner. With mobility in creeping and walking, we saw tracking (on sound cue) of the mother from room to room, independent exploration and return to the mother as a secure base.

As milestones in human attachment during the first two years of life, these achievements compare favorably with those of sighted children.

Note

1. This research has been supported since 1966 by grant no. HDO1-444 from the National Institutes of Child Health and Human Development and funds from the Department of Psychiatry of the University of Michigan Medical School and since 1969 by grant no. OEG-0-9-322108-2469(032) from the Office of Education.

8

One child's protolanguage

M.A.K. HALLIDAY
University of Sydney

1 Acts of meaning

A day-old child will stop crying to attend to his mother's voice. The
mother, for her part, will stop doing almost anything, including sleeping, to attend to the voice of her child. Each is predisposed to attend
to the sounds of the other.

Within a very few weeks, mother and child are taking part in ongoing exchanges of attention (Bullowa et al. 1964). The child is now
able to attend not only with his ears but also with his eyes: he can
watch as well as listen. Trevarthen (1974a) has beautifully documented the interaction of mother and child at this stage; his films show
the two of them facing each other engaged in animated mutual
address. The child is moving his face, his lips and tongue, his arms and
hands and his whole body, and the movements are directed towards
his mother: he is addressing her, and she is 'receiving' him. Simultaneously, she is addressing him with sounds and gestures of her own,
and he is receiving her (cf. France 1975).

There is a remarkable sense of identity between their actions, as if
the two were taking part in a single act. Not that they are superficially
similar – neither is imitating the other; yet they chime. When the
film is slowed down, the child is seen to be fractionally ahead; it is he
who is leading the dance. But the mother is dancing with him; it is a
duo, not a 'follow my leader'.

This is not yet language. M.C. Bateson (1975b) refers to the flow
of shared action and attention as proto-conversation; and Trevarthen
(1974b) describes the child's tongue and lip movements as pre-speech,
meaning by this that the child is contorting his articulatory organs in
a speech-like manner, perhaps flexing them for speaking later on. But
the exchange is not an exchange of meanings, and the acts are not
acts of meaning. What is significant about this early interaction is that

it provides a remarkable analogy for the child's development of language when this does begin to take place.

Trevarthen (1974b) characterises these as 'intersubjective' acts, meaning by this that mother and child share in the various creative processes that constitute the child's cognitive development. The term 'intersubjective' can equally well be applied to the processes of language development. Trevarthen's work provides in fact a point of departure for interpreting infant language development, enabling us to relate it to a general developmental perspective and to account for the very early age at which meanings begin to appear.

Psychologists and linguists have usually assumed that language development means the acquisition of the mother tongue; and that until a child begins to produce expressions that are recognisable to the investigator as words, typically (though with great variation) towards the middle of the second year, he has not yet embarked on language. But by the time a child does produce words, in the sense of elements that are coded lexically as distinct from imitations of word sounds, he has already been 'meaning' for a long time. Before the mother tongue comes the child tongue; and the child tongue comes into being considerably earlier, at a time that is likely to be nearer the middle of the first year of life than the middle of the second (cf. Bruner 1975a; Dore 1975).

A child tongue, though it differs from a mother tongue in one fundamental respect, namely that it has no lexicogrammar (its elements are simple signs, encoding content directly as expression without intermediate organisation, which is why it is referred to as a 'protolanguage'), is like a mother tongue in that both are resources for meaning (cf. Grieve & Hoogenraad forthcoming). An 'act of meaning' is the deployment of this resource: the actualising of the meaning potential, if such a ponderous phrase may be forgiven. But an act of meaning differs from the pre-symbolic acts of the first few weeks of life in that it is symbolic. It is an act whose success does not reside in its own performance, since it achieves success through representation. Up to this point, directed action by the child has not involved representations: either he was addressing someone, in which case the address constituted the act, and the act was successful if the address was received; or he was acting on some object (which may have been a person, i.e. a part of a person's body, but was an object for the purposes of the act, being acted on not addressed), in which case the act was successful if it achieved its aim, for example an act of reaching which made contact with the object that was its target.

It is not long before the child takes the step of combining these two modes of directed action, addressing (a person) and acting on (an object), into a single complex act in which the one is the representation of the other: in other words, making them into an act of meaning. An act of meaning is addressed to a person, but the success does not reside in the act of address itself: the address is a means of realising the intent. So if I 'reach for' the apple, not by extending my arm and grasping it but by addressing you with what you interpret as a request to hand it to me, I have performed an act of meaning.

Nigel had achieved this by the age of nine months, and he arrived at it by means of an intermediate step in which the mode of representation was iconic: that is, in which the act of address symbolised the intent in a non-arbitrary fashion. At eight months he had a system of three signs:

Meaning	Expression
(i) 'I want that'	grasp object momentarily, then let go
(ii) 'I don't want that'	touch object lightly and momentarily
(iii) 'do something with that for me to watch'	touch object firmly for measurable time

These were clearly acts of meaning: Nigel was not acting on the object, neither pulling it towards him nor pushing it away; moreover his eyes were on the person holding the object, not on the object itself. But the gestures were clearly related to the actions that would have been required to achieve the same goals by non-symbolic means.

There is reason for thinking, however, that in fact Nigel had already got further than this, and that he used iconic gestures not because he could not conceive of an arbitrary symbol but because he did not know how to construct one that would be understood. The three gestural signs were all pragmatic in function; but Nigel had already by this time created two other meanings which he encoded not by gesture but vocally:

Meaning	Expression
(iv) 'let's be together'	half close front rounded vowel on low falling tone
(v) 'that's interesting'	half close front rounded vowel on mid falling tone

Here the meaning is not active but reflective: not 'I want you to (give me that, do that for me)' but 'me and you, me and the world beyond'; and the expressions were his own invention and unrelated to the meaning. (Except perhaps in the analogic sense that the two meanings are, in terms of Nigel's developmental stage, nearly identical; both represent his growing awareness of self, with the wider pitch range on (v) symbolising the unboundedness of the non-self and the beginnings of exploration. That this may not be entirely farfetched is suggested by a consideration of the one sign that Nigel had developed before this stage, a short high-pitched squeak meaning 'what's going on?' that he used frequently for round about four weeks at six to seven months. It had disappeared by the time of the appearance of (i)–(v); but the association of high voice pitch with a search for explanation may in some as yet obscure way perhaps be 'natural'.)

The distinction that Nigel was making at eight months, between active meanings expressed gesturally and reflective meanings expressed vocally, was in any case short-lived; he was a child who pre-ferred the vocal mode, and by the age of ten months, when he had started meaning in earnest, all his meanings had come to be encoded as speech sounds (the one exception being the demand for music, which he expressed by 'beating time'). But Nigel's system fore-shadowed in a remarkable way what is in fact the basic functional distinction in the semantics of adult language, that between the inter-personal mode ('active') and the experiential mode ('reflective'). This infantile preview is the more striking because in the adult language too there is a clear tendency for the two modes of meaning to be realised in different ways; and the difference appears as a meta-phorical extension of the distinction that Nigel was making between the vocal and the gestural. Experiential meaning is typically realised in the form of constituent hierarchy, as what linguists call 'tree struc-tures', for example '(those + experts) + listen + ((young + children) + talking)' in the following sentence:

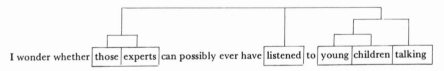

I wonder whether those experts can possibly ever have listened to young children talking

Here each piece of the wording represents some definable component in the configuration that makes up the thesis of the clause. Interper-sonal meaning is typically realised by prosodic patterns, strands run-

ning continuously through the discourse, for example 'I wonder . . .
can . . . possibly' together with the intonation contour, expressing the
speaker's judgment of 'I think it unlikely'. Here instead of discrete
segments representing different components there is a cumulative pattern whereby a rhetorical feature is distributed across the whole length
of the utterance. Nigel's brief period of specialisation, at eight months,
in the use of his expressive resources, though it was soon overtaken
by the demands of the systematic construction of a protolanguage,
provides a momentary glimpse, perhaps corresponding to a step in the
early development of language by the human species, of what later
becomes a central organising principle of the adult linguistic system.

At nine to ten months Nigel set about constructing his protolanguage in earnest, and by ten and a half months the number of
elements had grown to twelve. All were expressed vocally: Nigel had
found that he could create arbitrary vocal signs which were responded
to by his mother and the other two adults that were intimate with
him — that is, by all who constituted his 'meaning group'. These were
expressions like [nànànànà] 'give me that', demanding some visible
object; [ʒ̃] 'do that again', i.e. go on entertaining me; [ɞ̀ʒ] 'there
you are; now let's look at this (picture) together'; [ø̀] 'that's interesting'; [n̂ŋ] 'that tastes good'. These signs Nigel used frequently in his
daily interaction with the three people with whom he exchanged
meanings; they carried on the conversation with him and in so doing
shared in the creation of his first language.

2 Observing infant speech

The intensive study of the language development of a single child, in
the form of a journal kept by a parent or other intimate adult, was
rather unfashionable during the middle period of the twentieth century, when language development studies were largely the province
of psychologists; psychologists tended to prefer an experimental
approach involving large samples of children with the focus on a
single clearly defined problem, such as 'What is the probability that
a child of three years six months will be able to understand a sentence with a passive in it?' This sort of enquiry can be carefully controlled and monitored and the sample chosen to reflect any given
population; it is however subject to the limitation that children (like
everyone else) do tend to behave in untypical ways under experimental conditions. Recently many cognitive psychologists, and

psychologically inclined linguists, have favoured a semi-structured
approach in which medium-sized populations of children are recorded,
say, for half an hour in a playroom once a fortnight for six months;
their language and other behaviour is open-ended but some structure
is introduced, e.g. by the kinds of toys that are provided. The aim may
be to establish the range of linguistic functions typically engaged in
by children of the particular age range. The journal method, by comparison, is unstructured; the child is not asked any questions, or put
into any situations; nothing is elicited from him; he is simply observed,
under natural conditions. The disadvantages are clear: the 'sample' is
just one child, or at most two or three within the one family, and this
hardly justifies making general statements about how children learn
their language.

At the same time there are certain advantages. The natural setting
ensures that the developmental picture is a real one; not only in the
general sense that what is being recorded is natural behaviour and
not artificially structured or elicited, but also in that the leading edge
of language development, in the history both of the individual and of
the community, always lies in casual spontaneous speech. The family
context, with parent or other intimate as observer, ensures that the
greater part of what the child says is understood; and perhaps more
important, that the child understands what is being said to him.
Finally the uninterrupted ongoing interaction with the child, which
makes it possible to observe selectively and take note of whatever is
relevant, ensures that the record has no gaps in it, and that the investigator knows what the child's total system is at any one time. This
last is fundamental: every new development can be seen and interpreted against the background of the child's overall resources, in
terms of just what he is able to mean at the time. This is possibly only
with a continuous diary-type record.

In my own work I attempted to build up a picture of this kind,
tracking the semantic development of my own child from early infancy.
Having had the good fortune to be trained in linguistics as a dialect
field worker I was accustomed to being both participant and observer
at the same time, and to keeping an ongoing record of verbal interaction in varieties of phonetic script. All the essential material I
recorded with notebook and pencil, sometimes participating and
sometimes skulking; in this way I was able to filter out what was
irrelevant, and also to take note of whatever was relevant about the
context in which meanings were being exchanged — both these requir-

ing the sort of intuition that is not yet available in tape recorders. The child's utterances were taken down in phonetic notation; for accompanying adult speech I used ordinary orthography with the addition of symbols to mark intonation. The record was then written up as a continuous narrative, interspersed with interpretative commentary. Appendix 1 is a condensed account of the development of the protolanguage in the first three stages: (a) to nine months; (b) nine to ten and a half months; (c) ten and a half to twelve months.

3 Meaning in the protolanguage

If we look closely at the contexts of Nigel's acts of meaning at nine to twelve months, and at what he recognises as successful instances where the intention has been realised to his satisfaction, we can identify a small set of distinct semantic functions, present from the start, within each of which he is developing a potential for meaning. Let us label these (i) 'instrumental', (ii) 'regulatory', (iii) 'interactional' and (iv) 'personal'.

In function (i) Nigel is using language to get what he wants: to obtain goods-and-services, these being initially goods in the form of objects that are in sight but either withheld from him or out of reach. The acts are object-oriented, but person-mediated: objects can be acted on directly but not symbolically, so the meaning is addressed to a person and the act succeeds if that person's attention is directed to the object in question and she or he responds appropriately, by handing it to him. Nigel makes it quite clear whether he considers any such act of meaning successful or not. The act does not always succeed, of course; but it succeeds sufficiently often for Nigel to be able to code such meanings into his semantic system.

Function (ii) is also in the pragmatic or active mode, but it is person-oriented not object-oriented. The meaning is 'you do this!'; and whereas in the previous context it does not matter who delivers the goods, here the request is specific to the person addressed, who is being required to do something in which Nigel will share, such as sing a song or play a game.

Moving a step further away from the pragmatic end of the scale, in function (iii), 'interactional', Nigel is using language as a way of being together, of being 'in touch' with someone, typically his mother. Here the act of meaning is clearly oriented towards a person; but if the child is initiating the interaction it is often mediated by an object, so

that the togetherness takes the form of shared attention to something
in the environment (with Nigel this is usually a picture, an inherently
symbolic object whose function is just to be attended to), and the
meaning is something like 'let's look at this together'. Another early
instance of this type is the child's response to the calling of his name,
Nigel's long-drawn-out 'E-e-eh!' like a sigh, meaning 'yes? here I am!'

Function (iv) is referred to as 'personal', to suggest that the meaning relates to the child's development and assertion of self. The orientation is outward, towards the environment; but the mode is that of
reflection, not action, so it is the environment as it impinges on the
child, as a focus of his own thoughts and feelings. The meanings are
of the kind of 'I like' and 'I wonder'.

Nigel's earliest acts of meaning thus range over a continuum from
'most active' to 'most reflective'; within this we can recognise at first
four semantic functions, which provide the initial framework for the
development of his meaning potential, and its extension to the point
where he begins to move into the mother tongue (and cf. Wells 1974).
The transition from child tongue to mother tongue is of course gradual; it is foreshadowed in Nigel's acts of meaning already at fourteen
months, but the essential steps are taken a little later, at sixteen to
eighteen months. At twelve months, which is the point reached in
the narrative in appendix 1, Nigel is still clearly in the protolinguistic
stage, having now developed a semantic system which we could
represent as in table 1 (Halliday 1975).

Between twelve and seventeen months his further development
consists in enriching these functional—semantic resources, with the
addition of one new function, the 'imaginative' (meaning as play),
and the emergence of a sixth, the 'heuristic', by a transformation of
the 'I wonder' (personal) mode into a new kind of act of meaning
whose function is specifically the organisation of experience: 'what's
that?', 'that's a . . . ', leading at a much later stage to 'tell me why'.
The emergence of this 'meaning for learning' function is perhaps the
critical factor in the shift from protolanguage to language, the move
into the mother tongue.

The protolanguage may or may not represent a universal step in
infant language development. Whether it does or not, we can safely
assume that children who do develop a protolanguage do so in many
forms, differing both individually and socially. What is likely to be
common to all these is, first, the functional range along the 'action—
reflection' continuum, from language as doing to language as thinking,

Table 1 *Nigel at twelve months*

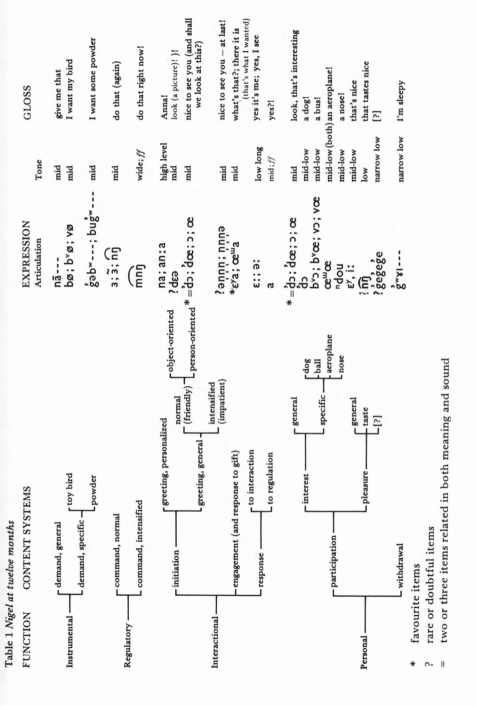

FUNCTION	CONTENT SYSTEMS				EXPRESSION Articulation	Tone	GLOSS
Instrumental	demand, general			toy bird	nã--- / bø; bˠø; vø	mid / mid	give me that / I want my bird
	demand, specific			powder	ˈgəbʷ---; bugʷ---	mid	I want some powder
Regulatory	command, normal				ɜ; ɜ; n̩ŋ	mid	do that (again)
	command, intensified				m̄n̄ŋ	wide; *ff*	do that right now!
Interactional	initiation	greeting, personalized			na; an:a	high level	Anna!
		greeting, general	normal (friendly)	object-oriented	ʔdɛə	mid	look (a picture)!)!
				person-oriented	*=ˈdɔ; ˈdɒɛ; ɔ; ɔɛ	mid	nice to see you (and shall we look at this?)
			intensified (impatient)		ʔɛn̄n̄; n̄n̄ɛ	mid	nice to see you — at last!
	engagement (and response to gift)				*ɔɛ̄ᵂa; ɔɛᵂa	mid	what's that?; there it is (that's what I wanted)
	response	to interaction			ɛ:; ə:	low long	yes it's me; yes, I see
		to regulation			a	mid; *ff*	yes?!
Personal	participation	interest	general		*=ˈdɔ; ˈdɒɛ; ɔ; ɔɛ / dɔ	mid	look, that's interesting
			specific	dog	bˠɔ; bˠɔɛ; vɔ; vɔɛ	mid-low	a dog!
				ball		mid-low	a bus!
				aeroplane	ɔɛᵂɔɛ	mid-low	(both) an aeroplane!
				nose	ⁿdou	mid-low	a nose!
		pleasure	general		ɛˠ, i:	mid-low	that's nice
			taste		ʔn̄ŋ	low	that tastes nice
			[?]		ˈgɛgɛgɛ	narrow low	[?]
	withdrawal				gʷʊ---	narrow low	I'm sleepy

* favourite items

? rare or doubtful items

= two or three items related in both meaning and sound

with perhaps something like Nigel's instrumental, regulatory, interactional and personal as particular modes of meaning; and secondly,
the nature of the protolanguage as a system that is different in kind
from adult language, in that it consists of a semantics and a phonology
(or other expressive means) with no lexicogrammar in between. Its
elements are discrete signs, each one being a direct pairing of content
with expression; there are no words, and no structures. The move
into the adult language lies in introducing a new, purely abstract level
of coding as intermediary between the two, so that meanings are
coded as (lexicogrammatical) forms, i.e. words-and-structures, and
these forms are encoded in turn as (phonological) expressions, so opening up the possibility of internal organisation at each of these levels:
a semantic system, a lexicogrammatical system and a phonological system. It is this tristratal organisation of adult language which makes
possible the construction of narrative and dialogue, and the combination of meanings of different kinds into a single integrated
whole.

By the middle of his second year, Nigel is firmly embarked on the
learning of his mother tongue. Appendix 2 gives a specimen of conversation from the day on which he reached eighteen months.

4 The social construction of language

Nigel had reached this point through constant interaction with others;
he had not got there by himself. The three adults in his meaning group
(there were no other children in the family; he interacted with other
children when the occasion arose, thrusting his toys at them and grab-
bing theirs, but as yet made no serious attempt to exchange meanings
with them) were unconsciously tracking his language, understanding
what he meant and responding with meanings of their own. Neither
Nigel nor the others were imitating; but all were participating in the
creation of his meaning potential. By their acts of understanding, the
others shared in Nigel's language at every stage; the language-creating
process was a social one, a product of the interaction between Nigel
and those with whom his experiences were shared in common.

This tracking of a child's language by his mother, and perhaps
others, is a remarkable phenomenon that has been paid very little
notice. It is something that takes place below the level of conscious
awareness; those involved cannot, as a rule, describe what they are
doing, and if the mother, for example, is asked what the child has
been saying she is quite likely to contend that he wasn't saying any-

thing at all — he can't talk yet. Of course he can't talk yet, in the mother tongue. But he is talking in the child tongue; and the mother is responding all the time in a way which can be explained in no other way than as a response to language. There is a direct continuity here from the early pre-linguistic exchanges described by Trevarthen; without noticing it, the mother has moved on with the child, and is responding to his vocal or gestural symbols as readily and as naturally as she did to the smiles and gurgles and other signs of animation that he gave in earliest infancy. At any given moment, she knows what he knows; not only does she understand him, but she knows the limits of his understanding, and talks to him so that he gets the message — not of course the literal message that the adult gets from it, but a message that he can interpret in the light of his own functional resources for meaning. Under favourable conditions this kind of tracking by others, who (again without being aware what they are doing) talk to a child in ways that stretch his understanding without going way beyond it, can persist throughout early childhood, and it probably has a great value for him in developing his linguistic resources, both in learning language and in learning through language.

At no stage is language development an individual matter. Meaning, and learning to mean, are social processes. From the moment of birth a child is one among others, a person among people. The recently dominant theories among linguists and psychologists, the so-called 'nativist' and 'environmentalist' approaches, which were often presented as opposite viewpoints, appear now rather as variants on a single theme, that of the child as an island, an individual existent who has to 'acquire' some ready-made object 'out there' that we call language. There is no need to labour the point that such theories are the product of Western individualist ideology. The important issue at the moment is not so much the particular intellectual model we choose to impose on the language-learning process, as the search for a greater understanding of the nature of early infancy, as we try to interpret the ontogenesis of language: how children begin to exchange meanings, how they construe in the course of their daily interaction a semantic system that gradually approximates to that shared by the others around them, and how while construing it they use it to construe reality — to make sense of their experience and organise it into a picture of the world that is likewise shared with the others. In understanding this we also begin to see more deeply into the nature of language itself, since ultimately language has been shaped by the functions it has to serve in the actions and reflections on reality by a child.

Appendix 1:
Development of Nigel's protolanguage

(a) To nine months

Nigel's first clearly identifiable act of meaning was in the last week of April at just under six months.

He was lying face downwards in his pram. Some pigeons took off noisily into the air. Nigel lifted his head, looked at his mother and said " ' ".

"Those are birds", she said to him. "Big birds. Pigeons. They all flew away."

Nigel's " ' " was a small sound, with no articulation, just a short high rising note. He used this expression frequently over the next three or four weeks, always when there was some kind of commotion around; and the three adults with whom he was in daily contact, his mother, his father and Anna, all took notice — they attended, and they responded. In other words, they interpreted it as an act of meaning. Since it was Nigel's first act of this kind, they were conscious of it and commented on it to each other; moreover they were in agreement as to 'what he meant' — that it could be translated into adult as 'What's that? What's going on?' Considering the nature of the signal this might seem surprising, until one takes account of the fact that, given the assumption that the meaning is contextually relevant (an assumption which they never questioned), there was not much choice. Since Nigel was not 'speaking adult', the question 'Was that what he really meant?' does not arise. He made it clear that he was satisfied with the response.

After a few weeks, Nigel stopped saying " ' ". He had found that he could 'mean' successfully — he could initiate an exchange, and be responded to. He now put meaning aside for a while, to be returned to later. Meanwhile, at six and three-quarter months (24 May) for the first time he laughed at something, the fluttering of a toy bird twirled on a stick; and at seven and a quarter months, just when he had learnt to sit up on his own, he gave his first response: his mother was saying a jingle to him, and Nigel responded by making rhythmic movements with his hands (hands clasped, bending alternate wrists). His first response in the form of an act of meaning came at just under eight months (in the interval on 21 June he had moved himself forward for the first time), when he took part in a conversation; his part was a short half-close front rounded vowel falling mid-low to low, [ø̞]. The conversation went something along these lines: "Nigel!" — "eu" — "Hello bootie!" — "eu" — "There's my bootie!" — "eu", and so on. We could translate Nigel's part as 'yes, we're together', which is more or less the meaning of his mother's part also. Here for the first time Nigel was exchanging meanings; the function of the exchange was interpersonal, a symbolic expression of togetherness.

It was shortly after this that Nigel first carried out a verbal instruction ("Clap hands!"); and at eight months, on the day after he learnt to play the 'dropping'

game, he first acted symbolically on an external object. I was making his toy cat
jump in the air. I stopped; Nigel leant forward, and touched the cat steadily for a
second with his finger, looking at me as he did so. The meaning was clear: 'do
that again'. I did, and Nigel showed he was satisfied. His act of meaning had succeeded.

This was the first instance of a little language that Nigel used for about six
weeks, from eight months (the beginning of July) to around nine and a half
months (the middle of August). The language consisted of five meanings, of
which three were expressed gesturally and two vocally. We could perhaps refer to
these elements as signs. A sign is a content/expression pair, remaining constant
over a period of time, where the expression is some bodily act (which may but
need not be a vocal act) and the content is functional in respect of the child's
intent; it forms part of a systemic set of signs, and its execution constitutes an
act of meaning. At this stage, then, Nigel's language consisted of five signs.

The second to appear was the 'I want' sign, expressed by grasping an object
firmly but momentarily, and then letting go; and this was followed almost
immediately by a contrasting sign 'I don't want', expressed by touching the
object lightly with outstretched finger and then taking the finger away. The contrast between these two was unmistakable. The expressions were, very clearly,
iconic; they were related to the meanings in a non-arbitrary way. Nevertheless
the act was a symbolic act. Nigel was not acting directly on the object itself — he
did not pull it towards him or push it away; he was addressing a person, and he
looked not at the object but at the person he was addressing. On other occasions,
of course, he did grab at objects or push them away, and then he looked at the
objects. What was noticeable was the sharp distinction between the two kinds of
act: the act of meaning, symbolic and person-directed (even though in the case
of 'I want' and 'I don't want' it is object-oriented), and the act projected
directly on to the object. It is interesting that the day on which Nigel first used
the 'I don't want' sign was also the day on which he learnt to demolish, repeatedly
knocking down a tower of beakers that was being built for him.

The fifth of the signs to emerge in this period was one that was expressed
vocally; it was oriented towards the environment, picking up the thread of the
" ' " of two months earlier. There were a number of what might be seen as preparatory steps leading up to this. On 9 July, Nigel first pulled himself up to a
standing position; on 14 July he went on his first voyage of exploration, and on
17 July he first got his knees and tummy off the ground and managed to creep
forward on forearms and toes. It was on that day that he first used this new
exploratory sign: watching birds in flight, when their wheeling movement reached
its peak of prominence, he said [ø̌] — a short half-close front rounded vowel falling mid to low. The expression differed only marginally from the 'togetherness'.
sign, perhaps starting on a slightly higher pitch. But the context, and the function,
were distinct; moreover this sign was addressed partly to himself — sometimes he
switched his gaze between the commotion and the person being addressed, and
sometimes he did not look at another person at all.

In the same week Nigel began playing with a ball, pushing it away from him,
and also trying to put it into a beaker. His language was now as follows:

Meaning	Expression	Function	Orientation
'give me that'	grasping firmly	instrumental	object
'don't give me that'	touching lightly	instrumental	object
'do that (with it)'	touching firmly	regulatory	other person
'yes, we're together'	[ø̰] mid-low to low	interactional	other and self
'look, that's interesting'	[ø̰] mid to low	personal	self and object

It is interesting to note that the distinction between the vocal and the gestural modes of expression anticipates the semantic contrast which will be Nigel's primary strategy for making the transition from protolanguage to adult language (second half of second year). In this later, transitional phase Nigel makes a systematic distinction between utterances of the 'do something' type, demanding a response, and those of the 'I'm learning' type which require no response; the distinction is expressed as an opposition of rising and falling tone:

	Mode of meaning	
	active	reflective
Age (months)	Mode of expression	
9	gestural	vocal
19–24	rising tone	falling tone

The distinction is lost in the intervening period; there is no trace of it in the developed protolanguage (ten to eighteen months). But it is interesting to see as early as nine months a glimpse of what is to become the primary functional contrast not only in Nigel's language-creating strategy but also, eventually, in the adult linguistic system.

(b) Nine to ten and a half months

Nigel could now pull himself up to a standing position; in the week in which he reached nine months he began putting things on things, and one week later made his first (and unsuccessful) attempt at standing one beaker on top of another. At this time his protolanguage underwent a significant change. Around nine and a half months he abandoned the three gestures, replacing them with vocal expressions; and he added a number of new signs, so that by ten and a half months the total had increased to twelve.

The 'I want' sign was now [na̰], usually repeated about four times; but it was never very frequently used. 'I don't want' had disappeared altogether. The 'do that' sign had two variants, a regular [ʒ̰] or [n͡ŋ], very frequent from ten months, and an intensified form [m͡n͡ŋ f] meaning 'do that — I insist!'. The general sign of attention to surroundings was still [ø̰], [œ̰]; but this now became symbiotic with other expressions [bø̰], [d̶ɔ̰], also on low falling tone, which may have originated as imitations of *bird* and *dog* and which were particularly associated with attention to rapid movement: 'look, a commotion'. Two new signs were added, also in the 'personal' realm of meaning but signalling pleasure rather than interest: [à] 'that's nice', and [n̂ŋ̂] 'that tastes good', both again on low falling tone.

In the interactional realm Nigel still had his sign for responding to address, 'yes? here I am'; this tended now to have the lips spread, [ɛ̀] , so that it sounded distinct from the expression of interest, which had the lips rounded. He now added two more. One, which was variously [ʔø̀], [ʔɔ̀], [ɑ̀ɔ] (always glottalised), meant 'nice to see you, and shall we look at this together?'; a favourite utterance, it was used to greet someone, especially someone coming in to see him when he had just woken up, and to create a bond of shared attention, either looking out of the window as the curtains were drawn back, or focussing on a picture, a symbolic object whose only function is to be attended to. The other was an intensified variant of the same thing, a repeated [əŋ̀ŋ̀ŋ̀ʃ] , loud and high falling in pitch, meaning 'nice to see you – and why didn't you get here before?'.

Meanwhile Nigel added one more sign of an 'instrumental' kind, [bø̀] meaning 'I want my bird'. This was Nigel's favourite possession, the same fluttering bird on a stick that he had laughed at some months earlier. It was kept high up on the wall, in sight but out of reach; Nigel would call for it with arms raised and face turning from the bird to the person being addressed: [bø̀, bø̀] . This was presumably an imitation of the adult syllable [bɜ̀:d] *bird*, and probably Nigel's only imitative expression. (If it was an imitation, it was an imitation of the syllable, not the word; Nigel is still far from being capable of abstracting words at this stage. Although this and the 'commotion' sign sometimes overlapped – and the syllable *bird* may have been one of the sources of that also – the two were quite distinct signs, with different meaning and context and different accompanying bodily postures.) The special significance of the bird, its value as a symbol of objectivity and continuity, was reflected in the fact of its being called for by a special sign, never by the sign [nǎ] which had the generalised meaning of 'I want'.

Finally there was the repeated [g̊ʷɤ̌ig̊ʷɤ̌ig̊ʷɤi . . .] , Nigel's version of the 'alternating prosody' that appears almost universally in infant babbling: essentially it is an alternation of the fundamental prosodic values of y and w, vocal postures that form the articulatory basis of contrasting phonological systems in adult languages the world over. The vowel qualities are simply the transitions between these two postures, and the w is often accompanied by some contact in the velar or uvular region, and sometimes glottalic closure. With Nigel the origin of the sound was quite clear: he had heard himself make it while falling asleep, a byproduct of the sucking movement with joint of thumb held against the lips. But instead of merely babbling with this sound, Nigel – who did very little babbling – put it to use in his protolanguage. It still sometimes came out while he was going to sleep; but he usually said it when he was not in his cot but wanted to indicate that he was feeling sleepy. He would curl up on the floor, look at his mother, close his eyes and say [g̊ʷɤ̌ig̊ʷɤ̌ig̊ʷɤi . . .] ; then open his eyes and look at her again. The message was 'I'm sleepy: shut the world out – and maybe someone will put me to bed?'

By this time Nigel could understand various sets of utterances addressed to him by the three adults with whom he exchanged meanings, his 'meaning group' of significant others:

Utterance type	Example	Nigel's response
where's . . . ?	Where's the window?	looked at it
	Where's teddy's eye?	pointed to it
go and get your . . .	Go and get your bib	fetched it
game routines	Round and round the garden	held our hand, palm upwards
do you want . . . ?	D'you want your bird?	smiled, sighed

Meanwhile at ten months Nigel had taken his first steps forward, holding on to someone or something, and had tried, unsuccessfully, to stand without support; the following week he managed to sit down voluntarily from a standing position. He now for the first time 'waved' goodbye — actually opening and closing his fist, with elbow bent and forearm pointing up. His only other gesture was a demand for music ('sing a song' or 'put a record on'), which he expressed by beating time with one arm, sometimes accompanied by the regulatory sign [ɜ̰́].

Summary of Nigel's protolanguage at ten and a half months.

Meaning	Expression	Function	Orientation
'give me that'	nã̀ . . . mid to low	instrumental	object
'give me my bird'	bø̀ mid to low	instrumental	favourite object
'make music'	gesture: beating time	instrumental	service
'do that'	ɜ̰́ , n̂ŋ mid to low	regulatory	other person
'do that — I insist'	m̂nŋ *f* high to low	regulatory	other person (intensified)
'yes? here I am'	ɛ̀ low	interactional	other and self (response)
'nice to see you; and let's look at this'	ʔø̀ , ʔɔ̀ , ɖ̀ɔ̀ mid to low	interactional	other and self (mediated by object)
'nice to see you — at last!'	əǹ̖ǹ̖ǹ̖ *f* high to low	interactional	other and self (intensified)
'goodbye'	gesture: opening and closing fist	interactional	other and self
'that's interesting'	ø̀, œ̀ mid-low to low	personal	self: cognitive
'look, a commotion'	bø̀ , ɖ̀ɔ̀ , ø̀ mid-low to low	personal	self: cognitive (prominence)
'that's nice'	à mid-low to low	personal	self: affective
'that tastes nice'	n̂ŋ̀ mid-low to low	personal	self: affective (taste)
'I'm tired'	g̊ʷɤi . . . low	personal	self: withdrawal

(c) Ten and a half to twelve months

At eleven months Nigel was able to get to his feet by steadying himself against a flat surface, such as a door or a wall, and to roll over and over continuously. He now fed himself for the first time, holding the spoon in his fist; one day he helped himself to an apple from the fruitbowl and tried unsuccessfully to gnaw it (he was just getting his second tooth). Next day was his first 'disobedience', the rejection of an act of meaning addressed to him: being told not to scratch the table, he went on doing so, looking expectantly at his mother for her response.

He still asked for his toy bird [bɵ̀], [vɵ̀], and now added another specific demand 'I want some powder (on my hands, so that I can hit the drums)'; this was a string of syllables [ɡə̀bʷɡ̀əbʷ ...] ("gabugabu ... " or "bugabuga ... ") in imitation of my ritual *a little bit of powder!* The general demand 'I want — ' was still [nà̰ ...] ; and both [ɟ̰̀] and its intensified form [m̄nn̄ŋ] were very frequent as the means of getting people to do things, usually forms of entertainment such as bouncing him on one's knee, making his rabbit jump in the air or tapping different objects to see what noise they made. Such expansion in his protolanguage as there was at this stage was mainly in the interactional and personal areas, and in responses.

Nigel now frequently expressed his personal involvement with his surroundings. As a sign of general interest, [ɵ̰̀] was now being replaced by [ɗɔ̀] or [dɛ̀ə], 'look!', the former being his own 'invitation to share attention' and the latter possibly an imitation of *there*. He now added signs for specific interest in various kinds of commotion: [ɗɔ̀] 'a dog commotion' (barking), [œ̀œ̀] 'an aeroplane commotion' (noise of aircraft overhead), and — being excited at the sight of a football game, with people running in all directions — [bɔ̀], [vɔ̀] 'a ball commotion'. As a sign of pleasure, [ɛˠiː] replaced [à] in the general sense of 'I like — ', [n̄ŋ] still being reserved for taste (and gradually disappearing). When he had had enough of the outside world, he shut it out with [ɡ̀ʷɤi ...] .

The form [dɔ̀] was still used as greeting: 'nice to see you; let's look at this picture together'. It was now used when the other person was already present, simply as a means of interaction. Nigel had a little board book of coloured pictures; he pointed to a picture, looked at the other person and said [ɗɔ̀] 'let's look at this'. This was the first step in the separation of the two components of interaction and attention; in this same context, Nigel introduced a new expression [ɛ̀ˠa] which was oriented less towards the other person and more towards the picture — the other person being invited to say its name, "Yes, it's a rattle". Here was the first intimation of the connection of a sign with (the demand for) a name; and Nigel sometimes used this same expression when something was named as it was being given to him: "Here's a rusk for you" — [ɛ̀ˠa] 'that's what it is (and that's what I wanted)'. It is interesting to note that in the same week Nigel used a personal name for the first time: [ānnā]. It was a greeting to Anna, and it was unique in being on a high level tone instead of the falling tone that was characteristic of all his other signs.

Nigel was now beginning to respond to acts of meaning with acts of meaning of his own. He had done this from the start in a context of simple interaction, responding to his mother's call, he still used [ɛ̀] in this sense, and now added an intensified variant [à:: *ff*], a raucous yell which he used only to respond when called from somewhere out of sight. But he now started responding in other contexts too — provided the response came within his functional competence, such

that the meaning was one that he could himself initiate. He could not respond to
a question seeking information, because he could not himself offer information,
and it would be the best part of a year yet before he could use language in an
informative function. But he could initiate acts of meaning with a sense of 'I
want'; and just before eleven months he learnt to respond verbally to offers, acts
of meaning by others where the response called for from him was '(yes) I want',
such as "Do you want a drink?" and "Shall I sing you a song?" Previously his
response to these had been a smile, together with a general bodily expression of
satisfaction; now he began to accompany these with a long breathy [ɛ̀ːː] on a
low falling tone. This was, in origin, a sigh, part of the total bodily response;
Nigel frequently sighed as a relaxing of concentrated attention when the attention had been rewarded. He now turned this into a linguistic sign, meaning 'yes,
that's just what I wanted!'

This step of turning a natural response into a symbolic one seemed to open
up for Nigel the potential of responding as a mode of meaning, and he now began
to use expressions that had hitherto served to initiate, in a responding sense also.
[nã̀...] is beginning to disappear, and is never used in this way; but the regulatory [ʒ̀] comes to function — without accompanying smile — in a response context, especially where some joint activity is suggested: 'Shall we go out for a walk?'
— [ʒ̀] 'yes let's'.

The long-drawn-out [ɛ̀ːː] still persists, and shortly afterwards it occurs in a
new setting. At just under twelve months, on the day Nigel first stood up on his
own, and first managed to put a holed disc on to a stick, he was turning over the
pages in his board book, looking carefully at each picture and saying [ɛ̀ʸa] as he
did so. He looked at me expectantly and, to make the meaning perfectly clear,
took hold of my finger and pressed it gently on to the picture: [ɛ̀ʸa]. "It's a
ball", I said. "E - e - eh!" — 'yes, *that's* what I wanted you to do'.

Nigel's responses now give some indication of the extent of his understanding
of the speech that is addressed to him. He can respond to a range of offers, such
as those mentioned earlier, with a 'yes please do that'; and to various instructions,
such as 'sing a song', by carrying them out. He shows understanding of particular
words: hearing "aeroplane", he said [œ̀ʷœ̀] ; hearing "big noise", he made one.
He now 'waves' (right hand raised, fingers opening and closing on palm) not only
on leaving, seeing someone getting ready to leave, or seeing them return, but also
in response to the word "byebye". Asked "Where's Nigel's nose?", he touches it.
Such situations were not entirely without ambiguity. On one occasion Nigel gave
his 'big noise' yell, apparently out of context; his mother looked startled, then
realised something she had just said, and laughed. "I said *nose*, not *noise*", she
said. Nigel gave a very convincing impression of being embarrassed by his mistake.

Appendix 2:
Specimen of Nigel's conversation on the day
he reached eighteen months

Nigel is sitting on the kitchen shelf having his syrup. He finds an old piece of rusk. [əɹòu] ('rusk') he says happily, starting to nibble it.

"You don't want more rusk after all that tea!" says his mother.

Nigel looks hopefully at the bottle of syrup. [nōumɔ̀] he says, slowly and deliberately.

This is a routine, and his mother responds appropriately. "No — more because — Dr — Thompson — said — no — more than — one — teaspoonful for a — little — boy!" She points to a bowl of fruit. "Now this is apricots and you'll have some tomorrow for tea."

[ɛ̀bkɔ]. This is a reasonable imitation of "apricots".

His mother lifts him down, and he runs to the front door. [dɔ̀] ('door'), he says five times, meaning 'I want to go outside'. She opens the door of the apartment, and Nigel runs out to the front door, just opposite. It is getting dark. Through the window at the side Nigel can see a clear sky, with the moon and stars.

[dà] ('stars'), he says. He points to the moon. [adᵛdà] ('what's that?'). "That's the moon", his mother says.

[mū:] ('moo!'). This is Nigel's imitation of an adult imitation of a cow.

"No it's not what the cow says", says his mother. "It's 'moon', not 'moo'!"

The cat appears. [bæ̀:] says Nigel ('pussy!'). [bæ̀:]

"Yes that's the pussycat."

Nigel looks hopefully at the main door. [nōumɔ̀], he says.

"No, we're not going out of the house any more today."

[nōumɔ̀] (nine times).

The end of the day; Nigel's mother is putting him to bed. "And when you get up in the morning, you'll go for a walk", she says.

[tìkᵃwa]

"And you'll see some sticks, yes."

[lòu]

"And some holes, yes."

[dà] (three times)

"Yes, now it's getting dark" (but he may have meant 'and I'll see the star' — a large poster he passes by in the street).

[ɔ̀] (thirteen times) ('I want')

"What?" says his mother.

[ɔ̀] (seven times); then plaintively [ōɔ́] ('please!')

"What do you want in bed?"

[ɔ́:]

"Jamie?" (his doll)

[ʒ̀ʒ̀] ('no!')

189

"You want your eiderdown!"
Nigel grins. [ɛ̀ːː] ('yes that's it!')
"Why didn't you say so? Your eiderdown!"
[àilə] (three times) ('eiderdown')
"There you are!"
Nigel clutches it contentedly, thumb in front of mouth.
[g̊ʷɤig̊ʷɪg̊ʷɤi] ('now I'm going to sleep')
He says a few last words to himself. [bà] (three times) ('buses'). [bɪ̵] (?)
[r̩ɪ̀GˣɔGˣɔ] (' and the weathercock') [dɵ̀] ('and stones') [tìkwa] ('and sticks')
[dà] ('and the star').

With this inventory of the sights of the day, or perhaps of the morrow, he falls
asleep.

9

Thickening thin data: the maternal role in developing communication and language[1]

KENNETH KAYE
University of Chicago

1 History

To many students of child speech . . . it seems that the linguistic data available to the child are so thin that we can only account for his knowledge by assuming that it is, in substantial degree, innate. It is possible, however, that the surface data seem as thin as they do because they are imagined in too static a form, as a set of still photos, unconnected model sentences. It may be as difficult to derive a grammar from unconnected sentences as it would be to derive the invariance of quantity and number from the simple look of liquids in containers and objects in space. The changes produced by pouring back and forth, by gathering together and spreading apart are the data that most strongly suggest the conservation of quantity and number. The changes produced in sentences as they move between persons in discourse may be the richest data for the discovery of grammar. (Brown 1968: 287–8)

In the decade since Roger Brown's Presidential Address to Division 8 of the American Psychological Association, these words have had remarkably little effect upon the way language development has been studied. The handful of investigators who have made parent–child discourse their subject of study have restricted themselves almost exclusively to analysis of mothers' utterances out of context (e.g. Snow 1972; Friedlander et al. 1972; Phillips 1973; Holzman 1974; Newport 1977; and unpublished studies reviewed by Slobin 1975) or limited types of contingency in verbal interaction (Cazden 1965; Brown et al. 1968; Brown & Hanlon 1970).

Recently a number of authors have discussed mother–child communication more generally, with language coming to be seen as essentially a subset of communicative skills, the development of language depending upon the prior development of communication itself (Bruner 1975b; Halliday 1975; Harris 1975; Lieven 1978, Moerk 1975; Riegel 1975). Our current work falls within this new tradition. In each of the papers just listed the evidence is extremely thin, and this chapter summarizes some recent attempts to thicken it.

What interests us about language is not grammar, but those features which linguistic skills share with communicative performance in general. Those features are also found in mother—infant discourse over the first year of life. While not explaining the development of language, this fact provides a new source of data by which our hypotheses may be enriched.

The *language-learning capacities* of our species have obviously been provided by evolution. *How* these capacities evolved is a question I cannot deal with; but *what* the capacities are, what it is with which we are endowed that makes language development possible, is what I take to be the question motivating a search for the precursors of language in infancy.

To find nothing in early communication but protolanguage and precursors of language would be virtually devoid of explanatory value. It is self-evident that everything one observes in adult language has an origin, and if one defines a phenomenon sufficiently broadly and vaguely one can always see some manifestation of it or analogy to it, in infancy or perhaps in the womb. Taken by itself this tells us nothing about the process by which the early form comes to be the later form. In fact it need not be the case that the formal similarity has any psychological, developmental reality at all.

Hence what should be looked for is neither linguistic *genius* in the human infant nor linguistic *training* in the human environment. Rather it is developmental *process*. Pre-speech communication, which is a matter of changing patterns of interaction over the whole course of the first year, is of interest because, among other things, it enables the child to *learn* language. Instead of looking at the complexity of human language and shaking our heads at how the child can ever master it, and rather than assuming that he is in some absurd sense born knowing it already, I would rather acknowledge that natural languages are just those, among the infinity of languages we might imagine, which happen to be very easy to learn given the developmental processes with which evolution has supplied us. While it is conceivable that the nature of language and the characteristics of specific languages exert some effects upon mother—infant interaction, I would emphasize the opposite point. It is almost a corollary of Darwinism: only those natural languages could have survived which happened to lend themselves to acquisition by one- to three-year-olds.

That this is an overlooked but potentially fruitful way of looking at language development may be illustrated with respect to the issue of 'critical period'. No satisfactory answer has been found to the question: what is there about the physical structure of the brain which makes it brilliant at acquiring language between the ages of one and ten, but rather stupid thereafter? Suppose instead we ask (among other questions): what is there about the behavior of the child in relation to other people which makes a certain kind of rule-learning possible in the early years and more difficult given his later modes of interacting?

Further, I would assume that developmental processes inhere in the social systems of which the infant is only a part, rather than in the infant himself. What it means to say that *homo sapiens* evolved as a linguistic creature is that processes of skill transmission evolved, largely depending upon interaction with the mother, which are fundamentally unlike anything occurring in other species.

Although the actual materials upon which evolutionary processes can work are those of the two organisms mother and child, as separate entities (reproductive physiology, neonatal reflexes, sensory and motor pathways etc.), the explanation for evolutionary changes at the level of each partner's behavior can be found only in the fit between the two — and more precisely, in the development of the individuals through interaction with one another. What is true of the newborn whale, kangaroo and penguin and of the newly hatched duckling is as true of the human. It is neither the baby whale's propensities for swimming nor his mother's propensities for pushing him to the surface which guarantees his survival and his subsequent exposure to the necessary and sufficient experiences for whaleness. It is instead the perfect design of each partner's behavior for the other's.

2 Theses

This chapter will present some findings which I think go beyond the formal correspondence between certain pre-speech communicative behavior of infants and properties of older children's or adults' language. Let me summarize my four claims with respect to these observations.

2.1

Each of the observations is merely suggestive. At the present state of our knowledge it is quite possible none of them has any relevance to the problem of how language develops. For example, they could be aspects of a general process of nonverbal communication, and language proper could be a separate system which begins to develop later, only later becoming coordinated with nonverbal communication. (This is, of course, not our contemporary view; but it is far from having been disproved.)

2.2

The observations, by myself and others, have a good deal of consistency despite their being drawn from a wide domain of ages, response modalities, situations and cultures. They suggest a set of basic processes by which infant and mother in the first year of life prepare and equip themselves for developing a broad range of skills in the second and third. Specifically, without rejecting either of the two broad approaches which have dominated theories of child language — that parents somehow teach language and that children are predisposed to learn it — I would add a third. The one- and two-year-old child has been prepared, by his prior interaction with primary caretakers, both to learn linguistic rules and to elicit instructive material under optimal circumstances for learning.

2.3

These notions can be formulated as testable hypotheses; that is, the idea that the essential skills for learning language develop systematically in mother—infant dyadic behavior is, while not yet proved, a provable or potentially disprovable theory.

2.4

The crucial evidence needed to test such hypotheses will come from studies of *individual differences* in mother—infant interaction and in early language development. There is little more to be learned in this particular area from studies of one, three, or half a dozen children. Formal analogy has its place, but to explain development we must find functional continuity.

3 The evidence

The Columbus Project takes its name from the community hospital in Chicago at which our fifty subjects delivered. We followed these subjects through five observations of mother—infant interaction (one in the hospital and four at home), ending when the infants were six months old; a series of return visits will begin at twenty-two months. Four standard, structured interaction situations form the core of the project, our principal method being microanalysis of sequences and temporal patterns. We are fortunate in that each of these situations is either identical or very similar to those studied by a growing number of other investigators around the world (see for examples Schaffer 1977a).

It is by now a commonplace to say that the avenues of interaction between mothers and infants are two-way streets: each partner adapts to the other over time. However, an important qualification of that theme emerges from the studies I will discuss. The kinds of effect infants have upon their mothers are very different from the kinds of effect which go the other way. The roles of the two partners in the dyad are different.

3.1 Feeding

The first of our observed situations is natural feeding. Kaye & Brazelton (1971) found that while mothers fit their 'jiggling' mainly into pauses between their infants' bursts of sucking and believe that this speeds up the onset of the next burst, in fact the jiggling (of the bottle or baby) tends to have the opposite effect, delaying the next burst. With our present sample we have found that the *cessation* of jiggling elicits a greater than chance probability of onset of sucking within about two seconds (Kaye 1977). This led us to predict that mothers would learn over the first two weeks to shorten their jiggling, changing from a (pause) — (jiggle) — (burst) — (stop jiggling) sequence to a (pause) — (jiggle, stop) — (burst) sequence. The prediction was confirmed for both breast-feeding and bottle-feeding mothers. In observational data, this dyadic phenomenon appears to result from a mechanism in the infant to resume sucking immediately when jiggling stops. A. Wells and I (in preparation) have recently confirmed such a mechanism experimentally, and have shown that the infant's response particularly reinforces his mother's tendency to short jiggling.

The dialogue-like turn-taking which we and others have seen in very early feeding sessions is a matter of the mother's fitting her behavior into the infant's natural rhythms. I have argued (Kaye 1977) that neurological immaturity is the infant's great asset, providing him with biological regularity through which his mother can quickly learn to anticipate his behavior. If it is true that the burst—pause pattern evolved because of its utility in establishing social exchanges between mother and infant, this still does not mean it has the quality of a social exchange from the infant's point of view. It is merely an endogenous cycle, onto which his mother imposes a discrete exchange of turns.

We should not use the term *dialogue* for interaction in which one partner's behavior, and perhaps the other's, too, is at the level of unintentional reflexes. However, the mother behaves *as if* it were a true dialogue. This fiction characterizes a number of her other activities in the first few months (Newson 1977).

3.2 Face-to-face play

The second situation upon which we focus is face-to-face play at six, thirteen and twenty-six weeks. Brazelton et al. (1974) had shown alternative cycling of arousal in five dyads filmed longitudinally through this period. They found individual differences, with a possible connection between the smoothness of cycling in early sessions and the extent to which an infant's attention to his mother increased over the five months. For his dissertation Fogel (1976, 1977) studied behavior within the cycles of attention and activity in a single mother—infant pair between six and thirteen weeks. In addition to the cycles of activity running horizontally in time, we see a vertical hierarchy in which behaviors are nested. Different units of analysis yield what Fogel calls temporal levels, his view being that the mother provides a frame with her gaze containing the infant's attention cycles, and at the same time fits her facial expression into those cycles from the temporal level 'below'.

Stern (1975; Stern et al. 1977) in a similar study has shown the repetitiveness of mothers' kinesic acts and vocalizations. He distinguishes two kinds of repetition: 'content runs', in which an act or utterance recurs in nearly identical form two or more times separated by short pauses, and 'temporal runs', in which different acts or utterances occur, all occupying nearly identical slots of time. Each of these types of 'run' includes roughly two-thirds of the stimuli which an infant gets from his mother (many runs are both temporal and content). Stern argues that this sort of variations-on-a-theme stimulation is optimal for holding the infant's attention. The work of Tronick et al. (1975) illustrates vividly what happens when mothers (with great difficulty) refrain from their normal modes of interaction, and approach their infants with a still face. Infants as young as ten weeks briefly smile and run through their repertoire of facial expressions, limb movements etc., attempting to initiate normal interaction. This failing, they avert their gazes entirely.

The opportunity to view videotapes of some fifty different pairs in face-to-face play impresses one with the consistency of individual mothers' behavior over a twenty-week period. However, the individual consistency appears less in specific responses such as facial exaggeration, tickling, playing with the baby's limbs etc. than in general strategies for interpretation of the task. How a mother conceptualizes the situation we have created for her — what agenda she seems to have for her infant — may vary among mothers, between mothers and fathers, and between cultural/racial groups. J. Callaghan and A. Fogel, under the direction of D.G. Freedman, videotaped twenty Hopi and sixteen Navajo mothers in the face-to-face situation. Freedman and I, together with our students, have been comparing these with the Columbus Project mothers by a variety of micro and macro techniques. One thing we can all agree upon is that our impressions of the three samples vary greatly with the methods by which we examine them. A global impression of a whole session can elude microanalysis, and on the other hand trends in the trees can fail to be validated by a look at the forest. One reason this may be the case is that one needs functional categories in place of or in addition to response categories. Coding 'attempts to provide attractive stimulus' or 'attempts to orient infant's body and head', for example, may prove more meaningful (and even more reliable) than coding the mother's hand movements objectively.

This aspect of our project, even within our Chicago sample, is still at the stage of coding and exploratory analysis. My own current notion is, however, that the two-way communication we see developing over the sessions at six, thirteen and twenty-six weeks involves considerably more subtlety on the mother's part than on the baby's. Let us consider the infant first. He periodically becomes more aroused and less aroused, through self-regulatory processes as well as in response to maternal stimulation (Thomas & Martin 1976). The infant also initiates activity: at six weeks this takes the form primarily of indexing his internal states, but by three months his role of social games takes the form of true signals, and by six months there is much independent exploration.

The mother adjusts her behavior to these developmental changes, but she also makes constant micro-adjustments to changes in her infant *within* each session. She seems to be processing information continuously in three different dimensions.

The first dimension is that of timing. There are moments when one can be sure of a maternal response, even though one cannot predict what it will be. The mother seems to be looking for slots into which she can insert her behavior — and this of course reminds us of jiggling and the burst—pause pattern in sucking. As Fogel (1976) points out, however, the mother's intention is not just to fit into the pattern but to alter it, to prolong the 'on' phase of her infant's attention and activity cycles and to generate in him a response to her. Since she has to act in the relatively short space of time when she can capture and maintain his attention, it is not surprising that in all these studies the best predictor of *when* a mother will respond is the moment when her infant's gaze shifts back to her (Brazelton et al. 1974; Stern 1974b; Fogel 1977).

A second dimension is the infant's arousal. Maternal responses can be classified along a continuum from 'turning on' to 'turning off' the infant. Mothers serve as buffers to keep their infants at moderate levels of arousal, neither too high nor too low. They do this partly for their own convenience and pleasure; but they also do it, I believe, for the same reason that an animal trainer maintains his animals at a moderate level of hunger. Performance and learning depend upon the infant's state, and mothers devote a great deal of energy and vigilance to the maintenance of an optimal state. Whether this is instinctive or a conscious purpose need not concern us here; I present it as a descriptive fact.

A third dimension is the balance between a mother's own agenda and her infant's. In our situation the mother has an idea of what we want, she has tricks which have worked on previous occasions which she wants to show us, and she has intuitions about new things to try. She is also constantly watching and listening for new initiatives from the infant. She imitates vocalizations, smiles, funny faces, tongue protrusions, flurries of limb movement etc. If she can produce or prolong a run of alternations between the infant and herself, she will do

so. When he stops performing his part in this 'dialogue' she may continue hers for a while, like a medic attempting heart resuscitation. It
is mainly when the infant offers nothing for a long time (5—10 seconds) that she goes back to her bag of tricks. Sometimes she will try
to initiate a game whose previous history is unknown to us. (Fogel is
currently gathering data on the introduction and history of social
conventions and games in a few subjects observed frequently.) Sometimes the mother will go back to a game we have seen working earlier
in the session. In each case she is likely to leave spaces between her
own repetitions for the infant to fit into if he can. To paraphrase an
example from the study by Stern et al. (1977), it is not just a matter
of repeated utterances or gestures strung together. The utterances or
gestures alternate with short pauses: 'You're my baby (pause) yes
you are (pause) yeah (pause) mommy's baby (pause) you're mommy's
baby.'

When the mother imitates, it is much more than a mirroring of her
baby. She pulls him from where he is in the direction of her own
agenda for him. For example, there is *maximizing* imitation: baby
opens his mouth and mother exaggeratedly opens her own mouth.
We can read her intention even without hearing the kind of remark
which sometimes accompanies such behavior: 'Yeah, come on, you
can do it.' Or there is *minimizing* imitation: baby begins a cry face
and mother responds with a quick cry face that lasts only an instant
and flows back to a bright expression. We are seeing the mother flash
to where her infant is, and attempt to draw him back to where she
wants him to be. Again, sometimes a vocalization will serve as a gloss
on this behavior: 'No don't cry.' Finally there is *modulating* imitation:
baby whines 'waaaah' and mother responds with the same pitch,
intonation and duration but mellows it to a sympathetic chanting
'awwwww'.

There is an important truth here about imitation. It is never a perfect match, always a variation, in the direction of an individual's personal style, a learner's incompetence or an instructor's agenda.

In this account I have been referring to 'the mother'. Of course
there are many mothers and a major task is to sort out what specific
aspects of their behavior are due to the situation, the infants' ages,
differences in the infants and differences in the mothers. After many
hours of observation, we can report that there are some mothers who
respond on all three of the dimensions listed above, quickly and sensitively. There are others who suffer from insensitivity or inconsistency

with respect to one or more dimensions. It may even be that the mother who is usually out of phase with her infant's own cycles and who fails to leave space for his responses is the same one who tries to achieve an inappropriately high level of excitement and the same one who pushes her own agenda while missing his initiatives.

If this sort of sensitivity versus insensitivity is indeed a consistent discriminator among mothers, does it have any consequences? After all, all of the infants will eventually learn to function in society and to speak English. In our sample the grammatical features of the language acquired by all of the children will be virtually indistinguishable. Still, some will acquire it faster than others. Furthermore the way language is *used* will vary across different dyads, and this in turn may have consequences for socialization and for the kinds of knowledge about the world which the children acquire in their preschool years.

An important observation is that each mother and infant develop a set of games of their own. If these conventional games are the foundation of later communication and language-learning skills, how is it that there are not certain games they all have to learn? Even if we say the games all share certain structural features (and they do), so that it does not matter precisely which ones a mother and infant play, we have still to account for the assiduousness with which each pair practices and perfects its own games, and introduces variations upon familiar themes. Instead of merely sampling the pool of potential games, a dyad goes into depth with particular ones. There is no particular response to a particular stimulus which has to be learned by all members of the species. Instead, what seems to be important is the *process* of conventionalization, the mutual topic-comment, the modularization (Bruner 1973) of dyadic routines of *some* kind, the learning to anticipate when and how a partner's behavior will change.

3.3 Detour reaching

When the infants in our project were six months old we observed them in our third structured situation, a teaching task. We noticed (Kaye 1970, 1976) that when mothers were asked to help their infants retrieve a toy from behind a plexiglass barrier their behavior could be reduced to three basic strategies. Of interest in addition to a mother's predominant instructional strategy was the question of her timing. We have found that the determinant of *when* she responds is the infant's gaze — just as in the face-to-face play studies, except that

CASH RECEIVED   9.95CR

| 1 | 1.3 | STATUS CODES: | OS - TEMPORARILY OUT OF STOCK
OPP - OUT OF PRINT AT PRESENT
NEP - NEW EDITION PREPARING
BDG - BINDING
NUS - NOT FOR SALE IN U.S. | NP - NOT YET PUBLISHED
RP - REPRINTING
OP - OUT OF PRINT
NR - DO NOT RECOGNIZE
NO - NOT OUR PUBLICATION |
| TOTAL QTY. SHIPPED | NET WEIGHT | | | |

ALL CLAIMS FOR SHORTAGES AND DAMAGED BOOKS MUST BE MADE WITHIN 5 DAYS AFTER BOOKS ARE RECEIVED. DO NOT RETURN ANY BOOKS UNLESS AUTHORIZED BY US TO DO SO.

here it is gaze aversion *from* the task which elicits maternal intervention. As in the face-to-face studies, *what* a mother does at these
junctures can vary enormously. We did find one factor affecting the
choice of strategy: the infant's behavior on a pretest. 'Showing' or
demonstration of the reaching path seemed to be the most common
strategy tried to some extent by nearly all mothers. 'Shoving' or
manipulation of the baby's arm and hand around the edge of the
barrier was a typical strategy when the infant had been active and
frustrated on the pretest, while simplification of the task for a gradual 'shaping' strategy was tried when infants had shown no signs of
being close to solution on the pretest, and relatively little interest in
the task. (All these results were previously found in a sample from
Cambridge, Massachusetts on whom we had no longitudinal data.)

In short, mothers use task analysis combined with baby analysis.
The detour reaching situation — and, we believe, instructional interaction in general — is responded to by the mother as if her task were
to adapt the infant's agenda to her own. She tries to meet him where
he is; she accommodates quickly to his behavior changes, but always
her behavior has a direction with respect to his. And success is a question of balance between the two agendas.

I have tried to show that this characteristic of instruction begins in
feeding as well as in play. We believe that, as in the case of the jiggling
behavior described above, mothers learn to be better and better at the
balancing act, though it also matters what kind of infant they have
and what their experience is together. These hypotheses require
analysis of individual differences in a longitudinal study with a fairly
sizeable sample. A great deal could be learned, in addition, if one
could cross mothers and infants temporarily as one would do routinely
with laboratory animals.

In looking for commonalities across studies of mother–infant interaction, one can focus on response modalities or on functional characteristics (just as one can when looking for consistency in individual
dyads). It is interesting that it should be the infant's gaze shifting that
determines so much of the timing of the mother's behavior. This too
may have origins in early feeding: too late in our work mothers' comments began to suggest that their infants' eye openness might explain
why the mothers chose to jiggle in some pauses and not in others.
Robson (1967) pointed out the dramatic changes produced in mothers'
perceptions of their infants at about one month, when eye contact
first becomes established. Collis & Schaffer (1975) have found that

when infants are in seats parallel to their mothers, their direction of
gaze is a strong predictor of where the mothers will look and even
where they will point. This last finding is an important one. It is not
the case that infants look where their mothers tell them to look; yet
mothers behave as if it were the case. They fit their own behavior
into the infant's so that the infant's subsequent behavior will seem to
be a contingent response. This is true in feeding, in face-to-face play
and in instruction. Gradually, the infant does come to fit his behavior
into his mother's dialogue. We still have very little understanding of
how mothers' false beliefs about their infants' behavior come true.

Note that behavior of a particular organ, e.g. the infant's eye and
head movements, can serve to develop far more general types of
behavior, signaling and responding, which are not limited to any
modality. This is exactly how we should expect evolution to have
worked. The adaptive consequences may be structural, system properties of the species; but the means of transmission must begin with
physical material, with the concrete behavior of sensory and motor
organs.

The mother, of course, responds in an unlocalized fashion from
the first. She may jiggle the infant, breast or bottle, stroke his cheek,
tweak his foot or call his name. The infant only gradually comes to
be free of his own fixed responses. He develops from a stage in which
his eye movements are merely interpreted as an index (our evidence
is that contrary to mothers' impressions he sucks better when they
are closed); to a stage when they really are an index and the mother's
behavior with respect to them matters (early face-to-face play); to a
stage when they are interpreted as a signal (later face-to-face play);
to a stage when they really are a signal.

3.4 Imitation

This brings us to imitation, the fourth task in which we have observed
all of our subjects. This observation, too, is made at six months, but I
am the mother. We developed a procedure for eliciting imitation
based on our own idealizations of face-to-face play and of the 'showing' strategy in maternal instruction (Kaye 1971). I alternate my turn
with the infant's turn, letting him control my behavior in the following manner. When he looks me in the eye, I make a series of five 'gold-
fish' movements with my lips; every time his eyes return to mine, I
repeat the 'burst' exactly. This proceeds for as many trials (typically
20—40) as he initiates, without any contingent response to his imi-

tative attempts. The first remarkable result of this method is that virtually all infants pick up the rule of the game, the fact that they can elicit my mouthing at will, within two trials. This knowledge is indicated by their sequence of acts: making their own imitative attempts, then becoming still, glancing at my eyes quickly as though flicking a switch, then looking immediately to my lips in *anticipation* of my response. The second remarkable result is that roughly two-thirds of the six-month-old infants achieve at least one *burst* of mouth movements (median trial number: 10), and one-third give bursts on three or more trials (Kaye & Marcus 1978). This is particularly surprising in view of the fact that the infant cannot see his mouth, and thus gets no feedback as to the correctness of his imitation.

We began analyzing each infant's sequence of imitative movements over trials in the hope of finding a systematic order through which all would move. For example, one immediately sees behavior of the following kinds, all of which can be shown to occur at a higher rate during trials than in the preceding two-minute baseline period: mouth movements, both opening and closing, from the baby's resting position; open—close movements of the hands; tongue movements; and rhythmic bursts of limb movement. We thought there might be some developmental order in these approximations of the model, an 'order of acquisition' (Brown & Hanlon 1970) within a single session. We found evidence for system within each infant's protocol — for example, they often put *mouth* movements together with limb *bursts* on the same trial before moving ahead to *mouth bursts* — but there are many paths to success. If one allows the infant to control the model's timing and his own arousal, his hypothesis-testing and skill-polishing resources by this age are already highly potent.

Our explanation for the infant's ability to imitate mouth movements without feedback from me is that he has already engaged in mouthing games with his mother and father, who have imitated his behavior in much the same way as he now imitates mine. This is an hypothesis which we can test using our longitudinal sample. At one level we must look for predictors of imitative success in the general smoothness and richness of face-to-face play at earlier sessions. At another level, however, in this case one must also predict specifically from mouthing games in the earlier sessions. Thus our ability to test this particular hypothesis depends upon the adequacy with which three videotape sessions sample the games in which mothers and infants engage daily.

4 Discussion

The unanswered question in the imitation study is precisely the same as in the other studies described here: how does the infant come to be able to make the kinds of contingent response to adults, which adults have been making to him over the preceding months? What am I to conclude when an eighteen-month-old, trying to put a raisin in my closed mouth, opens her own mouth exactly as mothers do when feeding their babies? Or when twenty-four-month-olds in a dissertation by Poppei (1976) use showing, shoving and shaping to teach eighteen-month-olds, with whom they have interacted for only 15 minutes in an unfamiliar playroom, how to operate a cookie dispenser?

The infant begins life with the capacity to elicit certain instructive kinds of behavior from adults. Somehow he gradually takes upon himself some of the aspects of the adults' role in interaction: imitation, adjustment of timing etc. This in turn gives him even finer control over adults' behavior, so that he gains further information and more and more models of motor skills, of communication, eventually of language. By the time his representational and phonemic systems are ready to begin learning language, he is already able to make his intentions understood most of the time, to orient himself in order to read and interpret others' responses, to elicit repetitions and variations. We are back to Brown's (1968) insights.

What we can add, on the basis of the recent studies of mother–infant interaction, is that there is a fundamental asymmetry of mother and child roles. In this paper I have discussed five asymmetries: (1) the mother's superior flexibility with respect to her own timing and anticipation of the infant's fairly regular cycling; (2) her agendas for the infant, always pulling him forward developmentally along a kind of intuitive curriculum; (3) her ability to monitor and code his changes of expression rapidly, switching gears and seizing opportunities for imitation; (4) her flexibility in substituting alternative means towards ends, as compared with the infant's relative fixedness in certain response modalities; and (5) her creativity in introducing variations in her own repetitions and in her part of the dyadic game. The last may be the most important, encompassing the other four. I have suggested elsewhere (Kaye 1977) that mothers violate conventions which are working well, just to test their own hypotheses that the apparent contingencies are real ones. The effect is to introduce disequilibrium for both partners, providing the raw materials for further negotiation

of conventions. Thus the process of differentiating dyadic schemata
is at least as important as the schemata themselves.

Our imitation paradigm is a kind of tissue culture for testing the
infant's capacities at a given age with the 'mother' held constant. It is
far too simple to be a model of how real mothers ever behave. Some
time ago L. Minnerly and I conducted an experiment in which mothers
were asked to read illustrated sentences to their two-and-a-half-year-
olds, alternating their own reading with pauses in which the children
could respond. We are still analyzing transcripts of these sessions, which
were taped daily over the course of a week. Pertinent to the studies
discussed above is the fact that every mother adapted our instructions
to her own style. Timing, motivation and balance of agendas seem to
characterize different mothers' responses to the task, and what can
be considered 'optimal' at any time in each of these dimensions may
be directly related to what the child has already achieved in his
language development.

We are therefore including the sentence-imitation procedure along
with spontaneous speech samples in our Columbus Project visits in
the third year. Will the mothers who had difficulty with timing,
arousal and the balancing of agendas in the first half-year of life still
have difficulties of the same kind? Will there be a chance for dyads
to succeed in their language interactions, even if they were relatively
unsuccessful in infancy? Or will patterns already be established, with
some dyads firmly on an upward spiral and others doomed downward?
Perhaps most important, will the child's own abilities to imitate, to
elicit imitations, expansions, and extensions, to make himself understood and to generalize linguistic rules depend in any way upon the
nature of his prior communicative experience?

The reader must regard this paper as an early observation, and
engage in longitudinal analysis of our theoretical development. This
will require patience over a period of years, for our conceptualizations
of the processes of communication between infants and adults necessarily develop more slowly than the processes themselves. It is half a
century since G.H. Mead wrote:

Gestures, if carried back to the matrix from which they spring, are always found
to inhere in or involve a larger social act of which they are phases. In dealing with
communication we have first to recognize its earliest origins in the unconscious
conversation of gestures. Conscious communication — conscious conversation of
gestures — arises when gestures become signs, that is, when they come to carry
for the individuals making them and the individuals responding to them, definite

meanings or significations in terms of the subsequent behavior of the individuals making them; so that, by serving as prior indications, to the individuals responding to them, of the subsequent behavior of the individuals making them, they make possible the mutual adjustment of the various individual components of the social act to one another, and also, by calling forth in the individuals making them the same responses implicitly that they call forth explicitly in the individuals to whom they are made, they render possible the rise of self-consciousness in connection with this mutual adjustment. (G.H. Mead 1934: 69)

Note

1. The research project described here has been funded by generous grants from the Spencer Foundation, and made possible by Richard Nachman MD and the staff of Columbus Hospital. I am also grateful to Alan Fogel, Lynn Barker, Janet Marcus, Lucia Minnerly, David Schwartz and Anne Wells for their collaboration in the studies discussed.

10

The growth of shared understandings
between infant and caregiver[1]

JOHN NEWSON
University of Nottingham

As the mother smiles when her child smiles . . . and clucks in response to his first
playful babbling, the child learns the world is a place in which people can recipro-
cate moods and meanings. (Mead & Hayman 1965: 18)

1 Theoretical considerations

Most of what a human infant learns is learned in the context of an ongoing, dynamic social interaction process. The inanimate environment,
in and of itself, provides the infant with only the most impoverished
stimulus towards an understanding, in human terms, of the world in
which he finds himself. It is, for example, noteworthy that up to
six months of age an infant may appear to be 'blind' to stationary
objects, even when they are clearly within his field of view. For
instance, a brightly coloured cube on a black table top may be stared
at and reached for only when special attention is drawn to it, and this
is normally done by jiggling it about or rattling it on the table top. It
is as if, in order to attract the infant's attention, an object must be
made artificially mobile, 'lively' and noise-producing, which is usually
accomplished by associating it with the mobile and lively human hand.
Certain types of spontaneously occurring events may momentarily
dominate the infant's attention or cause him to react in a quasi-reflex
manner, but a mere description of the classes of events which dominate
and hold an infant's sustained attention quickly leads one to the conclusion that the infant is biologically tuned to react to *person*-mediated
events, these being the only events he is likely to encounter which will
be phased, in their timing, to coordinate in a non-predictable or non-
redundant way with his own activities and spontaneous reactions. Pre-
programmed with some kind of sensitivity towards reciprocal social
interaction, the human infant undoubtedly is; but the very nature of
this pre-programming implies that within weeks — and perhaps within

days or mere hours — after birth, he is embarked upon the never-ending programme of social inter-communication with other self-conscious, intelligent and, above all, communicating human beings.

Much recent research in the field of infant perception has been directed towards discovering what features of an 'object' will make it naturally interesting or attention-compelling for a baby. The gist of this may be summed up by suggesting that the most obviously attention-commanding object will be a mobile, self-deforming, brightly coloured and noise-emitting device. Thus other living organisms will tend to monopolise the visual attention of a young baby whenever they come within his visual range. Responsive human caregivers, however, have an important additional stimulus property, which is that they tend to react selectively depending upon the immediately preceding activities of the baby himself. A mother's activity is thus by no means random with respect to the infant's own actions, and it is this simple fact of contingent reactivity which makes her an object of absolutely compelling interest to her baby.

1.1 Human babies become human beings because they are treated as if they already were human beings

Whenever grown-ups react sensitively towards a human infant, they do so by monitoring the moment-to-moment shifts in the child's own apparent interests; and, in so far as they impute to the baby meaningful intentions towards objects or meaningful gestures towards themselves, such as they naturally expect from other human beings, they time their interventions or gestures in ways which are reciprocally patterned. They make the assumption that the infant is attempting some form of meaningful dialogue, and out of this assumption the communication of shared meanings gradually begins to take place.

What is being suggested is that the human infant is biologically pre-programmed to emit 'signals', and that these signals are of such a kind that his mother will inevitably pay attention to them. She is equally bound to endow them with social significance. This insight does not rest upon mere speculative, armchair assertion. On the contrary, it derives from attempts we have made to analyse and describe the precise nature of mother—infant interactions as we have observed them, especially when we have used slowed-down audio-visual recordings. Human babies, right from birth — and even from well before birth — are biologically organised in certain very complex ways; and this complexity of organisation is no less striking in the field of behaviour

than it is in the field of anatomical brain growth and development. It
is misleading to suggest that behaviour ever issues from an infant as
an unpatterned or random event sequence. On the contrary, the
striking fact about infant behaviour is that it is so perfectly articulated
to serve functionally appropriate biological ends.

The infant emits potential behavioural statements which seem to
emerge pre-punctuated. Despite the biological immaturity of the
human baby at birth, his behaviour — like that of all living organisms
— comes pre-packaged in the sense that it is parcelled up in discrete
temporal chunks. Trevarthen (this volume), like ourselves, has analysed
slowed-down audio-visual recordings of human infants reacting to
objects and to their own mothers, and we fully endorse his conclusion
that infant behaviour always consists of chains of extremely brief but
quite distinct 'episodes', and that, in practice, these episodes take the
form of potential gestures which often last only for a second or two,
but which, within this time span, are none the less very highly organised as sequences of coordinated actions. Movements of head, eyes
and eyebrows, hands and fingers, arms and legs, together with vocalisations, are all beautifully articulated and synchronised. It is as if the
baby is already fluent in some universal organismic language of gesticulation long before he can interpret the significance of similar signs in
the behaviour of other organisms. As Trevarthen suggests, we are
probably able to begin communicating with babies right from the
moment of birth, for the same reason that we are able to communicate with each other and even, up to a point, with organisms of an
entirely different species from ourselves. Certainly this would account
for the strange fact that a human child can 'talk' to a cat nose-to-nose
and that when this happens the cat seems to respond appropriately to
what the child is 'saying'.

At birth, therefore, the human infant seems to be exceptionally
well endowed with those psycho-biological characteristics which
should suggest to us that social interaction and social communication
are destined to play a very special role in the whole course of human
psychological development. It is also important to add to this insight
the simple fact that human infants are utterly dependent upon the
ministrations of adult human beings for their physical survival, because
this in turn means that the social experience to which all infants are
naturally exposed is one in which one member of the interacting pair
is a highly sophisticated and culturally competent individual, whereas
the other is culturally completely naive.

1.2 'Mothering' as a communication skill

The viewpoint expressed in this paper is explicitly intended to take
account of the fact that, in the human case, cultural transmission
from generation to generation supersedes hereditary transmission
through the gene pool.

In opposition to the more conventional standpoint, we are suggesting furthermore that, in the case of the infant's own biological mother,
the naturalness of her behaviour resides not in any special maternal
intuition or instinctive heightened sensitivity towards babies, which
cannot be shared by other human beings: instead, it resides in the cultural assignment of responsibility for the welfare of her own offspring,
a cultural and moral imperative to behave with loving kindness and
tender concern towards a vulnerable, utterly helpless and dependent
member of one's family — to be human to one's own flesh and blood,
at the very least, if one is to be considered as human in the eyes of
one's fellow men.[2] Beyond this, however, sensitivity in communicating with any particular baby is very much a matter of practice in
communicating with that baby. Communicating with babies is
obviously possible long before the magic day when the child utters
his first spoken word. What is not so obvious is that it is a learned
skill available to anyone who is concerned to master it with any particular baby, i.e. by anyone who is motivated to make the necessary
effort and to give up the necessary time to establish a working dialogue
with one particular human infant.

What is called maternal intuition — a specialised form of social
responsiveness towards babies — seems, upon analysis, to be little
more than a form of the ordinary social responsiveness which all adult
human beings practise towards one another in intimate social intercourse. Of course, as Trevarthen emphasises, there must be a built-in
or biologically based foundation for this, as for any other functionally
useful behaviour; but it is equally important to emphasise that most
human beings are capable of responding socially towards other members of the human race, and that it is for this reason that mothers are
capable of responding socially towards their babies. All they need to
do is to credit them with human qualities and sensitivities and react
to them as potential human beings. It is the quality and consistency
of the attention-giving which matters, but the quality can be guaranteed simply by crediting the immature infant with having thoughts,
feelings and intentions much like all other members of the human

species. It is probably true that in the human case even a hoary old male of the species (e.g. a grandfather) could make a passable job of bringing up a human infant, so long as he followed the rule of crediting the infant with human sensitivities and potentialities, as a being whose wishes must be understood and respected even if not always met. Men can, and do, pick up babies to comfort them when they cry; with the decline of breast feeding, a human mammary gland is clearly no longer essential for feeding the baby. Men can certainly amuse babies, talk to them and play games with them, change their nappies, bring up their wind, detect if they are uncomfortable, rock them to sleep, sing them lullabies, kiss them tenderly and murmur sweet nothings in their ears. The major factor that prevents more men from adopting a complete 'maternal' role seems to be the fact that this role is normally culturally assigned to females, so that men are under social pressure to spend their time in different culturally approved pursuits, e.g. working at a desk, playing games in committees or fiddling about with machines. To make a man into an acceptable 'mother', it would probably be essential, within our cultural setting, to ensure that he and those with whom he was in social contact saw his baby-minding as his prime social responsibility. Possibly not as big a proportion of men as of women would be fully successful in bringing up emotionally healthy children, but the presumed biological risks connected with allowing men to function as caregivers for infants have probably been grossly overrated. It is normally the biological mother who carries this continuing responsibility for helping the human baby to become a humanly responsive member of the human society into which he is born, but this is partly for historical and practical reasons connected with the way our society is organised. It is not a simple matter of biological necessity.

The skill of baby caretaking lies in a sustained and moment-to-moment monitoring of what works, when one tries to stimulate and hold a particular young child's attention or to alleviate his distress. Furthermore, 'what works' rapidly comes to depend upon the unique social history of any given individual baby.

From birth, a mother interprets her baby's reactions by a process of adultomorphism; in other words, the infant is assumed to have fully human powers of social responsiveness: with wishes, intentions and feelings which can be communicated to others and which must, within limits, be respected. Furthermore, the baby's response 'tells her' whether or not any given interpretation which she makes is 'correct'. The baby mouths; is he perhaps hungry? If he rejects the nipple the answer is 'no'. Some alternative hypothesis leads the mother to try something else. This is also very reassuring for her, because she very soon realises that her baby can communicate most of his immediate needs to her in this simple way and in minute detail. The process does not, of course, imply that the baby is conscious of his own desires, or of his ability to communicate his needs. The mother is constantly monitoring her baby. The baby is not capable of monitoring his mother's behaviour in the same way, yet he is none the less constantly modifying his mother's response patterns to meet his own idiosyncratic needs.

The social programming to which an infant is subjected is continuous and cumulative. In an entirely natural way, anyone who cares about and cares for a human infant will find himself using interest-creating and interest-holding strategies, negatively to alleviate the baby's frustrations and discomforts, and positively to entertain and divert him. The infant, for his part, will respond initially with various pre-programmed proto-social gestures like smiling, intent and interested looking, crying, or satisfied sucking or snuggling, soon to be followed by active demanding and attention-seeking patterns in which attempts to attract or solicit caregiver attention rapidly become unmistakably deliberate and intentional. Babies very soon learn to operate as powerful social manipulators of those who care about and care for them: hence the perennial arguments among busy mothers about whether it spoils a baby to pick him up every time he cries.

1.3 Human caregivers programme social shared meanings and intentions into babies

During the first year, the establishment of a dialogue between a human infant and those who care for him throughout his waking life seems to be a matter of critical and fundamental importance. The mother or caregiver both reads in and then reads out meanings and intentions as significant factors which make the baby's behaviour intelligible to her. Initially, perhaps, the meanings are imputed and assumed before the baby himself recognises them or their significance. Over and over again, events which are at first only the results of automatic action patterns, or which are even quite accidental and beyond the control of either mother or child, are endowed with significance because of the way the mother reacts towards the child in the light of the event and its effect upon him. Any event which the mother knows to have significance and meaning in her own experience, she naturally assumes could come to have a similar significance and meaning to the baby himself. If the baby startles and cries to a loud noise, she assumes he is frightened and will convey some of this meaning in her attempt to comfort him. If the baby smiles, she assumes he is pleased at something – possibly at her own approach. If he spits out food, she reads the implied message that he does not want it, and, if he grimaces in a certain way at the same time, that he actively dislikes what he has been offered. The baby will automatically emit facial expressions which his mother can readily interpret. It is characteristic not only that he yawns, sneezes, coughs and spits out food, but also that he is pre-programmed to do these things in a highly articulate and adult-like way (Darwin 1872). Possibly it is irrelevant that the meaning of his own behaviour is not initially clear to the child himself; but it is a matter of supreme importance that meaning is imputed in some reliable and consistent way, because without this the human dialogue could never begin (Spitz 1957).

It is perhaps fortunate that in the case of normal healthy infants much of the initiative for establishing this pre-verbal dialogue will also tend initially to be highly situation-specific and situation-dependent. For example, the child suddenly arrests the ongoing pattern of his play activity in response to a new noise such as a car passing outside. His mother takes her cue from this shift in his attention to mark or 'comment' on his reaction by indicating that she too has noticed the intrusive noise. Perhaps she picks up the child to let him look out of the window and see the car as it disappears down the road, while the continuing noise of its engine gradually fades. The maintenance of communication in an incident of this kind is only accomplished by the fact that one of the two communicating persons is socially sensitive to the effect of what is happening to the other, moment by moment. The child's response needs to be monitored and adjusted to throughout the time when communication is occurring, whether it is one of fear, delight, frustration or indifference. It has to be reacted to in some appropriate way in order that the dialogue may be sustained. Only through this delicate ballet of action and reaction between a more experienced and a less experienced human communicator can shared meanings be arrived at.

The communication sequence just described was triggered by some fortuitous extraneous event. Other events may occur equally accidentally within the child's own body, as when the child sneezes and his mother reacts to his surprise by saying 'bless you'. Similarly, if he trips and falls she says 'Oh dear' or 'ups-a-daisy' accompanied by suitable gestures of concern for his discomfiture. Still other events may occur as a result of the child's more voluntary acts, such as when he knocks down a tower of bricks which clatter all round him. In this case, social mediation may at first sight seem to be rather irrelevant — except that the child's interest in such an event will rapidly wane unless he can find some human agent who will erect a tower of bricks for him to knock down again and again, just as his interest in throwing things from his pram will be greatly enhanced if some indulgent adult is present to pick them up and return them to him. These games in which the child can share with someone else the anticipation of some simple and predictable sequence of events under his own voluntary control are universally popular with children during the second half of the first year of life. Their importance is that they imply a high level of shared meaningful communication at a completely nonverbal level.

Last but not least, there are events which are deliberately created by caregivers for infants. The mother may, for example, produce and offer an object for the child to hold, or reach out to wipe his running nose, or pick him up to change his clothes. In all cases, however, the time course of the subsequent events will normally be sensitive to the way in which the child reacts to such events, and attempts will normally be made to make these arbitrary adult interventions in some way meaningful to the child himself, often by embedding them in some game-like ritual which will ensure the child's attentive cooperation.

The social programming to which normal infants are ordinarily subjected, because it occurs as a natural consequence of the care which is necessary for the infant's biological survival, is both massive and continuous. Its effect is to break up the ongoing stream of disordered experience into temporal chunks with defined beginning and end points, and into event sequences to which meaning can be attached. Because these recur day in and day out, they become familiar to the child, who soon shows his recognition of them by motor anticipation — which incidentally provides feedback to the caregiver that at some level a message has been conveyed and reacted to. The two-way interaction process is characteristic. In fact, the baby participates willynilly, whether he is being attracted towards events that someone has deliberately tuned to the vagaries of his own attention, or whether he is simple precipitated into massive physical, whole-body involvement, as when he is picked up and changed by a caregiver. Response to mere inanimate objects in his environment must wait upon the development of his ability to explore and exploit them, by incorporating them into his own voluntarily initiated action sequences; and it may only be when these action sequences are in turn incorporated into interactions with *persons*, who can present the objects in ways which highlight meanings related to what can be done with them, that the child can arrive at understandable and communicable concepts such as size, weight, shape, colour, texture, solidity, deformability and all the myriad notions which we all learn to operate in our everyday anticipatory judgements about the world. The great debt which developmental psychology owes to Piaget rests upon his insistence that the infant's mental conceptions, as distinct from his motor abilities, can only emerge slowly and as the consequence of his commerce with experience in a defined logical sequence of age-related stages (Newson & Newson 1976).

The importance of social mediation in conveying to the infant meaningful conceptions about which it will be feasible for him to communicate with other persons is, however, sadly underrated, not only by Piaget but by most other contemporary theorists in developmental psychology. In fact, certain of the more recent influences, derived from experimental studies using young babies, have tended to suggest (in sharp contrast to the theory being offered in this paper) that the child arrives in the world already innately equipped with the categories of experience which adults take for granted. Because, for instance, it can be shown that under optimal conditions of wakefulness and head support an infant may exhibit appropriate hand—eye coordination and visual localisation of objects in three-dimensional space, almost from birth, it has been argued that he must already have pre-programmed knowledge of objects and of distance and location. However, the ability of an infant to reach, with coordinated grasp movements in a manner appropriate to size and distance of objects, tells us virtually nothing about the way in which he comes to conceptualise, at a mental level, an out-there world of *differentiated* objects capable of being classified in terms of meaningful dimensions about which it might be possible for him to communicate with other human beings. Behavioural discrimination between different kinds of objects or events can be demonstrated at many different levels of phylogenesis,[3] but in comparative studies this is usually taken as evidence only that the nervous system and sensory receptors of the organism in question are so constructed that such behavioural discriminations are not impossible.

To be capable of behavioural discrimination may be a necessary, but certainly not a sufficient, condition for being able to communicate with other human beings about the similarities and differences between conceptual entities. The whole problem of conceptualisation must itself be faced and somehow accounted for. It is a central contention of the present argument that an essential characteristic of any form of conceptual categorisation is that it can, in principle, be shared with another human being. Moreover, it is suggested that the influence of other intelligent human beings who possess the power to communicate is always vitally necessary in order that shared categories of conceptualisation may be handed on from each generation to the next.

2 Research applications

The research work done in the Nottingham Child Development Research Unit in line with the concepts discussed in this chapter actually grew out of a research seminar held in 1972—3. S. Treble (now Gregory) started her thesis study in 1969 (Treble 1972), investigating the development of shape discrimination. The twenty infants studied were observed at monthly intervals for fourteen months, beginning at an average age of eight and a half months. In this work she asked mothers to teach their children to fit shapes to a formboard. The interactions were recorded on video-tape. In the course of what was originally intended as a study of the development of a cognitive capacity, it became apparent that each mother—child pair was constructing a shared understanding of the task, and developing ways of communicating intentions, even before the child was able to talk. In a shared context of reciprocal actions, intonation and gesture were clearly being used with great precision and effectiveness to communicate meanings. The observation that mothers select from the child's activity whatever is pertinent to the task, and single this out for emphasis and praise, thus marking the event as significant in a social context, led to important formulations of the mother's role as educator (Shotter & Gregory 1976; Wood & Middleton 1975). This highlighting of the child's success, even when the action was apparently inadvertent on the child's part, was found to be a characteristic and frequent maternal technique. This insight has fed back into the theoretical formulations and further investigations carried out in the unit.

Systematic and fine-grained analysis of episodes of mother–infant interaction preserved on video-tape and capable of being re-run as often as required — if necessary in slow motion — has been a technique of this research unit since Gregory's study. The method falls within the scope of 'ethological' studies since the interactions observed do not involve manipulation of the 'subjects', but rather observation of spontaneous behaviours, albeit in a somewhat circumscribed situation, and a biological and evolutionary basis is recognised. The same pairs have usually been observed repeatedly, frequently over months. Beside narrative descriptions of the activities captured on video-tape, several coding schemes have been developed, each relevant to the problem being probed.

A study focused on pre-linguistic communication was carried out by O. Jones (1977a, b). She set out to compare normal infants and infants with Down's syndrome in respect to their communication with their mothers. Six of each were selected for the study. The initial ages of the Down's children were thirteen to twenty-three months, and of the normal children eight to eighteen months. The normal children were individually matched to the Down's children on the basis of developmental age at the start of observation, as well as by sex, family position and social class. The taping was done in the children's own homes and mothers were asked to play with their babies as they normally would, both with and without toys. The 15-minute tapes (six for each pair taken at three-weekly intervals) were first analysed without predetermined categories, but rather transcribed within a framework of six major areas: gaze direction, vocalisations and non-vocal activities, for mother and for child. A form of transcription was devised which brings out the structure of the communication. Each line of the transcript represents approximately 1 second of real time. Simultaneous behaviours of both partners are recorded on the same line, sequential behaviours on adjacent lines. Jones cogently points out that

It was considered of great importance that a record of the simultaneous behaviour of both mother and child be kept, since records which only 'follow the action' as it flows between partners is an artifact of observational methods. Within the acting dyad, each partner is *continuously* aware of the other's behaviour — whether it be passive or active. In a study of interaction it is therefore essential that the investigator is aware of the cues being received by both partners at any one time. Observable 'listening' behaviour in the other is as important to the currently active partner as the act itself. (Jones 1977a: 382)

Since the issue was communication, behaviours were then coded into categories

according to whether they were obviously invitational to the partner; effectively invitational (i.e. recognisable only by the fact that the partner responded); or effectively responsive to the other's act. Each of the initial three areas, attention, non-vocal behaviour, and vocal behaviour, was coded into these categories. If none fitted they were noted simply as an 'act'. In this way it was possible to identify, for example, if the mother was inviting the child to attend, or to do something. Also, this made it possible to distinguish whether the mother was just responding to the infant 'as if' he had invited her. This particular situation was in fact very common and, of course, salient to the child's familiarity with his communicative role. It was, therefore, important to note these 'assumed invitations' even though this could only be done in retrospect at the point when a response was given. (Ibid: 383)

Through this method of analysis it was possible to show how the mother could keep up the appearance of a dialogue even when her child was continuing his ongoing behaviour. This was seen as crucial to the child in inducting him into his role as communicator.

The importance of attentional context was recognised and recorded. This helps to specify the possibility of two-way communication and the significance of breakdowns in communication. A method of diagramming the flow of communication was devised which makes the communicative strategies stand out clearly against a background of complex behaviours and interactions.

An interesting preliminary finding (since more fully confirmed) is that, *when matched for developmental age*, the rates of interaction were not significantly different for Down's and normal children. Because mothers looked at their children a great deal of the time, the responsibility for eye contact was usually with the child. Eye contact initiated by children was analysed in terms of three types: (1) directly personal situations such as approach for a hug, (2) in relation to games such as peek-a-boo and (3) referential looking from object to person. Normal children did not show a significantly higher rate of eye contact in general, but *referential* eye contact made up more of the total for the normal children. Child vocalisation was rated for communicative quality in terms of sophistication as a communication signal and also for context, i.e. whether the child paused long enough to permit a response. In the preliminary analysis, Down's children appeared to interfere with turn-taking more often than their normal counter-parts by rapid renewal of vocalisation without leaving space for the mother's response, and by simultaneous vocalising or 'clashing'. It was shown that, even in the pre-linguistic stage, all the Down's children were capable of communication with their mothers, i.e. they were able 'to provide sufficient feedback for their mothers to support them in interactive exchange' (ibid: 398). This is not to say that no differences were found, for the Down's children showed less initiative and their mothers were more often in control, as if striving harder to maintain dialogue continuity. A conclusion was that 'Over-all frequency counts often did not show any general differences between the groups. But when activities were considered in *relation* to the immediately preceding and subsequent inter-communicative activities, the same activity could be identified as having a different meaning, and a different effect in relation to the interactive exchange enclosing it' (ibid: 400).

The significance of this study for the theme of this volume is that a method of great generality has been devised for analysing inter-personal communication: one which is highly sensitive to interactive context, and so can identify subtle differences between individual communicating pairs and between clinically identified groups.

A somewhat different method, also based on video-recording, was devised by S. Pawlby for a study of imitative behaviour in infancy. Again, alternating actions of both the mother and the infant were considered so that the extent and use of mothers' imitations of their babies were brought into sharp focus. Eight mothers started bringing their infants to the laboratory at seventeen weeks and came weekly for twenty-six weeks. On one wall of the observation room was a mirror. The mother and infant were alone with the video camera and were positioned in relation to the camera and mirror so that both were recorded in full-face. Mothers were asked to play with their babies, but were not told of the researcher's concern with imitation. Toys were supplied but their use was left optional, and some object-less play invariably occurred during the 10 minutes recorded for each pair each week. A timing signal with divisions down to 0.1 seconds was superimposed on the tapes as an aid to indexing. General development was noted and all the children were within normal limits.

The tapes were scanned for episodes of imitation, of which over 1600 were found. All pairs participated frequently in imitative sequences. The behaviours of both partners were both described and coded, using a behaviour catalogue of sixty-four items. Statistical analysis of imitative sequences was based on five major groupings: behaviours involving (1) face/head movement, (2) hand/body movement, (3) speech sounds, (4) non-speech sounds and (5) manipulation of objects, i.e. indirect interaction. It was found that, although mothers' imitations of their babies were always much more numerous, infants' imitations of their mothers increased over time. Many mutually imitative sequences involved repeated cycles of action. Forty-nine different activities were observed to be imitated either by the infant or by the mother or by both. Nearly all the activities which were imitated by the infants were also found to be imitated by the mothers. There were, however, sixteen activities which were imitated only by the mother and never by the infant. Imitative sequences involving these activities occurred only rarely. It was suggested that these might be activities which mothers wished to discourage as socially unacceptable and therefore did not encourage the infants to imitate.

Speech sounds were the most frequently imitated group, whereas facial acts were relatively infrequently imitated and were imitated most often when the infants were four to six months old. Hand movements and non-speech sounds were most frequently imitated at six to eight months, and imitation of manipulation of toys peaked at eight to ten months.

This summary does not do justice to the richness of the data. The significance of the study lies in its identification of imitation starting early in infancy as one means of establishing a turn-taking dialogue-like type of communication, in the course of which infant and mother can develop mutual understandings. The findings were interpreted to indicate that 'the whole process by which the infant comes to imitate his mother in a clearly intentional way is rooted in the initial readiness of the mother to imitate her own infant' (Pawlby 1977). This sets up a context in which social learning can be communicated.

Application of this type of research to a practical problem is illustrated by the work of K. Mogford on the communication of young severely handicapped children (1972), a study of 106 children attending the counselling service of the Child Development Research Unit. The service helps parents, in a toy library setting, to alleviate their children's problems. The diagnoses varied, but all shared impaired ability to communicate through speech and language. The group

included children with Down's syndrome, defects of vision and hearing and various types and degrees of brain damage; some were multiply handicapped. In her paper Mogford points to the implications of
such handicaps for assessment of ability, and to the need to look into
the structure of the social interchange in which a child engages. A
secondary effect of lack of language can be seen in retarded learning
of the social meanings and skills which are usually transmitted through
play. The sheer demands on time to accomplish essential physical care
often pre-empts playtime which could have been used for face-to-face
interaction which would have fostered social learning. Rather than
write off the absence of speech as part of a general retardation, it is
necessary to find out what communicative skills a particular child
possesses. Video-recordings of play situations between these children
and their mothers has made it possible to analyse what can and what
cannot be transmitted without speech.

Several other studies are currently in progress. They share a basic
orientation which emphasises that infants can be involved in complex
and sophisticated dialogues of action and expressive gesture long
before the emergence of anything which could properly be called
speech. Because with their regular caregivers they share a familiar
context in which their actions take place, and a joint history of well-
practised interaction rituals within a dialogue format, babies gradually evolve a pre-verbal code of communication which fosters the
growth of a whole corpus of shared understandings. Upon this foundation the development of language can subsequently be built.

Notes

1. This chapter is in two parts. The first is an amended version of a paper which
   was originally prepared for circulation and discussion among members of a
   weekly seminar held in the Nottingham University Child Development
   Research Unit in the 1972–3 semester, and later published as a journal article
   (Newson 1974). The second part gives a brief account of some practical
   research applications which have developed out of this particular approach.
   For a fuller account of the theoretical position which has characterised the
   work at Nottingham, the reader may find it useful to consult some of the subsequent publications which are listed as references in the Bibliography by the
   author and the investigators whose work is reviewed in section 2, as well as by
   Shotter and by Wood & Middleton.
2. This is not to say that a mother may not go through a biologically based (probably hormonally induced) period of sensitivity (towards, for example, the

infant's cry), or may not experience a strong feeling of separation anxiety when she is parted from her infant.

3. Often, indeed, behavioural discriminations are programmed into animals by a process of experimental manipulation in order that the investigators may then claim to have discovered their existence!

I I

How wild chimpanzee babies trigger the onset of mother–infant play – and what the mother makes of it[1]

FRANS PLOOIJ
University of Nijmegen

1 Introduction

Even if one's ultimate interest is in the development of human babies, the study of the development of communication between mother and baby chimpanzees is interesting and significant. Why? Why would one study chimpanzees, for which one has to travel from Europe to another continent, when human subjects are available at home? The answer seemed straightforward when I started my field observations of free-living chimpanzee babies and their mothers in 1971: after initial observations under natural conditions there comes a time when one would like to start experimenting under more restricted conditions with newborn babies. This is not always possible with humans for ethical reasons. Therefore, man's closest relative was chosen as a model. Furthermore, in order to be able to formulate meaningful experiments with newborn chimpanzee babies, initial observations under natural conditions are needed (Tinbergen (1951) 1974, preface 1969: vi). This is the purpose of my study.

However, this point of view implies that animal work is relevant to research on human behaviour and the justifications for this assumption are not as solid any more as they seemed in 1971. The four major justifications for the relevance of animal research on human behaviour were discussed by Bernal & Richards (1973). It appears that three of the four justifications are very restricted.

The first justification that many behavioural processes, on a par with physiological and biochemical processes, are common to all mammals involves reductionist notions. Secondly, the assumption that it is better to start studying animal behaviour because it would be simpler, is not always justified. Thirdly, the argument that techniques of observation are developed in animal work which, there-

223

after, may be used in human studies can be used the other way around
as well: studies of human behaviour may lead to a better understanding of animals. This very study of free-living chimpanzees supports
these arguments (Plooij 1978).

So why would one study chimpanzees? I think that the fourth
justification for the relevance of such a study survives: 'knowledge of
living Primates does lead to an evolutionary perspective in which we
may place ourselves' (Bernal & Richards 1973). Comparative research
may render a better understanding of both the similarities *and* the differences in the behavioural development of various species. This may
show what is typically human, typically chimpanzean, typically apean,
typically monkeyan etc. In relation to this justification Bernal &
Richards (1973) stress the rôle of animal work in the formation of
general biological theory: 'in order to understand human development
we must understand biological development'.

Relatively little is known about the early development of behaviour
in wild chimpanzees (Lawick-Goodall 1968: 285). At the start of my
study it was impossible to observe it anywhere else in the wild except
for the one, unique place where I made this study. What makes the
place unique is that the chimpanzees living their have lost their shy-
ness of human beings and allow them within a close distance, even
within a few metres. This is necessary for the observation of babies
because they are so small and easily hidden behind the limbs of their
mothers. Furthermore, of all ape species, the chimpanzees are the
easiest to observe for two more reasons: (1) they spend a large proportion of their time on the ground, in contrast with orang-utans and
gibbons; (2) the chimpanzees' fur is short (compared with the fur of
the mountain gorilla), which allows the baby chimpanzee to be seen a
great deal.

I believe that it is best to start research into the development of
behaviour of a species of which so little is known with careful descriptions of the behaviour patterns involved. Originally these descriptions
were made with the purpose of sequential analysis of baby behaviour
in mind, in order to explore how the organization of behaviour
changed during development (for an explanation of the phrase 'organization of behaviour' see Baerends 1976). Since the pace of baby
behaviour sequences in chimpanzees is rather slow, I managed to
observe the behaviour of the babies' mothers as well. This chapter
will present a description of the interaction patterns between chimpanzee baby and mother during the first half year with the early

development of communication in mind. The major portion of our data and the methodology used will be reported in greater detail (my wife and I are writing a PhD thesis and a dissertation respectively). The sequential analysis will be included in my dissertation.

2 The field study

2.1 Methods and subjects

The study was done on free-living chimpanzees in the Gombe National Park, Tanzania, from June 1971 to February 1973. The park and its ecology was fully described by Lawick-Goodall (1968) and the way a feeding area was operated was described by Wrangham (1974).

For this chapter it is most relevant to describe the conditions under which the chimpanzee mother—baby pairs were observed. Chimpanzees were most likely to be met at the feeding area. I waited there for the appearance of the particular mother—baby pair I wished to observe at the time. As soon as they left the area I followed them on foot at a distance of at least 5 m. Whenever I was able to see both baby and mother completely (I call this 'spells of good observation'), I dictated a running commentary into a portable cassette tape-recorder strapped to my chest. I continued to follow the mother—baby pair until I had collected 300 minutes of running commentary (= good observation). Therefore I usually had to spend one to two days with the mother—baby pair in the field.

This running record consisted of occurrences of predefined behaviour units. The list of these units, comprising 45 units of baby behaviour and 190 units for the other age classes (of which 20 were typical maternal behaviours), grew out of my field experience during the first six months. During this time I was following a mother—baby pair of which the baby had just been born at the start of this project. In relation to the growth of this list the following quotation from Schneirla (1972: 5—7) is pertinent:

The field investigator must never be considered simply a 'watcher' . . . He is always a perceiver, who is not an unbiased registering instrument . . . Some ways in which an improvement in field perception may come about are suggested in Darling's discussion of observational techniques: . . . the fact remains that an observer has to go through a period of conditioning of a most subtle kind . . . He must empty his mind and be receptive only to the species of his focus and the signs of the country . . . This is quite severe discipline, calling for time and practice . . . It is necessary intellectually to soak in the environmental complex of the animal to be studied until we have a facility with it which keeps us, as it were, one move ahead. We must become intimate with the animal . . . in his state the observer learns more than he realizes. A cardinal point is that the observer must consider the single observation only a small part of his task, to be repeated, enlarged upon and varied as a matter of necessary control . . . This is a question of validity of sampling procedures.

The only way to repeat a single observation when studying behavioural development in fast-growing babies is to observe the next baby when he is born, and then the next. This is what I did, and I observed the next babies in terms of the list of behaviour units I developed during the observation of the first baby. Rare events which I had never seen before could be recorded, in addition to the predefined behaviour units, thanks to the use of the portable cassette recorder. In this way the observation of every successive baby was similar to repeating an experiment in order to make sure the results are not spurious. The account in this chapter is based on analysis of transcripts of these running commentaries.

Three male chimpanzee babies were born during my stay in the Gombe. Their names were: (1) Freud, son of Fifi, (2) Prof, son of Passion and (3) Wilkie, son of Winkle. For more biographical detail, see Lawick-Goodall (1971). I observed them from birth to the ages of twenty, fifteen and three months respectively. Freud was observed during my initial six-month period and the list of behaviour units was developed while watching him and his mother. In my dissertation the complete list of these behaviour units will be given (the list is available to anyone interested). The examples in the appendix should suffice to give an idea of the kind of units involved.

2.2 Findings

Chimpanzee birth has never been observed in the wild. Attempts to do so failed because one or two days before giving birth a chimpanzee mother tends to avoid both chimpanzee and human company. Even when I managed to follow a mother near term I was unable to observe anything because she made a nest high in a tree and gave birth there.

However, from the first postnatal day on, I had spells of good observation. The newborn baby is always on the mother's ventral side. He clings weakly (sometimes not at all) and has to be supported most of the time, especially when the mother is locomoting (see fig. 1). From the spells of good observation I got the impression that the new-

Fig. 1 Chimpanzee mother carries her newborn baby which is on her ventral side and not clinging at all.

born baby sleeps most of the time and wakes at intervals of one and a half hours. When the baby is awake he vocalizes frequently (mainly whimpering) while engaged in rooting and mountaineering. Mountaineering together with rooting may result in progression up the mother's body and reaching a nipple with the mouth.

The rôle of the chimpanzee mother in rooting and mountaineering is minimal. She may place her hand on the back of her baby and push him against her belly, a maternal behaviour unit called 'support'. This allows the baby to resume mountaineering and rooting if he has lost contact with the belly of the mother. She does not always look down at him while supporting him. One of the striking aspects of the neonatal period is the apparent lack of focus of maternal visual attention on her infant. While the chimpanzee mother is grooming her baby (see fig. 2) she is watching what she is doing as a human mother would while administering body care.

At about six weeks the three observed male babies started to bite

Fig. 2 Chimpanzee mother grooming her baby.

on or at everything that touched or came in front of their faces. The targets of one baby's (Prof's) bites are shown in fig. 3. Perioral stimulation was the predominant stimulation for biting. The orientation of the biting was very poor at first: often the baby bit his own limbs when they were in front of his face at a time when something else touched his face. Therefore we may conclude that the frequency with which objects are present near the face of a baby is a major determinant of how often these objects are bitten. The infant's own body, especially his hands and feet (see fig. 4), are most frequently bitten for obvious reasons. Because the infant is always on the body of the mother she comes second. Malorientation lasted for only two weeks.

Reaching was first observed to precede biting at seven to eight weeks. It was initially clumsy with a large lateral deviation. According to Bruner (1973), a goal is prefigured in such a motoric form. However, from week eight, if the infant did not manage to reach the eliciting stimulus, he invariably redirected the intended bite to his own

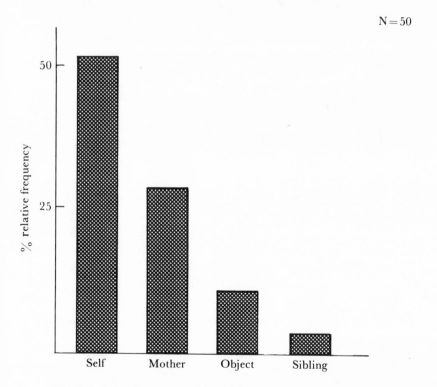

Fig. 3 Relative frequency with which targets were bitten by a chimpanzee baby (Prof) during observations between 6 and 12 weeks.

Fig. 4 Chimpanzee mother sitting and looking around while the baby
lies on his back in her lap biting one of his own feet.

body. The possible significance of this observation will be discussed
below.

'Playface' emerges at the same time as biting (see fig. 5). This facial
expression could also appropriately be called 'ready-to-bite-face', a
particularly apt description for chimpanzee babies. In the case of Prof,
34% of his bites were preceded by playface. In these cases I presume
that the playface was elicited by the same stimuli that elicited biting,
among which perioral stimulation predominated. However, sometimes
playface was observed without any observable prior stimulus and
without being followed by biting. At other times objects or individuals
just out of arms' reach would elicit playface, and reaching instead of
biting would follow.

During the first six weeks of the baby's life mother—baby interaction does not seem to be extensive. The mother cleans the baby just
after birth as she licks and gnaws the umbilical cord (Plooij 1974);
she also grooms him, and sometimes she briefly glances down at him

Fig. 5 Facial expression called 'playface'.

just after he vocalizes, but that seems to be about all the visual attention she accords him. In this context, I note that when the baby
starts to bite his mother's body and other things, he does not seem to
be treating her as an individual. For example, as the mother collects
food and eats it, the hairs of her upper arm may strike along her
baby's face, and provide perioral stimulation. The mother does not
attend at all to her baby before, while or after he bites her arm (see
fig. 6).

The mothers' behaviours changed drastically not long after week
six. They suddenly gave more visual attention to their babies. They
must have noticed, as I did, that perioral stimulation elicits playface
and biting because they started to stroke their babies' faces and to
place their index fingers against or in their babies' mouths. This
would start interactions in which a mother's stroking and poking
alternated with the baby's playface and biting. As a baby became
older he became progressively more likely to reach for his mother's
hand with a playface and bite it after she had stopped stroking or
removed her finger from his face. Thereupon she would stroke his
face again and the cycle would repeat. The range of things that were

Fig. 6 Baby holds and bites the hairs hanging down from mother's right upper arm. The baby is leaning with his back against the inside of mother's right leg. Her head is partly visible in the right upper corner of the picture.

bitten narrowed down by the age of twelve weeks; physical objects as well as the infant's own body ceased to be the target of biting. By the end of the third month the baby was biting only the mother's body.

One could say that the biting by the baby triggered the onset of mother–baby play. The mother, in turn, elaborated the initial mother–baby play. She started to touch and poke other parts of the baby's body in addition to the face, especially the belly, the neck-pocket and the groin-pocket. She started to gnaw the baby as well. Gnawing triggered the development of an interaction pattern between the baby and the mouth of the mother that was similar to the inter-action pattern between the baby and the hands of the mother: the mother would gnaw and then withdraw her mouth, the baby would reach for the mouth, the mother would gnaw again, and so on. Suddenly around the end of the third month or the beginning of the fourth month the babies paid increased attention to their mothers' faces. The relation of this to maternal gnawing behaviour is uncertain. In order to be able to touch the mother's face the baby stands bipedally, quite an achievement at this age. He touches his mother's mouth, her cheeks, her eyes, pulls her cheek-hairs and touches her lips with his own, resulting in a 'kiss'. On these occasions the mother lowers her face, chin on chest, and looks down into the baby's face, producing a considerable amount of face-to-face contact between mother and baby.

A chimpanzee baby of over six weeks uses all the means at his command to escape excessive stimulation including clinging to his mother, turning his face away from the stimulation and giving a stress vocalization. These behaviours completely inhibit the baby's playface and biting.

In mother—baby play the same thing happens in a milder form. The baby can regulate the strength of stimulation by partly withdrawing from it rather than escaping it altogether. If the mother stimulates in a more vigorous way than gently stroking the face, such as gnawing, poking and tickling, the baby will 'defend': this consists of arching the back and pulling up the legs to ward off the stimulation with hands and feet (see fig. 7). When the mother stops tickling, the baby switches from defending to reaching for her hand or mouth. If the mother tickles again, the whole sequence is repeated. If the mother, on the other hand, stops reacting, the baby not only reaches, but bites and may slap as well. If the mother then reacts to this by tickling again, the baby immediately switches from biting and slapping to defending. Early in life approach never occurs simultaneously with withdrawal, but, in mother—baby play, they do alternate frequently.

For the mother—baby play to continue, the stimulation provided by the mother should be very gentle: as soon as it is a little bit too much for him the baby shows full-scale escape. On the other hand, with too little stimulation, the baby will soon stop interacting. It seems that the mother has to adjust to the baby, rather than the baby to the mother. During play it is as if she constantly balances on an imaginary edge: the edge between approach and withdrawal by the baby. As the baby grows older and becomes an infant (six to twenty-four months) he received rougher stimulation: the tickling becomes more forceful. Not only can the infant withstand more stimulation than a baby, but a higher level of stimulation is required to keep mother—infant play going. Therefore I like to see the chimpanzee mother—infant play as balancing on an ever higher edge. On one side is a steep slope one can fall off (too strong stimulation by the mother and withdrawal by the baby), on the other side is a gentle slope which becomes longer and longer over development (see fig. 8).

Not long after biting and playface were observed for the first time

Fig. 7 Mother tickles with her right hand and the baby defends.

the babies were observed to 'laugh'. In fact this was during the third month of life. Laughter consists of staccato rhythmic breathing which sometimes escalates into galloping expellations of air. (This behaviour unit is not to be equated to human laughter.) The babies laughed when tickled by their mothers. However, not every tickling occasion produced laughter. On the one hand there were sequences where a baby did not laugh at all; on the other, a laughing baby could suddenly whimper and cling to its mother (thus withdrawing from the tickling). From these two observations I conclude that a baby's laugh indicates that he is receiving an amount of stimulation that he can just about handle. A little more would be too much. From this one might speculate that laughter from the baby is the necessary feedback for the mother through which she can tell that she is giving the optimal amount of stimulation, that she is close to the edge, so to speak (see fig. 8).

The phenomenon of laughter abruptly changing into whimpering or

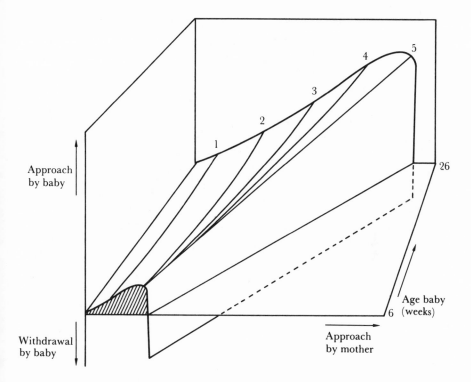

Fig. 8 Three dimensional 'edge' diagram plotting the approach—withdrawal by the baby against the approach by the mother over age. The numbers at the back of the diagram refer to specific maternal approach behaviour combined with approach or withdrawal behaviour of the baby: (1) mother close but passive, baby bites maternal body component; (2) mother strokes baby's face, baby bites her finger; (3) mother tickles, baby defends; (4) mother tickles harder, baby defends and laughs; (5) mother tickles too hard, baby withdraws and whimpers or even screams.

even screaming was observed frequently in chimpanzees of all age and sex classes including adulthood. In fact every observer at the Gombe Research Centre agreed that a rough-and-tumble play session between juveniles and/or adolescents combined with laughter that had already lasted for a few minutes was bound to be finished soon by one of the two partners screaming. From my former studies of a captive chimpanzee (unpublished material) I know that just tickling does not produce laughter. I really had to tickle this four- to five-year-old chimpanzee with all my force before he would laugh.

I plotted the frequency of mother—baby play resulting in laughter by the baby against the age of the baby (see fig. 9). At first sight these two graphs seem totally different. This is due to the strong individual differences between the mothers of the two pairs. Passion spent little time in play with her son Prof as compared to Fifi. She was always on the move to another food source, and only when there was nothing more to eat would she spend a few odd minutes in play with her son. Fifi, on the other hand, ate less frequently, rested much more and consequently had more time to spare for play. Nevertheless, both graphs show a peak in the first half year of life. Even Passion was observed to lie down, take Prof in her arms and play with him. I think this only strengthens the following argument. During the first half year a baby has hardly any interactions with other individuals that result in laughter. In the second half year the frequency of the mother–baby interactions resulting in laughter decreases, whereas

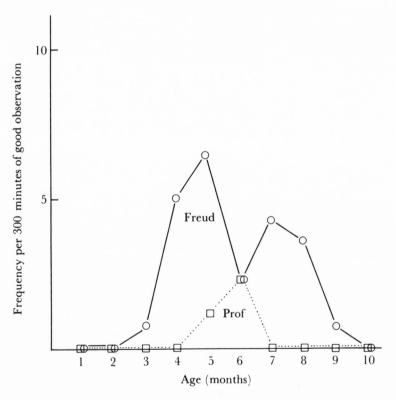

Fig. 9 Frequency of mother–baby play resulting in laughter by the baby, plotted against age for two individual chimpanzee babies, Prof and Freud.

the baby has an increasing number of such interactions with other individuals. Therefore, I suggest that the effect and a possible function of this graded mother—baby play is to prepare the baby for later interactions with other individuals by allowing him to become used to increasingly higher levels of stimulation.

This opinion is also supported by data on chimpanzees in captivity reported by Davenport (forthcoming). Chimpanzee infants which were separated from their mothers early in life avoid nearly all social interaction with other individuals and stimulate themselves a great deal. To extend my edge-imagery a little further: normal individuals are walking on an edge that is far too high and far too dangerous for the mother-deprived chimpanzee infants. And if mother-deprived infants are confronted with a social situation, as when an isolate is put in a cage with other individuals, they do not know how to balance close to the edge. They rush toward the edge (outrageous attack) and fall down the steep slope (withdrawal) (see fig. 8).

These captive chimpanzees, beside avoiding social interaction, showed high frequencies of self-stimulating behaviours. Davenport reported that the physical presence of the captive chimpanzee mother and only the mother in the first year of life prevented such abnormal behaviour. However, he acknowledged that he was not sure which aspects of the mother were essential.

Self-stimulating behaviours did occur in the Gombe chimpanzees, albeit in very low frequencies; they consisted of self-biting, 'lipflip' (folding the upper lip over the nose), sucking the cheeks inwards and rocking. Why were these behaviours ever observed in the Gombe chimpanzees where the mother was physically present? As we have seen, the Gombe chimpanzee babies at first bite their own bodies. Later in development they do so only when the eliciting stimulus is out of reach (see remarks about biting and playface). An unresponsive mother, though physically within arm's reach, is unavailable to the baby. This sounds paradoxical, but, when the mother does not respond at all to her baby's biting and pulling, she is unavailable, like a physical object which is out of reach. And it was exactly when the mother was unavailable in this sense that I observed self-stimulating behaviours in the Gombe chimpanzee babies and infants.

In summary, the behaviour of the mother which is contingent on the baby's bites directs his behaviour to herself, and thus, later on, to other chimpanzees, rather than to his own body and physical objects. It could be that the peak of mother—baby play resulting in laughter suggests a 'sensitive period' for the process described in this chapter.

3 Discussion

The results of my field procedure have suggested that it may be the absence of regular relationships between the behaviour of the mother and the behaviour of the baby that is responsible for most of the behavioural abnormalities accompanying social isolation. This contrasts with the suggestion that some mere quantity of stimulation is involved, as exemplified by the experimental approach of Mason et al. (1968: 446–7) and Davenport (forthcoming). My suggestion goes in the same direction as the one proposed by Hinde (1970: 216–17) for sensory or perceptual isolation. Rutter (1972) points out a tendency to regard both the experiences under and the outcomes of 'maternal deprivation' as a syndrome which can be discussed as a whole. On the contrary, he argues that little progress in our understanding is likely to occur until the basic variables indiscriminately combined under the term 'maternal deprivation' are differentiated and the separate effects of each determined. He presents evidence that physically present human mothers may still be depriving their children and concludes that privation is a more accurate term than deprivation (p. 85).

The frequent switching between approach and withdrawal during the chimpanzee mother–baby play seems to be one of these regular relationships, or, as Rutter (1972) puts it, 'basic variables'. Approach and withdrawal seem to be balanced in a delicate way. One can imagine that this balance is destroyed if either approach or withdrawal predominates for too long a period of time. The widely reported cases of social isolates may be understood in terms of disruption of this balance. The isolates are very withdrawn but may suddenly become incredibly aggressive, and then as suddenly withdrawn again.

This process of balance between approach and withdrawal is probably very widespread in the animal kingdom (Schneirla 1959), but there might be interesting species differences in the way it is brought about. Comparison between chimpanzees and monkeys (such as rhesus monkeys or olive baboons) showed that the sort of interaction that occurs in chimpanzee mother–baby pairs is absent in the monkeys (personal observation). The monkey babies do bite in a similar way to the chimpanzee babies but the monkey mothers do not react. However, there are other monkey individuals who do react to the bites of the monkey babies, namely siblings and peers. They provide the monkey babies with interactions that are similar to the interactions between chimpanzee mothers and babies. This helps to explain why Harlow & Harlow (1962a) found that the monkey peers were equally if not more important than the monkey mother, and it makes it all the more puzzling why Harlow & Mears (1977) recently presented 'self-motion-play' as the long-sought antecedent of social play. But one question remains: assuming for a moment that this is true for many more monkey species (see for instance Chevalier-Skolnikoff 1974), why did chimpanzees deviate from the pattern? Why is the chimpanzee mother providing her baby with what monkey infants get from their peers? One clue in the direction of an answer may be the group structure of chimpanzees. I observed that chimpanzee mothers with babies spend most of their time alone with their babies. As a consequence it is the chimpanzee mother who has to give her baby this sort of interaction if he is to get it at all. Knowing from the studies on captive chimpanzees at Yerkes Regional Primate Research Center (Davenport forthcoming) that the sexual, and therefore the reproductive, behaviour of at least the males is heavily impaired by deprivation, one can start to understand that there must have been a selection pressure for the kind of maternal behaviour which I have just described in free-ranging chimpanzees. The chimpanzee mother promotes her own genes by playing with her male baby in this way. Similar ideas have been expressed by Trivers (1971) among others.

Since only males were born during the time I was in the Gombe, I can say nothing about sex differences. It would be interesting to find out if and to what extent the same process occurs between the chimpanzee mother and her female baby. In the literature on humans it is repeatedly reported that mothers provide their male babies with more tactile stimulation than their female babies (see Korner 1974). Furthermore, primate male infants do indulge more in rough-and-tumble play than female infants (Mason 1960; Harlow & Harlow 1962b, 1965; Hinde 1971; Anderson & Mason 1975). The same is true for chimpanzees (personal observation). In fact, female chimpanzee infants and juveniles do engage in rough-and-tumble play, but they withdraw sooner as it becomes more rough. I predict that this is directly related to the extent to which the described process is present between mother and female baby. Only future research can answer this question.

The way in which the chimpanzee baby initially bites anything and everything and eventually narrows down to body components of his mother strongly reminds one of the 'imprinting' process in chicks as described by P.P.G. Bateson (1972). His theoretical model (1973), showing how the chick's strength of preference for an unfamiliar object varies with its difference from a familiar object and the chick's length of exposure to the familiar object, could apply to my chimpanzee data as well. Physical objects as well as the baby's own body become totally familiar and predictable, consequently the baby loses interest in them. The behaviour of the baby's mother, on the other hand, stays slightly unpredictable. A model similar to the one Bateson proposed can be found in the literature on humans under the name 'discrepancy principle' (Kagan 1972).

The way twelve-week-old chimpanzee babies interact with the body components of their mothers gives me the strong impression that they do not treat their mothers as whole individuals. It is as if a mother's hand were just a very interesting object. This impression may be caused by the absence of eye-to-eye contact, and the sudden increase in the baby's interest in the face of his mother around the age of three months may mark the very beginning of the formation of an internal representation of the mother as an individual. The development of 'fear of strangers' in chimpanzees starts only around six months (see dissertation). This suggests that the formation of an internal representation of the mother as an individual is a lengthy process in this species. The resemblance between the course and timing of development of playface and laughter in the chimpanzee baby on the one hand and the human smile on the other is striking (see Spitz & Wolf 1946; Ambrose 1961; Wolff 1963; Gewirtz 1965; Emde & Harmon 1972). Equally striking is the formation of a schema of the mother's face around the age of three months in both species (for humans see Kagan 1967; Lewis 1969). It is possible that a similar process is involved in both species; this view is supported by a human case-history that was reported by Brazelton et al. (1971) and Bullowa (1970). However, it should be stressed that the behaviour patterns involved are very species-specific. The human smile and the chimpanzee playface are not related in their biological evolution. The human smile is thought to have evolved from the 'bared-teeth-face' (Hooff

1972). Furthermore, biting, tickling and other proximal stimulation are typical for the chimpanzees, whereas gaze and other distal communication signals are rarely observed. It is an open question whether proximal stimulation plays an important part in human baby—adult communication (Bullowa & Putney in preparation), but gaze and other distal communication signals are certainly outstanding (Stern 1974b).

4 Summary

The chimpanzee baby triggers the onset of mother—baby play by biting the mother's body. When bitten the mother starts to tickle the baby and this biting—tickling grows into an alternating interaction, in which both mother and baby can take their turns many times in succession. Furthermore, chimpanzee mother—infant play can be looked upon as balancing on an ever higher edge between approach and withdrawal so that the baby becomes ready to interact with other individuals by the end of the first half year. Without this process the baby may develop abnormal behaviour in the very physical presence of the mother.

Note

1. This chapter was written while I was a guest in the Sub-Department of Animal Behaviour, University of Cambridge, at Madingley. The data on which it is based were collected in the Gombe National Park, Tanzania, at the Gombe Stream Research Centre, whose existence is due to the permission and cooperation of the Tanzanian Government and its officers in Dar es Salaam and Kigoma. The research would have been impossible without the initial encouragement of Dr H. Albrecht; Dr H.C.J. Oomen, lector in Animal Ecology, University of Nijmegen, and Professor Dr G.P. Baerends, professor of Zoology, University of Groningen, have given me invaluable help and support throughout the project. I am grateful to Dr Jane van Lawick-Goodall for admitting me to the Gombe Stream Research Centre to carry out my project, and I am indebted to Mrs H.H.C. van de Rijt-Plooij, Dr M. Simpson, Dr D. Shapiro, Professor G.P. Baerends and Professor R.A. Hinde for many stimulating and constructive discussions.

This research project was financially supported by the Netherlands Foundation for the Advancement of Tropical Research (grant no. W84-66) and the Dr J.L. Dobberke Stichting voor Vergelijkende Psychologie.

A talk based on this chapter was given at the XIVth International Ethological Conference, Parma, 27 August to 5 September 1975.

Appendix:
Sample behaviour units

Baby behaviour units

Bite	Taking something in between the jaws and closing them.
Clings mother	Clinging to the mother with the hands and sometimes with the feet as well.
Defend	Bringing the hands and, if possible, feet to a part of own body in order to repel tactile stimulation such as tickling and gnawing applied by another individual. Body parts which are frequently tickled are the belly, the neck-pocket and the groin-pocket. If the belly or the groin-pocket are tickled, the back is frequently arched as well. If the neck-pocket is tickled the chimpanzee may round its back and neck away from the source of stimulation.
Hand to hand	Chimpanzee infant brings his hand to the hand of another individual.
'Laughing'	Staccato rhythmic breathing which easily develops into rhythmic, sometimes hoarse grunting. The grunting rhythms may be irregular; within one bout of grunts the rate often suddenly accelerates and decelerates again. It is not the same as human laughter.
Mountaineering	Extending the arms and opening the hands combined with flexing the legs, alternating with flexing the arms and closing the hands combined with extending the legs. This may result in progression up the mother's body. Prechtl (1953) defined a similar behaviour unit for human babies.
Playface-half	The mouth is kept moderately to widely open. The mouth corners may be slightly retracted, but the lips maintain their normal relaxed position so that the upper teeth remain wholly or partly covered by the upper lip. Sometimes the upper lip is pulled down over and under the upper teeth to cover them completely. The lower teeth are bared.
Rooting	The very young infant moves his face repeatedly from side to side against the body of his mother. During each sweep the infant's head may move backward and forward several times. This behaviour has been designated 'rooting-reflex' for human infants by Prechtl (1958) and Prechtl & Beintema (1964) and for non-human primate infants by Hinde (1974: 166).
Whimpering	Series of short calls. During the series the frequency and the intensity of the calls rises and falls. The timbre is rather sharp.

242

Maternal behaviour units

Finger in mouth	Putting a finger (mostly the index finger) into the mouth or against the lips of another individual.
Gnawing	The chimpanzee mother puts her open mouth against the infant's body and makes quick nibbling movements either with the teeth or with the lips drawn down over the teeth.
Grooming	Picking through the infant's fur. Both hands and lips are used. One hand mainly pushes the hairs apart so that particles may be picked up with the other hand or with the lips.
Poking	The chimpanzee puts one or more fingertip with a sudden movement on the belly or in the neck-pocket of another individual. This has the same effect as tickling.
Support	The chimpanzee mother puts the palmar surface of her hand against the back of her ventro-ventrally clinging infant and may keep it there for a while.
Tickling	A chimpanzee puts one or both hands on the body of another individual and makes a series of alternating flexing and stretching finger movements in quick succession. The neck, the belly and the groin are favourite parts to be tickled.

12

Making sense of experience to make sensible sounds

Experimental investigations of early vocal communication in pre-verbal autistic and normal children

DEREK RICKS
Harperbury Hospital, Radlett

The problem with which this chapter is concerned can be stated quite simply: how do normal children first start to communicate vocally and in what way is this initial step prevented in many autistic children?

My own attention was focused on this problem some years ago by two events which occurred together. Part of my medical work in a children's psychiatric department at that time was to attempt to promote communication in a small group of resident autistic children. At the same time my son was just seven months old so that over the ensuing few months my own natural interest in his speech development was heightened by the practical difficulties of encouraging in my patients the same process as was unfolding in him. This interest prompted me to record our son at regular intervals, a procedure I was fortunately able to extend with the cooperation of five hospital colleagues who had children of similar age. Through their enthusiasm and interest I was able to discuss various details of their children's behaviour, babbling and earliest speech.

Two natural consequences arose from this early work, both of which had direct bearing on later investigations of the autistic children. One was the collection of records of normal babbling, roughly at monthly intervals, to see if I could discover how, if at all, the earliest words emerged from each child's babble. This enabled me later to compare the vocalisations of normal infants and autistic children. The second was a focusing of interest on the infant's response to his parents' efforts to stimulate speech. This led me to doubt my earlier ideas about stimulating speech in autistic children and to formulate new ideas which could be tested experimentally.

Hence a twofold project emerged: a comparison of the vocal behaviour of pre-verbal infants and non-verbal autistic children; and a study comparing the extent to which vocal behaviour in the normal child was influenced by imitating his parents with the ineffectiveness of such efforts for the autistic child. This led to a parallel programme of recording six selected autistic children, as young as possible, all living and recorded at home with their parents. Questions raised by discussion of these early recordings led to more structured experimental studies. These extended the study into three interrelated topics. These were (1) pre-verbal vocal communication, (2) the role of imitation and (3) the 'first word'.

1 Pre-verbal vocal communication

1.1 Experimental procedure

The investigation began in March 1966 with a recording of vocalisation of our own son, then aged seven months. He was recorded over a period of three days in a variety of situations: at meals, when lying in his cot, in his playpen etc. Each situation was specified with a brief recorded commentary on his activity at that time. All recording was on high-fidelity equipment. This procedure was extended to five other babies, three aged seven months and two aged five months initially. All of these babies were the first children of colleagues. The microphone and recorder, loaded with a 5-in reel of audio tape set for 3¾ in per second was loaned to the parents for a period of three days with the request that they record their baby in the way described above. Certain simple precautions were taken, e.g. placing the microphone on a different surface from the baby or the recorder to avoid vibrations, keeping the microphone about 2 ft from the baby. Each family was either already familiar with the use of a tape recorder, or learned quickly. The recording sessions were repeated for each child at one- to two-month intervals for a series of about nine sessions up to the age of approximately eighteen months. A final recording at about twenty-seven months was added later.

A major technical difficulty which became immediately apparent was that babies do not babble for the convenience of the experimenter. Since spontaneous as well as responsive babble was required, the problem arose how to record only as the child babbles. Spontaneous babbling had to be patiently awaited, although the mothers were very helpful in utilising anticipated 'chatty' periods. The only practical solution was simply to record over a likely period, later eliminating the silent stretches. During the three days a minimum of four and a half hours was recorded, producing a spontaneous record including silences. This was edited by listening to the whole tape and transferring the episodes of vocalisation and parents' commentary onto another tape. On each occasion I added to this edited record the date of recording and any further comments derived from discussions with the parents. Thereby a tape library of at least seventeen hours' duration was built up for each child containing serial edited recordings over the period of first speech acquisition.

A parallel series of recordings, using exactly the same procedures, was started in April 1966, using as subjects six autistic children between their third and sixth birthdays living at home. These children were recorded at about two-month intervals for about a year. Again the recorder was left with the families, who were instructed in the same way, and about four hours' edited recording was collected from each.

1.2 Vocal signals

Listening to the recordings of the normal children when they were eight months to one year old, I noticed that in certain situations each child made very similar noises. This impression was confirmed in discussion with their parents. For instance, each child seemed to make the same sort of noise when wanting something. This suggested a form of pre-verbal communication which warranted systematic investigation. That meant obtaining utterances in which the child conveyed a particular message to his parents which they would readily recognise. If these utterances were to be meaningfully compared, then not only must there be a common understanding between the two parents of the message conveyed, but, as far as possible, the utterance must be elicited in a standardised situation. Such situations, which each parent would accept as a likely stimulus for producing the appropriate message, should be presented identically to each child. To construct the experimental situation we had to select a few simple, clearly defined 'messages' which were unequivocal, regularly present, and elicited in controlled, specified but everyday situations. Listening to the tapes of spontaneous recordings suggested four such utterances: a requesting sound, a frustrated sound, a greeting sound and a sound expressing pleased surprise at a novel and exciting event. Discussion with the parents indicated that they too felt it likely that such mess-

ages would be expressed in a recognisable way which would enable
them to envisage fairly confidently what was happening to their child
if they themselves were to hear the sound uttered from the next room.
However, appreciating that such sounds were likely and eliciting them
when needed (i.e. when being recorded) were very different propositions.

1.3 Experimental procedure

The problem lay in constructing fruitful yet standardised situations
in which to record the child's responses. Two were quite simple (eliciting requesting and frustrated noises), two less so. When they were
eventually decided upon, the parents were instructed in the following
way:

1. *A request noise*: record the child while preparing a favourite meal
in his company when you know he is very hungry, then show it to
him.
2. *A frustrated noise*: repeat this situation but withhold the meal for
a few moments until you obtain what you recognise as a noise registering frustration.
(In both these situations, if a meal was not a satisfactory stimulus
then a favoured toy was kept out of sight for one day then produced
and used in the same manner as the child's meal.)
3. *A greeting noise*: record the child on waking either in the morning
or from his afternoon nap, obtaining his reponse to his mother when
she goes to his cot (if he then customarily makes a particular noise),
or when his mother returns to the room after an absence, e.g. shopping.
4. *A pleasantly surprised noise*: record the child when presented with
a novel and, it is hoped, pleasing event: either blowing up a coloured
balloon or lighting a sparkler firework.

These recordings were collected and used to construct a tape to test
the parents' recognition of these noises.

The experiment was arranged as follows. The twelve parents (six
with autistic children and six with normal babies) were presented with
a recorder and the tape and asked to reply to certain questions. They
were allowed to listen for as long as they wished. In the case of one
autistic child the parents did not agree in their answers and the
mother's answers were counted. To test the effect of the language
background an identical procedure was carried out with four normal

children of non-English-speaking parents (aged eight to twelve months). To test the effect of autism four retarded non-verbal but non-autistic children of the same age as the autistic group were recorded. Each tape was introduced by standard instructions followed by two sections.

The first section contained intonated utterances of four babies (or pre-verbal children), each baby being presented in turn as child A, B, C and D. For each child his respective noises were presented and termed A1, A2, A3 and A4, and so on for children B, C and D, making a total of sixteen vocal signals. However, for each child the order in which the signals were presented was different. For the normal parents' tape one of the babies was selected from a non-English-speaking family, and for the autistic children's parents one of the children was selected from the non-autistic group. On each tape one of the children was the parents' own child. The other two were taken at random from the remaining babies for the normal children's parents or from the remaining autistic children for the autistic children's parents. The parents were asked:
(1) to identify the messages of the four signals for each child and to state in which order they were presented;
(2) to identify their own child;
(3) to identify the non-English-speaking child (parents of normal babies), or the non-autistic child (parents of pre-verbal autistic children).

The second section consisted of the request signals of all six children presented one after the other and simply numbered child 1–6. The parents were asked to select the signals of their own child.

Results: see tables 1a and 1b. These tables show a striking contrast between the ability of parents of normal and of autistic children to recognise on the one hand the message of an intonated signal and on the other the identity of the child producing it. Parents of normal children found it easy to understand the message conveyed by intonated signals, not only of their own but of other normal children, whereas parents of autistic children could do this only in the case of their own child or a non-autistic child. However, parents of normal children had unexpected difficulty in selecting their own child, while the parents of autistic children did this with ease. These contrasts are the direct result of the marked similarity of signals conveying a particular message produced by ordinary children, so that one child uttering the signal sounds much like another even to parents. When conveying the same messages

Table 1a *Intonation experiment results: normal babies*

Mothers	Identification of 'intonated responses' (4 children : 4 responses each)				Identification of child		
	Own child (x4)	Non-English child (x4)	Other children (x8)	Total responses (x16)	Own child (out of 4)	Non-English child (out of 4)	Own child (out of 6 request noises)
A	4	4	8	16	Right	D.K.	Wrong
B	4	4	5	13	Wrong	Wrong	Wrong
C	4	2	8	14	Right	D.K.	Wrong
D	4	4	8	16	Right	Wrong	Right
E	4	4	8	16	Wrong	D.K.	Wrong
F	4	4	6	14	Right	D.K.	Right

Comparing cols. 3 : Rank Test: prob. 1:924 : T. Test, T. approx 12, P > 0.001.
Comparing col. 3 (table 1a) with col. 2 (table 1b) : no significant difference.
D.K. = Don't know.

Table 1b *Intonation experiment results: autistic children*

Mothers	Identification of 'intonated responses' (4 children : 4 responses each)				Identification of child		
	Own child (x4)	Non-autistic child (x4)	Other autistic children (x8)	Total responses (x16)	Own child (out of 4)	Non-autistic child (out of 4)	Own child (out of 6 request noises)
I	4	4	0	8	Right	Right	Right
II	4	4	0	8	Right	Right	Right
III	4	2	0	6	Right	D.K.	Right
IV	4	2	2	8	Right	Right	Right
V	4	4	0	8	Right	Right	Right
VI	4	4	1	9	Right	Right	Right

D.K. = Don't know.

the autistic children did not use this vocabulary of intonated signals; each had his own, and thus distinctive, signal in each situation. Hence both the signal and the child uttering it were readily recognisable to their parents but unintelligible to other parents.

This experimental evidence suggests that by the final third of the first year normal babies have acquired a number of intonated vocal signals, the utterance of which conveys to their parents (and, it seems, to any other parent) a particular message. This message enables the listening parent, without reference to any other information, to recognise that the child is in a particular situation and that he is responding to it in a particular way. It also implies that the child himself is able to identify each situation. Since all the normal subjects were first sibs from a variety of language backgrounds, such signals do not seem to be learned from the adult language. They have other important characteristics. Firstly they are strikingly common to normal babies, irrespective of the intonation patterns of the only language the babies hear; secondly they are entirely comprehensible to parents; thirdly they are consistent in response to a given situation; and fourthly they are of consistent form over a considerable period of time. They are also present in non-communicating retarded children of the same age as the autistic group. The essential and striking feature of these signals are that they are consistent, independent of language, and unlearned. They are absent in autistic children, at least from those three- to five-year-olds investigated. What seems significant is that the autistic children by this age *were* able in the same way as the normal babies to recognise consistently similar situations and were motivated to express vocally a response which was consistent for each child. Indeed it was the consistency of each particular autistic child's request signal which confirmed that he 'recognised' the eliciting situation. The autistic children were thus both cognitively equipped and motivated to produce the same messages but produced signals quite different both from the normal children and from each other.

The impressions presented to the child of eight months are varied and complex, yet he extracts from them the sense of 'something wanted'. It is difficult to see what common clues he utilises to arrive at the recognition needed in such diverse contexts to prompt his request signal, yet discussion with the parents revealed that such consistent responses may occur even before six months. This peculiar ability of the normal baby to impose some particular 'sense' on diverse sensory information may reveal a growing ability to categorise, expressed this early apparently without reliance on sophisticated perceptual skills. An exactly similar ability is employed in 'pointing' words (to be discussed later), a process which also seems to elude the autistic child.

What certainly is needed to enable a normal baby to vocalise these signals appropriately is the capacity somehow to identify a relevant situation and its precedents sufficiently to recognise its imminent recurrence, and thereby to establish, however simply, a horizon of expectations. Thus equipped he will know when a previous experience can recur. If it was previously enjoyable he will want it; he will know what is agreeably familiar and therefore to be greeted, and what is novel and therefore a surprise. In short he must be able to anticipate.

2 Experiments on imitation: vocal mimicry

The voices a child acquiring speech most often hears are his own and those of his parents. Many authorities suggest that learning to speak requires that the child monitor his own utterances to approximate to those of his parents. Often parents say words like 'Dada' and 'Mama' to elicit imitation, and in the experiments these are called Dada utterances. This presupposes the child recognises his own voice and those of his parents, so that, within the limits of the experimental situation, he would be expected to try mimicking them when he hears them. A series of experiments was carried out to test whether an antustic child will selectively attend to and mimic his own voice or his parents', and, if so, which of the two he is more likely to imitate. The normal children were similarly tested at one year.

The major problem in recording the scores of the children in these experiments was the criteria used to define which utterance was to be counted as an imitated response and which was not. However many responses were recorded in the interval between two presentations, they were regarded as all scoring one response, but what in fact defined any response as scoring presented difficulties which were different in the cases of the normal and the autistic children.

In the case of the normal children scoring of responses to 'Dada' was easy since their responses were readily detectable. Scoring responses of the baby to utterances from his own babble was not difficult, because the particular utterance, either complete or partial, was so distinctive that it was easy to detect as mimicked, particularly since on the very rare occasion on which it was mimicked this was preceded by a pause as if the child were listening.

Responses from the autistic children were even less ambiguous. None uttered any response to an adult utterance. Their own utterances, which were considerably longer than those of the normal babies, were responded to occasionally and, although the response would consist of a selected part, long sections of it were reproduced and the utterance itself was so distinctive and complex that imitation was very evident and far too distinctive to be produced at random.

2.1 First series of experiments

The six autistic children (aged three to five) and the six babies (aged one year) were each presented with a 'listening tape' with two recordings, one on each side, to which they listened on successive days. For each child the first side contained utterances used to encourage imitation, e.g. 'Dada' spoken by four adults, of whom two were the child's parents, the others unfamiliar male and female adults. The second side contained utterances spoken by the child himself and one other child (see table 2a).

The adult's utterance was repeated five times at regular 10-second intervals for each of the four adults (A, B, C, D). They were presented to the child in the following way: (A) five times, 30-second pause; (B) five times, 1-minute pause; (C) five times, 30-second pause; (D) five times. This comprised one section and was introduced on the tape by the author's announcing 'one' and terminated by the author's saying 'end of one'. The section lasted about 5 minutes. The parents were asked to select a time convenient to them when the child was settled, not just awakened nor drowsy, nor hungry nor satiated (at least 20 minutes after a meal) and to play the tape section to the child, at the same time recording the child's reponse on a second recorder (response tape). This procedure was repeated four times in one day, twice in the morning, twice in the afternoon, but arranged according to the convenience of the parents and the temperament of the child. These four repeats of the experiment permitted not only a greater opportunity for the child to respond taking into account possible variations in his responsive mood throughout the day, but also enabled the order of presentation of the four adult voices to be varied. At the end of the day's testing the child's responses to forty presentations of his parents' voices and to forty of non-parent adult voices had been recorded. All responses occurring in the interval between two presentations were counted as *one* response.

The child's utterances. A single isolated string of babble, lasting about 1 second and well inflected, was extracted from the spontaneous recording tape and transferred to another tape repeated ten times at 10-second intervals. A second utterance, if possible 'Dada' or 'Mama', was similarly extracted and transferred. The third was extracted from the recording taken from the same child two months previously, and the fourth was the utterance of another child of the same age. Each was repeated ten times and arranged in four sections like the adults' utterances. The responses were recorded as with the adults' utterances.

Results: see tables 2a and 2b. All the normals responded very little to the babble utterances but responded well to 'Dada'. The number of their responses was greater to an adult voice than to their own but there seemed little significant difference between the responses to their own parent's voice and to any other adult, and indeed in some cases there were more responses to a strange adult's voice than to their own parent's.

In the case of the autistic children there was no response to the adult phrases at all. To the presentation of utterances of babble the autistic children did show great interest, often by ceasing any current babbling or by suddenly stopping their rocking or manneristic movements. They also imitated a few times selectively, *always* in response to presentation of their own utterance. It did not matter whether the utterance presented was current or not.

2.2 Second series of experiments

The main general point which emerged from the first experiment was that normal one-year-old babies do not preferentially mimic an utterance from their own vocalisation, whereas chronologically older autistic children do. Since the preparation of each listening tape was quite an arduous and time-consuming task, a delay of about two weeks was inevitable between recording the child's current utterances and playing them back to him. An obvious query was whether, with such a delay, the one-year-old baby would fail to recall the phonetic content of the utterance or be unable to reproduce it. To test whether delay in the playback was significant, a second experiment was carried out in which six other pre-verbal normal babies aged between eight and fourteen months were tested in the same way as described above,

Table 2a *Responses to playback of babble and 'Dada' phrases: normal babies*

Child	Sex	Age in months	Response to babble phrase (out of 40 presentations)			Response to 'Dada' phrase (out of 40 presentations)			'Dada' phrase used
			Own current babble	Own previous babble	Other child's babble	Own 'Dada' phrase	Parents' 'Dada' phrase	Adult (non-parent) 'Dada' phrase	
a	Girl	12	0	0	0	7	10	7	Mama
b	Boy	13	2	0	1	8	12	13	Dada x2
d	Girl	12	1	1	1	7	13	10	Mama x2
e	Girl	12	2	0	1	5	11	6	Dada x2
f	Boy	12	1	0	0	4	8	8	Dada
g	Boy	12	2	2	1	5	14	15	Dada

Anal. of Variance : Comparing cols. 4 and 5; $F = 15.85$, $p > 0.01$: cols. 5 and 6; $F = 1.38$, No significant difference: cols. 4 and 6; $F = 7.027$, $p > 0.05$; cols. 6 + 5 and 4 (x2); $F = 15.6$, $p > 0.01$.

Table 2b *Responses to playback of babble and adult phrases: autistic children*

Child	Sex	Age in years	Response to babble (out of 40 presentations)				Response to adult phrase (out of 40 presentations)		Adult phrase used
			Own current phrase I	Own current phrase II	Own previous phrase	Baby's phrase	Parent's phrase	Adult (non-parent's) phrase	
1	Boy	$4\frac{2}{12}$	0	2	7	0	0	0	
2	Boy	$5\frac{6}{12}$	3	0	0	0	0	0	
3	Boy	$5\frac{9}{12}$	3	1	3	0	0	0	
4	Boy	$3\frac{2}{12}$	1	4	9	0	0	0	'Linda'
7	Boy	$3\frac{10}{12}$	3	3	5	0	0	0	'Key'
8	Boy	$5\frac{2}{12}$	0	9	6	0	0	0	'Hallo'

but in addition their spontaneous vocalisation recorded for 15 minutes was promptly played back to them. Their vocal response to this 15-minute record of their own vocalisations was recorded as well as the record of their later responses to a listening tape prepared in the usual way.

Results: none of the normals imitated any section of the tape recording of their own babbling during the 15 minutes when it was played back immediately after recording it. This suggests that delaying the play-back has in no way contributed to the absence of response to any imitation of their own babble.

2.3 Third series of experiments

The propensity of the autistic children to imitate their own voices raised further points to test, e.g. whether these children could discriminate their own vocal utterances (a) from that of any other autistic child (discriminate utterance content), or (b) from another child of the same age producing the same utterances as their own (discriminate different voice). To extract an utterance from the recording of another autistic child was simple since the utterances were already available from playback experiments with each of the six autistic children. To obtain a reasonable copy of a selected utterance made by each autistic child was difficult since the copy had to be produced by a child of similar chronological age. This was eventually achieved with the help of the author's son, then aged nearly four, who, after repeated encouragement, produced a series of copies of the utterances to be used. It was interesting to note how difficult a normal three-year-old finds the reproduction of a semantically unstructured 'noise' even if he is in a cooperative mood and quite used to being recorded on tape. Again these six autistic children were presented with a listening tape and their responses recorded as described.

Results: see table 3. Again the table shows the extent to which the autistic children selectively imitate their own utterance in a very striking manner. Each child, if he scores at all, imitates his own utterance spoken by himself, and does not respond at all to the utterance of another autistic child or to the imitation of his own utterance by another child.

2.4 Fourth series of experiments

This led to the question: is the autistic child's propensity to imitate distinctive or a feature common to non-verbal sub-normal children of

Table 3 *Responses of autistic children to playback of phrase of (a) own babble (b) babble of another autistic child (c) an imitation of their own babble*

Child	Sex	Age in years	Response to playback of phrases (out of 30 presentations)		
			(a) Own current phrase	(b) Other autistic child's phrase	(c) Imitation of phrase (a)
1	Boy	$4\frac{5}{12}$	4	0	0
3	Boy	$5\frac{11}{12}$	0	0	0
4	Boy	$3\frac{5}{12}$	3	0	0
5	Boy	$4\frac{11}{12}$	3	0	0
6	Girl	$5\frac{8}{12}$	??	0	0
8	Boy	$5\frac{6}{12}$	5	0	0

this age? To explore this point eight pre-verbal Down's syndrome children, a subnormal group with a reputation for mimicry, of the same age range and mental age as the autistic children, were tested with both playback experiments. Their vocalisation over 15 minutes was recorded and immediately played back to them while their responses to it were recorded. From this record a vocal utterance of about 1 second's duration was selected and coupled with an utterance of similar duration of another Down's child in the series and was incorporated into a listening tape in the usual manner and played back to them. Again the response of each Down's child was scored on the basis of a possible forty presentations (a) of his own utterance and (b) of another Down's child's utterance.

Results: of all the eight Down's children who listened to the playback of their own and another child's voice, only one child responded, and he, responding once only, imitated not his own utterance but that of the control. Again the results demonstrate that Down's children, like babies, may occasionally respond to other children, which would suggest that the discrimination of their own utterance, its selection and its imitation is not a characteristic of vocal responses of Down's children in spite of their reputed propensity to mimic.

2.5 Discussion

Normal one-year-olds very rarely mimic their own babble utterances when they are played back to them except when their utterances are of the 'Mama'—'Dada' type. Thus the normal baby at one year seems unresponsive to playback of babble utterances, whether these are his own or another child's, but imitates a played-back 'Dada' utterance — *and is as likely to respond to this type of utterance whether he himself, either parent or another adult speaks it.* Accepting the artificiality of the experimental situation, two cautious but interesting conclusions emerge from this finding. Firstly that the response of the babies did not occur more frequently and thus did not seem to be reinforced significantly by the voices of their parents compared with non-parental or indeed non-adult voices speaking the utterance. Secondly that already the childrens' greater propensity to imitate a 'Dada' phrase compared with a random, and equally repeatable, utterance of babble suggests a response related to 'content' or meaning in the utterances they hear. They are little concerned with qualities like accent or emphasis of the speaker's utterance, but are already abstracting some feature from the utterance independently of the voice that utters it, a feature which presumably stimulates them to mimicry.

The response of the autistic children was in sharp contrast. They paid no attention to playback of adult utterances spoken to provoke their imitation. However they did respond to phrases of their own, whatever their form, extracted at random from their babble and apparently 'meaningless'. Not only did they respond to their own utterances but, significantly, they responded to these alone. They were unaffected by playback of other autistic children's utterances, normal children's babble or by the 'same' utterance as their own spoken by different voices. In this ability to recognise selectively their own utterance they differed from a group of subnormal Down's controls and from normal one-year-old children.

3 Experiments on imitation and the child's 'first' word

Three to six weeks after the babies in the series had begun babbling 'Dada' words, which the parents tended to regard as their first words, each produced a new 'word' which, uttered in specific circumstances, seemed to have a definite 'pointing' quality. Identification of 'pointing' words did not prove difficult. They occurred in all the cases of normal children as an early addition to their limited vocabulary of 'Dada' words between the ages of about eleven and eighteen months. They were uttered in special circumstances, and had certain specific characteristics. They often appeared suddenly in the child's speech associated with a definite and *exciting* event such as the striking of a cuckoo clock, or reaction to a pet dog introduced into the home, or the first evident noticing of an aeroplane. They did not appear in the babble or word play as did the 'Dada' type of word, but only when the stimulus was presented either intentionally or unintentionally to the child with or without an audience, e.g. if a child being recorded lay in bed and heard an aeroplane or a striking cuckoo clock. The nature of the words seemed unimportant. Some resembled clearly a word said to the child, e.g. 'bow wow', but others had much more tenuous connections, e.g. 'ug uck' for 'cuckoo' and 'dis' for 'what's this'. With repeated usage these words were not modified by the child to resemble a more conventional term. Indeed the parents themselves used the child's term in context so that their own language was modified rather than that of the child. The 'pointing' word, once used, was frequently generalised to other objects over the course of several days. 'Ug uck' was used to refer to any dial, 'bow wow' to refer to any animal on four legs, 'birdie' to refer to all things in the air. The 'pointing' word was always expressed with great zeal and excitement, while the mention of the word usually captured the child's attention and alerted him as if to look for the object to which for him it referred. The mention of the word by a parent also very readily induced repetition by the child himself, and it was this last characteristic which gave rise to the specific series of experiments.

An interesting feature of this new utterance was that not only was it quite reliably evoked by certain stimuli, but it seemed more readily imitated when spoken to a child than were the 'Dada' words currently used by him and his parents. This suggested a hypothesis: the new word has a different communicating significance from his 'Dada' words, not only in respect to its referents but also in the social response it elicits in the child, i.e. in his greater propensity to respond to it by vocal imitation. This hypothesis was amenable to testing using the same experimental design.

3.1 First series of experiments

As quickly as practicable after this new 'pointing' word was reported in the child's speech, each of the six original normal children was presented with three listening tapes, each of four sections constructed in the usual way.

The first tape contained a 'Dada' word currently *used* by the child and his parents and spoken on the tape by four adults (father, mother, male and female adult) in turn but in varying order for four sessions.

The second tape contained the new 'pointing' word, spoken by four adults, similarly arranged, and presented in four episodes to the child over one day in the usual fashion.

The third tape contained a new but meaningless word, 'Dibby', spoken by his two parents and two other adults in the usual way. This word contained syllables which the children *could* produce, but it had not appeared as a word in any of their vocabularies nor was it used at home and so was a completely novel and meaningless stimulus.

Results: see table 4a. (The results here and for the second series of experiments (see below) are the scores for each individual child of his vocal responses to presentations of his earliest 'pointing' word.) Four out of the six children in this experiment responded more often to the 'pointing' word than to the 'Dada' word. In one out of the six

Table 4a *Responses to playback presentation of 'Dada', 'Dibby' and 'Label' phrases*

Child	Sex	Age in months	Response to 'Dada' phrase (taught) out of 40 presentations			Response to 'Dibby' phrase (novel) out of 40 presentations			Response to 'Label' phrase (novel) (untaught) out of 40 presentations			'Label' phrase used
			Parents	Adult (non-parents)	Total (out of 80)	Parents	Adult (non-parents)	Total (out of 80)	Parents	Adult (non-parents)	Total (out of 80)	
a	Girl	15	6	2	8	4	0	4	5	1	6	'Car-car'
b	Boy	18	4	10	14	2	1	3	19	10	29	'Birdie'
d	Girl	15	8	9	17	3	5	8	9	8	17	'Books'
e	Girl	18	11	9	20	1	8	9	23	11	34	'Birdie'
f	Boy	16	9	7	16	—	—	—	10	17	27	'Doggie'
g	Boy	17	9	4	13	4	0	4	14	4	18	'Owow'

Anal. of Variance: Comparing cols. 3 (tables 4a and b) with col. 9 (4a) and 6 (4b): $F = 18.2$, 13.29. Significant difference at 0.1% level. $p > 0.1$.

children the number of responses to 'pointing' and 'Dada' words was the same, and one out of the six children responded more to the 'Dada' word than to the 'pointing' word. All six children responded more to presentations to 'Dada' and 'pointing' words than to the novel meaningless word 'Dibby'. An interesting feature was that whereas in response to the 'Dibby' and 'Dada' words the frequency of the child's response did not seem to depend in any way on whether it was his parent or another adult who was speaking, they responded more to 'pointing' words when these were spoken by parents. Three out of the six children had a higher score of responses to 'pointing' words when these were uttered by parents rather than non-parents.

3.2 Second series of experiments

A series of similar design (but excluding the 'Dibby' word) was presented to another six normal children to test further the interesting findings of the first series.

Results: see table 4b. All five children responded more to the 'pointing' utterance, i.e. imitated it more frequently than the 'Dada' utterance. Again there was a striking difference in the response to the 'pointing' utterance when spoken by parents compared with non-parents. The children who responded much more frequently to 'pointing' words were all children with generally high response scores who could be considered 'chatty'.

3.3 Discussion

Between eleven and eighteen months a normal child produces a number of words; these include words like 'Mama', 'Dada' and 'Baba' which have loose referents, are used in babble without any referents at all, and may be imitated when spoken to the baby by adults. However at some stage another group of words appears, with which the 'Dada' words are used concurrently. The new words are produced clearly in response to a particular event and are used entirely in response to it, and so do not appear in the child's babble except when that event occurs. These early words seem little affected by reinforcement since they do not alter to approximate more closely to an adult form and are applied quickly and *spontaneously* to a variety of situations or objects, suggesting the child's growing ability to extract similar impressions from his world and to categorise them. Presumably it is for this reason he attaches a label to the category, an act he performs with enthusiasm in the cases studied, in contrast to the more

Table 4b *Responses to playback. Presentation of 'Dada'-type (taught) and 'label' phrases*

Child	Sex	Age in months	Responses to 'Dada'-type phrase (out of 40 presentations)				Responses to 'label' phrase (out of 40 presentations)			
			Phrase	Parents	Non-parents	Total (out of 80)	Phrase	Parents	Non-parents	Total (out of 80)
c	Girl	16	'Daddy'	3	6	9	'Doggie'	8	6	14
h	Girl	20	'Mummy'	10	9	19	'Teddy'	26	15	41
i	Girl	15	'Tata'	7	8	15	'Chair'	14	14	28
j	Girl	16	'Dada'	6	3	9	'Judy'	6	5	11
k	Boy	19	'Mummy'	5	4	9	'Teddy'	16	7	23

Anal. of Variance: Comparing col. 1 with col. 2 (both tables): F is less than 1. No significant difference. Comparing col. 7 (4a) and 4 (4b) with col. 8 (4a) and 5 (4b): $F = 10.05$. $p > 0.01$.

relaxed, amused responses he makes to 'Dada' words. The evidence of these experiments suggests that such 'pointing' words not only arise and are used in specific circumstances, but are more *socially* alerting to the child since he imitates them more readily than the 'Dada' words he is currently using. This greater propensity to imitate a spoken 'pointing' word is not due to its novelty, since a novel, but non-'pointing' word, when similarly presented, is hardly imitated at all, although the child is quite capable of enunciating it. It is interesting that although 'pointing' words, if not formulated entirely by the child, are certainly *applied* without reference to his parents' vocal reinforcement, yet their imitation is more likely when spoken by a parent than when spoken by any other adult. This does not occur with 'Dada' words, though ironically they are just the words spoken by the parents for the purpose of stimulating the child's imitation. The way in which a child establishes categories for labelling with his 'pointing' words seems very subtle. It requires quite sophisticated integration of sensory input, permitting at least primitive recognition and anticipation of certain situations. This must be already present several months before the child begins to label, if we are to explain his earlier repertoire of pre-verbal vocal signals. From the evidence available concerning the *situations* which excite 'pointing' words compared with those evoking request signals, there seems to be no indication that additional perceptual refinement is required. Not only does the mechanism for integrating sensory impressions seem to be already in operation, but the use to which the child puts it as he selects his categories for 'pointing' words seems very subtle and is certainly not at the level of simply establishing similarities, i.e. that A1 looks like A2 and thus warrants labelling as A. Indeed from any survey of first categories that the child establishes, it is often very difficult to know *what* similarities the child does find. The dissimilarity is striking between various cars, buses, lorries, bicycles, yet all may be labelled 'car' (because of mode of progression?), or between a light bulb, aeroplane, moon or bird, yet all may be called 'birdie' (because of location?). It is easy to supply a suggested reason for the categories, but they are the adult's and not the child's, and, even if correct, still pose the question: why is *this* grouping used?

This of course returns the discussion to motives, for which various explanations are put forward: that the child groups objects according to function, or to some problem, or to some role they play in his daily experience. What seems more important than the criteria adopted is the likelihood that the child's brain is not simply editing its sensory impressions and sifting out regularities, but is actively scanning the variety of impressions it receives, on the lookout, as it were, for categories which it is continuously in the process of establishing and modifying. Such a scanning process seems very likely in the child, if only to account for his zeal, for his early and vital capacity to anticipate, for the constantly changing criteria that he uses to categorise, and for the obvious self-generated quality of his early categories and labels. It is as if the growing child's brain is 'imposing' an order which it is constantly checking and adjusting. An executive conceptualising role is developing which converts the child from one who simply sees to one who looks and from one who hears to one who listens.

4 Conclusions

Perhaps the fundamental general conclusion of these experiments is that far from 'learning' his earliest steps in vocal communication by responding to social reinforcement, the normal child relies more on developing a capacity to make sense out of his experience. At first he does this independently of the language spoken to him or the verbal response he receives. This response seems more effective in guiding than in initiating his efforts, which are generated in some other way. Consequently it seems improbable that the autistic child's early imperviousness to social reinforcement has very much effect *in itself* on his language difficulty. The experiments too have demonstrated the normal child's early reliance on some primitive grasp of 'meaning' which he himself imposes to produce his earliest real words and, before them, his first vocal communications. The findings of these studies would seem to extend 'infantwards', providing evidence that the child's capacity to imitate utterances depends on his grasp of their meaning. When the child himself generates utterances, be they of single words or longer, he listens to and repeats them more readily than words provided by parents for his imitation. This suggests that the child, in his very first steps in language, already listens to content or meaning, and only then does the identity of the voice affect his response.

This early structuring imposed by the normal child presumably leads on from 'pointing' words to the developing grasp of language constraints. Its absence in the autistic child results not only in his inability to generate labels but in his early words and sentences being quite unlike toddler speech and prone to mistakes that no toddler would make. If one assumes, as seems likely, that such an ordering or structuring process is used by the normal child, not only in his language but in handling all his experience, then its absence would prevent the autistic child from appreciating or anticipating situations which normally would generate pre-verbal signals. It is in his inability to produce such signals and to generate 'pointing' words that the autistic child reveals the nature of his own distinctive language handicap and of those perceptual and conceptual deficits which may underly it.

I3

Talking and playing with babies: the role of ideologies of child-rearing[1]

CATHERINE SNOW, AKKE DE BLAUW,
GHISLAINE VAN ROOSMALEN
University of Amsterdam

It is a striking feature of early mother—infant interaction in North America and Western Europe that mothers spend a great deal of time talking to their babies. Caretaking activities are accompanied by almost constant maternal chatter, and play activities seem to be largely organised around verbal elements, such as verses and songs. The central place of maternal speech in mother—infant interaction calls for some explanation — especially since the mothers who spend so much time talking to their babies contend that the babies cannot understand them. Why, then, do they talk to them so constantly, and in a register especially adapted to the baby addressee?

It has been suggested (Snow 1977) that the fact that mothers talk to young babies, and many of the characteristics of the way they talk to them, can be explained if one assumes that mothers are trying to carry on conversations with their babies. Thus, mothers' speech to young babies should be seen not as a monologue, but as an attempt to establish a dialogue within which (a) turn-taking is required, (b) a wide variety of infant behaviours can be credited as turns and (c) infant behaviours can be interpreted as meaningful because of their occurrence within the context of the dialogue.

The hypothesis that mothers are trying to establish conversational interactions with their babies rests on the presumption that the mothers think of the babies as potential conversational partners, capable of having thoughts and feelings and of communicating about them. Mothers who talk to their babies, then, are treating them as one treats other human beings who speak the same language, not as one treats lower animals or inanimate objects with which inter-subjectivity cannot be established.

The belief that it is appropriate to treat a baby in this way may be

269

characteristic of only some cultural groups. Studies of various cultures have shown that the incidence of maternal vocalisations to babies is much lower among the Zincanteco, a Mayan group living in Mexico (Brazelton 1972), the Kikuyu in Kenya (Liederman & Liederman 1977), Indians and Spanish-speaking mestizos in Guatemala (Kagan & Klein 1973), the Japanese (Caudill & Weinstein 1969), the Dutch (Rebelsky 1967), Zambians (Goldberg 1972) and lower-class Americans (Tulkin & Kagan 1972) than for the middle-class Americans most often studied. It has also been reported that the South American, African and Dutch groups value quiet, obedient babies more than do American mothers, who want active, individualistic babies, that Japanese mothers see their babies as extensions of themselves whose needs and wishes are obvious without extensive interpersonal communication (Caudill & Weinstein 1969) and that lower-class American mothers believe it silly to talk to babies who cannot yet understand. There is some suggestion, then, that talking to babies is typical behaviour only for those mothers who see their babies as separate individuals with whom communication is possible and necessary. More direct evidence linking what mothers believe to how they talk to their babies comes from the study by Bingham (1971), in which mothers' beliefs about their babies' abilities to communicate and comprehend were found to correlate better with the way they talked to them than with their ages. Much more information needs to be collected about the way in which mothers' behaviour towards their babies is related to their beliefs about what babies are like and how to care for them.

The study reported here is a preliminary attempt to relate mothers' beliefs about children to various aspects of mother—infant interaction in two groups of mothers, Dutch and English. We will refer to the mothers' beliefs about babies as their ideologies of child-rearing. Information about three dimensions of the mothers' ideologies were collected:

(1) Rules and techniques for caretaking. Notions about how and when a baby should be fed, when solids should be introduced, how important sleep is to a baby's health, whether crying should be responded to immediately etc. This dimension is very likely to be directly affected by medical or written sources, what mothers have been told by their midwives or doctors or the advice given at well-baby clinics. This dimension of child-rearing ideologies is obviously

very important in determining details of the baby's daily life, and can also be a major factor in influencing other dimensions of the mother's ideology in that it regulates the sorts of experiences a mother has with her baby. For example, Rebelsky (1967) reported that Dutch babies, who were fed on schedule, were likely to fall asleep during a feed, whereas demand-fed American babies were livelier and more ready to play at the end of a feeding session.

(2) Beliefs about babies. To what extent are babies seen as individuals, with needs, desires and abilities of their own? Can they communicate their needs and desires? What means of communication do they have? How much do they comprehend of adult speech?

(3) Beliefs about the process of development. How much can the parent influence the child's development? What kind of stimulation is it important to provide to babies, e.g. interesting visual environment, motor stimulation, verbal stimulation?

In addition to collecting information about the mothers' ideologies, we observed mother—infant interaction in the two groups when the babies were three, four and a half and six months old. In discussing the data from the observation sessions, we will concentrate on the episodes of mothers' talking to their babies. These episodes are seen as attempts to establish communication with the babies, and thus reflect the mothers' beliefs about the ability of the baby to function as a communicative partner.

The study reported here was designed as exploratory rather than experimental, and for many reasons (some to be discussed below) no firm conclusions can yet be drawn as to direct relationships between ideologies and practices of child-rearing. However, we hope that the discussion of similarities and differences between the Dutch and English mothers will provide some insights into the way mothers' beliefs about babies affect their behaviour with babies, and the way their behaviour reflects otherwise untappable aspects of their beliefs.

1 Procedure

Observations were carried out on babies from nine English families living in the Cambridge area and eleven Dutch families living in Amsterdam. The Dutch and the English studies were planned and carried out separately by different observers (C.S. for the English and A.B. and G.R. for the Dutch families), which resulted in both planned and unplanned differences between the procedures employed. Nonetheless, the procedures were similar enough on the following points to make some comparisons fruitful:

(1) Age of the infants observed. Babies were observed at three, four and a half and six months, ± one week.

(2) Scoring. The observation sessions were tape recorded, and the observers made notes of what was going on with the help of a check-list, checking off the occurrence of certain maternal and baby behaviours at 15-second intervals. Specific details of the play activities of both mother and baby were also noted down.

(3) Social class of families observed. Both groups represented a range of social class, with a few working-class families in which neither parent had any post-secondary education, one middle-class family in which both parents had professional degrees, and the rest in between.

(4) Family constellation. The mother worked part time in two Dutch families and one English one. None of the English families and one of the Dutch had regular, part-time child-care help. The mother was the primary and practically the only caretaker in all the other cases. Ten of the eleven Dutch babies and five of the nine English babies had one brother or sister aged two to four, and one Dutch and one English baby had two older siblings. The two- to four-year-old sibling was present in the house all the time during the Dutch observations, but was often playing in the garden or at nursery school during the English observation sessions.

(5) Interviews. In both studies the observers asked the mothers questions after each observation session and also in a separate interview to obtain information concerning the baby's daily schedule, feeding and sleeping patterns and recent achievements, and the mothers' attitudes and beliefs about babies and raising children.

Potentially important differences between the observation procedures include:

(1) Length of the observation sessions. The English sessions were one and a half to two hours long, and the Dutch sessions one hour. The longer sessions made it more difficult for the English mothers to restrict their activities to those dealing only with the baby, and for the baby to be maximally happy and responsive during the entire session. Shorter periods of social interaction were thus observed in the English than in the Dutch families.

(2) Number of observers. The Dutch sessions were all carried out

by two observers, and the English by only one. The presence of two observers may have inhibited the mothers from interacting with the observers (or vice versa); there was considerably more conversation between the observer and mother in the English than in the Dutch study.

(3) Instructions to the mothers. In the English study, the mothers were told that the observations should be scheduled for a time when the baby 'is most likely to be awake and happy'. As the mothers differed in the extent to which they believed their presence was necessary to keep the baby happy, they also differed in whether they chose a time of maximum interaction or not. The Dutch mothers were told that the observation should be scheduled for a time when the baby was 'awake, happy, and when the mother and sibling were likely to be present'. The incidence of the mother's leaving the room or going on with her household tasks was much lower in the Dutch observation sessions.

Despite these dissimilarities between the studies, which result mostly in incomparability primarily on measures of length of social interaction, the questions of how, when and why mothers talk to and play with their babies can be addressed from both sets of data.

2 Results

2.1 Cross-cultural comparison of caretaking

The potential importance of such factors as professional advice given to mothers for babies' daily lives is quite clear from a comparison of the two groups on various parameters of caretaking (see table 1). The English babies were much more likely to be breast-fed. Breast-feeding is more encouraged by the medical establishment in England (at least, in Cambridge; large differences occur within Britain in the incidence of breast-feeding, see Newson & Newson 1963) than in Holland. Furthermore, Dutch mothers are advised to breast-feed until six weeks, whereas English mothers are encouraged to continue for six months. Hospital and post-natal care routine may also contribute to greater success at breast-feeding in Britain: Dutch babies are not suckled until the second or third day, when the milk 'comes in' whereas English babies are suckled from the first morning after birth at the latest; test-weighing babies is normal practice in Holland but not in England; and demand feeding is more likely to be practised in

Table 1 *Caretaking parameters in English and Dutch families (percentages)*

	English babies (n = 9)	Dutch babies (n = 11)
Breast-fed at 3 months	77.8	9.1
Breast-fed at 6 months	66.7	0.0
Demand-fed	77.8	0.0
Occasional middle-of-night feeds at 3 months	44.4	0.0
Occasional middle-of-night feeds at 6 months	44.4	0.0
Baby-chair used at 3 months	77.8	81.8
Playpen used at 3 months	0.0	27.3
Playpen used at 6 months	0.0	100.0
Toys/mobiles in cot	100.0	45.5

England (see Richards 1975 for a discussion of the factors contributing to success at breast-feeding).

The groups differed strikingly in where the babies were put to play on their own, when the mother wished to get on with her other tasks. By four and a half months all the Dutch babies were placed in a playpen for quiet play, as well as in their chairs or sometimes in bed. The English babies were more typically placed on a blanket or mat on the floor, often partially unclothed. All the English mothers reported independently and spontaneously that their babies greatly enjoyed kicking on the floor with no nappy on. No Dutch mother reported this or was observed to remove her baby's nappy for play periods. The English babies were also more likely to be placed in a pram in the garden and the Dutch babies in bed for periods of sleep and quiet play. This difference may reflect differences in the housing situations of the two groups rather than differences in beliefs about the importance of fresh air; all the English families but only two of the Dutch families had access to a private garden.

2.2 Cross-cultural comparison of beliefs about babies and development

The mothers in both groups said they could distinguish differences among the babies' various kinds of crying, and that the babies' vocalisations had some specific meaning, e.g. contentment or demand for attention. Furthermore, all the mothers felt, at least by six months, that their babies could understand some characteristics of adult speech, usually the tone of voice or combinations of often-repeated sentences with stereotyped situations. For example, one Dutch mother said her baby knew playtime was over and it was time to sleep if she put him in his cot and said decidedly 'Wel te ruste' (Sleep tight). However, all the mothers denied that their babies could understand more than a couple of words or stereotyped sentences.

The two groups differed rather more in the types of stimulation they considered important. The English mothers talked a great deal about what their babies liked to look at, and often placed them so they could look out of the window or at some interesting visual array. One English mother found she could amuse her son by opening all the cupboards in the kitchen and letting him look at the tins and boxes. Dutch mothers were less orientated to providing visual stimulation, as they showed by (among other things) their lesser tendency to provide hanging toys or mobiles in the cot. Motor development was not mentioned as particularly important by any of the mothers, though most did encourage their babies to sit, stand and reach for things, and many of the games and play sessions were based on eliciting motor responses.

In general, then, the Dutch and the English mothers differed considerably less in their beliefs about what babies are like and how development proceeds than in their rules and techniques for caretaking. The babies' daily lives were undoubtedly influenced by the differences in caretaking practices, but such differences in the parameters of caretaking may be relatively unimportant compared to the quality of social interaction experienced by the baby, if concomitant differences in the other dimensions of child-rearing ideologies do not exist.

2.3 Talking to babies in England and Holland

The mothers talked to their babies a great deal both in England and in Holland. The episodes of talking were occasioned for all the mothers by specific events (e.g. certain infant behaviours, certain maternal interventions), but some mothers also engaged in large amounts of 'talking for fun', playful talk which had no immediate initiating event. The similarities between the two groups of mothers in the way they talked to their babies and the occasions they chose for doing so can be related to the fact that both groups held very similar beliefs about the babies as potential communicative partners.

The amount of time spent talking to babies was much greater for the Dutch than for the English group (see tables 2 and 3). Unfortunately, the differences in the observation procedures (discussed above) make it impossible to decide whether this is a cultural difference or a situational difference. The findings of Rebelsky (1967) that Dutch mothers vocalised much less to their babies than American mothers are difficult to reconcile with our results. The difference may be accounted for by changes in Dutch child-care practices in the last ten years, or by the fact that Rebelsky was looking at younger infants (two to twelve weeks) than those in our study.

Means of the Dutch and English groups are presented in tables 2 and 3 for the following measures: frequency per hour of 15-second

Table 2 *Mean frequency of ISIs and mean frequency and length of ESIs for English and Dutch dyads at 3 and 6 months*

	English 3 months	6 months	Dutch 3 months	6 months
ISIs/hr	84.3	69.9	139.9	138.4
ESIs/hr	35.8	36.0	30.4	33.6
Mean length of ESIs (in intervals)	2.4	1.9	4.8	4.3

Table 3 *Mean frequency of ISIs and mean frequency and length of ESIs for the English dyads with and without an older child present, at 3 and 6 months*

	3 months present	absent	total	6 months present	absent	total
n	3[a]	5	8	5	4	9
ISIs/hr	53.4	98.1	81.3	54.3	89.5	69.9[b]
ESIs/hr	37.3	35.9	36.3	33.9	38.7	36.0
Mean length of ESIs (in intervals)	1.4	2.8	2.3[c]	1.6	2.3	1.9[c]

a One session in which the older sibling was present about a third of the time was not included.
b Difference between absent and present almost significant (p < 0.06), as tested with a Mann–Whitney *U*.
c Significant difference between present and absent, as tested with a Mann–Whitney *U*.

intervals during which the mothers talked to the babies (intervals of social interaction, ISIs), and the frequency per hour of episodes of social interaction (ESIs). An ESI is defined as one or more consecutive ISI unbroken by any 15-second interval of non-interaction. In all cases, the data are based only on periods of potential social interaction, i.e. when the mother and baby were in the same room, the baby was awake, and the baby was not being breast- or bottle-fed (mothers tended to talk very little to their babies during periods when the nipple was in the mouth; see Snow 1977). A greater portion of the Dutch observation sessions consisted of periods of potential interaction, since the Dutch mothers were less likely to be occupied in other rooms or with other tasks.

The generalisation that mothers talk a great deal to their babies holds true for both groups, despite the differences in length of interaction episodes (see table 2). The English mothers talked less to their babies, not because they were less likely to start to interact with them or because they were more likely to interact silently, but because they were more involved with other duties and activities during the observation session. Interestingly, only the length of ESIs, not their frequency, was affected. The importance of the mother's other activities in determining how much social interaction a baby experiences is made clear from the comparison of babies who were alone with their mothers during the observation and those whose older siblings were present (table 3). Babies who were alone experienced more ISIs, i.e. longer ESIs, than those with a sibling present. The English baby who had two older siblings present experienced the shortest periods of social interaction of all the babies (mean of 1.3 intervals at three months and 1.2 intervals at six months). Social class has also been found to affect length of ESIs, but not their frequency (Snow et al. forthcoming).

2.4 Occasions for talking to babies

The results considered above, showing that, although the length of ESIs was affected by these factors, their frequency remained quite constant across observational situations, social class of family and presence of other potential interactors, suggest that the occasions for starting to talk to a baby may be fairly constant across widely differing situations. This suggestion is supported by the observation that certain events, whose frequency is not directly a function of situation, social class or persons present, almost always caused the mother to start talking to the baby. Not all ESIs were started by such events, but the fact that such events could reliably start ESIs and did initiate a large proportion of ESIs decreases variability in the number of ESIs occurring.

Two events almost always caused all mothers to start talking to their babies: the occurrence of certain infant behaviours and the occurrence of certain maternal behaviours which affected the infant. Infant behaviours which almost invariably elicited a response from the mother will be referred to as quasi-communicational, to indicate that they were treated as communicational by the mother even though the baby's intent to communicate through those behaviours is doubtful or indeterminable. The quasi-communicational behaviour at three months included smiling, laughing, burping, sneezing, coughing, vocalising and looking intently at something or suddenly changing gaze direction. Many of these behaviours were still responded to reliably at six months, though the expansion of the baby's behavioural repertoire by six months meant that responses to the quasi-communicational behaviours played a less important role in the mother's speech. The mothers' responses to the quasi-communicational behaviours have been analysed in Snow (1977) as having the character of responses within adjacency-pairs, i.e. utterances which are obligatory according to the rules of conversation. The original analysis was based on 20-minute videotapes of only two mother–infant pairs; it is thus strong support for the notion that conversational rules play a role in normal mother–infant interaction that even in the much freer and longer observation sessions employed in the present study such responses were frequent components of maternal behaviour (see table 4).

The second situation in which mothers almost invariably started talking to their infants was when they intervened in some way in the infant's activities – e.g. when picking the baby up or putting him down, shifting his position, giving him a toy, taking something away

Table 4 *Mean frequency (per hour of potential social interaction) of responses to quasi-communicational behaviours by the English mothers at 3 and 6 months*

	3 months	6 months
Frequency	8.4	13.1
Range	0–27.0	3.3–30.6

from him, settling down to feed, removing the nipple, checking his nappy etc. During these activities, the mother talked about what she was doing, and very often in a way that made the baby a partner rather than an object of her intervention. Techniques used to treat the baby as a partner in these activities included (a) using the baby-talk pronouns 'we' or 'you' instead of 'I' to refer to the actor, (b) asking the baby for 'permission' to carry out the intervention and (c) giving reasons for the intervention. An example of this kind of talk is:

English mother putting six-month-old into baby-chair while she fetches his lunch: You've got to sit there and be good and quiet for a bit. All right?
A few minutes later, she returns with the food to feed the baby: Now are you ready for some food, Toti? Come on, we've got to undress you and take everything off.

Such utterances can be seen as marking out the major segments of the baby's life — feeds, playtimes, nappy changes and sleep periods were begun and ended by maternal intervention, and thus by content-related maternal utterances. There is evidence that the maternal utterances produced in such situations are highly repetitive and predictable, and that such maternal utterances may play an important role in the child's early language acquisition (Ferrier 1978).

A third situation which caused almost all the mothers to start to talk to the baby was talking to a third person about the baby. For example:

English mother to observer: He loves it when I take his nappy off.
Mother to baby: Dontcha? Hey? Always get a nice smile when I take his nappy off, don't I? (three months)

It seems from such examples almost as if the mother considered it rude to discuss the baby in his presence without including him in the conversation. It is a general rule of adult conversation in both Britain and the Netherlands that people are not talked about in their presence unless the discussants are clearly dominant over the discussed, e.g. teachers discussing a student, or wish to create some impression on the discussed, e.g. police officers discussing a captive. It is significant that the mothers observed did not treat their babies this way, but as potential interactors who should not be excluded from the discussion merely on grounds of immaturity.

Finally, a certain amount of the mothers' speech occurred without any clear occasion in the preceding situation. Quite often, mothers just started talking to babies 'for fun' — and they sometimes admitted that this was their motivation, as in the following examples:

English mother has just been playing extensively with three-month-old, and is standing holding him in face-to-face position after a game of 'aeroplane': You're no sagger, are you? You're not a sagger. Hooo. Well.
Baby vocalises.
Mother: Haaaaaa (imitation of vocalisation).
Baby vocalises.
Mother: Haaaaaa, Aaaaa. Mmmm. I could play with you all day, couldn't I? You'd like that. Play all day?
Baby vocalises.
Mother: I think you prefer it to eating sometimes, don't you? Playing. It's much better.

Dutch mother holding six-month-old on lap: Zo, nou moet ie naar bed (kus). Ik blijf altijd knuffelen met die kerel. Mm (kus). Daar smelt-ie van. Ja. Wordt ontzettend klein, die baby (kus). Andere babies worden groter, die wordt steeds kleiner. Van het opknuffelen. (So, now he has to go to bed (kiss). I always go on cuddling that fellow. Mmm (kiss). He melts from it. Yes. Gets terribly tiny, that baby (kiss). Other babies get bigger, this one gets smaller and smaller. From cuddling.)

Talking for fun was the most variable component of the social interactions. Responding to babies' quasi-communicational behaviours and explaining the mothers' interventions occurred predictably and reliably, even for the busiest mothers with the most distractions. If necessary, mothers would interrupt their conversations with others or their ongoing activities to respond and comment. 'Talking for fun' occurred if and when the mother had the time and inclination, and a few of the babies in both groups experienced little or none of this kind of social interaction. 'Talking for fun' will be discussed more fully in the next section.

2.5 Talking for fun

Talking for fun occurred primarily in three contexts: games, attempts to elicit specific responses (most often vocalisations) from the baby, and while offering toys or other objects to play with. Talking-for-fun episodes were often continuations of already established contact, e.g. talk while dressing the baby would develop into a game. Talking for fun was a highly variable component of maternal speech. Busy, distracted mothers had little time for this kind of talk. On the other hand, it would be misleading to suggest that adults are solely responsible for initiating talking for fun; passive babies or highly object-orientated babies elicited very little talking for fun, because they could amuse themselves. It was in most specific cases impossible to determine which of the partners initiated a talking-for-fun episode. Such episodes grew out of longer history of interacting, getting to know one another's preferences and learning to predict one another's responses, such that the question of who initiated a specific episode may be unanswerable.

2.6 Games

The kinds of games played in the English and the Dutch families were very similar, though of course the verbal and musical elements differed. Under games were classified all the standard games, rhymes and songs for playing with babies (e.g. 'Pat-a-cake' and the Dutch equivalent 'Klap es in je handjes', 'Peekaboo' and the Dutch 'Kiekeboe', bouncing games with rhymes such as 'Ride a cock horse' etc.), as well as games that had become institutionalised for one family or mother—child pair (e.g. an English mother had discovered that her daughter enjoyed a 'vowels game', in which the mother elicited laughter by slowly saying 'a-e-i-o-u' with exaggerated facial expressions). The criteria used to identify a game in this study were (a) turn-taking, (b) rules defining the appropriate response and (c) a definable beginning and end. Table 5 gives a summary of the kinds of games played by the mothers with the babies, and table 6 a summary of the frequency with which games were played in the observation sessions at three and six months for the English and Dutch families, and of the variety of games played by each pair. Tickling, bouncing and lifting games predominated in both groups. Frequency was about the same in the two groups, but the English mothers played more different games with their children. This

Table 5 *Kinds of games played by English and Dutch dyads at 3 and 6 months*

	English Game	Number of pairs playing	Dutch Game	Number of pairs playing
3 months	tickling	3	tickling	2
	lifting baby in air	2		
			looming and approach	1
			peekaboo	1
	jiggling feet	1		
	stretch	1		
	kick	1		
	imitation — facial expression	1		
	mirror — seeing self	1		
6 months	lifting baby in air	3	lifting baby in air	5
	looking and approach	2	looming and approach	4
	tickling and poking	4	tickling and poking	4
	bouncing	5	bouncing	1
	pulling to sit/stand	3	pull to sit/stand	4
	peekaboo	3		
	blowing on tummy	2		
	mirror — seeing self	1		
	a—e—i—o—u	1		
	catch it	1		
	patty cake	1		
	tug-of-war	1		
	tower-boom	1		

Table 6 *Mean frequency of games and mean number of different games played by English and Dutch dyads at 3 and 6 months*

	English		Dutch	
Age (months)	3	6	3	6
Frequency: mean	1.4	3.7	0.9	3.9
range	0—5	0—8	0—1	1—7
Different games: mean	1.1	3.0	0.4	1.5
range	0—3	1—6	0—1	1—3

difference cannot be accounted for by the greater length of the observation sessions in the English study, since the amount of potential interaction time was only slightly greater for the English babies.

All the game episodes observed had certain common characteristics, of which the most striking was the importance of the crucial verbal element. Even in 'body games' such as bouncing or tickling, the actions involved were accompanied verbally, sometimes by fairly simple formulations ('ticka-ticka-ticka'), but more often by quite complex rhymes or songs. The most commonly observed English tickling verse was:

> Round and round the garden
> Like a teddy bear, (said while tickling baby's palm in a circular motion)
> One step, two step, (walking fingers toward stomach or underarm)
> Tickle you under there! (said very fast, while tickling vigorously)

The equivalent Dutch rhyme is:

> Daar komt een muisje aangelopen.
> (There comes the mousie walking up) (Said while walking fingers slowly up arm or stomach)
> Die is in baby's nekje gekropen!
> (He has cralwed in baby's neck) (said very fast, while tickling vigorously)

Both these tickling games show the same structure: a slow initiatory phase with standard kinaesthetic and verbal components, and a fast, vigorous climax which can be varied as to timing and site of tickling. This structure enabled the baby, after he had learned the game, to anticipate the climax during the initiatory phase, but also to be surprised by the unpredictable elements of the climax. The variability of the final phase was also exploited by the mothers during prolonged episodes, when the game was repeated several times. During the repetitions, they tended to vary the site of tickling and to lengthen the pause between the initiatory and the climactic phases. Bruner (1975a) has discussed the ways in which such pause lengthening in well-established bouncing games can give the child the opportunity to produce signals that the mother should proceed to the awaited climax. Bruner was discussing somewhat older children; no clear 'get on with it' signals were observed from our three- to six-month-olds. However, the precursors to producing such signals — quietening, attending to the mother's face at the beginning of the game and responding enthusiastically to the climax — were observed regularly.

2.7 Elicitation sequences

Elicitations of vocalisations or other behaviours (reaching, kicking, smiling etc.) were similar to games in that turn-taking was clearly the mother's object. However, the rules about when the response was to occur were much less stringent than in games, and the elicitation episodes had no clear beginning or end. Failure on the baby's part to respond to a game caused the mother to stop playing it almost immediately, whereas eliciting talk might be continued for quite extensive periods with no response from the baby. Furthermore, whereas some elicitation sequences were aimed at eliciting a specific response, e.g. vocalisation, many elicited no particular response but just attention and heightened excitation from the baby:

English mother, kneeling in front of her three-month-old, who is lying on his back on the floor: Are you a good boy? Are you? Are you? Are you? Are you? There's a nice smile. Yes. Yes, there's a nice smile. Yes.
Baby laughs.
Yes. You old giggler. Are you a good boy? Are you a good boy? Are you a good boy? Are you a good boy? Are you a good boy?

Mothers used the acoustic properties of their speech to effect the elicitation. Speech during the elicitation sequences was invariably high-pitched, with exaggerated intonation contours, and tended to be quite rapid (unlike speech in games, which was often slowed down, at least in the first phase), and all these characteristics intensified as the sequence went on, as if the mother was literally trying to work the baby up to a higher pitch of excitement.

2.8 Object play

Increasingly during the age-span observed, mothers' play with their babies came to be centred around objects. At three months, all but one of the games observed involved only the baby's and/or the mother's body parts. At six months a number of episodes were observed in which an action begun with the body (e.g. looming and nuzzling in the baby's tummy with one's face) was repeated with a toy, such as a squeaking elephant or a teddy bear. Also, true object-

centred games such as building a tower for the baby to knock down
had been introduced. This greater incorporation of toys into play
with the babies reflected the evident greater interest of older babies
in inanimate objects (the percentage of vocalisations directed to
objects by the Dutch babies doubled between four and a half and six
months). The mothers were also responding to the ability of the six-
month-old to reach for and grasp objects, an ability which was only
minimally present at three months.

In addition to incorporating objects in games and elicitation episodes, mothers spent an increasing amount of time simply offering
objects to the baby. Some of these offers were fairly perfunctory,
giving the baby something to do so the mother could get on with
other activities, but a fair portion were elaborated episodes in which
the object was held up, the child's attention drawn to it, its properties
were demonstrated and various actions performed on it by the
mother before she gave it to the baby. These episodes were usually
accompanied by several utterances about the toy. For example:

Dutch mother offering a ball to six-month-old: Erik, pak de bal!
Pak'm. Goed zo! Hou'm vast. (Erik, take the ball! Take it. Well done!
Hold on to it.)

English mother offering mirror in the shape of a fish to six-month-old:
That's your fish. Well, I put it there and you threw it away. Look
(holding mirror-side up to baby's face). That funny old baby's Duncan.

Interestingly, even the rather perfunctory object-offer episodes were
almost always marked in the mother's speech, if only by 'Here' or 'Do
you want it?'

It can be seen from table 7 that the English mothers offered objects
considerably more frequently than the Dutch mothers (difference
significant at three months, $p < 0.002$, not at six months). It is tempt-
ing to relate the English mothers' greater frequency of object offers
at three months to their beliefs that babies enjoy and benefit from
looking at things. Possibly the talking-for-fun component of mothers'
speech is influenced by various aspects of the mothers' ideologies at
earlier ages, but as the babies become older and more active they play
an increasingly important role in creating their own social environments. Thus, the babies' obvious interest in objects may have caused
the Dutch mothers to offer more objects to play with at six months,

Table 7 *Mean frequency with which objects were offered to 3- and 6-month-olds by English and Dutch mothers*

Age (months)	English 3	6	Dutch 3	6
Mean	3.67	9.22	0.27[a]	5.55
Range	0—11	4—20	0—1	1—13

a Difference between Dutch and English significant at p < 0.002, as tested with a Mann—Whitney *U*.

whether or not they believed such object play was important to development.

2.9 Talking for fun as a way of establishing communication

The three contexts of talking for fun were not always clearly differentiable from one another; object offers were often combined with games or elicitations, and games sometimes changed into elicitations within a single episode. However, the category 'talking for fun' was quite clearly differentiable from the other, more 'business-orientated' maternal speech, acoustically as well as in content and structure. All the talking-for-fun episodes were characterised by the fact that the baby was given the opportunity to do something contingent on the mother's behaviour and on the content of her speech. Thus, talking for fun creates situations within which the mother can be most certain that she has in fact effectively communicated with her child.

In games, for example, the baby makes the 'correct' response at the right time — a reassuring sign that he knows the rules and knows the game is being played. Mothers are thus assured that, for the few moments they spend engaged in the game, at least, they and their babies are 'on the same wavelength', thinking about the same thing, engaged in seeking the same goals, in short, communicating. Similarly, success in eliciting a specific response implies that the baby has understood and is willing to comply with the request. Accepting a proffered object presupposes that the mother and the baby are both attending to that object and sharing the same goal. All these situations, then, create contexts within which communication can be *felt* to occur — quite independently of the extent to which the baby really does know the rules of the game, or knows which response his mother is trying to elicit, or is thinking about the object being offered. The importance of these moments of perceived communication in establishing the mother—infant relationship should not be underestimated. Much of what a baby does in his first few months of life is only minimally interpretable for adults, even familiar adults. The frustration involved in dealing with an infant who is crying or fussing for an unknown reason is reflected very clearly in the frequency with which mothers ask 'What's the matter?' of their babies (Snow 1978). Some mothers express their frustration even more explicitly, for example:

English mother to three-month-old: Well, what shall we do with you? I never know what to do with you.

The frustration of not knowing what a baby is fretting or crying about, and of not knowing what he is interested in or thinking about when happy, contrasts clearly with the satisfactory feeling of effective communication mothers receive from achieving eye-to-eye contact with their babies (Robson 1967), being smiled at (Ambrose 1961), recognising the meaning of certain cries or gestures, being imitated (Newson & Pawlby 1974), and being able to play games with and elicit specific responses from their babies. The way mothers talk to babies is well designed to create the feeling of effective communication, and the structure of games and other playful episodes is especially appropriate to that end.

3 Conclusion

Mothers who believe their babies are potential communicative partners talk to them in ways which serve both to strengthen that belief and to make it come true. The fact that the mother talks in predictable ways about recurrent events undoubtedly helps the child to structure his world, to segment events, to distinguish different types of activities and to anticipate future events. However, evidence from cultures within which maternal vocalisation to babies is infrequent should make us cautious about concluding that normal language acquisition requires that mothers talk to infants, play games with them, comment on objects and events, respond to quasi-communicational infant behaviours and treat the infants as conversational partners.

Dutch and English mothers were found to differ from one another in their beliefs about how babies should be cared for, and to differ considerably in the ways they organised their babies' daily lives. Nonetheless, their notions about what babies were like and how development proceeds were quite similar, and the way they interacted with the babies, talked to them and played with them were also very similar, at least between three and six months. More extensive and controlled observations might well result in findings of differences between the groups in parameters of mother—infant interaction other than those studied here, and perhaps in certain aspects of the ways the babies develop as well. Nonetheless, the most striking aspect of the mother—infant interaction in both Holland and England is the extent to which it rests upon and reflects the mothers' beliefs that their babies are potential communicative partners.

Note

1. The first author wishes to express her appreciation to the Unit for Research on the Medical Applications of Psychology, University of Cambridge, which provided facilities for carrying out the English study and preparing this paper.

14

Early tactile communication and the patterning of human organization: a New Guinea case study

E. RICHARD SORENSON

Smithsonian Institution, Washington, D.C.

Transmission of culturally specific human possibility, including communication, takes place as a growing child's neuromuscular system is patterned by the typical experiences provided by his milieu. Different milieux can provide quite different standard situations which, in effect, expose the infant and young child to alternative programs of sensory input, different gestalts of emotional organization, and different foci of perception and cognition.

Techniques of phenomenological inquiry, developed during the study of child behavior and human development among the Fore people of New Guinea,[1] revealed a previously unstudied kind of socio-sensual human organization which began in infancy during a period of almost continuous, unusually rich tactile interaction. From this foundation, a pattern of freely expressed exploratory play led ultimately to an economically adaptive personality which was unusually responsive to new opportunity and challenge, and socially flexible.

The Fore people had remained a small neolithic cultural enclave, isolated from the outside world until the mid 1950s.[2] Even through the 1960s they remained the beneficiaries of an ecological situation which fostered centrifugal segmentary dispersal into adjacent regions of economic opportunity. Differing from both hunter-gatherers and settled agriculturalists, the Fore had evolved their own behaviorally adaptive, territorially dispersive life-style. Their child handling and rearing practices sustained this way of life with a type of human behavior patterning which contrasts markedly with those of many other cultures.

When I first went to the Fore lands, I was impressed by the extensive bodily contact enjoyed by the very young, and the general absence of crying, infant frustration and striking out. And even in these early days of my research the absence of strife within the small Fore communities seemed in some still unfathomable way to relate to the lack of much discontent in the young. But it was not until I began to examine the daily life events of childhood in the research film record that the pervasiveness of early physical contact or its significance as a socio-sensual foundation to the Fore way of life became clear.

1 Method of inquiry

To study human behavior in an exotic culture presents special problems. Because the behavioral dynamics of the Fore protoagricultural way of life were not yet known, there was no way of knowing what was important to examine. As in any cross-cultural study, cultural blinders (blinkers) were a major problem. We cannot avoid the fact that we are all culturally conditioned beings with our own culturally specific patterns of awareness and understanding. There is no alternative to perceiving and talking about what we see in other cultures through the colored spectacles of our own backgrounds.

Yet only to the degree that we can extend awareness beyond this limitation can we escape the disjointed 'understandings' and invidious appreciations which so often accompany cross-cultural observation. Obviously there are epistemological weaknesses in inquiring into quite different patterns of human expression using the parameters of our own patterns.

The phenomenological data gathering ability of film provides a means to penetrate this cultural barrier to obtain human behavioral data not limited to those recognized or categorized by the culturally molded mental set of the observer. And with film we may inquire and document without first having to know what is significant to note.

For this reason I turned to cameras and film as my primary means of collecting data of Fore behavior in daily life.[3]

To realize the potential of film it was only necessary to develop a methodology of phenomenological inquiry which would take advantage of its facsimile quality. This required attention to sampling strategies, methods of handling unrealized data, strategies of analysis which could bring undifferentiated and unrecognized data to light, and a means to verify findings.

The sampling strategy took shape somewhat intuitively, at first, as a combination of three basic approaches: (1) opportunistic sampling,

(2) programmed sampling and (3) digressive search. These approaches put the data collection in an intellectual framework and provided an overall sampling rationale which would extend broadly into poorly understood situations.

Opportunistic sampling was the taking advantage of unanticipated events when they happened. It was particularly useful to the novel and unfamiliar situations so often provided by an alien culture, and it permitted a flexibility in approach which allowed greatest advantage to be taken of personal impression and insights.

Programmed sampling was focused on those things which were considered important in advance. It took advantage of the parameters and structural concepts already developed and proved significant in our own culture. Programmed samples drew from sources broader than individual personal awareness or interest and led to more comprehensive samples in tune with a larger body of existing scholarly knowledge. It led to documentation of types of events that would have been ignored by a filmer shooting only that which captured his personal interest.

Digressive search. Both programmed and opportunistic sampling, however, rely on forms of mind and habit which reflect one's own culture and background. They depend either on the state of publicly accepted knowledge, as developed through history, or on the sensory and cognitive abilities and habits which have emerged from one's own life experiences. The digressive search allows us to begin to move away from these limitations by adopting a deliberately random search strategy which gets into areas and events not yet appreciated or understood. It fosters an increased component of exotic, unrecognized and unplumbed information by putting the camera in new places ahead of understanding and intuition to document areas where significance is unknown, appreciation has not yet developed, and awareness is not attuned.[4]

Employing a mixture of these filming strategies I divided the study into three phases: (1) initial fieldwork and collection of visual data as research film; (2) analysis of research film records to discover culturally specific patterns of child activity, behavior, handling and socialization; (3) new fieldwork to test the hypotheses formed.

Phase 1. Because so little was known about Fore behavioral patterns and because there was behavioral diversity across the Fore territory, I emphasized opportunistic sampling and digressive search during my early filming. What programmed sampling there was was

very general: simply to shoot whatever child behavior and social interaction I saw and be sure I got such obvious things as nursing, handling,
grooming, response to aggression, sibling rivalry and social behavior.

Initially I tried to develop a randomness in sampling; but it proved
quite difficult to move randomly in the rain forest environment, and
there were cultural barriers as well which made it harder to film in
some locales (e.g. women's houses). The digressive search remained
semirandom.

So that the novel effect of my presence would not be too disruptive to the daily patterns of life, I chose two South Fore communities (Waisa and Yagareba) as sites for concentration. In these places
my presence came to be accepted as an everyday affair. My subject
of interest (child behavior) was also helpful in that infants and toddlers were seldom interested in my presence or behavior unless it was
very close to them or it directly affected their specific activities and
interests of the moment. It worked to my advantage that I was also
in the Fore region to investigate the epidemiology of the disease kuru.
This made my interest in social behavior less obvious.

I was also lucky, in 1963–4, that more Fore were not yet familiar
with cameras; there was no posing. Furthermore, the Fore use of eye
contact worked to my benefit. Looking into my camera effectively
broke off and precluded social interaction with Fore individuals
while I was filming. The Fore soon treated my photographic activities
very casually, probably because no ostensible effect could be
attributed to them and my cameras were almost as much a part of
me as my shoes (which attracted more attention because of their
obvious utilitarian nature).

Roaming the Fore lands and moving somewhat haphazardly from
one site to another, I conducted the digressive search for child behavior. A simple rule governed my use of the camera: when I had it with
me and whenever children were seen engaged in any kind of activity,
I pointed the camera and let it run until the film ran out, the activity
ceased, or I feared to use too much film on something that seemed
repetitious. Dramatic and aesthetic considerations did not affect this
filming rule; nor did a poor camera location or disadvantageous
lighting.

Sometimes my filming activity attracted the attention of those
being filmed; at other times it did not. This did not alter my approach
to filming. I felt that how attention was manifested in relation to me
and my activities was also of interest and would be useful. For

example, many of the data I accumulated on fear reactions of babies and toddlers were collected during my encounters with them on first visits to their hamlets. It was my close presence that caused the fear among these children who were not accustomed to seeing individuals they had not known all their lives.

I never asked to have any activity repeated in order to film it better; nor did I ask to have specific acts performed in order to film them.

By relying on my cameras to provide me with the behavioral data I needed, I did not have to discuss behavioral matters formally with the Fore during my 1963–4 fieldwork. This I felt was advantageous in that I was able to obtain data on the *actual* behavior, rather than on the *idealized* view the Fore might have of their own activities. Furthermore, reliance on cameras made it easier to avoid the problem of my Fore hosts being disconcerted by a too obvious and intrusive inquisitiveness. By depending primarily on the camera, I was able to limit my usual inquiries to those that might be expected of anyone new anywhere: where I was and what was going on around me. Inquiries about behavior seen came later, during phase 3.

Phase 2 of the study was preparation of the research film documents as a permanent scholarly resource and analysis of them. With the support of D.C. Gajdusek I devised a method intended to maximize the research potential of this undifferentiated data record by (1) preserving the total record in its original continuity, (2) appending time, place, person and event identifications and (3) indicating the selective bias of the cameraman. Following this method the full film footage was assembled as research film.[5]

When the job of assembly was complete, analysis began. Relying on the pattern-recognizing capability of the human mind, I simply examined and re-examined the research film record until those flashes of insight and intuition which characterize early stages of discovery began to reveal fragments of incipient principle and regularity. As these emerged, I re-examined the entire film record for all episodes which might have a bearing on these as yet untested 'eureka' appreciations to see whether they would hold.

Soon I was searching the films for episodes of infant handling, nursing, physical interaction, affectionate expression, exploratory behavior, aggressiveness, deference patterns, communicative activities, instruction, learning, peer relations, expressions of happiness and anger, and sharing. These emerged as categories important in the Fore way of life, ones in which the emerging patterns and style of Fore behavior seemed to fit. Because I retained my research film record, these categorizations did not foreclose future examination of other categories.

For some categories I had many events, for others only a few. All sequences falling into any one of the selected categories were viewed and compared; a norm was hypothesized on the basis of commonness, absence of contradictory behavioral events, or analysis of reactions of others present. Many sequences were observed in slow motion and stop frame in order to detect fleeting or subtle movements or expressions.

From repeated examination of the films against these selected categories of interest the patterns of Fore child behavior and development were postulated. If, for example, I could find no cases showing the breast being denied the child for nursing, I tentatively assumed that one of the features of Fore nursing practice was the availability of the breast when desired by the child. Similarly, if in all the sequences of aggressive behavior by toddlers I could find none where older children or adults became angry or retaliated when attacked, I assumed that the pattern of relation of elder to younger children was that of friendly tolerance to aggressive impulses. All assumptions were subjected to field verification during phase 3, the return fieldwork.

Phase 3 was the return to the field during which the validity of the results of research film analysis was subject to further inquiry. Observation was selective now, not random as before; informants were questioned. I deliberately searched for exceptions to my tentative findings, particularly when they did not correspond with what we would normally expect. For example, I made a special effort to look for incidents of aggressive behavior among children; I deliberately tried to find instances of older children insisting on precedence over younger. I asked men, women and children about the behavioral patterns I had postulated from the film analysis and whether such behavior was ever thought to be unusual, peculiar or intolerable. I also asked about possible exceptions to the behavioral norms I had postulated. New information was checked against further observation; more questions were asked as long as contradictions remained. Unsubstantiated hypotheses were discarded; uncontradicted hypotheses were accepted. In some cases new information led to additional findings; usually more precise formulations emerged. In nearly all cases, the findings derived from analysis of the research films were substantiated.

2 The basic patterns of Fore child handling and rearing discovered through film

Infants and toddlers were kept in almost continuous bodily contact with their mothers or their mothers' close associates, often on the laps or under the arms of their caretakers. The lap of the seated mother was the center of activity for infants, and they spent most of their time there, often at play with their own bodies or those of their mothers. From this vantage point of close and uninterrupted physical contact with their caretakers the young Fore children became aware of the world around them, while their physical needs, such as nursing, sleeping and stimulation, were satisfied without obstacle, almost without notice. They rested and slept, as they felt the need, against their mothers' bodies or laps (see fig. 1). They were not put aside even when she was otherwise occupied, as when food was being prepared or she had heavy loads to carry.

As the young children matured older children participated more and more in their carrying and handling. These caretakers were not assigned, but rather, their role developed from a mutual attraction established between themselves and the young children. The infants or toddlers could reject one older associate in favor of another, and as a result, they were accustomed to being in the hands of individuals whose presence they preferred.

Nursing was on impulse. The breast was always uncovered and always available for nourishment, nursing satisfaction or play. Infants and toddlers were expected to take advantage of it, according to their needs or pleasure. Considerable freedom was permitted to tug, pull and manipulate the breast. The reaction to breast biting was usually surprise and momentary withdrawal of the breast, followed immediately by affectionate playfulness with the annoyed child. This usually dispelled his pique or dismay.

Weaning typically took place gradually, as the child grew older and began to take greater interest in the other activities and foods provided by his environment. Often he sought solid nourishment in the same manner as he would seek his mother's milk. By the age of four or five self-weaning was usually complete, although occasional returns

Fig. 1 The early tactile setting. Small babies were occasionally carried as *in utero* in net bags against the backs of their mothers (a, b); but more frequently they were carried under their mother's arms. As the infants grew they were also carried on hips (c, d, e). Older children who partici- pated in the care and handling of toddlers also frequently carried them on their hips (f, g, i, j), but more often they carried their young associ- ates on their backs (k, l), which adults rarely did. When the toddlers were not being carried they were kept on laps (m—p).

to the breast occurred. Only in special circumstances, e.g. cases of terminal illnesses such as kuru, would mothers speed weaning by applying unsavory substances to their breasts. A Fore mother who had a second infant before the first child was weaned preferred to allow the older child to continue nursing rather than wean him. Both shared the mother's milk.

A considerable amount of attention and physical affection was lavished on infants and toddlers by their associates (see fig. 2). Sibling rivalry was almost impossible to detect, as much of the daily pleasure enjoyed by older and young siblings was that derived from affectionate play with each other. The demands for attention and affectionate contact by an infant or toddler were usually welcomed and virtually always tolerated by his older associates, who often sought the diversion and enjoyment this provided. Such play frequently included considerable caressing, kissing and hugging. Through the close, intimate personal rapport built up during such episodes Fore children were able to communicate needs, desires and feelings to a number of responsive caretakers by physical movement even before they could talk (fig. 2). Not only did this constant 'language' of contact seem readily to facilitate satisfaction of the infant's needs and desires but it also seemed to make the harsher devices of rule and regimen unnecessary. Infant frustration and 'acting out', traits common in Western culture, were rarely seen. The benevolent manner by which Fore mothers could deal with breast biting, or other types of 'accidental' aggression, stemmed from a close physical attunement which forestalled such disaffection.

Since this prelinguistic type of communicative interaction was well suited to expressing and requiting the major concerns of the young child (e.g. nourishment, security, comfort and stimulation), and since it proved well within the capability of the pre-verbal child, Fore infants and toddlers had a richer social life than is possible for their more physically isolated counterparts in other cultures.

The young Fore child made sorties out into the world from the sanctuary of his mother's body or that of one of her close associates. He was permitted to pursue his interests and predilections insofar as his physical capabilities and anxieties permitted. Initially, his interests were related to a desire for nourishment, warmth and stimulation which was communicated through touch. However, as awareness increased, the child's interests broadened to the things his caretaker did and on the objects and materials they used (see fig. 3). In this he

Fig. 2 Body talk. Infants and toddlers enjoyed extensive opportunities to indicate their interests and desires even before they could talk through messages of physical contact in a continually stimulating, socially engaging context.

Fig. 3 Inquiry and kinesthetic learning: the young child's exploration of the world around him from the vantage point of close physical association with caretakers.

was free to explore and play with those objects or materials he found about him, without interference and with minimal supervision. These included sharp or potentially dangerous objects such as knives, machettes, axes and fire (see fig. 4), which he could safely handle by the time he was able to walk. Thus the child came into contact with activities and materials of importance to his socio-economic welfare while very young and while directly in touch with those dealing with them.

The early pattern of exploratory activity included frequent returns to the mother. She served as the home base, the bastion of security, but not as a director or overseer of activities. Although she provided cues to safety or appropriateness which could be monitored by the child, she rarely attempted to control or direct his activities, interests or quests. Nor did she participate in his explorations or play, or try to be with him on his jaunts (fig. 5). Her child could be away whenever he wanted, but when he was away, he was, essentially, on his own until he returned. He could, however, depend on his caretakers to remain accessible.

Although older associates were almost always nearby, they did not go to 'rescue' the toddler when he became frightened or distressed. Instead it was up to each child to return to the security of personal

Fig. 4 Access to knives. Fore children frequently took advantage of their freedom in the choice of play objects to hold and use knives (a, b, c). Even toddlers who grabbed at knives being used by their mothers were not denied the right to interrupt their mother's work to examine her tools, techniques and materials (b, c).

physical association when he felt the need. When frightened, young children quickly sought bodily contact with their human bases, but not just for the security provided by physical association. They also sought the tactile response cues such contact provided. Even in the face of less stressful uncertainty, as when confronted by unexpected events, children tended to get themselves physically 'in touch' with an associate (fig. 6). Since the caretakers did not usually move very far away, a child was always able to return over not much more than the distance he had ventured. As soon as he could walk well, the excursions extended to the entire hamlet and gardens, and then with age-mates beyond. Developing without interference or supervision, this personal exploratory learning freely touched on whatever was around.

Eventually I discovered that this capability emerged naturally from the Fore infant handling practices in their milieu of close human physical proximity and tactile interaction. Touch and bodily contact lent themselves to satisfying the basic needs of young children and were nearly always a part of normal experience. This early tactile communicative experience fostered cooperative interaction between infants and their caretakers and provided the basis of the Fore kines-thetic way of learning. Infants and toddlers modeled their activity without ambivalence on what they touched and felt (fig. 3), learning in this nondirective way the forms of behavior and response character-

Fig. 5 Exploratory activity. A toddler is attracted by a bit of debris a short distance from his mother. After examining this, he moves a short distance further to investigate similar objects. The mother does not participate or intervene.

istic of Fore life. Muscle tone, movement and mood were components of this learning process. Formal instruction was not.

These basic early childhood experiences led to a confidence and realistic self-reliance which permitted independent experimental and inquisitive probings of surroundings at the discretion of the young growing child. Even after several visits, I continued to be surprised that the unsupervised Fore toddlers did not recklessly thrust themselves into unappreciated dangers, the way our own children tend to do. But then, why should they? From their earliest days, they enjoyed a benevolent sanctuary from which the world could be confidently viewed, tested and appreciated. This sanctuary remained ever available, but did not demand, restrain, or impose. One could go and come at will. In close harmony with their source of life, the Fore young were able confidently to extend their inquiry. They could widen their

Fig. 6 Tactile association and response to novelty. Older children, like infants and toddlers, often responded to novelty and challenge in bodily association with others, but unlike their younger colleagues, older children tended to turn more to their peers to provide the feeling of security from physical contact. Here children respond typically to the novelty of my presence and behavior in newly visited hamlets.

understanding as they chose. There was no need to be furtive or play tricks or deceive in order to pursue life.

Emerging from this early childhood was a freely ranging young child in tune with his older and younger hamlet-mates. This child was disinclined to act out his impulses and he possessed a capable appreciation of the properties of potentially dangerous objects, so he could

Fig. 7 Tactile interplay and early socialization. Much of the early social contact with age-mates tended to center on exploratory physical contact. Here two young children play near their mothers, who are making tapa (not seen in the pictures). The touching, caressing, hugging and hitting, much of which may be exploratory sensual play, is communicative and can thus be called social. Since it is voluntary, it is satisfying to each, otherwise the children would not remain with each other. Yet the interplay includes expression reminiscent of anger (c, g, o), displeasure (f, j), and demand (e), and hitting is involved (l, m, n). Adults gave little notice to such activities, neither overseeing them nor interceding in them. The Fore do not consider them to be indicative of displeasure, aggressive intent or hostility. That such play often continued for protracted periods, without squabbles or fighting, supports this assessment.

safely be permitted to move out on his own, unsupervised and unrestricted.

Common peer interests began to develop almost as soon as the toddlers became mobile; exploration of one another's reponses and reactions began to lead to consensual social objectives at an early age (fig. 7). Groups formed and reformed about the various activities at hand, as like-minded individuals began to move and act together.

Such a pattern of behavior development was well suited to the requirements of making one's livelihood by exploratory exploitation of new lands. It fitted the protoagricultural situation. Loosely stable groups emerged to explore, hunt, garden, cook, sleep, and play together. Food, shelter, and pleasure began to be obtained cooperatively in a socioeconomic development growing directly out of the tactile gestalt.

In keeping with this basic pattern, the social and residential groupings which emerged were informal and voluntary, lacking chiefs, medicine men or patriarchs. Affinity groups were the socio-political building blocks of Fore society; and personal affiliation was a more important force for solidarity than was formal kinship. This facilitated opportunistic movement into new lands with like-minded friends.

The two basic formative underpinnings of Fore child learning and social development (tactile association and freedom to pursue individual penchants) thus set the stage for the Fore cooperative type of social organization, in which socio-sensual appreciation of the excitement and values of life centered individualistic quests within a context of reciprocally supportive individuals.

Notes

1. I have already reported the larger study of the protoagricultural way of life of the Fore (Sorenson 1976) and discussed how the culturally specific patterns of child behavior development relate to the question of aggression (Sorenson 1978).

2. The Fore were a protoagricultural people who diverged and expanded through high virgin lands in a pioneer region. They lived on the edge of the forest and cut new gardens into it. They tilled these plots until fertility declined, then cut further into the forest, like hunter-gatherers. Grasslands sprang up over the abandoned sites. But, like farmers, they concentrated their effort and attention more narrowly on selected sites of production, on their gardens; they planted to live. They had child handling and rearing practices which sustained this way of life and which contrasted markedly with those of Western culture.

The traditional hamlets were small and impermanent. A single large men's house provided shelter for about ten to twenty men and boys and their visiting friends. The several smaller women's houses each normally sheltered two married women, their unmarried daughters, and their sons up to about six years of age. Not much attention was given to formal kinship. Friendship was more important. Friends formed hamlets and gardened together, and individuals from a hamlet or several hamlets could always get together to form a new hamlet. Dispersing centrifugally from the sites of their common origin, hamlets formed and reformed following the gardens ever further into the forest. There were no chiefs, patriarchs, priests, medicine men or the like; and a striking personal freedom was enjoyed even by the very young. During the day gardens became the center of life as friends, relatives and children went to one or more of the several garden plots to mingle their social, economic and erotic pursuits in a pleasant and emotionally filled gestalt of garden life. The boys and unmarried youths spent less time there, preferring to explore and hunt in the outlying lands. Daily activities were not scheduled. No one made demands, and the land was bountiful. Not surprisingly the distinction between work and play was never very clear.

3. The initial discussion of use of research film in the study of variation in child behavior development in different cultures appears in Sorenson & Gajdusek (1966).
4. More extensive discussion of these strategies appears in Sorenson & Jablonko (1975).
5. The theoretical foundations of this method are discussed in Sorenson (1968). The assembly method was developed as a means of increasing the research-ability of film records of vanishing and changing ways of life and culture (Sorenson 1967).

I5
Communication starts with selective attention[1]

KARIN STENSLAND JUNKER
Karolinska Institutet, Stockholm

1 Introduction

From his very first moment of postnatal life the baby is involved in continual communication with his environment through the giving and taking of signals different from those which were active before his birth. A major change is that the signals pass through different media. It is vital for the infant to develop the ability to recognize these signals to which it is important for him to pay attention, if he is to survive.

Communication is based on an exchange of signals which are decoded and adequately responded to by the use of commonly accepted rules. Language ability matures with increasing capacity to differentiate among signals, and discrimination forces the infant to choose the focus of his attention. We do not know how he learns to prefer certain signals over others, but he has the ability to use and respond to, in particular, those signals which bring satisfaction and reward.

We know now that the normal newborn alerts to the sound of a human voice and responds to human touch and to the sight of a human face. He is constitutionally geared to orient his whole body toward any signal that arouses interest. A baby's responsive smile is additional evidence of his potentiality for communication.

Communication as a subject for research covers a wide area, ranging over such fields as information theory, philosophy, sociology, linguistics, phonetics, biology, speech pathology, technical audiology, acoustics and medical psychology. Therefore such research calls for interdisciplinary teamwork. But, since hearing disorders usually are suspected when a child does not respond to speech, it is considered natural to assign most communicative disorders to the audiologist. The audiology literature describes the behavior which is to be expected from a normal baby on stimulation by sound. The first techniques for testing for communicative disorders were derived from this.

Failure to behave as expected in response to sound may be due to defective hearing, but there are other possible causes. A child might be restricted in movement because of muscular or neurological disease and so not show the expected behavior. He might simply appear indifferent to sound. My personal experience was to have such a child.[2] This challenged me to search for a simple and general testing method, which would provide an opportunity to assess an infant's ability to attend to signals appropriately.

A succession of research steps was required before it would be possible to institute such a program on a wide scale. The research led to the BOEL screening method for infants at eight months, now applied routinely in the well baby clinics not only in Stockholm where it was developed, but in a number of centers throughout the world. The search and the method are described in section 2.

The experience during the research for BOEL made me aware of the communication between child and caregiver that starts with birth, and that gives an opportunity for preventive work to be done with young people at the time they first become parents. A small pilot study on the feasibility of such work in the maternity hospital has been carried out.

2 BOEL — a program for early discovery of communicative disorders

The requirements for a testing method suitable for screening are that it should be applicable universally in a non-specialized environment. It should be quick, inexpensive and easy to administer and report by health personnel in routine contact with infants. This pointed to the well baby clinic and to the nurses who work there as the most available people.[3] The aim was a screening program for early detection of communication difficulties which had not been suspected. This purpose called for a testing method administered by only one person, in the often noisy milieu characteristic of well baby clinics. An additional problem was to discover the age at which such a procedure would be applicable.

2.1 Previous findings

Even a hundred years ago investigators knew how the unborn child reacted to certain auditory stimuli. Whether the reaction had the implication of communicative ability could not be answered until after birth. The auro-palpebral reflex in the neonate was long regarded as the most significant reaction to sound. Whispers, tuning forks, whistles, snappings, clappings, cow-bells and so on were used as sound sources. General 'muscle alarm state', pupil dilation and change in heart activity were thought to give the necessary information about the infant's reaction to sound.[4] Finally, when pure tone audiometry could be obtained shortly after birth, many audiologists felt that all problems regarding the preconditions for achieving speech were solved, if it could only be universally applied. They thought the only barriers consisted of lack of trained personnel and expense.

An important fact had been forgotten: hearing is one thing — listening is another. Linguistic communication demands the capacity for listening, i.e. understanding and discriminating between relevant and irrelevant sounds. Orientation towards a sound source, although noticeable already at birth, is far from giving the necessary information about the potentiality for perceiving spoken language.

2.2 Pilot studies

Having studied the traditional literature in the field of developmental psychology, visual perception, audiology, linguistics, communication theory etc., I turned to looking at babies in well baby clinics in different parts of Stockholm County. Instead of constructing a random sampling system I simply examined all available infants brought to the clinic on general check-up days in order to get as many potentially healthy children at a variety of ages as possible. My purpose was to discover and delimit the most suitable age for testing an infant sitting upright on an adult's lap face to face with the tester and within arms' reach, i.e. a method for one person to implement unaided.

Current, informal methods for assessing infant hearing included rattling a spoon in a mug or crushing tissue paper behind the baby's head. This usually called for the participation of two persons in addition to the mother. While actually carrying out these procedures alone, I noticed that the baby sometimes caught sight of what I was doing out of the corner of his eye, so I could not be sure that turning his head meant that he had heard rather than seen something which had captured his attention. I had reached a point where I realized that I had to find attractive sounds which could be presented without the source being seen by the baby. The sound sources should still be simple enough for wide application and not require elaborate equipment.

Furthermore I realized that I needed some aid to capture and hold the baby's visual attention. After trying out a number of bright colored objects I found that a simple red stick was sufficient to hold the baby's interest.

A pilot study on 134 infants, ranging from two to fourteen months, using six different sound sources, aimed at refining the testing method and at exploring the reaction patterns of infants at different age levels. Soon I found that the procedure I was using had no bearing on communication unless an initial social contact was well established, manifested through mutual gaze which I call 'you-and-I-contact'.

This pilot study was followed by an investigation of 480 additional Stockholm infants, ranging from three to thirteen months, 265 boys

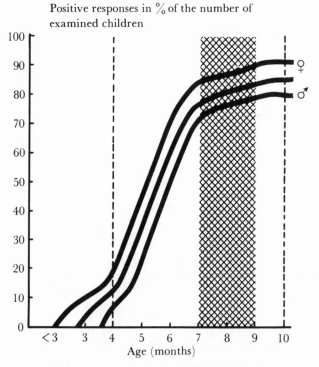

Fig. 1 Examination prior to the BOEL test of 480 infants registered at well baby clinics in Stockholm. The response criterion was turning the head after 4 sound presentations from 5 different sources preceded by firmly established eye contact.

and 215 girls (fig. 1). The age level for obtaining the expected responses was found to be optimal between seven and nine months. At earlier ages too few infants reached the established criterion, four responses on presentation of sounds from five different sources. At six months nearly 50% failed to reach the criterion and after nine months many infants lost interest in the test sounds.

During the investigation of suitable age level and sound sources I learned a lot about how to make contact with infants, and I realized that this had to be built into any testing procedure probing communication.

'Expected response' has to be explained. Although the criterion was expressed by 'head-turnings', it was rather the 'turning of attention' I was concerned with. I realized that it was necessary to observe and interpret, not only the direction of the infant's gaze, but also his facial expression. It should express 'searching', in other words interest and attention.

I also realized that the rapidly waning interest of infants would be a constraint on the screening procedure. This forced me to seek a sound source which would be at once the most attractive to the child and the most practical to administer. This called for compromise. It turned out that the sound source with the most favourable acoustic analysis was not suitable for a screening test because it required an accomplice. From among a variety of sounds tested, I found a small jingle bell to be the most practical. Its sound was interesting without being overwhelming. In addition the bell could easily be concealed in the closed fist and be made to sound without visible movement.

Out of the experience of exploring these practical issues, the realization of the importance of selective attention followed. By selective attention I mean the capacity to choose between signals. Since I believe that language is built up by a continuous choice among signals within a system, it appears reasonable to assume that the ability to direct the attention selectively is required for the development of functional language. If the infant, when still on the doorstep of speech acquisition, shows that he can turn his attention from one signal to another, he is likely to have one of the fundamental prerequisites for language development. Now I was ready to design all the aspects of the BOEL screening procedure.

2.3 The BOEL attention screening test for infants

The equipment includes two objects to capture visual attention: a red, shaped, polished, wooden, 20-cm stick (the 'gripper', fig. 2a) and two concentric silver rings (the 'spinner', fig. 2b). The inner ring rotates about a vertical axis when flicked with a finger. Four small silver sound sources are supplied to capture auditory attention: two 'balls' which are fastened to each index finger with thin, adjustable, open silver rings, and two 'bells' which are fastened to the ring fingers in the same way. The 'balls' produce a soft, rattling sound and the 'bells' produce a soft tinkle (fig. 2c). The frequency range for both sounds lies between 4000 and 12,500 Hz in free field and 5000 and 10,000 Hz when shielded by the tester's fist. This range was chosen to cover those components of speech sounds which are essential for certain important discriminations, and which are most frequently lost in cases of impaired hearing. The sound sources are so small that they can be completely hidden in a clenched fist and made to sound by a slight, imperceptible movement of the appropriate finger.

If the tester is not precise in the way she presents the sounds (if for instance she glances at her own hand), she risks obtaining a spurious response. Speed, care and firmness are essential.

The test is carried out in the following way. It is very important to create a social atmosphere from the start, so the tester should have everything ready, including the sound sources on her fingers, before approaching the mother and baby. The contact may be initiated with an intimate, friendly chat directly with the baby in the waiting room.

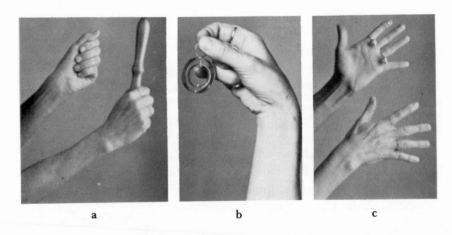

a   b   c

Fig. 2 a, c: the sound sources are small enough to be easily hidden in the clenched fist (frequency range 4000–12,500 Hz); b: the silver 'spinner'.

The tester should try to maintain contact with the infant throughout the procedure. She may continue to talk to the baby in a soft voice throughout the test, provided she is sufficiently trained.

The mother sits with the infant seated forward on her knees, facing the tester who sits on a lower chair so that her eyes are at the same level as those of the baby. The tester has to be close enough to reach behind the baby's head with an enclosing movement, while maintaining face-to-face contact. Diagnoses of hearing are meaningless unless visual communication is first secured. Therefore firm eye contact is established first, if possible combined with a smile (fig. 3a). The tester presents the 'gripper'. The normal baby usually attempts to grasp the 'gripper' and investigate it with his mouth (fig. 3b).

The tester then checks that the baby's eyes can follow the 'gripper' as it is moved first to the right, i.e. to the baby's left (fig. 3c), then to the left about half a meter in front of the infant, then up and down (figs. 3d, e). At last the infant is allowed to grasp it, take it and put it into his mouth (fig. 3f).

Then the tester brings up her right hand about 20 cm to the side and behind the infant's left ear without the infant's noticing it (fig. 3g), because of the firmly established social contact. The 'ball' is made to sound, and, if the child perceives it, he will break face-to-face contact in order to search for the sound (fig. 3h). His attention is brought back to the 'gripper' before the tester presents the other 'ball' to his right ear with her left hand.

The contact from the front is renewed before bringing up the right hand again on the left side of the baby, then the left one on his right side, to repeat the testing with the 'bells'.

The test procedure is completed with a repeated check on the eye movements and visual attention, this time using the 'spinner' and moving it in the same way as the 'gripper' was moved at the beginning. This gives the tester an opportunity to check for eye asymmetry which might turn into strabismus (crossed eyes).

The influence of different cultural patterns has to be taken into consideration. In our country, for example, many immigrants from very disparate cultures have settled, and I have personal experience of trying to do BOEL testing with children who had been forbidden to grasp an object and put it into the mouth.

BOEL is applied to infants aged between seven and ten months, preferably at eight months ± fourteen days. All the functions and patterns of behavior mentioned above are recorded on a small chart

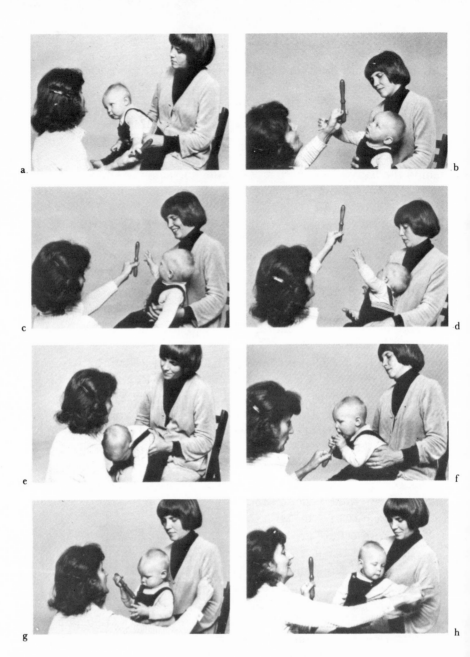

Fig. 3 The BOEL test procedure. a: establishing firm eye contact with the infant before testing; b: presenting the red 'gripper'; c—e: checking that the eyes can follow the 'gripper' horizontally, up and down; f: allowing the infant to grasp the 'gripper' and put it in his mouth; g: moving the hand unnoticed by the infant 20 cm behind his right ear; h: sounding the bell, infant breaking face-to-face contact to search for the sound source.

which is backed with adhesive and can be attached to the clinic record (fig. 4).

2.4 Prevalence of BOEL screening and follow-up programs

BOEL screening was, in the fall of 1977, being carried out in nearly all well baby clinics in Stockholm County. Ten instructors have been trained to teach the method of administering and recording the test to nurses who are new within the district.

One district in Gothenburg, Sweden, has made a one-year study of 1432 infants, the result of which was presented at the International Pediatric Congress in New Delhi in 1977. A Swedish parliamentary committee has proposed that BOEL screening become routine in child health centers in Sweden. At present we lack sufficient trained people to give proper instruction to testers if we are to extend the BOEL program throughout the country, but training is in progress here, as it is throughout Denmark. A pilot study in the greater Helsinki area in Finland on more than a thousand infants aged eight months ± fourteen days has now been followed up. It may result in a decision to go on with BOEL screening as fast as personnel can be trained. BOEL screening programs have also started in Groningen, The Netherlands; in Milan; in Chapel Hill, North Carolina; and in Cairo.

Table 1 shows the results of screening a sample of about 9000 Stockholm infants. Of these infants 5.8% failed to respond in the expected way. The table is presented with the caveat that follow-up has so far not been possible on deviations other than lack of response to sound signals.

This screening was performed by well baby clinic nurses who had had a brief training, and whose experience with mental health obser-

Table 1 *Sample from BOEL screening in Stockholm County 1971–4*

Total number of children	9051	100%
Deviations involving:		
Eye contact and/or visual attention	21	0.2%
Auditory attention	110	1.2%
Motor behavior	57	0.6%
Social contact	77	0.9%
Asymmetrical eyes and other deviations	236	2.6%
Total incidence of deviations	501	5.5%

		BOEL
☐ Head held steady	☐ Eyes symmetrical	Insert X in
☐ Firm eye contact	☐ Responsive social vocalization	appropriate square
☐ Reaches for gripper	☐ Explores with mouth	
☐ Reaches for spinner	☐ Searches for sound of ball, left	
☐ Holds gripper	☐ Searches for sound of ball, right	
☐ Holds spinner	☐ Searches for sound of bell, left	
☐ Responsive contact smile	☐ Searches for sound of bell, right	
☐ Gaze follows	☐ Sits without support	

☐	☐
well baby clinic	home

Date	Signature

Fig. 4 BOEL chart attached to the infant's case record.

vation within the well baby clinic routine was limited. We followed up the 110 cases involving deviations of auditory attention. Stockholm County provides a good opportunity for critical evaluation of BOEL as a method for screening of hearing for a unique reason. All children from the entire county who suffer from hearing defects will, sooner or later, be seen at the audiological department of Karolinska Hospital. This means that the department eventually discovers any hearing impairment which has not been detected by the nurse during the BOEL test or which has developed later.

Most of the 110 infants who did not search for the sounds appeared to have had an upper respiratory infection from which they had recently recovered, or they still had one when examined. Binaural otosalpingitis, secondary to the infection, was usually assumed to have caused a temporary hearing defect, and after treatment in the usual way most of the children proved to have normal hearing.

In a few cases, however, the routine treatment for otosalpingitis did not restore hearing. In spite of the infants' being very young, it was necessary to resort to adenoidectomy and the insertion of plastic tubes to attain permanent good hearing. In three cases in which hearing had been defective for a long time, a dramatic, favorable effect on the child's whole development occurred along with the improvement of his hearing. In five cases deafness was detected in children whose parents had not at all suspected that they could not hear. They are now participating in the rehabilitation program of the audiological department at Karolinska Hospital. Two cases of deafness were found through the audiological department which had not been found by the nurses.

Since a general follow-up, at this stage, was impossible, I had to design a study which would compare the results of BOEL screening, performed by one skilled tester, with BOEL performed within the general routine by different nurses. This led to the Helsinki study mentioned above (for results see table 2).

BOEL's emphasis on defective attention makes us hope that the screening may contribute to early detection of many lesser behavior disturbances which are difficult to label. These may include disorders classified as minimal brain defects or dysfunction (MBD), and the still more diffuse concept 'understimulation'.

So far we have experienced, both in Sweden and in Finland, how the BOEL screening has had an important side effect. We know that it is one thing to aim at finding deviations early and to diagnose them. Quite another thing is to do something for the children and their families. However, we have already made a start toward offering help in addition to the medical procedures traditionally thought sufficient for children with communicative defects (see section 2.5). It is hoped that in the future children showing poor social contact may be helped to overcome their difficulties before the pattern becomes fixed. The BOEL screening program increases awareness of the importance of very early communication for the child's whole development.

2.5 Play habilitation as the necessary follow-up of a screening

When all possible medical care has been given to a child suffering from communication disability, there is need for an active program for everyday life. Although practical handling of the child may be outlined, this remains an unsolved problem.

For a child, play is medicine in the same way as creative activity is for an adult. Nowadays we are conscious of play as an important part of pediatric medical care. From personal experience I was well aware of this fact when the 'lekotek' idea evolved. It developed a new form of play habilitation.

'Lekotek' is a new word, coined by analogy with the Swedish word for playthings, 'leksaker', and for library, 'bibliotek'. The first lekotek was the joint creation of myself and a fellow parent, E. Blid, who had the professional background of a preschool teacher for special education and, also, the personal experience of being the mother of a boy with muscular dystrophy. Thus we both had personal and painful experiences of communication disorders in our own families. We knew the helplessness that harasses parents confronted with the lack of meaningful occupation for their handicapped children, whether physically or mentally disabled.

At the beginning the main purpose of our lekotek was to lend toys

Table 2 *BOEL screening in the Greater Helsinki area, Finland, September 1974—June 1975, with follow-up 1977*

			Percentages
Total number of BOEL-tested infants:			
Boys	541		
Girls	521	1062	100.0
Referrals for:			
Ophthalmological examination	56		5.3
Audiological examination	20		1.9
Neurological examination	115		10.8
Psychiatric examination	15		1.4
Number of referrals	206		19.4
Number of children referred		186	17.5

		Percentages
Findings on follow-up:		
Ophthalmological follow-up		
Manifest strabismus	3	0.28
Temporary strabismus and/ or changing, to be checked up at 2 years	21	1.98
Undetermined diagnosis, recommended follow-up at 2 years	8	0.75
No findings, recommended sight check-up at 3 years	23	2.17
	55	5.18
Audiological follow-up		
Deafness (binaural hearing impairment)	1	0.09
Difficult to examine and/or monaural hearing impariment	7	0.66
No findings, 'social hearing' intact	10	0.94
	18	1.69
Neurological follow-up		
Unspecified deviations for follow-up	7	0.66
Dead	1	0.09
Recommended follow-up at 3 years	64	6.03
No findings	28	2.64
	100	9.42
Psychiatric follow up		
'Problem families'	2	0.18
No findings in the infant's behavior	11	1.04
	13	1.22

and play-tools to parents free of cost, and to advise them in their appropriate use to help their children as much as possible. We felt that the parents would be better equipped to help their child if they got a feeling of being able to do something therapeutic to further his development. This helps relieve the sense of guilt, so usual in parents of defective children. The family atmosphere becomes brighter, and doors open up to the outside.

Well- and correctly designed play-tools are often too expensive for the ordinary, private family budget. This was an additional motive for the lekotek. Knowledge is also necessary for making optimal use of good toys. This requires professional skill. A lekotek staff must be well trained, observant and experienced in infant and preschool stimulation and in developmental diagnosis.

The traditional, professional knowledge of sensory training which concentrated on the ability to identify, discriminate, associate and generalize impressions of form, color, structure, weight, taste, sound, smell etc. had to be extended. An understanding of what we now know about communication in infancy had to be included. This communication is founded primarily on things that happen at close range between infant and caregiver and makes use of intimacy more than of toys.

The importance of communication is emphasized to the parents by showing how the baby's face comes to life when he is talked to face-to-face. Furthermore we advise the use of a baby carrier (which holds the baby in frontal body contact with the parent) as a way of establishing and maintaining communication. Two aspects are pointed out: the close body contact and the stimulation from social participation which is quite different from being in a crib. For infants under one year a baby carrier of Japanese type (the Kodomó) is demonstrated and lent to the parents.

3 Conclusion

Whenever parents express anxiety about their child, clinicians should listen with sensitivity. There is usually some truth hidden in verbalized anxiety. Unfortunately parents' fears are often regarded as exaggerated and treated with scepticism. When a baby looks normal superficially, the pediatrician, who is the one parents usually turn to first, often avoids talking about things which are not physically tangible. This approach may be understandable but it is no longer acceptable. The blanket reassurance usually given to anxious parents when no obvious physical defect is discovered shows both ignorance of the fundamental prerequisites for human communication and lack of concern founded on the traditional 'wait and see' attitude.

We no longer need to look the other way when a baby gives early evidence of communicative handicap from whatever cause. Preventive measures are now available for families in which communication problems are suspected and early intervention brings hope of improved outcome for babies with diagnosed disorders which affect communication and, therefore, total life adjustment. However, the most effective approach to problems involving human communication is to widen awareness of its significance among both professionals and the general public. This should start with awareness of its importance even at or before birth.

Notes

1. For their work in the specialist follow-up of the Helsinki study described in this chapter I would like to acknowledge Hilkka Schugk, Sirkka Kruus, Maija Wilska, Tapani Jauhiainen, Christina Raitta, Vappo Taipale, Sinikka Maliniemi, Ole Wasz-Höckert and Olivia Olilla. The study was financed by the Swedish Scouts' Association's Foundation for Handicapped Children and the First-of-May-Flower Campaign for Children with Difficulties (Förstamajblomman). Karolinska Sjukhuset (the Children's Clinic) and the Wenner-Gren Research Laboratory provided facilities. References to relevant literature may be found in the bibliography.
2. The name of my autistic daughter is Boel; her story is told in *The child in the glass ball* (1964). Her insoluble problem of communication resulted in the choice of the name BOEL for the screening procedure described. BOEL is also an acronym of the Swedish 'Blicken orienterar efter ljud' ('Gaze orients after sound').
3. The attendance at well baby clinics in Sweden (as well as in Finland) is virtually 100%.
4. Compare Stensland Junker 1972: 14, 17—45.

16

Communication and cooperation in early infancy: a description of primary intersubjectivity

COLWYN TREVARTHEN
University of Edinburgh

1 Introduction

In film and television recordings of face-to-face interactions of
mothers with their infants aged one to three months, my students
and I have observed extremely complex behaviours that have led us
to accept the idea that human beings are equipped at birth with a
mechanism of personality which is sensitive to persons and expresses
itself as a person does. Obviously such a mechanism must be formulated largely within the brain before birth without benefit of imitation or training, but the anatomy required seems to be unknown.
Beyond question the acts of communication in early infancy are very
immature, but they appear powerful enough to take charge of the
process by which the cognitive processes of the mind develop. In the
first few months, before manipulation is effective in exploring
objects, an infant establishes the basis for a deep affectional tie to his
mother and other constant companions. He does so by means of this
delicate and specifically human system for person-to-person communication.

In this chapter I wish to review this behaviour of young infants to
see how far the unspoken part of human communication is present
long before the infant can speak and to investigate whether there are
riduments of speech activity as well. Such an inquiry is forced upon
us when we admit that language may be part of the larger function
of interpersonal communication that grows in the child.

1.1 Subjectivity and intersubjectivity: definition of terms

Human beings understand one another intimately and at many levels.
To analyse this ability of persons to act together and to share experience in harmony, we have first to view communication in relation to

the private activities of conscious, purposeful action. All voluntary actions are performed in such a way that their effects can be anticipated by the actor and then adjusted within the perceived situation to meet the criteria set in advance. Interpersonal communication is controlled by feedback of information, as is all voluntary behaviour. But there is an essential difference between a person doing things in relation to the physical world and the control of communication between persons. Two persons can *share* control, each can predict what the other will know and do. Physical objects cannot predict intentions and they have no social relationships.

For infants to share mental control with other persons they must have two skills. First, they must be able to exhibit to others at least the rudiments of individual consciousness and intentionality. This attribute of acting agents I call *subjectivity*. In order to communicate, infants must also be able to adapt or fit this subjective control to the subjectivity of others: they must also demonstrate *intersubjectivity*.[1]

By subjectivity I mean the ability to *show* by coordinated acts that purposes are being consciously regulated. Subjectivity implies that infants master the difficulties of relating objects and situations to themselves and predict consequences, not merely in hidden cognitive processes but in manifest, intelligible actions.

Acts that make subjective processes overt include the following: focussing attention on things, handling and exploring objects with interest in the consequences, orientating or avoiding while anticipating the course of events and meeting or evading them. Acts of these kinds have been found in research with infants that obeys the observational tenets of Piaget in his studies of cognitive development (1936). Of recent work on infant cognition in this tradition, Bower's (1974) is the most comprehensive. Infants one or two months of age may be observed to look at, listen to and touch objects with the beginnings of alertness for the changes in experience that follow what they do. They also perform rudimentary acts of grasping and manipulation, stepping, avoidance or withdrawal which, while ineffectual, have already enough adaptive form to be identified with these purposes (Trevarthen 1974b, forthcoming). Such patterned and intelligible activity, guided by its effects, shows the subjectivity of infants in their dealings with physical *things*.

Infants also show distinctive behaviours to *persons*. In the second month after birth their reactions to things and persons are so different that we must conclude that these two classes of object are dis-

tinct in the infant's awareness (Trevarthen forthcoming). They seek
physical objects as sources of perceptual information or interest, and
also as potentially graspable, chewable, kickable, step-on-able or
otherwise usable (Trevarthen 1974b, 1975). But persons are communicated with by expressive movements.

It seems at first sight confusing that infants exhibit affective
relations to objects over which they are attempting mastery in perception and action. They seem to be trying to communicate feelings
to things as well as to people. But is this really what they are doing?
This emotional aspect of infant behaviour, which goes beyond either
regulation of an internal state of arousal or perception of contingency,
has been little studied simply because most psychologists have rejected
it out of hand. Nevertheless, pertinent observations have been made.
Emotionality in young infants has, for example, been recorded and
recognised to be of great importance in relation to learning and cognitive prediction by Papoušek (1967, 1969) and Papoušek &
Papoušek (1977). Piaget (1936, 1946) records expressions of 'pleasure
in mastery' and 'serious intent' with respect to cognitive tasks, and
Wolff (1963, 1969) observed that smiling and cooing or crying of
young infants may accompany and signal recognition of a familiar
toy.

Facial expressions closely similar to those of adults for the emotions
of pleasure, displeasure, fear, surprise, confusion and interest may be
distinguished in newborns, or young infants (Charlesworth & Kreutzer
1973; Oster & Ekman forthcoming). These movements are automatically perceived as 'emotional' by adults. They move other people and
strengthen the apparent personality of the infant. Some, such as the
smile, are clearly related to events over which the infant has claimed
some degree of predictive control. A six-week-old may show pleasure
at predicting correctly and displeasure at failure, even if satiated and
refusing a physiological 'reward'. The expression of pleasure relates
to the cognitive (subjective) prediction itself (Papoušek 1969;
Zalazo 1972). In any attempt to understand infants as communicators
it must be noted that the effect of the emotional expression can only
be interpersonal. Only another person capable of emotion can be
influenced by an emotional sign. Like adults, infants act as if they
both *know* and *care* about events in their world. Indeed their relationships with other persons would be impossible without the aspects of
subjectivity manifested by their prolific but organised emotional
expressions.

1.2 The sample, and methods of research

The following account is focussed on evidence of intersubjective processes between mothers and their infants. This evidence is gleaned from films and video recordings of 165 'staged' encounters with their mothers of thirty-four (fifteen male, nineteen female) infants in their second and third months, some at the Harvard Center for Cognitive Studies but most at the Department of Psychology, University of Edinburgh.[2]

The techniques used have been designed to obtain detailed records of both mother and infant while they are in close communication. The artificial setting does not inhibit rich and close interaction. Mothers visit the laboratory from the time their babies are two to three weeks old. The baby is supported in an infant chair facing, but separate from, the mother. This allows free limb movement. The mother, seated close to her infant, is simply asked to talk to her baby. With the aid of a mirror, both mother and infant behaviours are recorded in near full face on video and film. Combination of video recording including sound with short selections on silent film permits survey of samples of behaviour lasting an hour or more on video and detailed analysis of patterns of action lasting seconds to a few minutes on film. The film is inspected frame by frame on a Perceptoscope projector with variable speed of projection. A back-projection arrangement permits tracing of the film to prepare graphic montages of patterns of action.

The films are of infants with their mothers. A few samples with other females or fathers as partners show that mothers are not absolutely unique, but there are not enough of these to permit comparative statements.

For convenience, expressive and receptive functions of infant and mother will be considered separately. This separation helps start analysis, but it is unnatural both with respect to the way each subject integrates experience with what he or she does and with respect to the intimate cooperation between them. Eventually we will have to put actions and reactions together again to determine how their form depends on their relations within an interplay controlled by both partners.

2 Communicative expressions of young infants

Here I am confining attention to expressions which lead to interpersonal communication, leaving aside well-known feeding, defensive or distress behaviour and signals of physiological state, all of which, while invoking others, are self-regulatory for the infant and disruptive of reciprocal intersubjectivity. The most familiar early expressions, cooing and smiling, are not the only ones pre-adapted to intersubjective exchange. Some of the less familiar expressions seem more important to psychological development. All appear clearly about the end of the first month.

Cooing, also known as pleasure, positive or non-crying vocalisation, is effective as communication only if other persons hear it. Neonates coo weekly, often when alone. When coos become clear and strong in the second month, adults find them pleasing. Coos are easily stimulated by friendly attention and speech, and by toys, such as rattles, if they are moved before the baby's eyes (Wolff 1969). Babies coo when not distressed and especially when distress has been overcome. The appropriate mouth opening and shaping for cooing is often made silently by infants less than two months old (fig. 1). Our films show that mouth movements are patterned separately for speech before the motor coordination of vocal organs with the respiratory apparatus is adequate to produce reliably controlled sound. Vocalised cooing

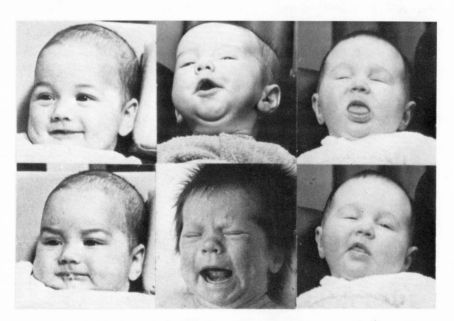

Fig. 1 Infant expressions. Left: smile and scowl with set jaw (boy, 12 weeks); centre: above, coo (boy, 6 weeks), below, crying (girl, 6 weeks); right: simulations of disgust and sneer (girl, 6 weeks).

develops in the second month, apparently at least partly in independence of auditory feedback from self or others (Lenneberg et al. 1965). Neither babbling nor laughter develops until after the third month.

Smiling develops parallel to cooing (Washburn 1929; Spitz & Wolf 1946; Ambrose 1961; Wolff 1963). Even premature infants smile and recognisable smiles may occur within minutes of birth (Leboyer 1974). Neonates smile in response to attention, but more weakly and unpredictably than they will a few weeks later. They also smile spontaneously, usually in a fragmentary or ill-formed way, during irregular sleep or drowsiness (Herska 1965; Wolff 1966; Oster & Ekman forthcoming) (fig. 2). In the second month smiling becomes an effective social signal. Even totally blind two-month-olds smile to a voice or tickling, so the infant smile cannot be an imitative response to seeing the smile of others (Freedman 1964; Fraiberg 1968, this volume). Like cooing, it must be based on a motor pattern formed before birth.

Almost all adult facial expressions can be found in photographs and video records of newborns and infants (Darwin 1872; Herska 1965; Ekman 1973; Charlesworth & Kreutzer 1973; Leboyer 1974; Oster & Ekman forthcoming). Some infant expressions appear differ-

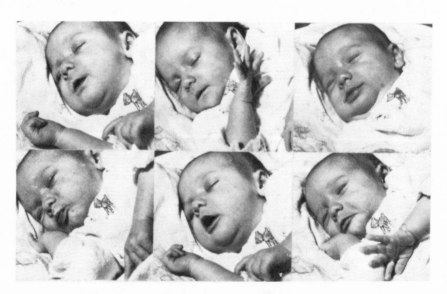

Fig. 2 24-day-old girl asleep. Born approx. 10 days post-mature, but typical of a neonate.

ent from adult expressions, in correlation with differences in facial structure (Oster & Ekman forthcoming). Cross-cultural studies of adults and children give evidence for an innate, pan-human facial 'vocabulary' of emotional signs (Ekman 1973; Ekman & Friesen 1971, 1975; Ekman et al. 1972; Eibl-Eibesfeldt 1970).

Our films confirm that emotional expressions can be recognised in infants (figs. 1 and 2). They also show facial movements which have little to do with emotion or mood. In relation to language the most significant non-emotional expressions are the lip and tongue movements which I have named 'prespeech' (fig. 3). Like other expressions mentioned, prespeech movements exist at birth, becoming much more distinct by the second and third months when most of our films were made.

By producing prespeech in systematic relation to the signals from a partner in face-to-face communication (see below), infants appear to express a rudiment of intention to speak to that person, although the movements differ from adult speech and are usually not voiced. For example, since young infants lack teeth, there can be no exact matches for the movements for sounds such as /th/, /v/ and /f/. Infant lower jaws are proportionately small, affecting mouth configurations used for vowel sounds and also limiting tongue mobility. Nevertheless, as fig. 3 shows, the movements closely resemble lip opening, tightening, pursing and closing and lip and tongue appositions essential to forming adult speech sounds. In photographs these configurations are distinguishable from all other forms of expression. The details of prespeech movements suggest that they are, from their first appearance, already part of a specific mechanism for speech. Furthermore, by directing illumination upward through the open lips during prespeech we have observed that the tongue is exceedingly mobile inside the mouth as well as at the front. Prespeech is emitted in episodes or bursts, often mixed with expressions for happiness, anger, disgust or surprise. But the speech-like movements may occur also when the face is otherwise at rest and quite free from expression of emotion or mood (fig. 3).

All such mouth movements of infants have been explained as being evolved from non-linguistic actions, like kissing or biting, and non-intersubjective acts, like turning to the breast, pushing out food, vomiting and breathing (Eibl-Eibesfeldt 1970; Andrew 1963; Blurton Jones 1971). The tenable hypothesis that these speech-like movements are related to speaking has not been explored.

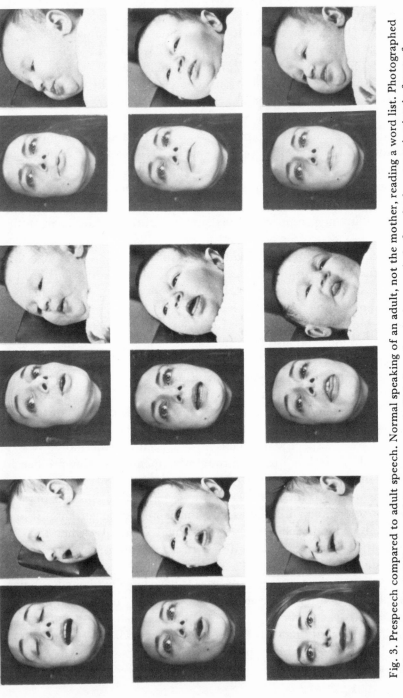

Fig. 3. Prespeech compared to adult speech. Normal speaking of an adult, not the mother, reading a word list. Photographed with a motor-driven Nikon at 4 frames per second. Girl, 7 weeks, during a period of excited communication in front of mother, but with gaze averted. Only climax postures shown.

Posturing of the head, which turns up, down or to the side in many forms of expression, and of the trunk and limbs, seems to be systematically related to particular facial expression (fig. 4). This observation leads to the working hypothesis that total patterns of body expression are present in infants. The most economical theory is that the patterns of expression through posture, which become stereotyped in dance

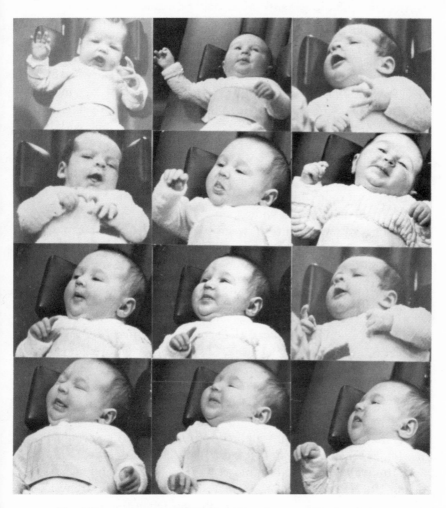

Fig. 4 Gestures in communication. Top: large, waving hand above shoulder, extending fingers wide while vocalising (6—7 weeks); upper centre: touching two index fingers together, opposing index finger and thumb (7 weeks); lower centre: pointing index finger with pre-speech, pursed lips (7 weeks); bottom: 'disdain' or 'disgust', hand held to side, flexed down (7 weeks).

and theatrical mannerisms, are based on innate templates as Darwin (1872) proposed. Study of these patterns requires repeated analysis of videotapes or films or sorting of many photographs. Since it is impossible to attend adequately to several parts of the body in real time, pencil and paper or keyboard encoding from ongoing behaviour are unreliable.

Particular hand movements are closely associated with particular facial expressions, forms of vocalising and prespeech (fig. 4). Some gestures are more often combined with 'big' open-mouthed expressions or calls like those adults make in greeting or attracting attention, or to express excitement, surprise or anger (Darwin 1872; Eibl-Eibesfeldt 1970; Ekman & Friesen 1969). This category includes vigorous hand waving and large open-handed or fisted movements. In contrast, index-finger pointing and finger-thumb closing with the hand held up over the shoulder or near the face are often synchronised with the climaxes of prespeech and the formulation of a new focus for visual attention (fig. 4). The association of lip-pursing or tongue protrusion with index-finger pointing or index-thumb closing, and of open-mouthed calling with wide open hand recalls Peiper's concept of 'spreading' of movements between eyes, mouth and hand to produce a pattern of simultaneous opening or closing (Peiper 1963). But the combinations are far too numerous and subtle for this to be a satisfactory explanation.

By the second month infants show improved visual focus and their eye movements communicate the changing direction of their visual attention. A two-month-old can elect to look at things of interest and can reject or avoid by looking away. Systematic eye movements to or away from the hands and face of a partner, especially to the eyes or mouth, are important signals in person-to-person interaction (Caron et al. 1973; Maurer & Salapatek 1976). The fact that infants select organs used for expression (eyes, mouth, hands) as foci for attention suggests that looking is a pre-adapted response to particular signal patterns (fig. 5). Eye-to-eye contact has been used as a defining feature of face-to-face communication between young infants and others (Robson 1967; Stern 1974b). The development of deliberate well-aimed visual orientating to the mother's eyes when the infant is about six weeks old is the main event of which she is aware at the start of 'strong' communication (Wolff 1963; Robson 1967). At six to eight weeks focussed looking with knitted brows giving way to smiling and prespeech are clearly differentiated in an intelligible and appealing

pattern of communicative intent (Rheingold 1961; Stern et al. 1975).
Even blind infants orientate to faces. They are well coordinated when
they direct their eyes toward voices as well as when they link aiming
the eyes with head rotation and attempts to reach and grasp. Blindness easily goes undetected in early infancy because looking movements seem normal (Freedman 1964; Fraiberg this volume).

The whole complex of actions just described seems to imply that
the infant has a clear commitment to intentional communication. But
do infants adjust their expressions in relation to other people or are
their different experessive movements entirely the result of changes
in a vague protocommunicative state, one that is pure output stimulated by recognition of a face but is blind and deaf to signals from
communicative acts of persons? To answer this question we must
examine the sensitivity and responsiveness of infants to signals from
people who desire to communicate with them.

3 Infants adapt to expressions of the mother

Young infants respond adaptively to a wide range of human signals
and these responses demonstrate their elaborate perception of persons.

Infants mimic expressions of adults. Maratos (1973) has shown
that infants under one month of age may imitate pitch and duration
of sounds, tongue protrusion and mouth opening, but she did not
obtain imitation of head rotation, babbling or leg displacement at
this age. Meltzoff & Moore (1977) report discriminating imitation of
hand gesture, tongue protrusion and jaw drop with open mouth by
neonates. I have observed that infants in the second month may imitate hand opening or bringing the two hands together. Piaget (1946),
in his careful study of imitation, without the aid of film or video,
underestimated the initial imitative competence of infants. When
reproducing tongue protrusion or a voice sound even the one-month-
old infant shows signs of searching for the right effect, making
repeated responses with variations. The search for a desired pattern
of movement must be regulated by a process of matching. It does not
necessarily depend on body sensations caused by movement of the
limbs or face or comparison of seen and felt movements, but some
kind of adjustment of the 'image' of a movement to be made to that
of a movement seen must be taking place in the brain. In order to
imitate, the infant must have a cerebral representation of persons.

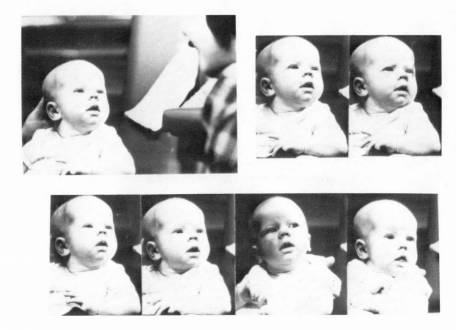

Fig. 5 Girl (6 weeks) spoken to softly watches face intently, brow furrowed and mouth open, then stirs and makes start of prespeech.

Maratos (forthcoming) found that imitation of facial expressions and simple voice sounds declined in the second to fifth months. Deliberate and more accurate reproduction of babbling and crying sounds after thoughtful watching appeared in the fourth and fifth months. Piaget (1946) described similar regulation of imitative accommodation. Observations by Uzgiris (1972) confirm that a more deliberate manner of imitation of expressive movements and vocalisations is characteristic of infants of five months or older. On the basis of my own film data I have called the early form of imitation 'magnetic' and the later 'discretionary' to emphasise the increased deliberation (a more developed self-awareness?) in the second period (Trevarthen 1978).

All movements imitated by infants resemble movements they may formulate on their own. The models offered are themselves imitations of babyish acts (Piaget 1946). Imitation is certainly not passive incorporation of 'new' experiences; it is more a remodelling and integration of components already in spontaneous expression. Therefore, the fact of imitation gives no licence to an unqualified empiricist approach to the growth of communicative abilities in man. It merely suggests how

the infant may pick up new variants of expressions in collaboration
with adults (Trevarthen 1974c).

To imitate, an infant must discriminate the model expression, but
more cogent evidence that two- to five-month-olds perceive expressions
is the subtle way in which the baby *translates* or *complements* the
mother's acts. Even when not imitating, infants in our films show
sensitive and specific replies to the communications of their mothers.
A smile may elicit a call or a wave. Raised eyebrows may elicit a smile.
Frowning may cause the expression of surprise, fear or even sudden
crying. The temporal correlations between behaviours in such
exchanges have recently been emphasised by authors who describe
the 'interactions' of 'rhythmical' and 'cyclical' in a 'communicative
network' or 'dyad' (Brazelton et al. 1974; Lewis & Freedle 1973;
Schaffer 1977b). Imitation is evidently a special case of intersubjectivity mirroring (Trevarthen 1974c; Sylvester-Bradley & Trevarthen
1978).

The reaction of an infant of three or four weeks to the approach
of an adult and to speech and touching is orientation to the face with
gaze fixed on eyes or mouth, facial expression of interest or mild surprise (wide open eyes, brow 'knitted', everted lips, mouth slightly
open) and smiling (fig. 5). Experiments with artificial stimuli show
that even neonates prefer to look at simplified face-like patterns
(Fantz 1963). They seem to explore the configuration of the face,
being most attracted to the eyes (Lewis 1969; Carpenter et al. 1970;
Wolff 1963, 1969). They are more interested in upright faces (Watson
1972), which adults also see more easily. Experiments show that
looking to faces and preference for looking at eyes increases in the
second month and is usual thereafter (Caron et al. 1973; Maurer &
Salapatek 1976). Infants discriminate colour, evidently by means of
built-in categorisation of wavelength into a code of the primaries: red,
yellow, green, blue (Bornstein 1975). Light reflected from the skin
of humans of all races is reddish. This may explain the preference
infants show for a patch of red in a non-red field, a preference which
could aid them in finding a face or hand. Two-month-olds will try to
communicate with a televised image of a human face and this permits
many experimental manipulations and tests of their understanding of
communication behaviour (Papoušek & Papoušek 1974; Murray
forthcoming).

Perception of human sounds is acute in very young infants. Speech
is reacted to with particular interest. The pitch characteristics of the

voice are preferred to non-voice sounds, and the female voice is preferred to the male (Eisenberg 1975). There is evidence from sucking
tests based on operant conditioning that by one month consonant
formant transitions[3] in synthetic speech sounds are distinguished
(Eimas et al. 1971; Trehub 1973). The mother's individual voice or
manner of speaking is recognised and preferred early (Mills &
Melhuish 1974).

Finally, the strong response of a newborn to the periodic motion
of an object in an otherwise inactive field must contribute to his perception of persons and their communication signals. All voluntary
movement is periodic (Bernstein 1967). It has rhythmic coherence,
a hierarchical structure of cadences and a strong tendency to synchrony of beats. Movements of different parts of the body demonstrate 'self-synchrony' (Condon this volume). Condon & Sander
(1974a) have presented evidence that the speech sounds of adults
may act as pacemakers for limb movements of listening neonates. It
is possible that the neonate becomes locked into adult speech, but
much of the periodicity observed in limb movements of neonates is
contributed by the infant's own motor pacemakers (Trevarthen
1974b). I believe that they are less passive in their entrainment than
has been suggested, and doubt that synchronisation of this kind contributes to the development of language.

We find that close integration of rhythm of mother and baby is
one of the clearest features to emerge from microanalysis of happy
communications between two-month-olds and their mothers (figs. 7,
8 and 10). Coordinated action with synchronisation about a common
beat is the framework on which reciprocal exchange of complimen-
tary messages is based (Brazelton et al. 1974). Two-month-olds can
stop and start activity, a capacity which is essential for reciprocal
exchange. Reply movements by sound making and gesture may
extend the same beat as the baby talk of the mother and the head and
face movements or touching which accompany her speaking.

When adults are unresponsive, avoiding or aggressive, two-month-
olds show tension or distress by facial expressions of fear, yawning,
grimacing and frowning, as well as by gaze avoidance, crying, startle
movements and threshing or struggling. L. Murray in my laboratory
has used an interruption of communication to test the predictions of
the infant about communication (Murray forthcoming). Mothers are
asked to stop reacting and to freeze their expressions for one minute
in the middle of a happy communicative exchange. The infants give

complex emotional responses. They may move as if to shout with sudden waving of the arms and grimaces of excitement while staring at the partner's face. These appear to be acts of appeal or solicitation. Brazelton et al. (1975) report the same results from interruption of exchanges with mothers, and Papoušek & Papoušek (1975, 1977) have studied the cognitive basis for distress when the infant is confronted with maladapted or artificially distorted maternal signals. These reactions prove that an eight-week-old may respond predictably to unfriendly actions from a familiar person (Tatam 1974; Murray forthcoming). Signals of distress or protest include self-stimulatory, avoiding and aggressive acts, like those of children who have been chronically isolated from human contact or who are diagnosed as autistic (Clancy & MacBride 1975).

The signs of anxiety and distress when communication is broken show the close integration of subjective emotional states with interpersonal communication. They also show how the infant may move to recover communication if the mother fails to display affection. The infant makes forced, abrupt and large gestures which attract attention, then shows passivity and sadness or grimaces and gestures of distress which stimulate comfort and concern. In a test of the infant's intermodal perception of the mother, Aronson & Rosenbloom (1971) found that one-month-old infants made complex expressions of distress, including crying, when loudspeakers were placed to create an artificial separation between the perceived location of the mother's voice and the location of her face seen through a window. This observation is consistent with what we have seen after disruption of communication.

The infant is clearly equipped to perceive and interpret input from the mother's personality. Indeed, adaptive forms of reply to what the mother does give the infant a considerable control over the communicative exchange from the start. On this base learning will later permit the infant to achieve much more elaborate expressions and more subtle recognition of the mother, adding strength and content to their growing affectional and communicative attachment.

4 The mother generates expressions adapted to her infant's interest

Our mothers were skilled human communicators. All those who agreed to participate had busy lives. Most were married to men with pro-

fessional or intermediate classes of occupation and the majority had
at least secondary school education and were fluent in spoken
language. Our films show that individual mothers differed in the style
or range of their expression according to their personalities. Nevertheless, all made the facial expressions and gestures of surprise,
amusement, anxiety and so on. Each mother mixed the pan-human
language of expressive communication with socially cultivated mannerisms, and with speech that varied widely in content.

There is great richness and variety of structure in adult-to-adult
communication, and the infant could conceivably be equipped to
respond to some of it at least. However, it is not the adult forms of
communication in the other's behaviour to the infant which interest
us most, but a special manner which most of the observed mothers
developed for capturing the infant's interest (Papoušek & Papoušek
1977; Stern 1974b; Snow 1972; Sylvester-Bradley & Trevarthen
1978). Differences in playfulness, sensitive encouragement and contingent pacing of mothers in the home when the baby is three
months old are prognostic of the quality of the relationship (security
of 'attachment') when the baby is nine months old (Blehar et al.
1977). Clearly there is an optimal adaptation of the mother to the
baby.

As soon as a mother begins to talk to the baby her movements
become regular and subdued. She speaks more quietly and more
gently and becomes highly attentive, spending as much time waiting
and watching as speaking. The form of speech is changed in consistent
ways towards the regularity, repetition and musical, questioning
intonation known as 'baby talk'. Alternatively, the mother may
become active and playful, or teasing, making rhythmical and exaggerated movements of her head, trunk and whole body, or reach to
touch the infant in emphatic ways. When playing in this way she
tends to use nonsense sounds. In visible records of the sounds of baby
talk the overall effect is that of repeating patterns as in simple music.
Apparently baby talk is regulated to create short dramatic episodes
of action, with controlled change of intonation to a short succession
of marked climaxes. The same may be said of the mother's playful
movements of the head and face, of her touching with the hands and
of her singing or nonsense syllables to create voice games. It is probable that baby talk obeys unconscious rules of expression, and that
these rules are also applied automatically through the whole range of
expressive movements whenever communication is attempted with

any being that is conceived to have limited comprehension. The manner of baby talk is close to that sometimes used in speech to animals, foreigners and mentally defective or extremely aged persons. However, I do not believe that simplification is the main purpose of baby talk. A solicitous or caring intent, leading to watchful gentleness, seems more fundamental. It is a specific, assisting form of intersubjectivity, and not simple at all.

In general this automatic adaptation of a mother's behaviour would seem to match infants' perceptions and communicative capacities. Papoušek & Papoušek (1977) consider the mother's baby talk and associated orienting and patterned body movement to be highly adapted to the cognitive, learning and information processing competence of the infant and to give strong support to the initial development of cognition. Most mothers, even when unaware of doing so, tend toward similar patterns of rhythm and repetition. This behaviour of mothers, closely fitted to the baby's needs, makes it possible for the investigator to use baby talk and vocal games to detect infant behaviours which indicate changes in communicative intelligence (Sylvester-Bradley & Trevarthen 1978). It also offers a sensitive way of comparing the communicative styles of mother—infant pairs. This aspect of intersubjectivity with infants, in spite of rules that transcend cultural groups, varies widely in certain details between different individual mothers, and these differences show marked correlations with social class (Blehar et al. 1977; Moss et al. 1969; Lewis & Freedle 1973; Stern 1974b).

In a very few of our recording sessions the mother was unable or unwilling to submit to the special requirements of communication with a young infant under laboratory conditions. Then her infant was fretful or avoiding. Individuals less experienced or less involved with an infant than the mother may likewise fail in communication. This is because they fail to support the infant's expressions of pleasure or his prespeech and gestures. It is important to note that our method using staged communicative exchanges in an institutional environment may intimidate the mother, the infant or both and cause a breakdown of intersubjectivity or its change to a distressed form. However, it does not take much observation in homes to determine that 'normal' human communication with infants is very varied in quietness and success. The 'studio' situation does not appear to be outside the range of natural interactions. Even in the home and under optimal conditions the mother has to adapt deliberately to her infant to obtain communication. These observations of failure in communication give strong support to the claim that both infant and mother are sensitive to the quality of each other's expressions.

5 Mothers respond to the expressions of infants

The films show that mothers are captivated and emotionally involved with their infants (fig. 6). As soon as the infants join in communication the behaviour of most mothers quickly becomes subdued and attentive to and dependent on what the infants do. In our films mothers are usually watchful and questioning or show signs of surprise or disbelief. They react as agents who are *subordinate* to acts of babies. Smiling, baby talk, touching and moving the face in and out

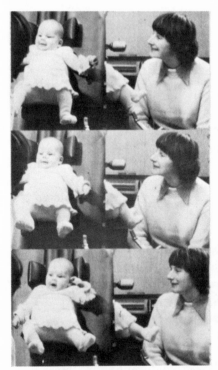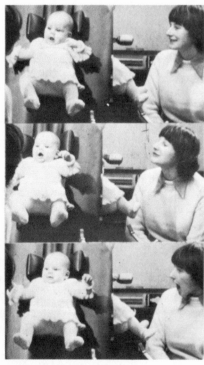

Fig. 6 Mother mirroring 2-month-old daughter (from ciné film). Left, top to bottom: they smile, then the infant makes an utterance with gesture; right, top to bottom: at the climax the infant is not smiling, the mother imitates calling out with mocking exaggeration. Interval between climaxes of expression of infant and mother = 1 second.

towards the infants cease, and are succeeded by attentive stillness and orientation to the infants' faces, and by imitation of certain infant expressions.

In the communications we have observed, close imitation of the infants by the mothers is characteristic (figs. 6 and 7). The imitated behaviours, often reproduced with playful exaggeration or gentle mockery, include excitement and vigorous calls. Mothers imitate tossing back the head, raising eyebrows in surprise or emphasis, opening the mouth, frowning and laughing. Some mothers include conscious or semiconscious humorous, sometimes teasing or aggressive, reproductions of comical expressions in their imitations, including poking out the tongue or grimacing (fig. 6). But most of the imitation in our sample is unconscious following of the infants' most vigorous or most prominent gestures. The behaviour may be described as mirroring, although, since it is often slightly after the infant in time, 'echo' describes it better. At other times, mothers synchronise with or even slightly anticipate what infants will do. Reflecting excited or melo-

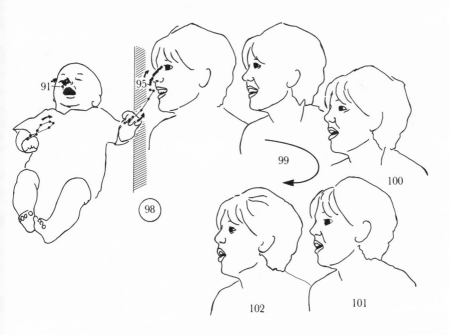

Fig. 7 Imitation with close following of boy (12 weeks) by mother. Infant moves head and vocalises; 4 frames later (= ¼ second) mother moves head back to exclaim in reply. (From ciné film; same episode as fig. 10, to which frame nos. refer.)

dramatic behaviour evidently plays a role in sustaining communicatio
This is what Stern et al. (1975) call 'coaction'. It does not form the
sole basis for early communication because infants are quite capable
from the start of a more subdued dialogue-like alternation of 'utterances' (M.C. Bateson 1975b, this volume). As a rule, prespeech with
gesture is watched and replied to by exclamations of pleasure or surprise like 'Oh, my my!', 'Good heavens!', 'Oh, what a big smile!',
'Ha! That's a big one!' (meaning a story), questioning replies like
'Are you telling me a story?', 'Oh, really?' or even agreement by
nodding 'Yes' or saying 'I'm *sure* you're right'. Since mothers reproduce infants' demonstrative acts, it is all the more interesting that
they do not usually imitate prespeech and small hand movements
such as pointing, but reply to these with baby talk. What they say
gives us access to how they perceive infants. The content of baby
talk to one two-month-old infant girl, in films taken under the conditions we have standardised, has been analysed by Sylvester-Bradley
(Sylvester-Bradley & Trevarthen 1978). He discovered that the
mother rarely talked about what needed to be done to attend to the
baby's physiological needs. Nearly all the mother's utterances were
about how the baby felt, what the baby said and what the baby
thought. A mother evidently perceives her baby to be a person like
herself. Mothers interpret baby behaviour as not only intended to be
communicative, but as verbal and meaningful. They may not remem-
ber these complex and elaborate interpretations but this does not
detract from the psychological significance of what they do.

   In summary: mothers' responses to two-month-old infants are
stimulating, attentive, confirmatory, interpretative and highly supportive. They inject meaning into the infants' expressions, but at this
stage verbal meaning has no influence on the infants' minds. *What*
the mothers say does not tutor infants. Because infants already perceive speech, they are able to assimilate baby talk as a carrier of
maternal subjectivity along with changes in maternal appearance and
cadence of movement, taking them into their own patterns of communicative expression and deriving organisation from what the
mothers do. They take what they require and let the rest go by.

6 Dyadic communication

The described responses and actions give us the essentials for analysis
of intersubjective communication between two- and three-month-old

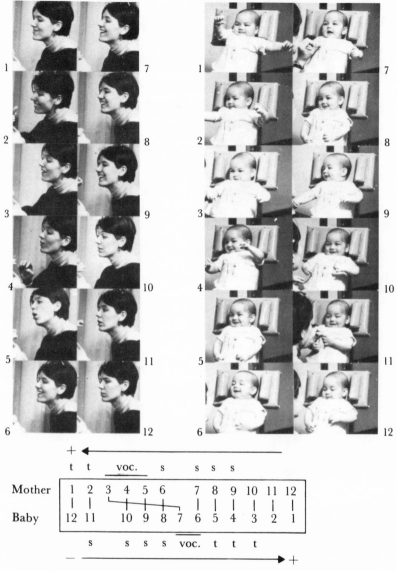

Fig. 8 Interaction of interpersonal initiatives. Photographs taken over
2 minutes in which several exchanges of utterances between mother and
11-week-old son took place. The pictures of the infant and of the mother
in a mirror were cut apart and separately ordered with respect to intensity
of communication. 1 = highest, most assertive initiative; mother teasing
and touching, infant acting as if angry. 12 = lowest degree of intimi-
dation or weakest initiative; mother looking worried, infant avoiding
gaze. Below: the rank order of mother and infant expressions were subsequently compared when the pictures were reassembled as originally
paired; there is an almost perfect reciprocal relationship of intensity of
communication or motivation (t = teasing smile; voc = vocalisation;
s = intimidated or amused smile).

infants and their mothers. The four main functions discussed are as
follows:

1. *Infant expressions* include a wide repertoire of indications of subjective mood and of intent to transmit specific contents of experience
and purpose, even though these contents themselves are poorly differentiated at this age.

2. *Infant responses* show attention to and imitation of expressions of
mothers, including mood and speech.

3. *Maternal expression* tends to a specialised mode of communication
adapted to the perceptual capacities of infants.

4. *Maternal responses*, largely unconscious, complement infant
expressions and follow them closely.

Putting these together we may create a diagram of mutual interaction
(fig. 9). A system like this has many possible states. Most important

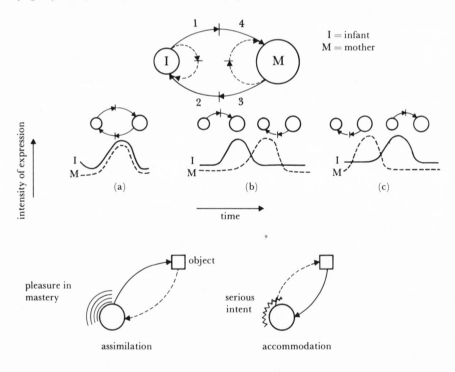

Fig. 9 Diagrams of primary intersubjectivity. Above: the cycle of interaction; synchronisation (a) and alternation (b and c). Below: Piagetian
assimilation and accommodation to an object have different emotional
correlates. Similar states alternate in communication.

are states of closely synchronised activity (fig. 9a) and states of reciprocal or complementary activity (fig. 9b and c). There is no reason to assume that the partners are equally active, and there may be considerable asymmetry of intention. Since one partner is psychologically very immature, asymmetry is likely and must be taken into account. Analysis of filmed exchanges reveals that while the pattern of communication between mother and infant is regulated by *both* partners, it is indeed one-sided and the infant tends to assume control of the course of communication after mother and baby become mutually orientated. I consider the finding that a two-month-old baby may take purposeful initiative in communication as important as the discovery of an innate form of intention to speak with an accompanying code of gestures (see fig. 8). The communicative processes of infants are not merely latent precursors of language; they are already functional in directing communication with adults. Thus infants control the social stimulation on which their own development depends.

Evidence for infant control is presented in a diagram of the sequence of events in a communicative exchange (fig. 10).

Stimulated by a simple request to 'talk to' or 'chat with' her baby the mother begins by efforts to attract the infant's attention, principally to obtain eye contact. If the infant is relaxed and alert this is usually achieved in a few seconds. Then the mother smiles and speaks gently, bringing her face close in front of the baby who watches fixedly what she is doing. The first sign of response from the baby is almost always a smile, but he may begin mouth movement or make some other expression.[4] If the mother receives a sign of pleasure or interest from her baby she reacts immediately by imitating his expression or by increasing her solicitations in movement and baby talk or singing etc. But good communication involves reticence on the part of the mother. She must step down as soon as the infant appears ready to make an 'utterance'. Watching, admiring and withdrawing to make way are signs of the mother's willingness to become subordinate to any communicative initiative from the infant (fig. 8). When the infant makes an elaborate gesture, vocalisation or prespeech with gesticulation, the mother reacts with receptive expressions of surprise, pleasure and admiration. We distinguish between the mother's response to more animated and vocal displays of excitement, which she tends to shadow or mirror, and more concentrated unsmiling

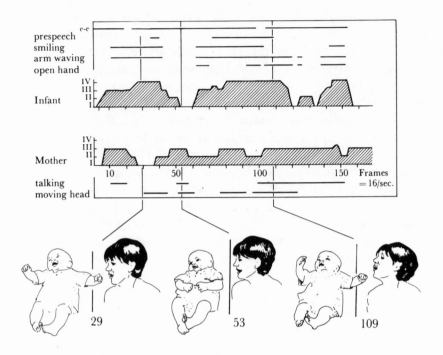

Fig. 10 A communicative exchange analysed frame by frame. I—IV = levels of general animation in body action; e—e = infant in eye-to-eye contact with mother. Mother looks at infant throughout. The infant makes two full utterances each lasting about 3 seconds, then truncates on a third, looking away. The mother acts reciprocally, adjusting to the infant and giving overlapping and turn-taking stimulation. The infant attends closely when not making an utterance.

prespeech which she watches passively and then replies to at the end (cf. Stern et al. 1975).

This accommodative patterning of the mother's reponse allows the infant to form sequences of activity that take the form of utterances 1—5 seconds long separated by pauses in which the infant watches the mother. Thus phrasing of the exchange results from a cooperative effort. The infant reacts to the mother's attentions, much affected by her shadowing reinforcement of smiling, vocalising etc., by becoming stimulated to expressive activity before returning to the relaxed state (Bateson 1975b; Reingold 1961; Stern et al. 1975).

During prespeech the infant's eye contact and smiling may disappear to give way to an expression of concentration (figs. 3 and 8). It seems likely that these indications of withdrawal, with reduction in attention to the mother, are responsible for the mother's deferentially withholding baby talk and other expressions during the infant's utterances. As soon as the infant shows signs of ending his utterance, with reduction in all forms of expression, the mother actively approves and replies. If the infant does not respond, the mother's efforts increase. They are phrased with regular questioning climaxes which may succeed in eliciting immediate response. Quick, precisely tuned responses of the baby to the mother's climax pauses show that he is following the pattern of the mother's behaviour and that he is particularly sensitive to her more marked signals. If the mother becomes assertive and teasing, the infant at this age may withdraw and cease to communicate. Each partner watches and joins in step with the patterned utterances (or signal displays) of the other. The exact form of the infant's utterances seems mainly determined by his own spontaneous brain processes. Immaturity of comprehension of what the mother does results in his assertiveness which she acknowledges (fig. 8).

The mother finds out what her infant can do as she becomes familiar with him. She creates interpersonal games which become ritual exchanges commenting on or emotionally marking familiar patterns of their companionship. Each mother—infant pair develops conventions of communication. When mothers and infants are interchanged to make pairs of 'strangers' the communication becomes less elaborate and more cautious and seems out of tune. Games and play rituals are characteristic of communication between mothers and their infants older than three months (Trevarthen & Hubley 1978) but the process of personal friendship begins earlier. The restraint in the behaviour of a two- or three-month-old when he is required to communicate with an unfamiliar woman may be due partly to immediate recognition of her different identity, but details of observed behaviour indicate that the process is much more complex. It involves variation in the pattern of response of *both* partners. Women are less confident, less relaxed with a strange infant. Infants often show surprise at an unfamiliar woman's hesitant behaviour. Nevertheless, experienced and confident mother-substitutes can elicit cheerful communicative responses from infants. In these exchanges the communication can be more excited and more playful than the typical exchanges of the infant with his own mother.

We conclude from these observations that the learning by both infant and mother within their communicative interaction is a major

factor in the creation of the personal bond between them. Attachment does not appear to be a simple imprinting of the infant to facial
appearance or signals from body contact, odour etc. However, I do
not wish to conclude on the basis of the artificial exchanges we film
that this kind of active communicative practice at two months, enjoyable though it is for infant and mother, is essential to the psychological growth of the infant. Its value to me as an investigator is that it
brings out what the infant and mother are capable of and willing to
do to achieve communication. What we have seen makes it impossible to ignore the significance or innate intersubjectivity in the mental
growth of the infant.

7 Comment

It is often thought that the main cause of development in communication during infancy is the fabrication of structure for the infant by
the mother. According to this view the infant's immature acts have
rhythm and impulse, but are at the outset exceedingly simple in
variety of form. The mother attributes intentions to these seemingly
pointless movements, maintaining development by transfer of her
intentions and understandings to the infant. This view of the development of communication neglects the regulation of development from
within the mind of the child and leaves the child's psychological
growth unexplained.

Our findings with infants two to three months of age lead us to
conclude that a complex form of mutual understanding develops even
at this age. It is both naturally accepted and strongly regulated by the
infant. Two-month-olds exhibit many different expressions, some
highly emotional, and they make a variety of attempts to gain the
lead in an exchange with another person. They also are sensitive to
subtle differences in the mother's expression.

The dependent acts of the mother show that she is adapting to the
infant, and apparently each pair develops a unique style of communication and a private code. But in primary intersubjectivity there is
innovation of meaning by the infant as well as by the mother. Furthermore, inside the earliest communications of man may be observed the
embryonic forms of communication by speech itself. In this sense we
may cautiously refer to the 'protoconversational' character of these
exchanges. The mother, we believe, is right. The infant, though telling
her nothing, *is* speaking to her.

Even more important is the precocity of a general interpersonal understanding. In the first functional stage of human communication, before transactions with objects are developed beyond a few simple orientating reactions and thoughtless explorations, the infant recognises the mother and invites her to share a dance of expressions and excitements. The infant needs a partner but knows the principle of the dance well enough, and is not just a puppet to be animated by a miming mother who 'pretends' her baby knows better.

Notes

1. I use the word 'intersubjectivity' in the sense of Habermas (1970, 1972) when he considers the origins of language from a psychoanalytic viewpoint. It is not a graceful word, but it does specify the linking of subjects who are active in transmitting their understanding to each other. The relating is 'interpersonal', but we need to penetrate the psychological process by which conscious intending subjects relate their mental and emotional processes together. I feel that 'intersubjective' emphasises this.
2. Grateful acknowledgement is given of support from the United States Public Health Service to Professor Jerome Bruner at the Harvard Center for Cognitive Studies, and from the Social Science Research Council of the United Kingdom.
3. When consonants are articulated the flow of air is stopped. Different consonants combined with the same vowels stop the voice for different times. The differences, though of the order of a few thousandths of a second, are perceived by young infants.
4. If the baby has been fretful or sleepy, sight of the attentive mother usually triggers grimaces of sadness, fussiness or crying. We do not persist long in recording this kind of behaviour as our aim is to obtain information about exchanges expressive of complex mental processes of the infant rather than mere physiological or emotional states. An unhappy infant is taken from the chair and left to be attended by the mother.

I 7

Structure of early face-to-face
communicative interactions

E. TRONICK
University of Massachusetts, Amherst
H. ALS
Children's Hospital Medical Center, Boston
L. ADAMSON
Wellesley College, Massachusetts

1 Introduction

Human social interaction is a culturally modified species-specific process in which message-carrying displays, both verbal and non-verbal,
are mutually exchanged by the interactants. The exchange of these
messages insures our survival and integrates each new individual into
the culture. Our goal has been to describe the ontogenetic development of this system of interchange and to uncover the principles that
govern its organization. Moreover, the necessity of this system for
our survival implies that our adaptations or capabilities are initially
and primarily oriented toward intersubjective demands, and thus the
performance of both interactants in such interchanges should be most
revealing of these adaptations.

In studying the development of this system, a primary fact to
recognize is the initial 'inequality' of the partners. The adult partner
exists in a cognitive and temporal domain different from that of the
infant. The initial structuring of the interaction and its change over
time is most likely to reflect this imbalance. The system is the *Anlage*
of the adult communication system but in its early structuring it is
constrained by the capabilities of the partners and not by its ultimate
goal. For example, the initial communication system does not contain language, although clearly it will develop in such a manner as to
permit linguistic interchanges. Therefore, to look at the early development of the system solely in terms of its pre-linguistic properties
would be to miss its current organization and the change of that
organization.

In our attempts to understand this process of communication we have chosen to study face-to-face interactions. Interchanges in this setting should most clearly demonstrate the structure of the communication process since it lacks the constraints inherent in caregiving situations or play situations with objects which modify the communication process (see fig. 1). For example, diapering or feeding have a temporal structure that is independent of the communication process per se. It is possible to change a sleeping infant or feed a non-reactive three-month-old, but it is not possible to maintain successful communication with a sleepy, unresponsive infant.

2 Procedure

2.1 Subjects

Our subjects were twelve mothers and their normal full-term healthy infants. All the mothers had been delivered at the Boston Hospital for Women. Contact was made with all of the mothers prior to their coming into the laboratory to participate in the study. A mother was told that we were videotaping and then analyzing the development of normal social capabilities during the first six months of infant life and that in some conditions we would ask her to play with her infant and in others we would ask her to distort the way she normally played with her infant. We encouraged her questions at the time of initial contact and throughout all the sessions. Immediately after the recording was completed we watched the tape of that session with the mother and discussed how the infant behaved. Our contacts with the mothers were relaxed. We had known them from the time of the

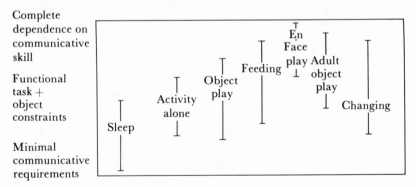

Fig. 1 Relative communicative requirements of different infant activities.

birth of their infants and we felt that we and they were engaged in a mutually shared project.

Infants were brought into the laboratory as soon as the mother felt comfortable in taking her infant out. This varied from eleven to twenty-eight days. All the infants were seen at least once before they were one month old and weekly through the second month. Visits were two or three weeks apart from the third through the sixth month. All the infants missed occasional sessions but at least eight sessions were recorded for each infant.

2.2 Method

The mother would bring the infant into the laboratory where his outer clothing and shoes were taken off and he was diapered if necessary. Feeding was done at home or in the laboratory, depending on the infant's schedule and the mother's sense of her infant's needs. We then placed the infant in a modified infant chair which had an adjustable back rest and movable foam pads to help support him, including a seat pad hollowed out for his rump which helped to prevent him from slipping forward. This arrangement left his limbs free and allowed for some postural shifts on his part. The chair was set on a 30-in high table surrounded on three sides by curtains and facing a

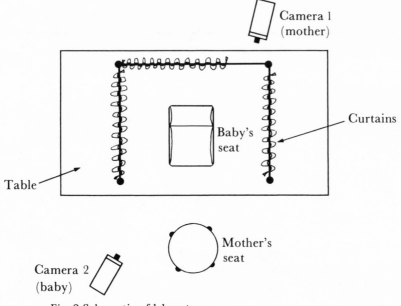

Fig. 2 Schematic of laboratory.

blank white wall (see fig. 2). After being placed in the chair the
infant was left alone and his behavior was recorded on videotape for
30 seconds. Then the mother approached him from behind the curtains and seated herself on a stool facing him. After 3 minutes she
left and the infant was recorded alone for 30 seconds. Then she re-
appeared for another 3-minute recording session with her baby (see
below).

Videotaping was done with two cameras. One camera focused on
the infant. It was located on a tripod 5 ft away and obliquely to the
right of the infant. The camera recording the mother was located
behind a slit in the curtains behind the infant. No special lighting was
required to achieve high-resolution pictures. The output from the two
cameras was fed into a split screen generator that gave a viewer an *en
face* view of both the mother and the infant (see fig. 3). In addition
an electronic timer calibrated in minutes, seconds and hundredths of
seconds was fed into the tape deck and recorded along with the
images of the mother and infant. Sound was recorded from a single
microphone placed under the infant seat. The taped image contained
the infant seated in the chair on one half of the picture, the mother
from the waist up on the other half and a real time digital display
along the bottom. The video recorder operated at a rate of 60 frames
per second and had complete resolution even when stopped.

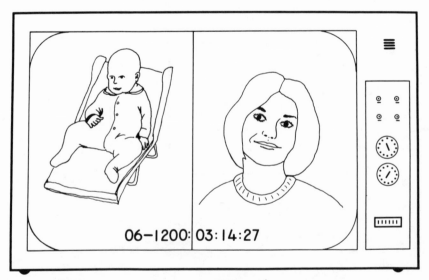

06–1200: 03:14:27

Fig. 3 Schematic of picture on TV monitor.

2.3 System of description

The tapes were analyzed with a detailed microbehavioral categorizing system. For the infant we scored 10 behaviors, each having from 2 to 13 possible categories, and for the mother we scored 6 behaviors, each having from 2 to 13 categories (see appendix). The infant behaviors scored were vocalization, direction of gaze, head left or right, head position, facial expression, body position, amount of movement, blinks, specific hand movements and specific foot movements. The mother's behaviors were vocalization, specific handling of the infant, facial expression, direction of gaze, head position and body position. Scoring was always done with two observers at the same time. If they disagreed on a category for a particular piece of behavior they would rerun the tape until they came to agreement. Reliability was checked by scoring segments of tapes without discussion and evaluating the interobserver agreement. Reliability for each behavioral category was well over 0.9 each time it was checked. Usually only one behavior was scored on each run and thus as many as sixteen slow-motion runs might be required to score one tape. Each mother and infant behavior was written on a data record sheet and then punched onto computer cards. In addition the sessions were described by two observers in a narrative form arrived at by consensus which characterized the quality and tempo of the infant—mother communication as well as the impression the session made on them.

Our categorizing of the displays of the mother and infant is done on the basis of a 'dynamic second', and not on stopped frames. The tape is played back at its slow-motion rate of $\frac{1}{7}$ normal speed. This allows us to view a communicative event which took 1 second of real time for 7 seconds. We can tell the real time duration of an event because the timer was recorded simultaneously with the event and so it, too, is slowed to $\frac{1}{7}$ speed. When a real time second has passed we stop the tape, categorize and record the quality of the particular behavior that we are scoring on that run. There is no blurring during the slow-motion playback, during the time when the tape is stopped after the 1-second scoring period or when the tape starts moving again for the next period. We are able to watch an event without losing its dynamic qualities. Slowing down its rate of occurrence allows us to see how the behavior is changing. In addition, since some events such as a yawn or smile are harder to identify when slowed down, we often check the slow-motion description with normal-speed runs. The normal-speed run is always used when scoring mother and infant vocalizations.

This method of categorizing is based on the view that the information conveyed by social displays is carried by transformations of the stimulus array (Gibson 1966). The message contained in a facial expression is not contained in a single static facial configuration nor even in a strung together series of such configurations. Static configurations contain at best degraded information about expressions. Expressions are plastic transformations of the stimulus array. These transformations carry the information which specifies the meaning of an expression. They take a specific amount of time to occur and to use stop-frame analysis would be to forfeit information.

3 The dyadic phases of infant—caregiver social interaction

Looking first at the quality of the infant—mother communication process we have found the following phases typical for a three-month-old infant and his mother: (1) initiation, (2) mutual orientation, (3) greeting, (4) play-dialogue and (5) disengagement (see fig. 4).

Initiation occurs when the mother's face brightens and she baby-talks to a sober baby, or a baby vocalizes and smiles to a caregiver

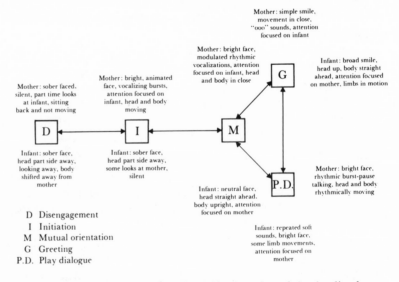

Mother: simple smile, movement in close, "ooo" sounds, attention focused on infant

Mother: bright face, modulated rhythmic vocalizations, attention focused on infant, head and body in close

Mother: bright, animated face, vocalizing bursts, attention focused on infant, head and body moving

Mother: sober faced, silent, part time looks at infant, sitting back and not moving

Infant: broad smile, head up, body straight ahead, attention focused on mother, limbs in motion

Infant: sober face, head part side away, looking away, body shifted away from mother

Infant: sober face, head part side away, some looks at mother, silent

Infant: neutral face, head straight ahead, body upright, attention focused on mother

Mother: bright face, rhythmic burst-pause talking, head and body rhythmically moving

Infant: repeated soft sounds, bright face, some limb movements, attention focused on mother

D Disengagement
I Initiation
M Mutual orientation
G Greeting
P.D. Play dialogue

Fig. 4 Phase transit diagram: a schematized version of the dyadic phases of a 3-month-old's interaction with a caregiver. The boxed portions are exemplars of behaviors that make up the phases for infant and caregiver.

who has paused too long. Mutual orientation may take place with neutral or bright faces, with the caregiver talking or the infant making isolated sounds. Greeting occurs with mutual smiles that can be either simple or broad smiles. There may be much or little hand and body movement but both partners must be looking at one another. Play-dialogues occur when the mother talks in a burst—pause pattern and the infant vocalizes during the pauses. Disengagement may occur when one of the partners looks away from the other while that partner is still oriented.

Phases are defined by a set of clusters of behaviors, never by a single behavior. Thus certain behaviors can substitute for other behaviors as in initiation, when tapping is substituted by the mother for moving into the infant's line of vision. Each of these phases reflects the current state of the communication and the intent of the partners. This means that not every phase is entered in every interaction. Initiation may not occur when both partners successfully maintain mutual orientation. Greeting may not occur in an interaction that does not go beyond mutual orientation. Moreover, a sequence of phases may be repeated several times in one interactive communication and only once in another. Thus, there may be many cyclings back and forth between mutual orientation—greeting—mutual orientation, or only one of these cycles, or many disengagement—mutual orientation—disengagement cycles. These sequences of phases, their recurrent characteristics and the times spent within each phase give every communication a unique quality.

3.1 A schematic example

At the beginning of an idealized communication sequence (presented in fig. 5) the partners are disengaged. Both are neutral-faced and looking away from one another (fig. 4 and fig. 5 point a). In the initiation phase (fig. 5 point b), the mother's goal is to achieve an *en face* position with the infant. She does this by moving her face into the infant's line of vision and/or modulating her voice in a staccato burst pattern as in 'Hi! Hi!' or by calling the baby's name repeatedly. If the infant stays disengaged the mother may try additional strategies to get him to orient to her such as touching him or turning his head. This phase reflects dyssynchrony between the partners, one involved, the other not, the mother's aim being the establishment of mutuality. When the infant does orient, they achieve a state of mutual orientation

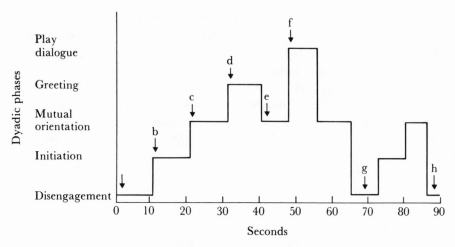

Fig. 5 Phase flow diagram: a schematized version of the movement from
one dyadic phase to the next in a 3-month-old and adult interaction. It
illustrates the flow of affective involvement.

(fig. 5 point c). At this point the infant often has a neutral or bright
face. The mother's voice quality shifts to a smoothly modulated pattern and her face brightens, or she may smile. The amount of time
they stay in the mutual orientation phase varies. The mother talks to
the baby and may touch him. Her face goes through many changes.
She may be smiling, then animated bright, then smiling again. The
infant stays neutral or possibly bright. Mutuality of attention has
been established.

The next phase is greeting (fig. 5 point d). Its crucial element with
an infant of this age is the smile (see above). As the baby smiles and
his limbs go into motion, the mother becomes increasingly animated.
She smiles, either at the peak of his smile or just after the peak. Then
they both decelerate to bright or neutral faces. Often the infant
shifts his gaze briefly during deceleration. They are back to the
mutual orientation phase (fig. 5 point e) and ready to move toward
another greeting (or play-dialogue or disengagement). If they move
into the play-dialogue phase (fig. 5 point f), the mother begins a carefully modulated burst—pause pattern of talking. The infant either
actually vocalizes or makes movements of intention to do so. The
mother marks the infant's vocalizations with a change in facial
expression or with a single burst of vocalization that breaks the
burst—pause pattern. These phases — greeting and play-dialogue —
reflect positive, affective mutuality.

As the typical communication proceeds the periods of mutual orientation last longer while those of greeting and play-dialogue are briefer. The affective level is decreasing, and the infant eventually looks away with a neutral or even sober face (fig. 5 point g). The mother tries to re-elicit the infant's attention, as in the initiation phase. If they re-orient, they tend to remain in that phase until the mother leaves (fig. 5 point h).

This sequencing of phases produces a characteristic waxing and waning of affective involvement (fig. 5). In the schematized example, there is a movement toward mutuality of attention. The partners are at first not joined to each other. This is the phase of disengagement. Initiation is an attempt to establish mutuality and make possible more positive affective states. With the establishment of mutual attention, greeting and play-dialogue become possible. These are highly positive emotional states reflecting attentional and affective synchrony.

3.2 Two communication sequences

Two actual sequences from two different pairs can illustrate these points, emphasizing both their universal and their idiosyncratic aspects. The infant in sequence I is a boy eighty days old. This sequence begins with a greeting phase and not an initiation phase (fig. 6a point a). As soon as the mother enters the infant's visual field they are looking at each other, the mother smiling and the baby bright. In seconds 2 and 3 they are smiling while maintaining mutual regard. The sequence decelerates at second 5 but then they resume greeting (fig. 6a point b). Both partners cycle again through the greeting—mutual orientation phases and then go into prolonged play-dialogue (fig. 6a point c). The infant vocalizes for 2 seconds, pauses, vocalizes, pauses and again vocalizes. The total phase of play-dialogue lasts 21 seconds. He is looking at his mother the whole time. His face is bright and occasionally he even smiles. During this time the mother's attention is fixed on the infant. She is talking with a burst—pause pattern that becomes more sing-song as the phase continues. Her hands are gently holding the baby and her face is bright, then shows a simple smile, then she smiles broadly. At the close of this phase there is a momentary (2 seconds) disengagement (fig. 6a point d). The infant stops vocalizing and briefly glances away but his head continues to face his mother. His face is at first neutral and then sober for 1 second. The mother does much the same. She continues

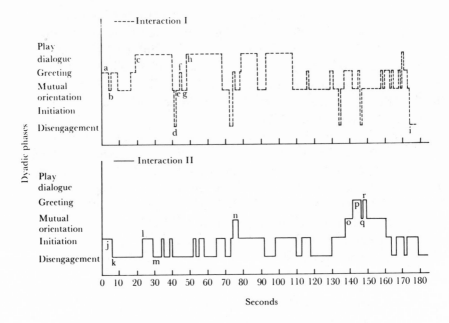

Fig. 6 Phase flow diagram for interactions I and II.

talking but her voice loses the burst—pause pattern and has little
modulation. Her face becomes neutral and then sober, and she glances
briefly from the infant's face to his body. Following this brief disengagement, the mutual attention—vocalizing—disengagement cycle
(fig. 6a points e, f, g, h) begins again and continues in much the same
way until the interaction ends when the mother leaves (fig. 6a
point i).

Sequence II is quite different in its patterning of phases and its
affective rhythmicity. The infant is an eighty-six-day-old girl. It
begins with an initiation phase (fig. 6b point j). The infant is silent
and looking away with her head part side down (chin tucked down
and to one side). The mother is smiling, making rhythmic 'Hi! Hi!'
sounds, while using her hands to contain the baby with light rhythmic
movements. This initiation lasts about 6 seconds, but then changes
into a disengagement phase (fig. 6b point k). The infant remains disengaged and the mother's voice becomes rapid, tense and higher in
pitch. She is no longer touching the infant, and her expression, at
first bright, becomes neutral. Both partners then go back into an

initiation phase: the infant is looking away with a neutral then sober expression, not vocalizing and head part side down. The mother is talking in an adult conversational tone which is soft but lacking modulation; her hands are holding the infant; she is smiling and shifting her body from side to side (fig. 6b point l). Another disengagement phase follows in which the baby is looking away with a neutral face; the mother is silent; her hands contain the baby, and her expression is bright but lacks animation (fig. 6b point m). Initiation–disengagement cycling continues until it is interrupted by mutual orientation when the still slumped infant brightens and looks toward her mother who is bright-faced and talking softly (fig. 6 point n). But this phase is brief and the initiation–disengagement cycle is resumed until a mutual orientation–greeting–mutual orientation–greeting sequence is achieved toward the end of the interaction (fig. 6b points o, p, q, r). During the mutual orientation (fig. 6b, point o) the infant and mother look at each other. At first the infant is grimacing but then her face brightens and her limbs start moving. Her mother is whispering and her face is bright as she moves in close to the infant. They move into a greeting (fig. 6b point p). The infant smiles and makes large movements of her limbs and sustains a vertical position. The mother is talking in baby talk, gently holding the baby, smiling and leaning forward. They then decelerate to a mutual orientation state (fig. 6b point q) followed by a second greeting (fig. 6b point r). After this they resume the initiation–disengagement cycles characteristic of the major portion of the sequence.

The two communication sequences are unique but they share many characteristics such as an accelerative–decelerative flow of affective involvement, and cycling through a sequence of particular phases. In each there is an intermeshing of behaviors, of performance and reception, which are particular to the phase. But each pair enacts each phase uniquely, with its own particular timings and behaviors.

The flow through the phases illustrates the cyclic aspects of affective attention in the two sequences (see fig. 6). Both are characterized by increasing and decreasing cycles of affective involvement: in the first (I, fig. 6a) a waxing and waning from very positive to 'pausing' phases (greeting to mutual attention), in the second (II, fig. 6b) between disengagement and initiation, two somewhat negative phases (see also fig. 7). There appear to be limits to how long any given phase may last, especially the more positive states. Moreover the build-up to these states appears to require a decelerative component.

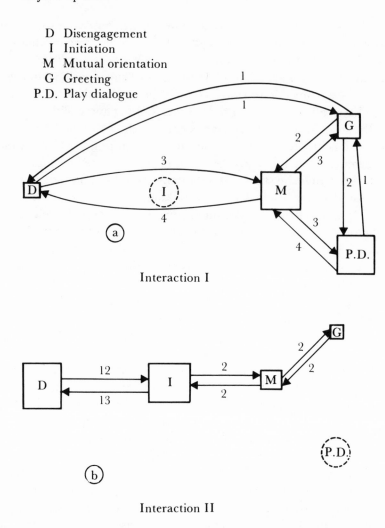

D Disengagement
I Initiation
M Mutual orientation
G Greeting
P.D. Play dialogue

Interaction I

Interaction II

Fig. 7 Phase transit diagram for interactions I and II. Numbers are the number of transitions from one phase to next. Relative size of phase box represents proportion of time spent in that phase (the initiation phase is not entered in I nor play-dialogue in II).

This suggests a homeostatic function that maintains the level of affective involvement within certain limits.

The phase transit diagrams (fig. 7) show the qualitative differences in the sequence and the repeated occurrence of states. In interaction I (fig. 7a), most of the transits are spent cycling through a sequence of mutual orientation to greeting and back, or from mutual orientation to play-dialogue. Mutual orientation appears to function as a decelerative pause when entered from greeting or play-dialogue but can also act as a foundation for accelerating into one of these phases. Larger decelerations into disengagement occur only five times in this sequence (and one is at the end of the sequence, see fig. 6a). Initiation, a phase in which one of the partners is attempting to engage the other partner in interchange, is not entered at all. Both mother and infant move smoothly together into and out of these phases with no need to re-establish the cycling.

This is not the case for interaction II. Sequencing and cycling through mutual attention and greeting occurs only four times and then only briefly (fig. 7b). The sequence takes place predominantly in the initiation—disengagement phases and transits between them. The mother initiates many attempts to engage the infant in inter-action but she is not successful and so she, too, moves into the dis-engagement phase. When the mutual orientation—greeting cycle is achieved it appears to be much the same as in sequence I but it happens only twice. The partners do not get into a play-dialogue. It may be that play-dialogue occurs only after successful greeting phases have occurred.

4 Each partner's contribution to the communication

4.1 The caregiver's activities

In the laboratory, and we think in other situations as well, the care-givers, in their attempt to achieve an understanding of the infant's intention and to have a smooth interchange, engage in particular kinds of activities in particular kinds of ways. Many of their care-giving activities are the background or foundation of face-to-face communication.

(1) *Preparatory activities.* The caregiver (a) reduces the interference of physiological needs such as hunger or lack of sleep; (b) contains the interference of reflexes and other disorganizing motor activity; and (c) soothes and calms the infant when he is upset (Brazelton et al. 1974). The meeting of these needs in a fashion that is appropriate to a particular infant provides for the freeing of the infant from the dominance of his physiological level. It allows him to engage in other activities that are based on a different time-scale and which have dif-ferent intentional goals and performatory requirements (Gibson 1966).

(2) *State setting activities.* The caregiver sets and often has to re-set the infant for face-to-face interaction. These activities include adjusting the infant's body to symmetry around his midline and supporting it if necessary. This activity helps orient the infant toward the caregiver. If the infant fails to orient the caregiver may lean quite far over in a plane parallel to the infant or raise herself in an attempt to move into the infant's line of vision. The caregiver often vocalizes in a staccato manner while making these postural readjustments. Interaction II included many of these activities.

(3) *Maintaining a communicative framework.* There is an almost continuous stream of actions, which we call 'continuates', presented by the caregiver. Continuates include almost constantly modulated speech, rhythmic patting and tapping and rhythmic movements of her body. Continuates such as slight but frequent head nodding occur in adult-to-adult communication, but they are less dramatic and less frequent. In infant—adult communication continuates are always occurring, providing the infant with a constant focus for attention and action, a set of markers for timing responses and expanding the duration of his focused activity.

(4) *Infant-like modification of adult actions.* Just as the constant provision of continuates is a modification of what goes on in adult—adult communication, so all the actions of the caregiver with an infant show a similar kind of modification. It has been shown (Brazelton et al. 1974; Stern 1974a) and we confirm that the caregiver's activities vary in rate, modulation of intensity, amplitude and quality from those of adult-to-adult communication. Almost everything the caregiver does is exaggerated and slowed down. The voice assumes 'baby talk' characteristics (Ferguson 1964) where pitch, syntax and pronunciation are altered. Adult facial expressions become 'baby faces', slowed down and exaggerated. There are also 'baby movements', such as coming in close, always orienting straight ahead, and moving the body both perpendicularly and parallel to the infant. Finally, there is an overall modulation of all activities, a cyclic increase and decrease in the number of activities of the caregiver at any time. Almost all of these infant-like modifications would appear bizarre in communication with an adult. They appear to increase the information content of the caregiver's activities while facilitating the intermeshing of the infant's activities with the actions of the caregiver.

4.2 The infant's contribution to the communication

This characterization of the caregiver's contribution seems to indicate that she is making all the adjustments to an insulated and non-responsive flow of infant activities. This condition could be thought of as a duet of maestro and inept pupil. In that situation the pupil is apparently dominant. The pupil plays on and the master makes all the adjustments because the pupil is not yet able to move out of a single-minded and non-receptive flow of musical performance. But in fact it is the master who controls the situation. If the master, like the caregiver, did not provide the necessary framework and adjust to the inadequacies of the performance, the pupil's performance would be totally inadequate. There is interplay between apparent and objective dominance: the pupil feels in control, the master is in control.

4.3 Perturbations of the normal interaction and infant adaptability

To explore the adaptability of the infant, we have experimentally perturbed the actions of the caregiver in several ways. Our first manipulation was to have the caregivers slow down their already infant-like rate of speech by counting aloud very, very slowly, i.e. less than one number vocalized per second. This procedure has the effect of slowing down all their actions. It was difficult for the caregivers to change their normal rhythms with their infants (even though it is easy for them to go from adult to infant rhythm and back), and often a caregiver reverted back to her usual infant-like rhythm, indicating a limit on adult adaptability. But when the requested slowing down was achieved, we often saw extremely successful communication. The infants' smiles and vocalizations were more frequent and sustained. In general they appeared to achieve a higher level of affective involvement and to maintain that peak longer than was usual. There were periods when the infants seemed perplexed; they would sit back and watch and then return to the interchange. This watching demonstrated their awareness of the change but they were not 'disturbed' and were able to adjust to it.

Two other perturbations were used to explore the adaptability of the infants. In one we had the mother seat herself in front of the infant and remain still-faced, and in the second she showed only her profile to the baby. In the still-faced setting the infant watches the mother and gives her a smile of greeting. This greeting is sometimes repeated but with the mother's continued lack of response (a very difficult task for the adult), the infant's face slowly sobers and he looks away with his chin tucked down and to the side. From this position he shoots quick glances at the mother — sometimes with fleeting smiles — followed by long looks away. As this perturbation continues the infant may turn fully to the side then turn toward her with a smile, only to look down and away again. Very few of the infants have cried in this situation. Some do not turn 'full side away', but with sober face sit, head straight on, looking at the mother and then, while maintaining the straight-on head position, they look away. This lack of head—eye alignment is a non-typical head—eye position for an infant (Tronick & Clanton 1971). When the mothers leave after 3 minutes of the still-face condition, almost all of the infants turn their head and eyes to follow her even if they were looking away from her just prior to her leaving.

Fig. 8a—d illustrates this pattern in a time sequence of photographs of a seventy-four-day-old infant. Fig. 8a shows the infant greeting. Then in 8b and 8c he warily looks away and then checks back toward his mother again. In 8d he withdraws with a sober facial expression, eyes averted, head turned full away. The sequence took 30 seconds.

When the mother is in profile the infant acts differently. The infant sits and watches her. He seldom smiles but makes cooing, calling vocalizations and often leans forward in his seat. He also may cry but the cries seem faked. This vocalizing is interspersed with long periods of intense looking at the mother. The infant's orientation remains straight ahead and with gaze fixed on the mother throughout the whole period. The infants do not go into the greeting phase and they often get fussy as the session proceeds. Our mothers report that a similar type of performance often happens while they are driving their car and unable to maintain an *en face* position with their infants.

These performances by the infant are organized and appropriate. They clearly indicate that the infant is not simply exhibiting a rigid and unmodifiable pattern of behavior into which the mother fits herself. Rather the infant is adjusting his responses appropriately to the actions of his partner. In the still-face condition the infant greets the mother, and then, when communication fails to ensue, he repeats the greeting. With repeated failures he begins a new pattern of wary looking and checking which keeps open the possibility of reinstating

Fig. 8 A—D: A time series of photos taken from the recorded video image of a still face condition. Infant 74 days old.

communication. When the mother has her profile to her infant, the dyad appears to be in a continuous initiation phase with the infant attempting to call the mother so as to 'get' her to enter into communication. As in slowed down communication, the infant is able to cope with these new conditions.

All of these examples give evidence that the infant is aware of his partner's communication. We see it in the wary reactions the infants have to us and other strangers. We see the limits of this adaptability when the infant gets upset during a communication sequence. This may occur because the person is mis-timing and mis-matching displays with the infant that exceed his experience and capabilities. Such may be the essence of the stranger.

5 Discussion

5.1 Implicit knowledge

The caregiver's performance gives evidence of tremendous implicit knowledge about the physiological and psychological capabilities and limitations of the infant. The infant can be characterized as living within a limited phenomenal world as compared to an adult's (Aronson & Tronick 1971). Infants have a slower rate of processing information than do adults. Younger infants observing an experimental spatio-temporal event see it as a single event in motion while older children can see it as two separate events (Pollack 1966). In experiments involving disappearance of objects, Bower (1967) demonstrated that infants perceive an occlusion as annihilation of the object because it occurs too quickly for them to see it as simple occlusion, while older infants perceive the disappearance. A similar limitation occurs spatially. Infants have a shrunken phenomenal space, a narrower peripheral field and a shorter straight-ahead space than do older children and adults (Koffka 1924; Tronick 1971). Added to these input processing limitations are the infant's limitations in producing responses. For example, it takes a three-to-four-week-old infant longer to organize his initial reach in the presence of an object than it does a three-to-four-month-old (Bower et al. 1970a). Moreover the infant has a shorter and less developed memory (Watson 1972). Compounding all these limitations are the physiological demands of sleep, hunger, activity, respiration and the like in a still immature organism.

However, despite these limitations, the three-to-four-week-old infant's world is well structured. He perceives distance, depth and the path of approach of an object (Ball & Tronick 1971; Bower et al. 1970b). He also perceives solidity and the disappearance of objects (Bower 1967). He even detects the difference between animate and inanimate objects (Brazelton et al. 1974), and, within the animate realm, can make very fine distinctions about animate events.

Implicit knowledge of these limits and abilities is reflected in the caregiver's actions. In the first place there is the fact that successful communication sequences occur. It is extremely difficult to know when the infant is ready for face-to-face communication; it is a rare event. Successful prediction of its possibility requires that the caregiver be able to read the infant's signals for sleep, food, emotional discharge and the like, detect the periodicity of those events and fit face-to-face communication in at the appropriate time. Also the exaggerated, slowed and simplified qualities of the caregiver's displays, their bizarreness in adult terms, reflect the limits of the infant's ability to process information. The adult has modified her displays to fit the infant's information processing limitations.

The continuates (cf. section 4.1(3)) provide a constant focus and support for the infant's limited attentional capabilities. Bullowa (forthcoming a) has observed that the infant is organized in a simpler way alone than when in interaction with an adult, and we have observed that infants show a more staccato build-up and decrease of activity when they play with an object. These differences may in part be accounted for by a lack of continuates in these situations. Also, such 'inanimate events' as rocking, music or rhythmic displays may be calming because they resemble continuates. This suggests that closer observation of interspecies communication and communication of children with infants might reveal the temporal quality of continuates and their species and developmental limitations.

5.2 Mis-matching and development

Despite this knowledge it is not possible for the caregiver to intermesh exactly with the intentions or actions of the infant. That would require a perfect signalling system for the infant, a perfect decoder and action generator for the adult. So mis-matching in face-to-face interaction must occur. Mis-matching can occur in the timing and rate of caregiver actions, for even as slowed down as the caregiver is, the slowed down perturbation indicates that this normal infant-like slowing may not be optimal for communication. The important quality of a sensitive caregiver's mis-matching is that is it not far beyond the infant's capabilities and that it offers an expanded and more complicated social environment for the infant.

One form of mis-matching is 'overloading'. The caregiver performs too many display components for the infant's limited capacity and the infant turns away. The sensitive caregiver then decelerates and adds on components more slowly the next time. The caregiver's substitution of one display component for another can also be a form of mis-matching. A caregiver might have typically responded to an infant's vocalization with a vocalization, but after repeated vocalizations her reponse may become a head shake. This substitution, too, may exceed the infant's abilities.

In 'exemplification' the caregiver performs too many display components, but in this case the display is one that will eventually become part of their communicative repertoire, whereas in overloading the caregiver just does too many things. For example, caregivers respond to a neonate's eye-contact with a display that is similar to the display they will enact in response to a ten-week-old's smile (Als 1975). Or there is the brief attempt to play the twelve-week-old game of pat-a-cake with a six-week-old.

In each of these situations it is unlikely that the infant processes all the information in the display or is able to react to all of it. The caregiver sometimes matches and sometimes mis-matches the infant's abilities. This contradictory quality is inherent in the infant's environment and it functions to provide the infant with an expanded environment into and within which he can develop. Matching displays to the infant's abilities allows the infant to function within his limitations: to act on the basis of the qualities of the displays as they now occur and to organize and practise his current capabilities. But the *mis*-matching provides more complicated events to learn about, so that as his capabilities develop at one level, there is an environment to develop into. An environment that always perfectly matched the infant's abilities (were it possible) might not allow for the operation of this dialectic. Communication might be better at that moment, but it would not provide for growth. The normal social environment, then, is an environment for both maintenance and growth.

5.3 The rule-governed nature of social communication

Successful communication depends on mutual following and enactment of rules: rules specifying the meaning of displays and their sequencing, and rules specifying how to interact with a conspecific. The goal of both partners who intend to engage in communication is to maintain reciprocity of intention. In the mother—infant communicative system, despite the greater capabilities of the mother, this process is engaged in and shared by both partners. Each strives to have the other detect his intention. This is the fundamental characteristic of the system and it is the necessary condition for meanings to be exchanged.

The analogy of a duet between maestro and pupil can be extended and made more explicit to clarify this process further. The intention of the two musicians is to produce music that follows a score. Each player has a level of skill in playing his instrument and reading the musical score, a knowledge about the rules of playing together and a level of skill in following them. In either case one partner may read and play perfectly but be unable completely to follow the rules for playing together, or he might be able to coordinate his actions with the other player although his own performance is less than ideal. Each partner strives to know and be skillful with the syntax of his instrument and the syntax of communication. In communication sequences this corresponds to performing skills of sending messages and knowledge of their meaning and knowledge of communication rules and skill in enacting them (Ryan 1974). Thus the infant must be able to send and receive meaning carrying displays at the appropriate times in relation to his partner.

In normal face-to-face communication the joint possession of rules accounts for the synchronous movement of caregiver and infant through different phases. Never is one partner *causing* the other to do something. One musician does not cause the other to play the next note. In the same manner neither the mother nor the infant causes the other to greet or to attend. They are mutually engaged in an activity.

Rule enactment explains the success of the slow interaction. It *is* an enormous change from the usual but it allows for and follows the rules. In that sense it is not a violation. It is similar to changing the tempo of a piece of music. The sequence of notes, their relative length and so on does not change. The musicians are still enacting the score.

Rule enactment applies to the other perturbations as well. In the side-face condition the mother's performance signals disengagement. The infant, following the rules, moves into an initiation phase but is unsuccessful in moving the dyad into mutual orientation. In the still-faced condition the mother is enacting two contradictory rules of performance at the same time. With her entrance she is enacting a rule for initiation of communication, but with her failure to proceed and act she is enacting a rule of disengagement. The infant has knowledge of these rules and is trapped between them: he acts first on the initiation and then on the disengagement. He greets her, then sobers, then greets her again. He does not fully break down because he acts and is trapped within the framework of the communicative rules.

Language is not yet a part of this system, but many of the characteristics of communication through language are already present. There is a lexicon of expressions that serve to regulate the pragmatics of the interchange as well as to convey intention and the inner emotional state of the communicant. This lexicon is most clearly evident in the perturbed sequences. There may well be transformational rules for categorizing a particular phase of an interaction (Chomsky 1968). This would be the case where what comes before a phase determines how that phase is categorized. For example, in sequence I mutual attention after greeting might better be categorized as a decelerative pause, while when it follows withdrawal, it might be categorized as an accelerative connecting pause. Categorization of phases would then require transformational rules and would introduce a syntactical generative component that would account for the infinite variety and uniqueness of communication.

The infant's reactions in the still-faced condition also raises an interesting question about the possibility of negatives in non-linguistic forms of communication. Watzlawick et al. (1967) argue that since language is 'digital' it can express negatives, while behavior is analogical and inherently ambiguous. This seems true enough for any non-conventionalized single behavior but it may not be true for a sequence of communicative behaviors. In the still-faced condition the caregiver enacts one rule and then another which negates the first. The infant demonstrates his understanding of this negation by turning away. This could be detection of a non-linguistic negative.

The capabilities for social communication, the rules, the implicit knowledge of the partner and the intention to communicate must all have a phylogenetic base. As with language, it would be impossible to induce the rules or syntax of communication, given the infant's experience and the complexity of the process. It is the phylogenetic base that accounts for the infant's performance and the smoothness of communication.

Appendix:
Behaviors scored for mother and infant

Infant

1. Vocalization
1. none 2. isolated sound 3. grunt 4. coo 5. cry 6. fuse 7. laugh

2. Direction of gaze
1. towards mother's face 2. away from mother's face 3. follows mother 4. looking at toy or hand mother is using as part of interaction

3. Head orientation
1. head towards, nose level 2. head towards, nose down 3. head towards, nose up 4. head part side, nose level 5. head part side, nose down 6. head part side, nose up 7. head complete side, nose level 8. head complete side, nose down 9. head complete side, nose up

4. Facial expression
1. cry face 2. grimace 3. pout 4. wary/ sober 5. lidding 6. yawn 7. neutral 8. sneeze 9. softening 10. brightening 11. simple smile 12. coo face 13. broad smile

5. Body position
1. leaning forward and doubled over 2. body turned completely to one side 3. arching or leaning very far back 4. slumped and/or off to one side 5. neutral 6. adjusted by adult 7. hip jerk forward 8. movement up in the vertical plane 9. body vertical with neck extended, trunk elongated and/or head off back rest 10. leaning forward with straight back

6. Head position
1 left 2. right

7. Amount of movement
1. ¾ limbs, large movements 2. ½ limbs, large movements 3. ¾ limbs, medium movement 4. ½ limbs, medium movement 5. ¾ limbs, small movement 6. ½ limbs, small movement 7. no movement 8. mother moving infant

8. Blinks
1. yes 2. no

9. Specific hand movements
1. eye wiping 2. hand to mouth 3. swipe 4. fidgets 5. all lower limbs extended forward

10. Specific foot movements
1. kick 2. startle

371

Mother

1. Vocalization
1. abrupt shout 2. stern, adult narrative
3. rapid tense voice 4. whispering 5. little
or no vocalizing 6. rhythmic sounds with
little modulation 7. burst—pause talking
8. single bursts in rapid succession with
wide pitch range 9. burst of sound that
peaks with much change of modulation and
pitch

2. Direction of gaze
1. towards infant's face 2. towards infant's
body 3. away from infant but related to
interaction 4. away from infant and not
related to interaction

3. Head orientation
1. towards and down 2. towards and up
3. towards and level 4. part side and down
5. part side and up 6. part side level
7. toward and level 8. toward and up
9. toward and down 10. thrusting
11. nodding 12. nuzzling 13. cocked head

4. Facial expression
1. angry 2. frown 3. serious, sad, sober
4. lidded 5. neutral flat 6. brightening
7. animated 8. simple smile 9. imitative
play face 10. kisses 11. exaggerated play
face 12. broad full smile 13. 'ooo' face

5. Body position
1. turns body full away 2. sits back and
still 3. slumping 4. neutral—slight forward
5. sideways shifts 6. slight rocking 7. large
sideways shifts into line of vision
8. medium close forward 9. going close
and staying close 10. large shifts forward
and back

6. Specific handling of the infant
1. abrupt shift of baby's position 2. abrupt
but no shift 3. jerky movement of limbs
4. no contact 5. gentle containing 6. small
rhythmic backing 7. rhythmic movements
of limbs 8. intensive movement, fast
rhythm

Bibliography
(and citation and names index)

Note. * indicates a relevant work not cited in the text.

Aaronson, D. & Rieber, R.W. (ed.) 1975. *Developmental psycholinguistics and communication disorders.* New York: New York Academy of Sciences. **18.**

Adamson, L.B., **60–1, 349–72.**

Adamson, L.B. *see* Brazelton et al. 1975; Tronick et al. 1975.

Adelson, E. *see* Fraiberg & Adelson 1973; Fraiberg et al. 1969.

Advances in Child Development and Behavior 1963– (annual). New York: Academic. **35.**

Ainsworth, M. 1972. Attachment and dependency: a comparison. In *Attachment and dependency,* ed. J. Gewirtz, pp. 97–137. New York: Wiley. **104.**

Ainsworth, M.D.S. *see* Blehar et al. 1977.

Aldrich, A.A. & Aldrich, M.M. 1938. *Babies are human beings.* London: Macmillan. **32.**

Aldrich, M.M. *see* Aldrich & Aldrich 1938.

Allen, D.H. *see* Blank & Allen 1976.

Als, H., **60, 349–72.**

Als, H. 1975. The human newborn and his mother: an ethological study of their interaction. PhD dissertation, University of Pennsylvania. **368.**

Als, H. *see* Brazelton et al. 1975; Tronick et al. 1975.

Altman, M.M. & Shenhav, R. 1971. Methods for early detection of hearing loss in infants. *Journal of Laryngology and Otology,* 85: 35. *

Altmann, J. 1974. Observational study of behaviour: sampling methods. *Behaviour,* 49: 227–67. **114, 116.**

Altmann, S.A. 1965. Sociobiology of rhesus monkeys II: stochastics of social communication. *Journal of Theoretical Biology,* 8: 490–552. **113.**

Altmann, S.A. 1967. The structure of primate communication. In *Social communication among primates,* ed. S.A. Altmann, pp. 325–62. Chicago: University of Chicago Press. **120.**

Ambrose, A. 1961. The development of the smiling response in early infancy. In Foss 1961, pp. 179–96. **240, 287, 326.**

Ambrose, A. (ed.) 1969. *Stimulation in early infancy.* New York: Academic. **34.**

Anderson, C.O. & Mason, W.A. 1975. Early experience and complexity of social organisation in groups of young rhesus monkeys (Macaca mulatta). *Journal of Comparative and Physiological Psychology,* 87: 681–90. **239.**

Anderson, H., Barr, B. & Wedenberg, E. 1973. Epidemiology of hearing loss in childhood. *Audiology,* 12: 426–37. *

Anderson, J.W. 1972a. On the psychological attachment of infants to their mothers. *Journal of Biosocial Science,* 4: 197–225. **128.**

Anderson, J.W. 1972b. Attachment behaviour out of doors. In Blurton Jones 1972, pp. 199–215. **44, 128.**

Andrew, R.J. 1963. Evolution of facial expression. *Science*, 142: 1034–41. **327.**

Argyle, M. & Cook, M. 1976. *Gaze and mutual gaze.* Cambridge: Cambridge University Press. **119.**

Argyle, M. & Ingham, R. 1972. Gaze, mutual gaze and proximity. *Semiotica*, 6: 32–49. **114.**

Aronson, E. & Rosenbloom, S. 1971. Space perception in early infancy: perception within a common auditory-visual space. *Science*, 172: 1161–3. **335.**

Aronson, E. & Tronick, E. 1971. Perceptual capacities in early infancy. In *Human development and cognitive processes*, ed. J. Eliot, pp. 216–25. New York: Holt, Rinehart & Winston. **366.**

Ashby, R. 1952. *Design for a brain.* London: Chapman & Hall. **93.**

Babkin, P.S. 1958. The establishment of reflex activity in early postnatal life. Translated from the *Sechenov Physiology Journal of the USSR*, 44, 10: 922–7. In *The central nervous system and behavior*, pp. 24–31. Bethesda, Md.: National Institutes of Health, 1959. **82.**

Baerends, G.P. 1976. The functional organization of behaviour. *Animal Behaviour*, 24: 726–38. **224.**

Ball, W. & Tronick, E. 1971. Infant responses to impending collision: optical and real. *Science*, 171: 818–20. Repr. in Stone et al. 1973, pp. 735–8. **366.**

Barr, B. & Stensland Junker, K. 1972. Functional contact test for babies as a screening test. In *International symposium on speech, communication ability and profound deafness*, ed. G. Fant. Washington, D.C.: Alexander Graham Bell Association for the Deaf. *

Barr, B. *see* Anderson et al. 1973.

Barrett, P.H. *see* Gruber & Barrett 1974.

Bates, E., Camioni, L. & Volterra, V. 1975. The acquisition of performatives prior to speech. *Merrill-Palmer Quarterly*, 21: 205–26. **30, 120.**

Bateson, G. 1972. *Steps to an ecology of mind.* New York: Chandler. Repr. New York: Ballantine, 1975. **67.**

Bateson, G. *see* McQuown et al. 1971.

Bateson, M.C., **51–2, 63–77.**

Bateson, M.C. 1968. Linguistics in the semiotic frame. *Linguistics*, 39: 5–17. **75.**

Bateson, M.C. 1971. The interpersonal context of infant vocalization. *Quarterly Progress Report of the Research Laboratory of Electronics*, 100: 170–6. Boston, Mass.: Massachusetts Institute of Technology. **19, 37, 65.**

Bateson, M.C. 1972. *Our own metaphor: a personal account of a conference on conscious purpose and human adaptation.* New York: Alfred A. Knopf. **51.**

Bateson, M.C. 1975a. Linguistic models in the study of joint performances. In *Linguistics and anthropology: in honor of C.F. Voegelin*, ed. M. Dale Kinkade et al., pp. 53–6. Lisse: Peter de Ridder. *

Bateson, M.C. 1975b. Mother–infant exchanges: the epigenesis of conversational interaction. In Aaronson & Rieber 1975, pp. 101–13. **37, 65, 77, 117, 171, 340, 344.**

Bateson, M.C. 1975c. Ritualization: a study in texture and texture change. In

Religious movements in contemporary America, ed. I. Zaretsky & M.P. Leone, pp. 150—65. Princeton: Princeton University Press. **74, 75, 77.**

Bateson, P.P.G. 1972. The formation of social attachments in young birds. *Proceedings of the XVth International Ornithological Congress*, ed. K.H. Voous, pp. 303—15. Leiden: E.J. Brill. **240.**

Bateson, P.P.G. 1973. Internal influences on early learning in birds. In *Constraints on learning: limitations and predispositions*, ed. R.A. Hinde & J. Stevenson-Hinde, pp. 101—16. New York: Academic. **240.**

Bayley, N. 1969. *Manual for the Bayley scales of infant development*. New York: Psychological Corporation. *

Beavin, H.J. *see* Watzlawick et al. 1967.

Beebe, B. *see* Stern et al. 1975, 1977.

Béhar, M. *see* Lechtig et al. 1975.

Beintema, D. *see* Prechtl & Beintema 1964.

Bellugi, U. *see* Brown et al. 1968.

Bennett, S.L. *see* Stern et al. 1975, 1977.

Bergman, A. *see* Mahler et al. 1975.

Bernal, J.F. & Richards, M.P.M. 1973. What can the zoologists tell us about human development? In *Ethology and development*, Clinics in Developmental Medicine, 47, ed. S.A. Barnett, pp. 88—103. Spastics International Medical Publications. London: Heinemann Medical Books. **223, 224.**

Bernstein, N. 1967. *The coordination and regulation of movements*. London: Pergamon. **334.**

Bertalanffy, L. von (1933) 1962. *Modern theories of development*. New York: Harper & Brothers. **5.**

Bever, T.G. *see* Bullowa et al. 1964.

Bingham, N.E. 1971. Maternal speech to prelinguistic infants: differences related to maternal judgements of infant language competence. Unpubd paper, Cornell University. **270.**

Birch, H.G. *see* Cravioto et al. 1966.

Birdwhistell, R.L. 1970. *Kinesics and context: essays on body motion communication*. Philadelphia: University of Pennsylvania Press. Repr. Harmondsworth: Penguin, 1971. **64, 65, 72, 122.**

Birdwhistell, R.L. *see* McQuown et al. 1971.

Blank, M. & Allen, D.H. 1976. Understanding 'why': its significance in early intelligence. In *Origins of intelligence: infancy and childhood*, ed. M. Lewis, pp. 259—78. New York: Plenum. **62.**

Blauw, A. de, **58, 269—88.**

Blauw, A. de, *see* Snow et al. in preparation.

Blehar, M.C., Lieberman, A.F. & Ainsworth, M.D.S. 1977. Early face-to-face interaction and its relation to later mother—infant attachment. *Child Development*, 48: 182—94. **336, 337.**

Blurton Jones, N. 1971. Criteria for use in describing facial expressions of children. *Human Biology*, 43: 365—413. **128, 327.**

Blurton Jones, N. 1972. *Ethological studies of child behaviour*. Cambridge: Cambridge University Press. **4.**

Boismier, J.D., Chappell, P.F. & Meier, G.W. 1970. A behavioral inventory for assessing states of arousal in the human newborn. Paper presented to the Southeastern Psychological Association, Louisville, Ky. **108.**

Boismier, J.D. *see* Chappell et al. 1973.

Bornstein, M.H. 1975. Qualities of colour vision in infancy. *Journal of Experimental Child Psychology*, 19: 401–19. **333.**

Bower, T.G.R. 1966. The visual world of infants. *Scientific American*, 215, 6: 80–92. Offprint 502(a). **29.**

Bower, T.G.R. 1967. The development of object permanence: some studies of existence constancy. *Perception and Psychophysics*, 2: 411–18. **366.**

Bower, T.G.R. 1971. The object in the world of the infant. *Scientific American*, 225, 4: 30–8. **29.**

Bower, T.G.R. 1972. Object perception in infants. *Perception*, 1: 15–30. **30, 39.**

Bower, T.G.R. 1974. *Development in infancy*. San Francisco: W.H. Freeman. **29, 322.**

Bower, T.G.R., Broughton, J.M. & Moore, M.K. 1970a. The coordination of visual and tactual input in infants. *Perception and Psychophysics*, 8: 51–3. **366.**

Bower, T.G.R., Broughton, J.M. & Moore, M.K. 1970b. Infant response to approaching objects: an indicator of responses to distal variables. *Perception and Psychophysics*, 9: 192–7. **366.**

Bowlby, J. 1951. *Maternal care and mental health*. Geneva: World Health Organization. **32.**

Bowlby, J. 1965. *Child care and the growth of love* (based on Bowlby 1951, abridged and ed. Margery Fry with two new chs. by M.D.S. Ainsworth). Harmondsworth: Penguin. **32.**

Bowlby, J. 1969. *Attachment and Loss. Vol. I. Attachment.* New York: Basic Books; London: Hogarth. Repr. Harmondsworth: Penguin, 1971. **32–3, 85.**

Bowlby, J. 1973. *Attachment and Loss. Vol. II. Separation, anxiety and anger.* London: Hogarth. **32–3.**

Brazelton, T.B., **52, 79–88.**

Brazelton, T.B. 1961. Psychophysiologic reactions in the neonate: I. The value of observations of the neonate. *Journal of Pediatrics*, 58: 508–12. **83.**

Brazelton, T.B. 1972. Implications of infant development among the Mayan Indians of Mexico. *Human Development*, 15: 90–111. **270.**

Brazelton, T.B. 1973. *Neonatal behavioral assessment scale*, Clinics in Developmental Medicine, 50. Spastics International Medical Publications. London: Heinemann Medical Books. **80.**

Brazelton, T.B., Scholl, M.L. & Robey, J.S. 1966. Visual responses in the newborn. *Pediatrics*, 37: 284–90. **28.**

Brazelton, T.B., Young, G.G. & Bullowa, M. 1971. Inception and resolution of early developmental pathology: a case history. *Journal of the American Academy of Child Psychiatry*, 10: 124–35. **240.**

Brazelton, T.B., Koslowski, B. & Main, M. 1974. The origins of reciprocity: the early mother–infant interaction. In Lewis & Rosenblum 1974, pp. 49–76. **84, 196, 198, 333, 334, 361, 362, 366.**

Brazelton, T.B., Tronick, E., Adamson, L., Als, H. & Wise, S. 1975. Early mother–infant reciprocity. In Ciba 1975, pp. 137–54. **335.**

Brazelton, T.B., Tronick, E., Lechtig, A., Lasky, R. & Klein, R. 1977. The behavior of nutritionally stressed Guatemalan neonates. *Developmental Medicine and Child Neurology*, 19: 364–72. **85.**

Brazelton, T.B. *see* Kaye & Brazelton 1971; Tronick & Brazelton 1975; Tronick et al. 1975.

Brosin, H.W. *see* McQuown et al. 1971.

Broughton, J.M. *see* Bower et al. 1970a, b.

Brown, R., **56, 62.**

Brown, R. 1968. The development of WH questions in child speech. *Journal of Verbal Learning and Verbal Behavior*, 7: 279–90. **191, 204.**

Brown, R. & Hanlon, C. 1970. Derivational complexity and order of acquisition in child speech. In *Cognition and the development of language*, ed. J.R. Hayes, pp. 11–53. New York: Wiley. **191, 203.**

Brown, R., Cazden, C.B. & Bellugi, U. 1968. The child's grammar from I to III. In *Minnesota symposium on child development*, vol. II, ed. J.P. Hill, pp. 28–73. Minneapolis: University of Minnesota Press. **191.**

Bruner, J.S., **31, 62.**

Bruner, J.S. 1973. Organization of early skilled action. *Child Development*, 44: 1–11. **200, 229.**

Bruner, J.S. 1975a. The ontogenesis of speech acts. *Journal of Child Language*, 2: 1–19. **121, 172, 283.**

Bruner, J.S. 1975b. From communication to language — a psychological perspective. *Cognition*, 3: 255–87. **191.**

Bruner, J.S. 1977. Early social interaction and language acquisition. In Schaffer 1977a, pp. 271–89. **31.**

Bruner, J.S., Olver, R.R. & Greenfield, P.M. 1966. *Studies in cognitive growth.* New York: Wiley. **61.**

Bruner, J.S. *see* Connolly & Bruner 1974; *Developing Child, The*; Scaife & Bruner 1975.

Bullowa, M., **1–62, 77.**

Bullowa, M. 1967. The onset of speech. Paper presented to the Society for Research in Child Development, New York. Unpubd mimeo. **16.**

Bullowa, M. 1970. The start of the language process. *Actes du Xe congrès international des linguistes, Bucarest, 28 août–2 septembre 1967, III*, pp. 191–200. Bucarest: Editions de l'Academie de la Republique Socialiste de Roumanie. **22, 240.**

Bullowa, M. 1975. When infant and adult communicate, how do they synchronize their behaviors? In Kendon et al. 1975, pp. 95–129. **36, 50.**

Bullowa, M. 1977. From performative act to performative utterance: an ethological approach. *Sign Language Studies*, 16: 193–218. **10.**

Bullowa, M. forthcoming a. Non-verbal communication in infancy. Paper presented at the First Congress of the International Association for Semiotic Studies, Milan, 1974. **367.**

Bullowa, M. forthcoming b. Infants as conversational partners. In *The development of discourse and conversation*, ed. T.F. Myers. Edinburgh: Edinburgh University Press. **72.**

Bullowa, M. & Putney, E. in preparation. A matrix for language structure in the communicative milieu of the human infant. Paper presented at the 21st Annual Conference of the International Linguistic Association, New York, March 1976. **40, 241.**

Bullowa, M., Jones, L.G. & Bever, T.G. 1964. Development from vocal to verbal behavior in children. *Monographs of the Society for Research in Child Development*, 29, 1: 101—14. Repr. in *The acquisition of language*, ed. U. Bellugi & R. Brown, pp. 101—14. Chicago: University of Chicago Press, 1971. **26, 171.**

Bullowa, M., Fidelholtz, J.L. & Kessler, A.R. 1975. Infant vocalization: communication before speech. In *Socialization and communication in primary groups*, ed. T.R. Williams, pp. 253—81. The Hague: Mouton. Repr. in *Language and man: anthropological issues*, ed. W.C. McCormack & S.A. Wurm, pp. 67—95. The Hague: Mouton, 1976. **25.**

Bullowa, M. *see* Brazelton et al. 1971.

Burlingham, D. 1972. *Psychoanalytic studies of the sighted and the blind.* New York: International Universities Press. **9.**

Burlingham, D. *see* Freud & Burlingham 1944.

Burns, P., Sander, L.W., Stechler, G. & Julia, H. 1972. Distress in feedings: short-term effects of caretaker environment of the first 10 days. *Journal of the American Academy of Child Psychiatry*, 11: 427—39. **90.**

Burns, P. *see* Sander et al. 1969, 1970, 1972.

Byers, P. 1972. From biological rhythm to cultural pattern: a study of minimal units. PhD dissertation, Columbia University. **17.**

Byers, P. 1976. Biological rhythms as information channels in interpersonal communication behavior. In *Perspectives in ethology*, vol. II, ed. P.P.G. Bateson & P.H. Klopfer, pp. 135—64. New York: Plenum. **16.**

Byers, P. *see* Mead & Byers 1968.

Caldwell, B.M. 1964. The effects of infant care. In *Review of Child Development Research*, vol. I, pp. 9—87. **35.**

Caldwell, R.C. *see* Caron et al. 1973.

Callaghan, J., **197.**

Camioni, L. *see* Bates et al. 1975.

Camp, B.W. *see* Frankenberg et al. 1971.

Caron, A.J., Caron, R.F., Caldwell, R.C. & Weiss, S.J. 1973. Infant perception of the structural properties of the face. *Developmental Psychology*, 9: 385—99. **330, 333.**

Caron, R.F. *see* Caron et al. 1973.

Carpenter, G.C., Tecce, J.J., Stechler, G. & Friedman, S. 1970. Differential visual behaviour to human and humanoid faces in early infancy. *Merrill-Palmer Quarterly*, 16: 91—108. **333.**

Caudill, W. 1973. Tiny dramas: vocal communication between mother and infant in Japanese and American families. In *Mental health research in Asia and the Pacific*, vol. II, *Transcultural research in mental health*, ed. W.P. Labra. Honolulu: The University Press of Hawaii. **77.**

Caudill, W. & Weinstein, H. 1969. Maternal care and infant behavior in Japan and America. *Psychiatry*, 32: 12—43. **270.**

Cazden, C.B. 1965. Environmental assistance to the child's acquisition of grammar. PhD dissertation, Harvard University. **191**.

Cazden, C.B. *see* Brown et al. 1968.

Center for Cognitive Studies, Harvard University 1966–7. *7th Annual Report.* 1967–8. *8th Annual Report.*

Chappell, P.F., **53, 89–109**.

Chappell, P.F. 1970. The validation of a behavioral inventory for assessing states of arousal in the human newborn. Unpubd paper, George Peabody College for Teachers, Nashville, Tenn. **108**.

Chappell, P.F., Boismier, J.D. & Meier, G.W. 1973. The infant's entering repertoire. Paper presented to the Society for Research in Child Development, Philadelphia, Pa. **108**.

Chappell, P.F. *see* Boismier et al. 1970; Sander et al. 1975.

Charlesworth, W.R. & Kreutzer, M.A. 1973. Facial expressions of infants and children. In Ekman 1973, pp. 91–168. **323, 326**.

Chevalier-Skolnikoff, S. 1974. The ontogeny of communication in the stumptail Macque (*Macaca arctoides*). *Contributions to primatology*, vol. II, ed. H. Kuhn et al. Basle: Karger. **239**.

Chomsky, N. 1959. Review of B.F. Skinner's 'Verbal behavior'. *Language*, 35: 26–58. Repr. in *The structure of language: readings in the philosophy of language*, ed. J.A. Fodor & J.J. Katz, pp. 547–78. Englewood Cliffs, N.J.: Prentice-Hall, 1964. **67**.

Chomsky, N. 1967. The formal nature of language. In Lenneberg 1967, pp. 397–442. **67**.

Chomsky, N. 1968. *Language and mind.* New York: Harcourt, Brace, Janovich. **370**.

Ciba 1975. *Parent–infant interaction.* Ciba Foundation Symposium, n.s. 33. Amsterdam: Elsevier. **34**.

Ciba 1976. *Breast-feeding and the mother.* Ciba Foundation Symposium, n.s. 45. Amsterdam: Elsevier. **34**.

Clancy, H. & McBride, G. 1975. The isolation syndrome in childhood. *Developmental Medicine and Child Neurology*, 17: 198–219. **335**.

Clanton, C. *see* Tronick & Clanton 1971.

Clark, E.V. (ed.) 1974. *Papers and reports on child language development*, 8. Stanford, Calif.: Committee on Linguistics. **25**.

Cohen, L.B. & Salapatek, P. (ed.) 1975. *Infant perception: from sensation to cognition*, vols. I and II. New York: Academic. **33**.

Cole, M. *see Developing Child, The.*

Collis, G.M., **54, 111–30**.

Collis, G.M. 1977a. Body movements and some relations with gaze and vocal behaviour in mother–infant interaction. Unpubd paper, University of Strathclyde. **38, 49**.

Collis, G.M. 1977b. Visual co-orientation and maternal speech. In Schaffer 1977a, pp. 355–75. **118, 119, 121, 122, 128**.

Collis, G.M. & Schaffer, H.R. 1975. Synchronization of visual attention in mother–infant pairs. *Journal of Child Psychology and Psychiatry*, 4: 315–20. **115, 118, 201**.

Collis, G.M. *see* Schaffer et al. 1977.

Condon, W.S., 54–5, 73, 131–48.

Condon, W.S. 1963. Synchrony units and the communicational hierarchy. Paper presented at the Western Psychiatric Institute, Pittsburgh, Pa. 136.

Condon, W.S. 1964. Process in communication. Paper presented at the Western Psychiatric Institute, Pittsburgh, Pa. 136.

Condon, W.S. 1977. A primary phase in the organization of infant responding behaviour? In Schaffer 1977a, pp. 153–76. 138.

Condon, W.S. & Sander, L.W. 1974a. Neonate movement is synchronized with adult speech: interactional participation and language acquisition. *Science*, 183: 99–101. 17, 122, 139, 334.

Condon, W.S. & Sander, L.W. 1974b. Synchrony demonstrated between movements of the neonate and adult speech. *Child Development*, 45: 456–62. 17, 139.

Connolly, K.J. (ed.) 1970. *Mechanisms of motor skill development.* New York: Academic. 34.

Connolly, K.J. & Bruner, J.S. (ed.) 1974. *The growth of competence.* New York: Academic. 34.

Cook, M. *see* Argyle & Cook 1976.

Cravioto, J., DeLicardie, E.R. & Birch, H.G. 1966. Nutrition, growth and neuro-integrative development: an experimental and ecologic study. *Pediatrics*, 38: 319–72. 79.

Danehy, J.J. *see* Pittenger et al. 1960.

Darwin, C. (1872) 1965. *The expression of the emotions in man and in animals.* Chicago: University of Chicago Press. 8, 213, 326, 330.

Davenport, R.K. forthcoming. Some behavioral disturbances of great apes in captivity. Paper prepared for the Burg Wartenstein Symposium 62: The behavior of great apes. July 1974. In *Perspectives in human evolution*, ed. D. Hamburg & J. van Lawick-Goodall. 237, 238, 239.

Davenport, R.K. Jnr *see* Mason et al. 1968.

Davis, B.B. *see* Friedlander et al. 1972.

Delgado, H. *see* Lechtig et al. 1975.

DeLicardie, E.R. *see* Cravioto et al. 1966.

Delius, J.D. 1969. A stochastic analysis of the maintenance behavior of skylarks. *Behaviour*, 33: 137–78. 115.

Denes, P.B. & Pinson, E.N. 1963. *The speech chain.* Baltimore: Waverly Press. 15.

Dev, P. *see* Schmitt et al. 1976.

Developing Child, The 1977– (series). Ed. J.S. Bruner, M. Cole & B. Lloyd. London: Fontana/Open Books. 33.

Dodds, J.B. *see* Frankenburg & Dodds 1973.

Dore, J. 1975. Holophrases, speech acts and language universals. *Journal of Child Language*, 2: 21–40. 172.

Downs, M.P. & Sterritt, G.M. 1971. A guide to newborn and infant hearing screening programs. In *Hearing measurement*, ed. I.M. Ventry et al. New York: Appleton-Century-Crofts. *

Dubber, C. *see* Snow et al. in preparation.

Eckerman, C.O. *see* Rheingold & Eckerman 1970.

Eibl-Eibesfeldt, I. 1970. *Ethology: the biology of behavior.* New York: Holt, Rinehart & Winston. (2nd edn). 327, 330.

Eibl-Eibesfeldt, I. 1971. *Love and hate.* New York: Holt, Rinehart & Winston, 24.

Eimas, P.D., Siqueland, E.R., Jusczyk, P. & Vigorito, J. 1971. Speech perception in infants. *Science,* 171: 303—6. Repr. in Stone et al. 1973, pp. 1180—4. 334.

Eisenberg, R.B. 1975. *Auditory competence in early life: the roots of communicative behavior.* Baltimore: University Park Press. 28, 334.

Ekman, P. (ed.) 1973. *Darwin and facial expression.* New York: Academic. 326, 327.

Ekman, P. & Friesen, W.V. 1969. The repertoire of nonverbal behavior: categories, origins, usage and coding. *Semiotica,* 1: 49—98. 39, 330.

Ekman, P. & Friesen, W.V. 1971. Constants across cultures in the face and emotion. *Journal of Personality and Social Psychology,* 17: 124—9. 327.

Ekman, P. & Friesen, W.V. 1975. *Unmasking the face.* Englewood Cliffs, N.J.: Prentice-Hall. 327.

Ekman, P. & Friesen, W.V. 1976. Measuring facial movement. *Environmental Psychology and Nonverbal Behavior,* 1: 56—75. 24.

Ekman, P., Friesen, W.V. & Ellsworth, P. 1972. *Emotion in the human face: guidelines for research and an integration of findings.* New York: Pergamon. 13, 327.

Ekman, P. *see* Oster & Ekman forthcoming.

Ellsworth, P. *see* Ekman et al. 1972.

Emde, R.N. & Harmon, R.J. 1972. Endogenous and exogenous smiling systems in early infancy. *Journal of the American Academy of Child Psychiatry,* 11: 177—200. 240.

Emde, R.N. & Koenig, K.L. 1969. Neonatal smiling, frowning and rapid eye movement states. II. Sleep-cycle study. *Journal of the American Academy of Child Psychiatry,* 8: 637—56. 157.

Erasmi, T. 1975. *Language development and social influence.* Linköping University studies in education dissertations series, 7. Linköping, Sweden. *

Fantz, R.L. 1963. Pattern vision in newborn infants. *Science,* 140: 296—7. Repr. in Stone et al. 1973, pp. 314—16. 333.

Feldstein, S. *see* Jaffe & Feldstein 1970.

Ferber, A. *see* Kendon & Ferber 1973.

Ferguson, C.A. 1964. Baby-talk in six languages. In *The ethnography of communication* (= *American Anthropologist,* 66, 6/2), ed. J. Gumperz & D. Hymes, pp. 103—14. 362.

Ferguson, C.A. *see* Snow & Ferguson 1977.

Ferrier, L. 1978. Some observations on error in context. In Waterson & Snow 1978. 279.

Fidelholtz, J.L. *see* Bullowa et al. 1975.

Flavell, E.R. *see* Lempers et al. 1977.

Flavell, J.H. *see* Lempers et al. 1977.

Fogel, A., 197, 199.

Fogel, A. 1976. Gaze, face, and voice in the development of mother—infant face-to-face interaction. PhD dissertation, University of Chicago. **196, 198.**

Fogel, A. 1977. Temporal organization in mother—infant face-to-face interaction. In Schaffer 1977a, pp. 119—51. **129, 196, 198.**

Foss, B.M. (ed.) 1961, 1963, 1965, 1969. *Determinants of infant behaviour*, vols. I—IV. London: Methuen. **34.**

Fouts, R.S. 1975. Capacities for language in great apes. In *Socioecology and psychology of primates*, ed. R.H. Tuttle, pp. 371—90. The Hague: Mouton. **13.**

Fraiberg, S., **19, 55, 149—69, 326, 331.**

Fraiberg, S. 1959. *The magic years: understanding and handling problems of early childhood.* New York: Scribners. **55.**

Fraiberg, S. 1968. Parallel and divergent patterns in blind and sighted infants. *Psychoanalytic Study of the Child*, vol. XXIII, pp. 264—300. New York: International Universities Press. **153, 161, 326.**

Fraiberg, S. 1971a. Intervention in infancy. *Journal of the American Academy of Child Psychiatry*, 10: 381—405. **153.**

Fraiberg, S. 1971b. Smiling and stranger reaction in blind infants. In Hellmuth 1971, pp. 110—27. **157.**

Fraiberg, S. 1977. *Insights from the blind: comparative studies of blind and sighted infants.* New York: Basic Books. *

Fraiberg, S. & Adelson, E. 1973. Self representation in language and play: observations of blind children. *Psychoanalytic Quarterly*, 42: 539—62. Repr. in Lenneberg & Lenneberg 1975, vol. II, pp. 177—92. **166.**

Fraiberg, S. & Freedman, D. 1964. Studies in the ego development of the congenitally blind child. In *Psychoanalytic Study of the Child*, vol. XIX, pp. 113—69. New York: International Universities Press. **153.**

Fraiberg, S., Siegal, B. & Gibson, R. 1966. The role of sound in the search behavior of a blind infant. In *Psychoanalytic Study of the Child*, vol. XXI, pp. 327—57. New York: International Universities Press. **161.**

Fraiberg, S., Smith, M. & Adelson, E. 1969. An educational program for blind infants. *Journal of Special Education*, 3: 121—39. **153.**

France, M.N. 1975. The generation of the self: a study of the construction of categories in infancy. PhD dissertation, University of Essex. **171.**

Frank, L.K. 1957. Tactile communication. *Genetic Psychology Monographs*, 56, 209—55. **39.**

Frankenburg, W.K. & Dodds, J.B. 1973. *Denver developmental screening test.* Manual/workbook for nursing and paramedical personnel. Denver: University of Colorado Press. *

Frankenburg, W.J., Goldstein, A.D. & Camp, B.W. 1971. The revised Denver developmental screening test: its accuracy as a screening instrument. *Journal of Pediatrics*, 79: 988—95. *

Fraser, G.R. 1974. Epidemiology of profound childhood deafness. *Audiology*, 13: 335—41. *

Freedle, R. *see* Lewis & Freedle 1973.

Freedman, D.G., **150, 197.**

Freedman, D.G. 1964. Smiling in blind infants and the issue of innate versus acquired. *Journal of Child Psychology and Psychiatry*, 5: 171—84. **326, 331.**

Freedman, D.G. 1974. *Human infancy: an evolutionary perspective.* Hillsdale, N.J.: Lawrence Erlbaum. Repr. New York: Halsted, 1975. *

Freedman, D.G. *see* Fraiberg & Freedman 1964.

Freud, A. & Burlingham, D. 1944. *Infants without families.* New York: International Universities Press. 9.

Friedlander, B.Z., Jacobs, A.C., Davis, B.B. & Wetstone, H.S. 1972. Time-sampling analysis of infants' natural language environments in the home. *Child Development,* 43: 730—40. 191.

Friedman, S. *see* Carpenter et al. 1970.

Friesen, W.V. *see* Ekman & Friesen 1969, 1971, 1975, 1976; Ekman et al. 1972.

Gajdusek, D.C., 293.

Gajdusek, D.C. *see* Sorenson & Gajdusek 1966.

Garfinkel, H. 1967. *Studies in ethnomethodology.* Englewood Cliffs, N.J.: Prentice-Hall. 5.

Gesell, A. 1934. *An atlas of infant behavior: a systematic delineation of the forms and early growth of infant behavior patterns, in two volumes, illustrated by 3200 action photographs.* New Haven: Yale University Press. 24.

Gesell, A. 1940. *The first five years of life.* New York: Harper & Brothers. 50.

Gewirtz, J.L. 1965. The course of infant smiling in four child-rearing environments in Israel. In Foss 1965, pp. 205—48. 240.

Gibson, J.J. 1966. *The senses considered as perceptual systems.* Boston: Houghton Mifflin. 354, 361.

Gibson, R. *see* Fraiberg et al. 1966.

Glasersfeld, E. von 1974. Signs, communication, and language. *Journal of Human Evolution,* 3: 465—74. 107.

Goldberg, S. 1972. Infant care and growth in urban Zambia. *Human Development,* 15: 77—89. 270.

Goldberg, S. 1976. Some stimulus properties of the human infant. Unpubd mimeo, Brandeis University. 85.

Goldstein, A.D. *see* Frankenburg et al. 1971.

Gould, J. *see* Sander et al. 1975.

Gray, H. forthcoming. Learning to take an object from the mother. In Lock 1978, pp. 159—82. *

Greenfield, P.M. *see* Bruner et al. 1966.

Greenough, W.T. 1973. *The nature and nurture of behavior: developmental psychobiology.* San Francisco: W.H. Freeman. 33.

Gregory, S. *see* Shotter & Gregory 1976; Treble, S.

Grieve, R. & Hoogenraad, R. forthcoming. First words. In *Studies in language acquisition,* ed. P. Fletcher & M. Garman. Cambridge: Cambridge University Press. 172.

Griffiths, R. (1954) 1967. *The abilities of babies.* London: University of London Press. *

Gruber, H.E. & Barrett, P.H. 1974. *Darwin on man.* New York: Dutton. *

Gruber, J.S. 1973. Correlations between syntactic constructions of the child and of the adult. In *Studies of child language,* ed. C.A. Ferguson & D. Slobin, pp. 440—5. New York: Holt, Rinehart & Winston. Rev. as Performative-constative transition in child language. *Foundations of Language*, 12 (1975): 513—27. 10.

Habermas, J. 1970. Introductory remarks to a theory of communicative competence. In *Recent sociology*, vol. II, ed. H.P. Drietzel. London: Macmillan. 347.
Habermas, J. 1972. *Knowledge and human interest*. London: Heinemann. 347.
Habicht, J.P. *see* Lechtig et al. 1975.
Hall, E.T. 1969. *The hidden dimension*. New York: Doubleday. 42.
Hall, E.T. 1976. *Beyond culture*. New York: Anchor/Doubleday. 9, 16, 17, 139.
Halliday, M.A.K., 55, 171—90.
Halliday, M.A.K. 1975. *Learning how to mean: explorations in the development of language*. London: Edward Arnold. 178, 191.
Halperin, S. *see* Menzel & Halperin 1975.
Hanlon, C. *see* Brown & Hanlon 1970.
Harlow, H.F. 1963. The maternal affectional system. In Foss 1963, pp. 3—33. 119.
Harlow, H.F. & Harlow, M.K. 1962a. Social deprivation in monkeys. *Scientific American*, 207, 5: 136—46. 239.
Harlow, H.F. & Harlow, M.K. 1962b. The heterosexual affectional system in monkeys. *American Psychologist*, 17: 1—9. 239.
Harlow, H.F. & Harlow, M.K. 1965. The affectional systems. In *Behavior of non-human primates: modern research trends*, vol. II, ed. A.M. Schrier et al., pp. 237—334. New York: Academic. 239.
Harlow, H. & Mears, C. 1977. The power and passion of play. *New Scientist*, 73, 1038: 336—8. 239.
Harlow, M.K. *see* Harlow & Harlow 1962a, b, 1965.
Harmon, R.J. *see* Emde & Harmon 1972.
Harris, A.E. 1975. Social dialectics and language: mother and child construct the discourse. *Human Development*, 18: 80—96. 191.
Harris, R.M. *see* Kendon et al. 1975.
Hayman, K. *see* Mead & Hayman 1965.
Heider, G.M. 1966. Vulnerability in infants and young children: a pilot study. *Genetic Psychology Monographs*, 73: 1—216. 79.
Hellmuth, J. (ed.) 1967. *Exceptional infant. Vol. I. The normal infant*. New York: Brunner/Mazel. 33.
Hellmuth, J. (ed.) 1971. *Exceptional infant. Vol. II*. New York: Brunner/Mazel. *
Herska, H.S. 1965. *Das Gesicht des Säuglings: Ausdruck und Reifung*. Basle and Stuttgart. 326.
Hinde, R.A. 1970. *Animal behaviour*. London: McGraw-Hill (2nd edn). 238.
Hinde, R.A. 1971. Development of social behavior. In *Behavior of nonhuman primates: modern research trends*, vol. III, ed. A.M. Schrier & F. Stollnitz, pp. 1—68. New York: Academic. 239.
Hinde, R.A. 1974. *Biological bases of human social behaviour*. London: McGraw-Hill. 242.
Hinde, R.A. 1976. On describing relationships. *Journal of Child Psychology and Psychiatry*, 17: 1—19. 129.

Hockett, C.F. 1960. The origin of speech. *Scientific American*, 203, 3: 87–97. 72.
Hockett, C.F. *see* McQuown et al. 1971; Pittenger et al. 1960.
Holzman, M. 1974. The verbal environment provided by mothers for their very young children. *Merrill-Palmer Quarterly*, 20: 31–42. 191.
Hooff, J.A.R.A.M. van 1972. A comparative approach to the phylogeny of laughter and smiling. In *Non-verbal communication*, ed. R.A. Hinde, pp. 209–41. Cambridge: Cambridge University Press. 240.
Hoogenraad, R. *see* Grieve & Hoogenraad forthcoming.
Horowitz, F.D. *see* Young-Browne et al. 1977.
House, A.S. *see* Stevens & House 1972.
Howe, C. 1975. The nature of social class differences in the propositions expressed by young children. PhD dissertation, University of Cambridge. 121.
Hubley, P. *see* Trevarthen & Hubley forthcoming.
Huxley, R. & Ingram, E. (ed.) 1971. *Language acquisition: models and methods.* New York: Academic. 34.
Hymes, D. 1964. Towards ethnographies of communication. In *The ethnography of communication* (= *American Anthropologist*, 66, 6/2), ed. J. Gumperz & D. Hymes, pp. 1–34. 75.

Ingham, R. *see* Argyle & Ingham 1972.
Ingram, E. *see* Huxley & Ingram 1971.
Inhelder, B. *see* Tanner & Inhelder 1956a, b, 1958, 1960.

Jablonko, A. *see* Sorenson & Jablonko 1975.
Jackson, D. *see* Watzlawick et al. 1967.
Jacobs, A.C. *see* Friedlander et al. 1972.
Jaffe, J. 1968. Computer assessment of dyadic interaction rules from chronographic data. In *Research in psychotherapy*, vol. III, ed. J. Shlein, pp. 260–76. Washington, D.C.: American Psychological Association. 114.
Jaffe, J. & Feldstein, S. 1970. *Rhythms of dialogue.* New York: Academic. 114.
Jaffe, J., Stern, D.N. & Peery, J.C. 1973. 'Conversational' coupling of gaze behavior in prelinguistic human development. *Journal of Psycholinguistic Research*, 2: 321–9. 72, 114, 118.
Jaffe, J. *see* Stern et al. 1975, 1977.
Jakobson, R. (1941: *Kindersprache, Aphasie und allgemeine Lautgesetze.* Stockholm: Almqvist & Wiksell) 1968. *Child language aphasia and phonological universals.* The Hague: Mouton. 26.
Jerauld, R. *see* Klaus et al. 1972.
Jones, L.G. *see* Bullowa et al. 1964.
Jones, O.H.M. 1977a. Mother–child communication with pre-linguistic Down's syndrome and normal infants. In Schaffer 1977a, pp. 379–401. 217, 218, 219.
Jones, O.H.M. 1977b. Mother–child communication with young Down's syndrome and young normal children. PhD dissertation, University of Nottingham. 217.
Julia, H. *see* Burns et al. 1972; Sander et al. 1969, 1970, 1972.

Jusczyk, P. *see* Eimas et al. 1971.

Kagan, J. 1967. The growth of the 'face' schema: theoretical significance and methodological issues. In Hellmuth 1967, pp. 335–48. 240.

Kagan, J. 1972. Do infants think? *Scientific American*, 226, 5: 74–82. 240.

Kagan, J. & Klein, R. 1973. Cross-cultural perspectives on early development. *American Psychologist*, 28: 947–61. 270.

Kagan, J. *see* Tulkin & Kagan 1972.

Karmiloff-Smith, A. forthcoming. The interplay between syntax, semantics and phonology in language acquisition processes. Paper presented at the Stirling Conference on the Psychology of Language, June 1976. 62.

Kaye, K., 55–6, 191–206.

Kaye, K. 1970. Maternal participation in infants' acquisition of a skill. PhD dissertation, Harvard University. 200.

Kaye, K. 1971. Learning by imitation in infants and young children. Paper presented to the Society for Research in Child Development, Minneapolis. 202.

Kaye, K. 1976. Infants' effects upon their mothers' teaching strategies. In *The social context of learning and development*, ed. J.C. Glidewell. New York: Halsted. 200.

Kaye, K. 1977. Toward the origin of dialogue. In Schaffer 1977a, pp. 89–117. 115, 129, 195, 196, 204.

Kaye, K. & Brazelton, T.B. 1971. Mother–infant interaction in the organization of sucking. Paper presented to the Society for Research in Child Development, Minneapolis. 84, 195.

Kaye, K. & Marcus, J. 1978. Imitation over a series of triads without feedback. *Infant Behavior and Development*, 1: 141–55. 203.

Kaye, K. & Wells, A. in preparation. The micropsychology of feeding in the first two weeks of life. 195.

Kendon, A. 1972. Some relationships between body motion and speech: an analysis of an example. In *Studies in dyadic communication*, ed. A.N. Siegman & P. Pope, pp. 177–210. New York: Pergamon. 13, 15, 139.

Kendon, A. & Ferber, A. 1973. A description of some human greetings. In *Comparative ecology and behaviour of primates: proceedings of a conference held at the Zoological Society, London, November 1971*, ed. R.P. Michael & J.H. Crook, pp. 591–668. New York: Academic. 42.

Kendon, A., Harris, R.M. & Key, M.R. (ed.) 1975. *Organization of behavior in face-to-face interaction*. The Hague: Mouton. *

Kennell, J.H. *see* Klaus & Kennell, 1970; Klaus et al. 1972, 1975.

Kessler, A.R. *see* Bullowa et al. 1975.

Key, M.R. *see* Kendon et al. 1975.

Klaus, M.H. & Kennell, J.H. 1970. Mothers separated from their newborn infants. *Pediatric Clinics of North America*, 17: 1015–37. 85.

Klaus, M.H., Jerauld, R., Kreger, N.C., McAlpine, W., Steffa, M. & Kennell, J.H. 1972. Maternal attachment: importance of the first post-partum days. *New England Journal of Medicine*, 286: 460–3. 85.

Klaus, M.H., Trause, M.A. & Kennell, J.H. 1975. Does human maternal behaviour after delivery show a characteristic pattern? In Ciba 1975, pp. 69–85. 40.

Klein, R. *see* Brazelton et al. 1977; Kagan & Klein 1973; Lechtig et al. 1975.

Kloot, W. van der & Morse, M.J. 1975. A stochastic analysis of the display behavior of the Red-breasted Merganser. *Behaviour*, 54: 181—216. **115.**

Koenig, K.L. *see* Emde & Koenig 1969.

Koffka, K. 1924. *The growth of the mind.* New York: Littlefield, Adams. **366.**

Koopmans-van Beinum, F.J. forthcoming. Infant speech development during the first months of life. **26.**

Korner, A.F. 1974. The effect of the infant's state, level of arousal, sex, and ontogenetic stage on the caregiver. In Lewis & Rosenblum 1974, pp. 105—21. **239.**

Korner, A.F. & Thoman, E.B. 1972. Relative efficacy of contact and vestibular proprioceptive stimulation in soothing neonates. *Child Development*, 43: 443—53. **83.**

Koslowski, B. *see* Brazelton et al. 1974.

Kreger, N.C. *see* Klaus et al. 1972.

Kreutzer, M.A. *see* Charlesworth & Kreutzer 1973.

Lafon, Jean-Claude (ed.) 1974. *Prélangage. Bulletin d'Audiophonologie*, suppls. 5, 6, 7. Besançon. **25.**

Laguna, G.A. de (1927) 1963. *Speech: its function and development.* Bloomington: Indiana University Press. **26.**

Landes, J.E. 1975. Speech addressed to children: issues and characteristics of parental input. *Language Learning*, 25: 355—79. **128.**

Lasky, R. *see* Brazelton et al. 1977; Lechtig et al. 1975.

Lawick-Goodall, J. van 1968. The behaviour of free-living chimpanzees in the Gombe Stream Reserve. *Animal Behaviour Monographs*, 1, 3: 161—311. London: Tyndall; Paris: Ballière. **224, 225.**

Lawick-Goodall, J. van 1971. *In the shadow of man.* London: Collins. **226.**

Leboyer, F. (1974: *Pour une naissance sans violence.* Paris: Editions du Seuil) 1975. *Birth without violence.* London: Wildwood; Repr. London: Fontana, 1977. **40, 326.**

Leboyer, F. 1976. *Shantala, un art traditionnel le massage des infants.* Paris: Editions du Seuil. **40.**

Lechtig, A., Delgado, H., Lasky, R., Yarbrough, C., Klein, R.E., Habicht, J.P. & Béhar, M. 1975. Maternal nutrition and fetal growth in developing countries. *American Journal of Diseases of Childhood*, 129: 553—6. **79.**

Lechtig, A. *see* Brazelton et al. 1977.

Lee-Painter, S. *see* Lewis & Lee-Painter 1974.

Lempers, J.D. 1976. Production of pointing, comprehension of pointing and understanding of looking behavior. PhD dissertation, University of Minnesota. **119, 120.**

Lempers, J.D., Flavell, E.R. & Flavell, J.H. 1977. The development in very young children of tacit knowledge concerning visual perception. *Genetic Psychology Monographs*, 95: 3—53. **119, 120.**

Lenneberg, E., **166.**

Lenneberg, E. 1967. *Biological foundations of language.* New York: Wiley. **17.**

Lenneberg, E. *see* Lenneberg & Lenneberg 1975.

Lenneberg, E.H. & Lenneberg, E. (ed.) 1975. *The foundations of language development*, vols. I and II. New York: Academic. *

Lenneberg, E.H., Rebelsky, F.G. & Nichols, I.A. 1965. The vocalization of infants born to deaf and hearing parents. *Vita Humana (Human Development)* 8: 23–37. **326.**

Lewin, R. (ed.) 1975. *Child alive: new insights into the development of young children.* London: Temple Smith; New York: Anchor/Doubleday. **33.**

Lewis, M. 1969. Infants' responses to facial stimuli during the first year of life. *Developmental Psychology*, 1: 75–86. Repr. in Stone et al. 1973, pp. 648–55. **240, 333.**

Lewis, M. (chairperson) 1971 (1972). Cross-cultural studies in mother–infant interaction: description and consequences. *Human Development*, 15. **33.**

Lewis, M. 1972. State as an infant–environment interaction: an analysis of mother–infant interaction as a function of sex. *Merrill-Palmer Quarterly*, 18: 95–121. **114.**

Lewis, M. & Freedle, R. 1973. Mother–infant dyad: the cradle of meaning. In *Communication and affect: language and thought*, ed. P. Pliner et al., pp. 127–55. New York: Academic. **114, 333, 337.**

Lewis, M. & Lee-Painter, S. 1974. An interactional approach to the mother–infant dyad. In Lewis & Rosenblum 1974, pp. 21–48. **114.**

Lewis, M. & Rosenblum, L.A. (ed.) 1974. *The effect of the infant on its caregiver.* New York: Wiley. **18.**

Lezine, I. 1972. Influence du milieu sur le jeune enfant. In *Milieu et développement: symp. de l'association de psychologie scientifique de langue française, Lille 1970.* Paris: Presses Universitaires de France. **9.**

Lieberman, A.F. *see* Blehar et al. 1977.

Liederman, G.F. *see* Liederman & Liederman 1977.

Liederman, P.H. & Liederman, G.F. 1977. Economic change and infant care in an East African agricultural community. In Liederman et al. 1977, pp. 405–38. **270.**

Liederman, P.H., Tulkin, S.R. & Rosenfeld, A. 1977. *Culture and infancy: variations in the human experience.* New York: Academic. **33.**

Lieven, E.V.M. 1978. Conversation between mothers and young children: individual differences and their possible implication for the study of language learning. In Waterson & Snow 1978. **191.**

Lind, J. (ed.) 1965. *Newborn infant cry.* Uppsala: Almqvist & Wiksell. **25.**

Lind, J. 1973. Die Geburt der Familie in der Frauenklinik. *Medizinische Klinik*, 68: 1597–1601. Repr. as The newborn family. *Swedish Medical Journal*, Stockholm, 1975. *

Lind, J. *see* Wasz-Höckert et al. 1968.

Lisina, M.I. 1974. Ch. 4 of *Razvitiie obshcheniya u doshkol'nikov (The development of communication in preschool children)*, ed. A.V. Zaporozhets & M.I. Lisina, pp. 113–52. Moscow: Pedagogika. Translated as Aspects of the communication of young children engaged in joint activity with adults. *Soviet Psychology*, 4, 3 (1976): 50–93. **9.**

Lloyd, B. *see* Developing Child, The.

Lock, A. (ed.) 1978. *Action, gesture and symbol: the emergence of language.* New York: Academic. 30.

Lorenz, K. 1970—1. *Studies in animal and human behavior* (translated by Robert Martin), vols. I and II. Cambridge, Mass.: Harvard University Press. 66, 68.

Luria, A.R. (1957) 1961. *The role of speech in the regulation of normal and abnormal behaviour,* ed. J. Tizard. New York: Pergamon. 9.

McAlpine, W. *see* Klaus et al. 1972.

McBride, G. *see* Clancy & McBride 1975.

MacFarlane, A. 1975. Olfaction in the development of social preferences in the human neonate. In Ciba 1975, pp. 103—17. 41.

McGraw, M.B. 1935. *Growth: a study of Johnny and Jimmy.* New York: Appleton-Century. 30.

McGraw, M.B. (1943) 1956. *The neuromuscular maturation of the human infant.* New York: Hafner. 24.

MacKay, D. 1972. Formal analysis of communicative processes. In *Non-verbal communication,* ed. R.A. Hinde, pp. 3—25. Cambridge: Cambridge University Press. 106—7.

McQuown, N.E., Bateson, G., Birdwhistell, R.L., Brosin, H.W. & Hockett, C.F. 1971. *The natural history of an interview.* Microfilm Collection of Manuscripts in Cultural Anthropology, ser. 15, nos. 95—8. Chicago: University of Chicago Library. 65.

Mahler, M.S., Pine, F. & Bergman, A. 1975. *The psychological birth of the human infant.* New York: Basic Books. *

Main, M. *see* Brazelton et al. 1974.

Mair, M., 139.

Maratos, O. 1973. The origin and development of imitation in the first six months of life. PhD dissertation, University of Geneva. 331.

Maratos, O. forthcoming. Trends in the development of imitation in early infancy. In *Proceedings of the OECD Conference on Dips in Learning,* St Paul de Vence, March 1975, ed. H. Nathan. Paris. *

Marcus, J. *see* Kaye & Marcus 1978.

Marler, P. 1967. Animal communication signals. *Science,* 157: 769—74. 119.

Martin, J.A. *see* Thomas & Martin 1976.

Martin, J.G. 1972. Rhythmic (hierarchical) versus serial structure in speech and other behavior. *Psychological Review,* 79: 487—509. 139.

Mason, W.A. 1960. The effects of social restriction on the behaviour of rhesus monkeys. I. Free social behavior. *Journal of Comparative and Physiological Psychology,* 53: 582—9. 239.

Mason, W.A., Davenport, R.K. Jnr & Menzel, E.W. Jnr 1968. Early experience and the social development of rhesus monkeys and chimpanzees. In *Early experience and behavior: the psychobiology of development,* ed. G. Newton & S. Levine, pp. 440—80. Springfield, Ill.: Thomas. 238.

Mason, W.A. *see* Anderson & Mason 1975.

Maurer, D. & Salapatek, P. 1976. Developmental changes in the scanning of faces by infants. *Child Development*, 47: 523–7. **330, 333.**

Mead, G.H. 1934. *Mind, self and society.* Chicago: University of Chicago Press. **206.**

Mead, M. & Byers, P. 1968. *The small conference: an innovation in communication.* International Social Science Council, 9. The Hague: Mouton. **33.**

Mead, M. & Hayman, K. 1965. *The family.* London: Macmillan. **207.**

Mears, C. *see* Harlow & Mears 1977.

Meier, G.W. *see* Boismier et al. 1970; Chappell et al. 1973.

Melhuish, E. *see* Mills & Melhuish 1974.

Meltzoff, A.N. & Moore, M.H. 1977. Imitation of facial and manual gestures by human neonates. *Science*, 198: 75–8. **331.**

Mencher, G. 1976. *Early identification of hearing loss.* Novia Scotia conference on early identification of hearing loss. Halifax, Novia Scotia, 1974. Basle. *

Menzel, E.W. Jnr 1971. Communication about the environment in a group of young chimpanzees. *Folia Primatologica*, 15: 220–32. **119.**

Menzel, E.W. Jnr 1973. Leadership and communication in young chimpanzees. In *Precultural primate behavior*, ed. E.W. Menzel Jnr, pp. 192–255. Basle: Karger. **111.**

Menzel, E.W. Jnr & Halperin, S. 1975. Purposive behavior as a basis for objective communication between chimpanzees. *Science*, 189: 652–4. **119.**

Menzel, E.W. Jnr *see* Mason et al. 1968.

Merrill-Palmer Quarterly. Detroit, Mich.: Merrill-Palmer Institute. **35.**

Messer, D.J. forthcoming. The integration of mothers' referential speech with joint play. *Child Development.* **121.**

Messer, D.J. *see* Murphy & Messer 1977.

Michelsson, K. 1971. Cry analyses of symptomless low birth weight neonates and of asphyxiated newborn infants. *Acta Paediatrica Scandinavica*, Stockholm, suppl. 216. **25.**

Middleton, D. *see* Wood & Middleton 1975.

Mills, M. & Melhuish, E. 1974. Recognition of mothers' voice in early infancy. *Nature*, 252: 123–4. **334.**

Moerck, E.L. 1975. The multiple channels of the young child's communicative behavior. *Linguistics*, 169: 21–32. **191.**

Mogford, K. 1972. Communication of young severely handicapped children. Unpubd paper, University of Nottingham. **220.**

Montagu, A. 1971. *Touching: the human significance of the skin.* New York: Columbia University Press. **39, 41.**

Moore, M.H. *see* Meltzoff & Moore 1977.

Moore, M.K. *see* Bower et al. 1970a, b.

Morris, D. 1971. *Intimate behaviour.* New York: Random House. **39.**

Morse, M.J. *see* Kloot & Morse 1975.

Moss, H.A. 1965. Methodological issues in studying mother–infant interaction. *American Journal of Orthopsychiatry*, 35: 482–6. **85.**

Moss, H.A., Robson, K.S. & Pederson, F. 1969. Determinants of maternal stimulation and consequences of treatment for later reaction to strangers. *Developmental Psychology*, 1: 239–47. **337.**

Murphy, C.M. forthcoming. Pointing in the context of a shared activity. **10.**

Murphy, C.M. & Messer, D.J. 1977. Mothers, infants and pointing: a study of a gesture. In Schaffer 1977a, pp. 325—54. **24, 120, 121.**
Murphy, L.B. *see* Stone et al. 1973.
Murray, L. forthcoming. Infants' capacities for regulating interactions with their mothers and the function of emotions. PhD dissertation, University of Edinburgh. **333, 334, 335.**

Newport, E.L. 1977. Motherese: the speech of mothers to young children. In *Cognitive theory*, vol. II, ed. N.J. Castellan et al. Hillside, N.J.: Lawrence Erlbaum. **189.**
Newson, E. *see* Newson & Newson 1963, 1974, 1976, forthcoming.
Newson, J., **56, 207—22.**
Newson, J. 1974. Towards a theory of infant understanding. *Bulletin of the British Psychological Society*, 27: 251—7. **221.**
Newson, J. 1977. An intersubjective approach to the systematic description of mother—infant interaction. In Schaffer 1977a, pp. 47—61. **196.**
Newson, J. 1978. Dialogue and development. In Lock 1978, pp. 31—42. *
Newson, J. & Newson, E. 1963. *Infant care in an urban community*. London: Allen & Unwin. Repr. Harmondsworth: Penguin, 1965. **273.**
Newson, J. & Newson, E. 1974. Cultural aspects of childrearing in the English-speaking world. In Richards 1974b, pp. 53—82. **32.**
Newson, J. & Newson, E. 1976. On the social origins of symbolic functioning. In *Piaget, psychology and education*, ed. V.P. Varma & P. Williams, pp. 84—96. London: Hodder & Stoughton. **215.**
Newson, J. & Newson, E. forthcoming. People as playthings: some research background. In *Toys and playthings in development and remediation*. Harmondsworth: Penguin. *
Newson, J. & Pawlby, S. 1974. On imitation. Unpubd paper, University of Nottingham. **287.**
Newson, J. & Shotter, J. 1974. How babies communicate. *New Society*, 29, 618: 345—7. Repr. in *Growing up: a New Society social studies reader*. IPC Magazines, 1976. *
Nichols, I.A. *see* Lenneberg et al. 1965.

Olver, R.R. *see* Bruner et al. 1966.
Osofsky, J. (ed.) forthcoming. *Handbook of infancy*. **33.**
Oster, H. forthcoming. Facial expression and affect development. In *The origins of behavior: affect development*, ed. M. Lewis & L.A. Rosenblum. New York: Plenum. *
Oster, H. & Ekman, P. forthcoming. Facial behavior in child development. In *Minnesota symposia on child psychology*, 11, ed. A. Collins. New York: Thomas Y. Cromwell. **24, 323, 326, 327.**
Ostwald, P. 1972. The sounds of infancy. *Developmental Medicine and Child Neurology*, 14: 350—61. **25.**

Papoušek, H., **31.**

Papoušek, H. 1967. Experimental studies of appetitional behaviour in human newborns and infants. In *Early behaviour*, ed. H.W. Stevenson et al., pp. 249– 77. New York: Wiley. **323.**

Papoušek, H. 1969. Individual variability in learned responses in human infants. In Robinson 1969, pp. 251–66. **323.**

Papoušek, H. & Papoušek, M. 1974. Mirror image and self-recognition in young infants. I. A new method of experimental analysis. *Developmental Psychology*, 7: 149–57. **333.**

Papoušek, H. & Papoušek, M. 1975. Cognitive aspects of preverbal social interaction between human infants and adults. In Ciba 1975, pp. 241–69. **31, 335.**

Papoušek, H. & Papoušek, M. 1977. Mothering and the cognitive head-start: psychobiological considerations. In Schaffer 1977a, pp. 63–85. **31, 39, 323, 335, 336, 337.**

Papoušek, M. *see* Papoušek & Papoušek, 1974, 1975, 1977.

Parsons, G. *see* Schaffer et al. 1977.

Partanen, T.J. *see* Wasz-Höckert et al. 1968.

Pavenstedt, E. 1961. A study of immature mothers and their children. In *Prevention of mental disorders in children: initial explorations*, ed. G. Caplan, pp. 192–217. New York: Basic Books; London: Tavistock. **90.**

Pavenstedt, E. 1964. Description of a research project on the influences of the maternal character structure on the development of the child's personality. *Japan Journal of Child Psychiatry*, 5: 19–28. **90.**

Pawlby, S., **219.**

Pawlby, S. 1977. Imitative interaction. In Schaffer 1977a, pp. 203–24. **220.**

Pawlby, S. *see* Newson & Pawlby 1974.

Pederson, F. *see* Moss et al. 1969.

Peery, J.C. *see* Jaffe et al. 1973.

Peiper, A. 1963. *Cerebral function in infancy and childhood.* New York: Consultants Bureau. **32, 330.**

Peters, A.M. 1976. Language learning strategies: does the whole equal the sum of the parts? *Berkeley Working Papers in Linguistics* 8: 1. **26.**

Phillips, J.R. 1973. Syntax and vocabulary of mothers' speech to young children: age and sex comparisons. *Child Development*, 44: 182–5. **191.**

Piaget, J., **215.**

Piaget, J. (1936: *La naissance de l'intelligence chez l'enfant*) 1952. *The origins of intelligence in children.* New York: International Universities Press. **164, 322, 323.**

Piaget, J. (1946: *La formation du symbole chez l'enfant: jeu et rêve image et representation*) 1962. *Play, dreams and imitation in childhood.* New York: Norton. **160, 323, 331, 332.**

Pine, F. *see* Mahler et al. 1975.

Pinson, E.N. *see* Denes & Pinson 1963.

Pittenger, R.E., Hockett, C.F. & Danehy, J.J. 1960. *The first five minutes: a sample of microscopic interview analysis.* Ithaca, N.Y.: P. Martineau. **65.**

Plooij, F., **56–7, 223–43.**

Plooij, F.X. 1974. In het voetspoor van de chimpansee. *Vakblad voor Biologen*, 54, 22: 362–6. **228.**

Plooij, F.X. 1978. Some basic traits of language in wild chimpanzees? In Lock 1978, pp. 111—31. 224.

Pollack, R.H. 1966. Temporal range of apparent movement as a function of age and intelligence. *Psychonomic Science*, 5: 243—4. 366.

Poppei, J. 1976. Problem-solving through peer imitation in toddlers. PhD dissertation, University of Chicago. 204.

Poyatos, F. 1975. Cross-cultural study of paralinguistic 'alternants' in face-to-face interaction. In Kendon et al. 1975, pp. 283—314. 39.

Prechtl, H.F.R. 1953. Die Kletterbewegungen beim Säugling. *Monatsschrift für Kinderheilkunde*, 101, 12: 519—21. 242.

Prechtl, H.F.R. 1958. The directed head turning response and allied movements of the human baby. *Behaviour*, 13: 212—42. 242.

Prechtl, H.F.R. & Beintema, D. 1964. *The neurological examination of the fullterm newborn infant*, Clinics in Developmental Medicine, 12. Spastics International Medical Publications. London: Heinemann Medical Books. 42, 242.

Psychoanalytic Study of the Child 1945— (annual). London: Hogarth (current publisher). 32.

Putney, E. *see* Bullowa & Putney in preparation.

Raffler-Engel, W. von. 1964. *Il prelinguaggio infantile*. Brescia: Paideia. 26.

Rebelsky, F. 1967. Infancy in two cultures. *Nederlands Tijdschrift voor de Psychologie*, 22: 379—85. 270, 271, 276.

Rebelsky, F.G. *see* Lenneberg et al. 1965.

Review of Child Development Research (series). Vol. I, 1964 and vol. II, 1966, ed. M.L. Hoffman & L.W. Hoffman. New York: Russell Sage Foundation. Vol. III, 1973, *Social policy*, ed. B. Caldwell & H.N. Ricciuti; vol. IV, 1975, ed. F.D. Horowitz & E.M. Hetherington; vol. V, 1975, ed. E.M. Hetherington. Chicago: University of Chicago Press. 35.

Rheingold, H.L. 1961. The effect of environmental stimulation upon social and exploratory behaviour in the human infant. In Foss 1961, pp. 143—77. Repr. (abbreviated) in Stone et al. 1973, pp. 789—95. 331, 344.

Rheingold, H.L. & Eckerman, C.O. 1970. The infant separates himself from his mother. *Science*, 168: 78—83. 128.

Richards, M., 61—2.

Richards, M.P.M. 1974a. The development of psychological communication in the first year of life. In Connolly & Bruner 1974, pp. 119—32. 3.

Richards, M.P.M. (ed.) 1974b. *The integration of a child into a social world*. Cambridge: Cambridge University Press. 33.

Richards, M.P.M. 1975. Feeding and the early growth of the mother—child relationship. In *Modern problems in pediatrics. XV. Milk and lactation*, ed. N. Kretchmer et al. Basle: Karger. 274.

Richards, M.P.M. *see* Bernal & Richards 1973.

Richer, J. forthcoming. The partial noncommunication of culture to autistic children — an application of human ethology. In *Infantile autism: reappraisal of concepts, characteristics and treatment*, ed. M. Rutter & E. Schopler, pp. 47—61. New York: Plenum. 19.

Ricks, D.M., 19, 57, 245—68.

Rieber, R.W. (chairperson) 1975. Discussion. In Aaronson & Rieber 1975, pp. 156—70. *

Rieber, R.W. *see* Aaronson & Rieber 1975.

Riegel, K.F. 1975. Semantic structure of language: language as labor. In *Structure and transformation: developmental and historical aspects*, ed. K.F. Riegel & G.C. Rosenwald, pp. 167—92. New York: Wiley. **191.**

Rimland, B. 1964. *Infantile autism.* New York: Appleton-Century-Crofts. **143.**

Robey, J.S. *see* Brazelton et al. 1966.

Robinson, R.J. (ed.) 1969. *Brain and early behavior: development in the fetus and infant.* New York: Academic. **34.**

Robson, K.S. 1967. The role of eye-to-eye contact in maternal—infant attachment. *Journal of Child Psychology and Psychiatry*, 8: 13—25. Repr. in *Annual progress in child psychiatry and child development*, ed. S. Chess & A. Thomas, pp. 92—108. New York: Brunner/Mazel, 1968. **24, 30—1, 155, 201, 287, 330.**

Robson, K.S. *see* Moss et al. 1969.

Roosmalen, G. van, **58, 269—88.**

Roosmalen, G. van *see* Snow et al. in preparation.

Rosenbloom, S. *see* Aronson & Rosenbloom 1971.

Rosenblum, L.A. *see* Lewis & Rosenblum 1974.

Rosenfeld, A. *see* Liederman et al. 1977.

Rosenfeld, H.M. *see* Young-Browne et al. 1977.

Roskies, E. 1972. *Abnormality and normality: the mothering of thalidomide children.* Ithaca, N.Y.: Cornell University Press. **155.**

Rutter, M. 1968. Concepts of autism: a review of research. *Journal of Child Psychology and Psychiatry*, 2: 1—25. **143.**

Rutter, M. 1972. *Maternal deprivation reassessed.* Harmondsworth: Penguin. **238.**

Ryan, J. 1974. Early language development: towards a communicational analysis. In Richards 1974b, pp. 185—213. **107, 369.**

Salapatek, P. *see* Cohen & Salapatek 1975; Maurer & Salapatek 1976.

Sander, L.W., **53—4, 89—109.**

Sander, L.W. 1969. The longitudinal course of early mother—child interaction: cross-care comparison in a sample of mother—child pairs. In Foss 1969, pp. 189—227. **90, 95.**

Sander, L.W. 1975. Infant and caretaking environment: investigation and conceptualization of adaptive behavior in a system of increasing complexity. In *Explorations in child psychiatry*, ed. E.J. Anthony, pp. 129—66. New York: Plenum. **16, 90.**

Sander, L.W. 1977. The regulation of exchange in the infant—caretaker system and some aspects of the context—content relationship. In *Interaction, conversation and the development of language: the origins of behavior*, vol. V, ed. M. Lewis & L. Rosenblum, pp. 133—56. New York: Wiley. **104.**

Sander, L.W., Stechler, G., Julia, H. & Burns, P. 1969. Regulation and organization in the early infant—caretaker system. In Robinson 1969, pp. 311—33. **90.**

Sander, L.W., Stechler, G., Julia, H. & Burns, P. 1970. Early mother—infant interaction and 24-hour patterns of activity and sleep. *Journal of the American Academy of Child Psychiatry*, 9: 103–23. **90, 104, 105.**

Sander, L.W., Julia, H., Stechler, G. & Burns, P. 1972. Continuous 24-hour interactional monitoring in infants reared in two caretaking environments. *Psychosomatic Medicine*, 34: 270–82. **90.**

Sander, L.W., Chappell, P., Gould, J. & Snyder, P. 1975. An investigation of change in the caretaker–infant system over the first week of life. Paper presented to the Society for Research in Child Development, Denver, Colo. **94.**

Sander, L.W. *see* Condon & Sander 1974a, b; Burns et al. 1972.

Scaife, M. & Bruner, J.S. 1975. The capacity for joint visual attention in the infant. *Nature*, 253: 265–6. **119.**

Schaffer, H.R. 1971a. *The growth of sociability*. Harmondsworth: Penguin. **33.**

Schaffer, H.R. (ed.) 1971b. *The origins of human social relations*. New York: Academic. **34.**

Schaffer, H.R. 1977a. *Studies in mother–infant interaction*. Proceedings of the Loch Lomond Symposium, Ross Priory, University of Strathclyde, September 1975. New York: Academic. **35, 195.**

Schaffer, H.R. 1977b. Early interactive development. In Schaffer 1977a, pp. 3–16. **333.**

Schaffer, H.R., Collis, G.M. & Parsons, G. 1977. Vocal interchange and visual regard in verbal and pre-verbal children. In Schaffer 1977a, pp. 291–324. **115, 116, 117, 121, 122, 129.**

Schaffer, H.R. *see* Collis & Schaffer 1975.

Scheflen, A.E. 1964. The significance of posture in communication systems. *Psychiatry*, 27: 316–31. **42.**

Scheflen, A.E. 1972. *The stream and structure of communicational behavior*. Bloomington: University of Indiana Press. **64.**

Scheflen, A.E. 1975. Micro-territories in human interaction. In Kendon et al. 1975, pp. 159–73. **42.**

Schmitt, F.O., Dev, P. & Smith, B.H. 1976. Electrotonic processing of information by brain cells. *Science*, 193: 114–20. **134.**

Schneirla, T.C. 1959. An evolutionary and developmental theory of biphasic processes underlying approach and withdrawal. In *Nebraska symposium on motivation*, 7, ed. M.R. Jones, pp. 1–42. Lincoln, Nebr.: University of Nebraska Press. **238.**

Schneirla, T.C. 1972. The relationships between observation and experimentation in the field study of behavior. In *Selected writings of T.C. Schneirla*, ed. L.R. Aronson et al., pp. 3–29. San Francisco: W.H. Freeman. **225.**

Scholl, M.L. *see* Brazelton et al. 1966.

Shenhav, R. *see* Altman & Shenhav 1971.

Shotter, J. 1974. The development of personal powers. In Richards 1974b, pp. 215–44. **32.**

Shotter, J. 1978. The cultural context of communication studies: theoretical and methodological issues. In Lock 1978, pp. 43–78. *

Shotter, J. & Gregory, S. 1976. On first gaining the idea of oneself as a person. In *Life sentences: aspects of the social role of language*, ed. R. Harré, pp. 3–9. New York: Wiley. **32, 216.**

Shotter, J. *see* Newson & Shotter 1974.

Siegal, B. *see* Fraiberg et al. 1966.

Simon, N. 1975. Echolalic speech in childhood autism. *Archives of General Psychiatry*, 32: 1439–46. **143.**

Sinclair-de Zwaart, H. 1974. On pre-speech. *Papers and Reports on Child Language Development*, 8: 1–10. Stanford, Calif.: Committee on Linguistics. **25, 26.**

Siqueland, E.R. *see* Eimas et al. 1971.

Slater, P.J.B. 1973. Describing sequences of behavior. In *Perspectives in ethology*, vol. I, ed. P.P.G. Bateson & P.H. Klopfer, pp. 131–53. New York: Plenum. **113.**

Slobin, D.I. 1975. On the nature of talk to children. In Lenneberg & Lenneberg 1975, pp. 283–98. **191.**

Smith, B.H. *see* Schmitt et al. 1976.

Smith, H.T. *see* Stone et al. 1973.

Smith, M. *see* Fraiberg et al. 1969.

Snow, C.E., **57–8, 269–88.**

Snow, C.E. 1972. Mothers' speech to children learning language. *Child Development*, 43: 549–55. **191, 336.**

Snow, C.E. 1977. The development of conversation between mothers and babies. *Journal of Child Language*, 4: 1–22. **269, 277, 278.**

Snow, C.E. 1978. The conversational context of language acquisition. In *Advances in the psychology of language: language development and mother–child interaction*. NATO Conference Series 4a, ed. R. Campbell & P. Smith. **287.**

Snow, C.E. & Ferguson, C.A. (ed.) 1977. *Talking to children*. Cambridge: Cambridge University Press. **32.**

Snow, C.E., Dubber, C., Blauw, A. de & Roosmalen, G. van in preparation. Sex and social class differences in mothers' talking to babies. **277.**

Snow, C.E. *see* Waterson & Snow 1978.

Snyder, P. *see* Sander et al. 1975.

Soddy, K. (ed.) 1955. *Mental health and infant development*, vols. I and II. London: Routledge & Kegan Paul. **34.**

Sorenson, E.R., **58–9, 289–305.**

Sorenson, E.R. 1967. A research film program in the study of changing man. *Current Anthropology*, 8: 443–69. **305.**

Sorenson, E.R. 1968. The retrieval of data from changing culture: a strategy for developing research documents for continued study. *Anthropological Quarterly*, 41: 177–86. **305.**

Sorenson, E.R. 1976. *The edge of the forest: land, childhood and change in a New Guinea protoagricultural society*. Washington: Smithsonian Institution Press. **303.**

Sorenson, E.R. 1978. Cooperation and freedom among the Fore of New Guinea: a nonaggressive expression of human adaptation which altered as settled agriculture emerged. In *Learning nonaggression: the experience of non-literate societies*, ed. A. Montagu. Oxford: Oxford University Press. **303.**

Sorenson, E.R. & Gajdusek, D.C. 1966. *The study of child behavior and development in primitive cultures. Pediatrics*, 37, 1, 2: 149–243 (suppl.). 305.

Sorenson, E.R. & Jablonko, A. 1975. Research filming of naturally occurring phenomena: basic strategies. In *Principles of visual anthropology*, ed. P. Hockings, pp. 151–63. The Hague: Mouton. 305.

Spitz, R.A. 1957. *No and yes: on the genesis of human communication.* New York: International Universities Press. 213.

Spitz, R.A. 1965. *The first year of life: a psychoanalytic study of normal and deviant development of object relations.* New York: International Universities Press. *

Spitz, R.A. & Wolf, K.M. 1946. The smiling response. A contribution to the ontogenesis of social relations. *Genetic Psychology Monographs*, 34: 57–125. 240, 326.

Stechler, G. *see* Burns et al. 1972; Carpenter et al. 1970; Sander et al. 1969, 1970, 1972.

Steffa, M. *see* Klaus et al. 1972.

Stensland Junker, K., 59, 307–21.

Stensland Junker, K. 1964. *The child in the glass ball.* Nashville, Tenn.: Abington Press. 59.

Stensland Junker, K. 1971. *Lekoteket på blockhusudden, a program for training through systematic play activity.* Stockholm. *

Stensland Junker, K. 1972. *Selective attention in infants and consecutive communication behavior.* Acta Paediatrica Scandinavica. Repr. Stockholm: Almqvist & Wiksell. 320.

Stensland Junker, K. *see* Barr & Stensland Junker 1972.

Stern, D., 114, 121.

Stern, D. 1971. A micro-analysis of mother–infant interaction: behavior regulating social contact between a mother and her 3½ month-old twins. *Journal of the American Academy of Child Psychiatry*, 10: 501–17. 118, 123.

Stern, D. 1974a. The goal and structure of mother–infant play. *Journal of the American Academy of Child Psychiatry*, 13: 402–21. 362.

Stern, D. 1974b. Mother and infant at play: the dyadic interaction involving facial, vocal and gaze behaviors. In Lewis & Rosenblum 1974, pp. 187–213. 114, 118, 122, 128, 198, 241, 330, 336, 337.

Stern, D. 1975. Infant regulation of maternal play behavior and/or maternal regulation of infant play behavior. Paper presented to the Society for Research in Child Development, Denver, Colo. 196.

Stern, D. 1977. *The first relationship: infant and mother.* London: Fontana/Open Books. 33.

Stern, D., Jaffe, J., Beebe, B. & Bennett, S.L. 1975. Vocalizing in unison and in alternation: two modes of communication within the mother–infant dyad. In Aaronson & Rieber 1975, pp. 89–100. 114, 116, 129, 331, 340, 344.

Stern, D., Beebe, B., Jaffe, J. & Bennett, S.L. 1977. The infant's stimulus world during social interaction: a study of caregiver behaviours with particular reference to repetition and timing. In Schaffer 1977a, pp. 177–202. 84, 122, 128, 196, 199.

Stern, D.N. *see* Jaffe et al. 1973.

Sterritt, G.M. *see* Downe & Sterritt 1971.

Stevens, K.N. & House, A.S. 1972. Speech perceptions. In *Foundations of modern auditory theory*, ed. J.V. Tobias, pp. 1—62. New York: Academic. **140.**

Stone, J.L., Smith, H.T. & Murphy, L.B. 1973. *The competent infant*. New York: Basic Books; London: Tavistock, 1974. **8, 33.**

Strain, B.A. & Vietze, P.M. 1975. Early dialogues: the structure of reciprocal infant—mother vocalisation. Paper presented to the Society for Research in Child Development, Denver, Colo. **116.**

Sudnow, D. (ed.) 1972. *Studies in social interaction*. New York: Free Press. **5.**

Sylvester-Bradley, B. & Trevarthen, C. 1978. Baby-talk as an adaptation to the infant's communication. In Waterson & Snow 1978, pp. 75—92. **333, 336, 337, 340.**

Tanner, J.M. & Inhelder, B. (ed.) 1956a, b, 1958, 1960. *Discussions on child development*, vols. I—IV. London: Tavistock. Repr. as one vol., London: Tavistock, 1971. **34.**

Tatam, J. 1974. The effects of an inappropriate partner on infant sociability. MA dissertation, University of Edinburgh. **335.**

Tecce, J.J. *see* Carpenter et al. 1970.

Thoman, E.B. *see* Korner & Thoman 1972.

Thomas, E.A.C. & Martin, J.A. 1976. Analyses of parent—infant interaction. *Psychological Review*, 83: 141—56. **197.**

Tinbergen, N. (1951) 1974. *The study of instinct*. Oxford: Oxford University Press. **223.**

Tinbergen, N. 1963. On aims and methods of ethology. *Zeitschrift für Tierpsychologie*, 20: 410—29. **111.**

Trause, M.A. *see* Klaus et al. 1975.

Treble (now Gregory), S. 1972. The development of shape perception in young children. PhD dissertation, University of Nottingham. **216.**

Trehub, S.E. 1973. Infants' sensitivity to vowel and tonal contrasts. *Developmental Psychology*, 9: 91—6. **334.**

Trevarthen, C., **17, 25, 59, 209, 210, 321—46.**

Trevarthen, C. 1974a. Conversations with a two-month-old. *New Scientist*, 62, 896: 230—5. **171.**

Trevarthen, C. 1974b. The psychobiology of speech development. In *Language and brain: developmental aspects, Neurosciences Research Program Bulletin* (Boston), 12, ed. E.H. Lenneberg, pp. 570—85. Repr. in *Neurosciences research symposium summaries*, 11, ed. F.O. Schmitt et al. Boston, Mass.: Massachusetts Institute of Technology Press, 1975. **171, 172, 322, 323, 334.**

Trevarthen, C. 1974c. Intersubjectivity and imitation in infants. *Proceedings of the British Psychological Society Annual Convention*, Bangor, p. 33. **333.**

Trevarthen, C. 1975. Early attempts at speech. In Lewin 1975, pp. 57—74. **323.**

Trevarthen, C. 1977. Descriptive analyses of infant communicative behavior. In Schaffer 1977a, pp. 227-70. *

Trevarthen, C. 1978. Modes of perceiving and modes of acting. In *Modes of per-*

ceiving and processing information, ed. H.L. Pick & E. Saltzman, pp. 99—136. Hillsdale, N.J.: Lawrence Erlbaum. **332.**

Trevarthen, C. forthcoming. Basic patterns of psychogenetic change in infancy. In *Proceedings of the OECD Conference on Dips in Learning*, St Paul de Vence, March 1975, ed. H. Nathan. Paris. **322, 323.**

Trevarthen, C. & Hubley, P. 1978. Secondary intersubjectivity: confidence, confiding and acts of meaning in the first year. In Lock 1978, pp. 183—229. **345.**

Trevarthen, C. *see* Sylvester-Bradley & Trevarthen 1978.

Trivers, R.L. 1971. The evolution of reciprocal altruism. *Quarterly Review of Biology*, 46: 35—57. **239.**

Tronick, E., **21, 60, 349—72.**

Tronick, E. 1971. Stimulus control and the growth of the infant's visual field. *Perception and Psychophysics*, 11: 373—6. **366.**

Tronick, E. & Brazelton, T.B. 1975. Clinical uses of the Brazelton Neonatal Scale. In *Exceptional infant. Vol. III. Assessment and intervention*, ed. B.Z. Friedlander et al., p. 137. New York: Brunner/Mazel. **85, 86.**

Tronick, E. & Clanton, C. 1971. Infant looking patterns. *Vision Research*, 11: 1479—86. **364.**

Tronick, E., Adamson, L., Wise, S., Als, H. & Brazelton, T.B. 1975. Infant emotions in normal and perturbated interactions. Paper presented to the Society for Research in Child Development, Denver, Colo. **197.**

Tronick, E. *see* Aronson & Tronick 1971; Ball & Tronick 1971; Brazelton et al. 1975, 1977.

Tulkin, S. & Kagan, J. 1972. Mother—child interaction in the first year of life. *Child Development*, 43: 31—41. **270.**

Tulkin, S.R. *see* Liederman et al. 1977.

Uzgiris, I.C. 1972. Patterns of vocal and gestural imitation in infants. *Proceedings of the Symposium on Genetic and Social Influences* (International Society for the Study of Behavioural Development, Nijmegen 1971). Basle: Karger. Repr. in Stone et al. 1973, pp. 599—604. **332.**

Valamme, E. *see* Wasz-Höckert et al. 1968.

Vietze, P.M. *see* Strain & Vietze 1975.

Vigorito, J. *see* Eimas et al. 1971.

Volterra, V. *see* Bates et al. 1975.

Vorster, J. 1975. Mommy linguist: the case for motherese. *Lingua*, 37: 281—312. **128.**

Vuorenkoski, V. *see* Wasz-Höckert et al. 1968.

Washburn, R.W. 1929. A study of the smiling and laughing of infants in the first year of life. *Genetic Psychology Monographs*, 6: 398—537. **326.**

Wasz-Höckert, O., Lind, J., Vuorenkoski, V., Partanen, T.J. & Valamme, E. 1968. *The infant cry: a spectrographic and auditory analysis*, Developmental Clinics in Medicine, 29. International Medical Publications. London: Heinemann Medical Books. **25.**

Waterson, N. & Snow, C.E. (ed.) 1978. *The development of communication: social and pragmatic factors in language acquisition*. Paper presented at the Third International Child Language Symposium. New York: Wiley. **25.**

Watson, J.S. 1972. Smiling, cooing and 'the game'. *Merrill-Palmer Quarterly*, 18: 323–39. **333, 366.**

Watzlawick, P., Beavin, H.J. & Jackson, D. 1967. *The pragmatics of human communication*. New York: Norton. **370.**

Wedenberg, E. *see* Anderson et al. 1973.

Weinstein, H. *see* Caudill & Weinstein 1969.

Weiss, S.J. *see* Caron et al. 1973.

Wells, A. *see* Kaye & Wells in preparation.

Wells, G. 1974. Learning to code experience through language. *Journal of Child Language*, 1: 243–69. **178.**

Wetstone, H.S. *see* Friendlander et al. 1972.

Whipple, D.V. 1944. *Our American babies*. New York: M. Barrows. **32.**

Wise, S. *see* Brazelton et al. 1975; Tronick et al. 1975.

Wolf, K.M. *see* Spitz & Wolf 1946.

Wolfenstein, M. 1955. Fun morality: an analysis of recent American child-training literature. In *Childhood in contemporary cultures*, ed. M. Mead & M. Wolfenstein, pp. 168–78. Chicago: University of Chicago Press. **32.**

Wolff, P.H. 1963. Observations on the early development of smiling. In Foss 1963, pp. 113–38. **157, 240, 323, 326, 330, 333.**

Wolff, P.H. 1966. *The causes, controls and organization of behavior in the neonate*. Psychological Issues, 5: 1–99 (monograph 17). **73, 326.**

Wolff, P.H. 1969. The natural history of crying and other vocalizations in early infancy. In Foss 1969, pp. 81–109. Repr. in Stone et al. 1973, pp. 1185–98. **323, 325, 333.**

Wood, D. & Middleton, D. 1975. A study of assisted problem solving. *British Journal of Psychology*, 66: 181–97. **216.**

Wrangham, R. 1974. Artificial feeding of chimpanzees and baboons in their natural habitat. *Animal Behaviour*, 22: 83–93. **225.**

Yarbrough, C. *see* Lechtig et al. 1975.

Young, G.G. *see* Brazelton et al. 1971.

Young-Browne, G., Rosenfeld, H.M. & Horowitz, F.D. 1977. Infant discrimination of facial expression. *Child Development*, 48: 555–62. *

Zalazo, P.R. 1972. Smiling and vocalizing: a cognitive emphasis. *Merrill-Palmer Quarterly*, 18: 349–65. **323.**